AF470605

Tiffany

(1848-1933)

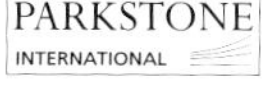

PARKSTONE
INTERNATIONAL

Page 4:
Louis Comfort Tiffany, c. 1908

Author: Charles de Kay

Layout:
Baseline Co Ltd
61A-63A Vo Van Tan
District 3, Ho Chi Minh City
Vietnam

ISBN: 978-1-84484-858-4

Printed in China

"I have always striven to fix beauty in wood, stone, glass or pottery, in oil or watercolor by using whatever seemed fittest for the expression of beauty, that has been my creed."

— Louis Comfort Tiffany

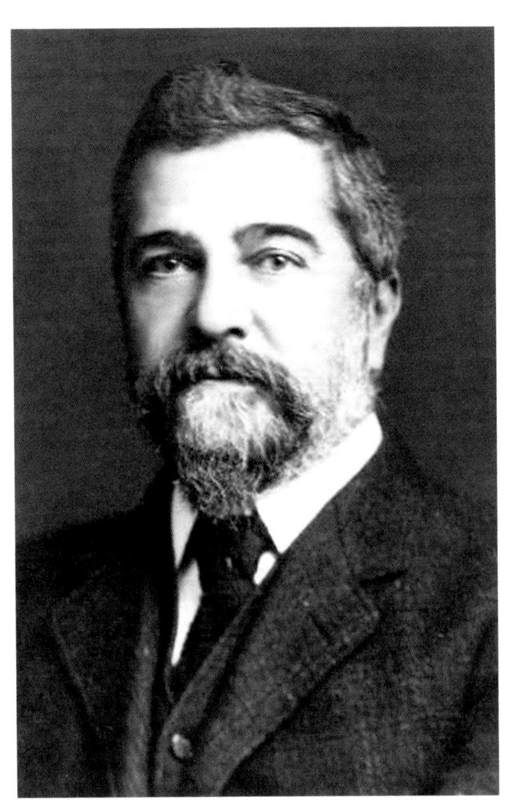

Biography

1848: Louis Comfort Tiffany is born to Charles Lewis Tiffany, the founder of Tiffany & Co., and his wife Harriet Olivia Avery Young on February 18th in New York City.

1866: Tiffany studies under American landscape artist George Inness.

1872: As his interest shifts from painting to glassmaking, Tiffany begins working in glass houses in Brooklyn.

1879: Louis Comfort Tiffany and Associated American Artists is formed with Candace Wheeler, Samuel Colman and Lockwood de Forest.

1882: Tiffany is asked to redesign several rooms in the White House.

1885: Tiffany breaks away from L.C. Tiffany and Associated American Artists in order to form his own Tiffany Glass Company.

1893: Tiffany Glass Company opens a new factory in Queens, New York, later called the Tiffany Glass Furnaces, which starts to manufacture the glass that is famously known as "favrile".

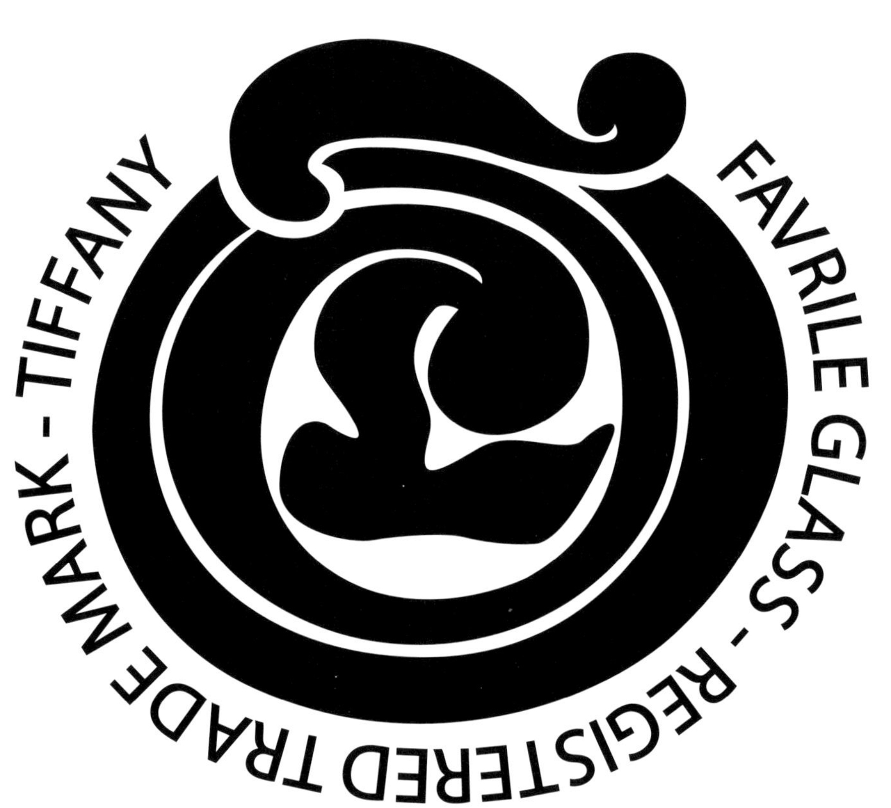
TIFFANY
FAVRILE GLASS
REGISTERED TRADE MARK

1894:   The Tiffany Glass Company trademarks the term "favrile", which later comes to refer to all

           the glass, enamel and pottery that the company produces.

1895:   Tiffany Glass Company begins to commercially produce its famous lamps.

1900:   Tiffany's exhibits at the Paris Exposition Internationale earn him a gold medal and the title of

           Chevalier of the Legion of Honor.

1902:   Tiffany becomes the first Design Director for his father's company, Tiffany & Co.

1904:   A new line of pottery, copper enamels and jewellery is exhibited at the Louisiana Purchase

           Exposition in St. Louis, Missouri.

1906-1916: In addition to the pottery, lamps and jewellery already produced by the company, Tiffany

           Studios expands its line to gift items like cigar and jewellery boxes, pictures frames, clocks

           and dishes.

1919:   Tiffany retires from active participation in Tiffany Studios, but retains his title as president.

1933:   Louis Comfort Tiffany dies at the age of eighty-five in New York City.

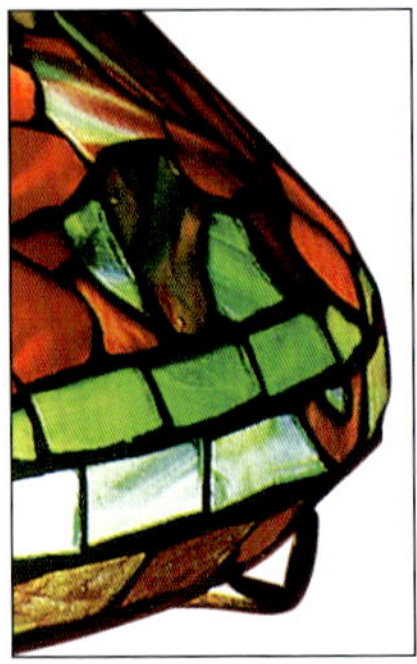

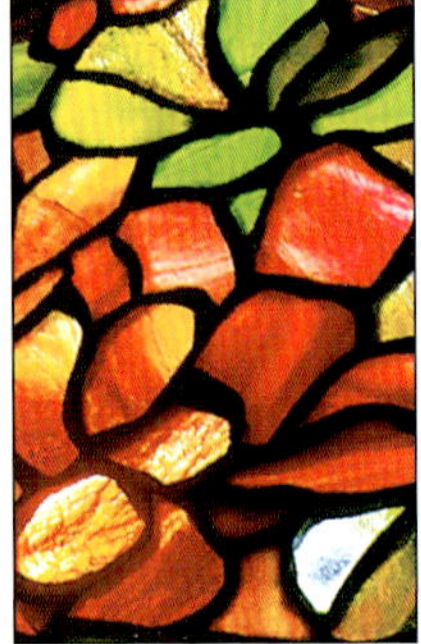

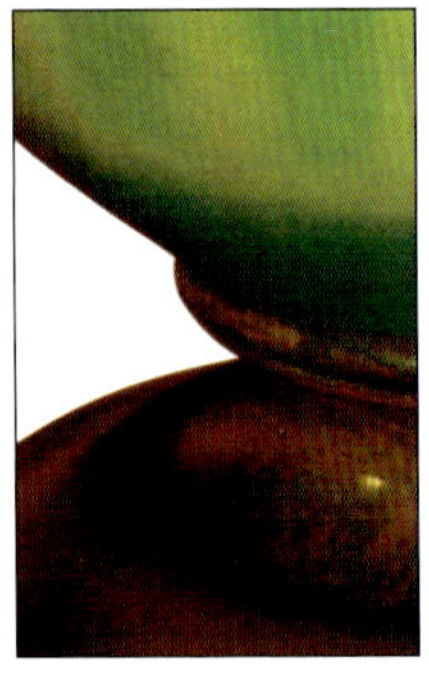

TIFFANY THE PAINTER

Louis Comfort Tiffany was born with a golden spoon in his mouth, but the spoon was immediately tucked away and he was seldom permitted to remember its existence. His father, the eminent goldsmith and jeweler Charles Lewis Tiffany, and his mother, who was Harriet Olivia Young before her marriage, did not believe in spoiling children by allowing them to live on a scale such as their fortune warranted.

Floral Oil Lamp

Leaded favrile glass and bronze.

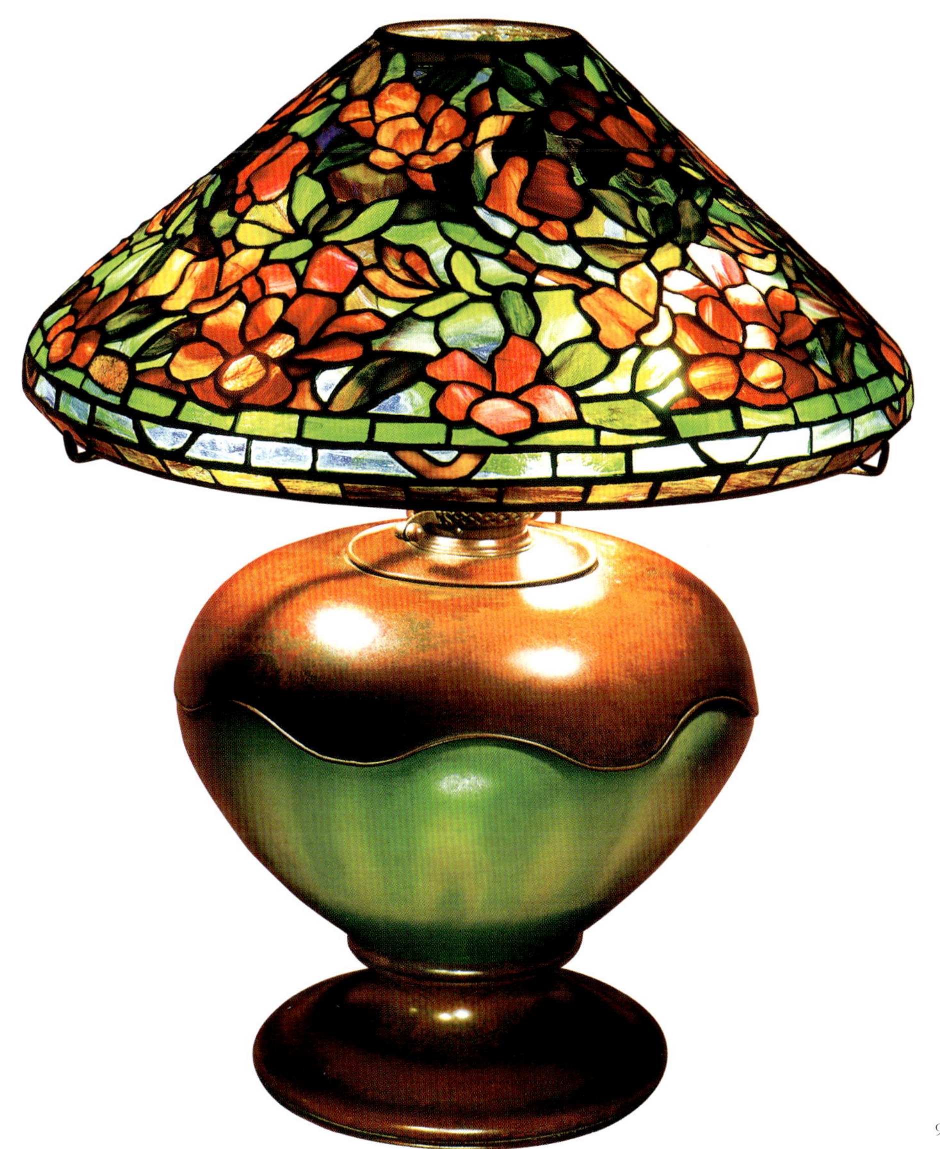

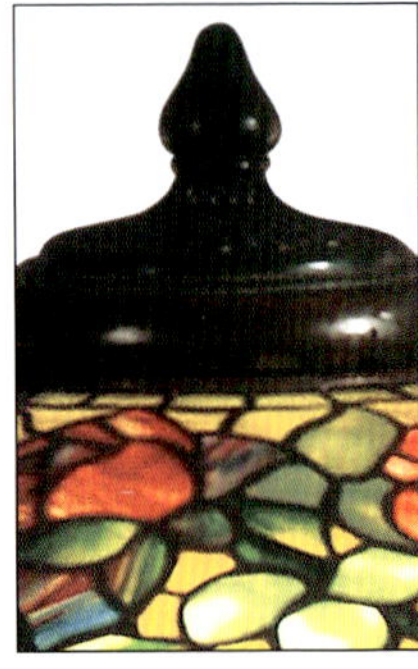

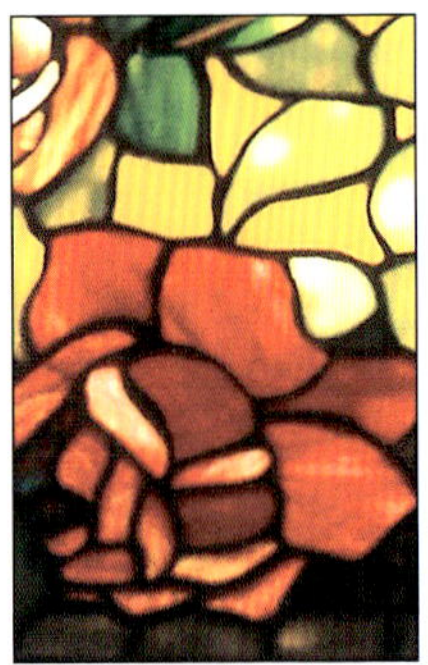

Education should be thorough, but luxuries few and spending money curtailed. Born February 18th, 1848, their son was still at school when the Civil War was fought, but like many other school boys of that period we can imagine how he deplored the fate of having been born too late to take any part in the contest. Some of his fellow artists in later life such as George B. Butler, Elihu Vedder, and Winslow Homer had been to the war.

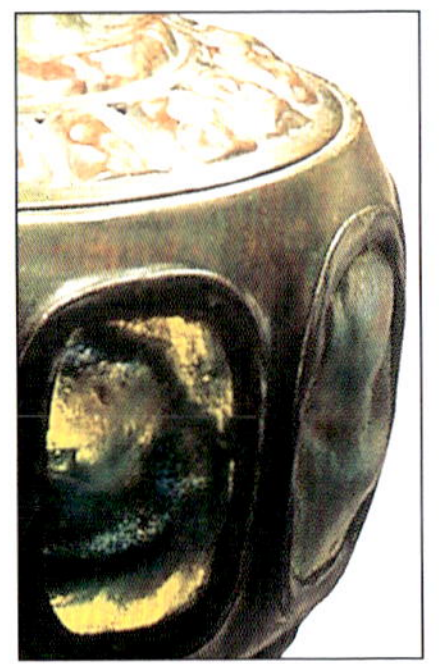

Rose Design with Flared Shade

Leaded glass and bronze.

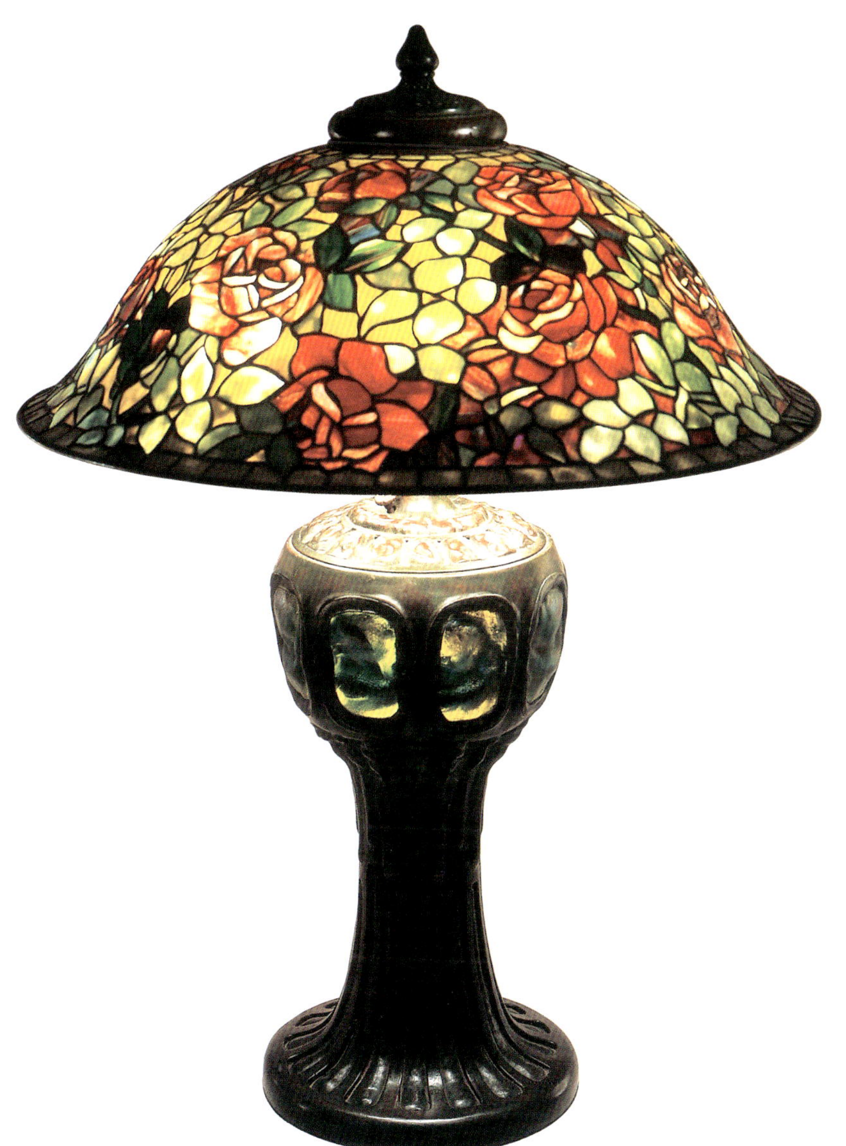

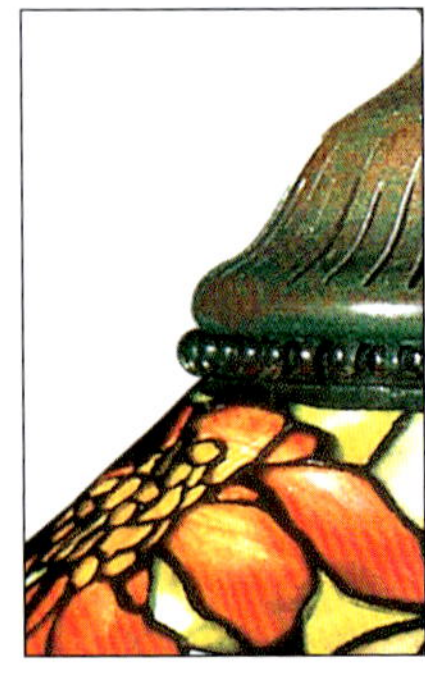

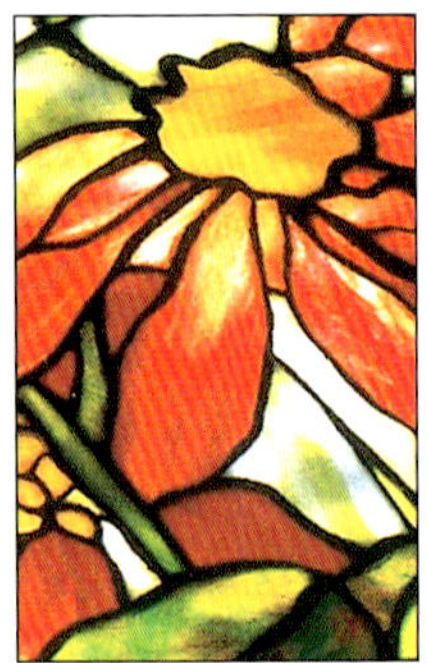

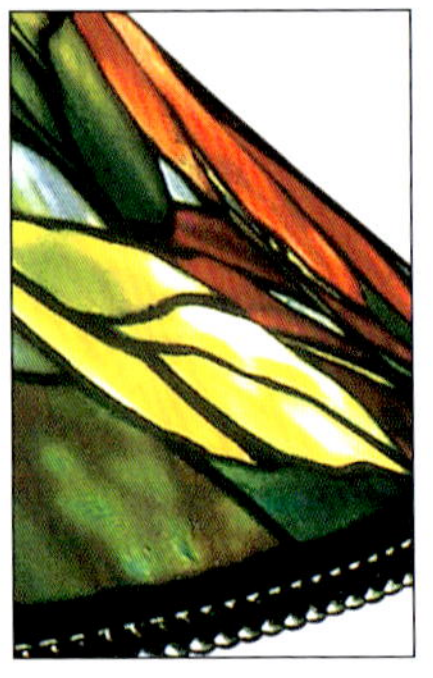

As he grew up he felt the longing for expression which indicates the coming artist and usually makes him cold toward a college career, so that at the age when a youth in his circumstances is pretty sure to be at the university, he was haunting the studios of George Inness, N. A., and Samuel Colman, N. A., the latter being one of the founders and first presidents of that Society of Painters in Water Colors which became the

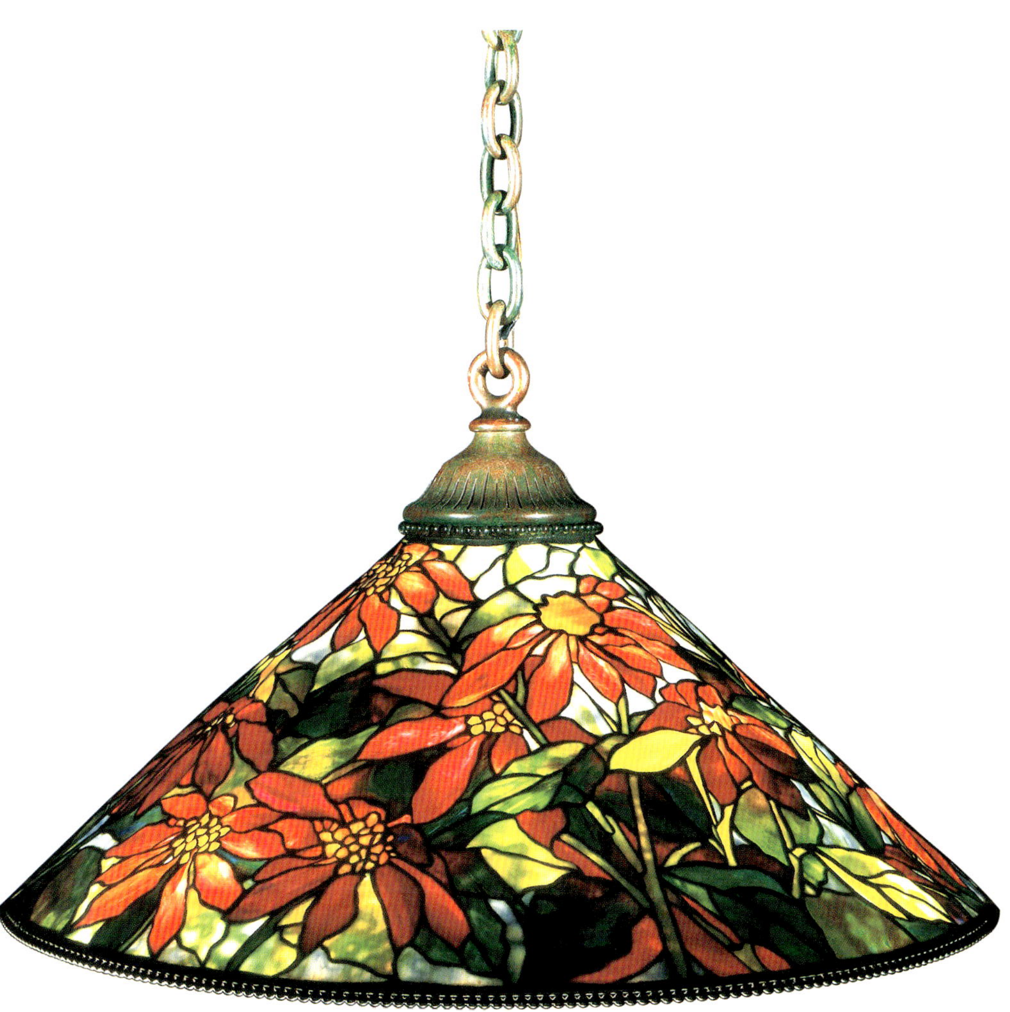

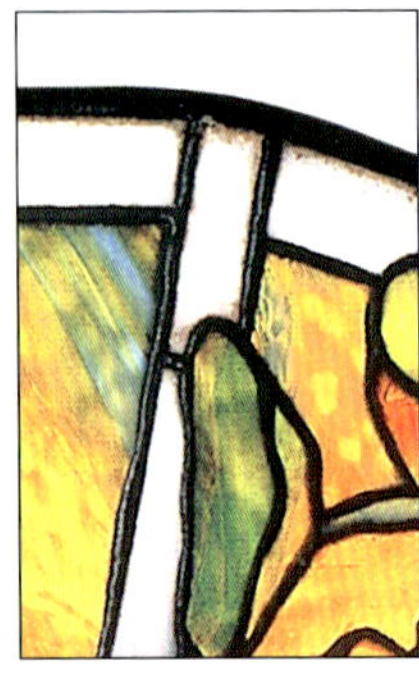

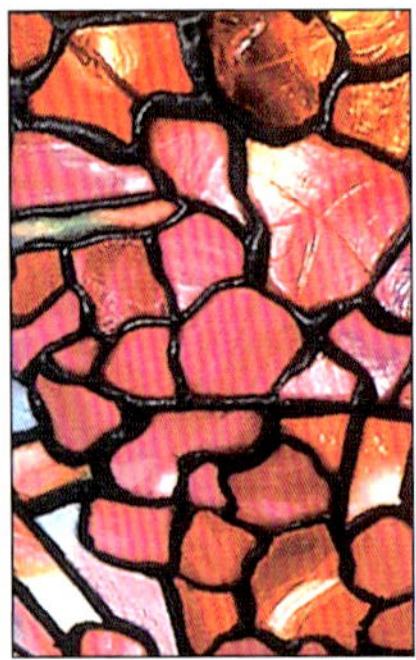

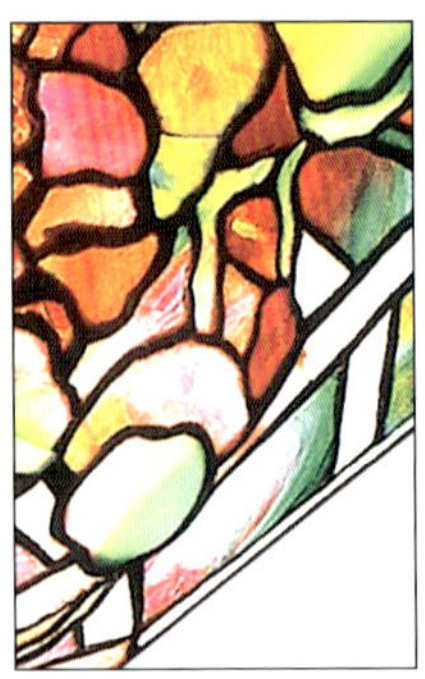

American Water Color Society and also one of the original members of the Society of American Artists, merged later into the National Academy of Design.

George Inness was a man peculiarly fitted, through certain sides of his character, to rouse the interest of a pupil. His incisive, outspoken views on art were supplemented by a stimulating if somewhat chaotic philosophy in which the sublime ideas of Swedenborg took a

Floral Ceiling Light

Leaded glass and bronze.

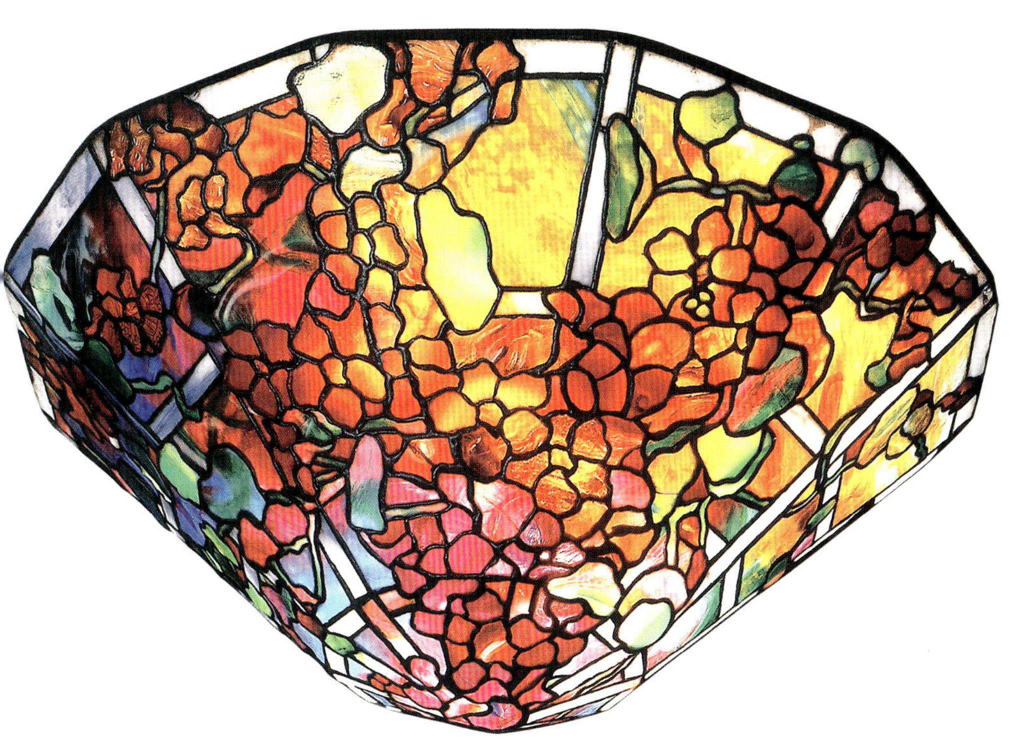

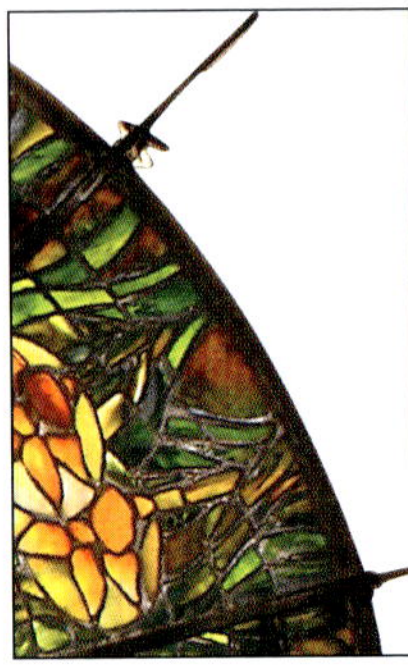

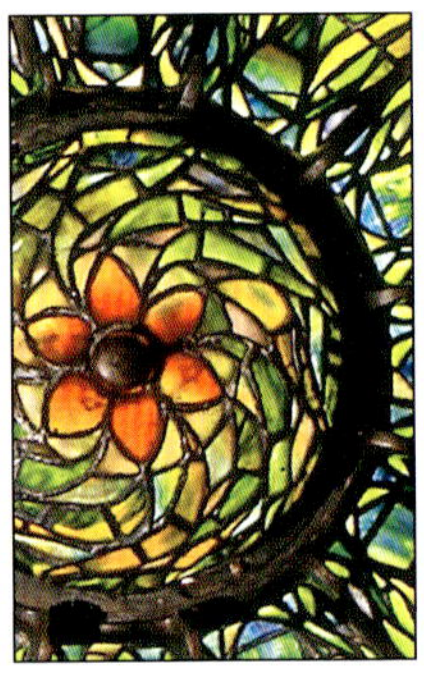

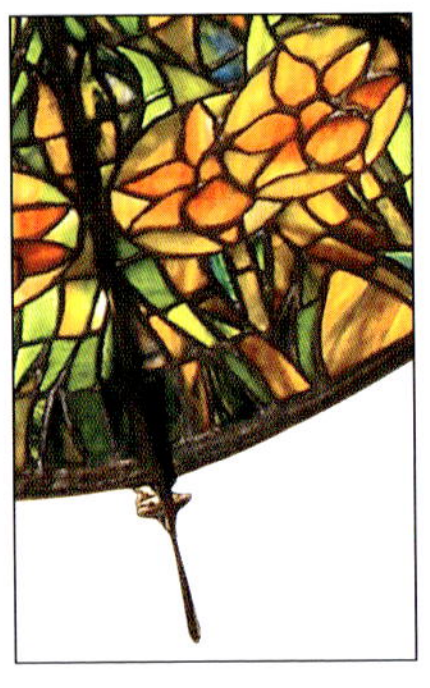

prominent place. I remember hours passed in his studio in the old University building on Washington Square when he would stand before his easel making and unmaking a picture with rapid strokes of his brush, all the while pouring forth a stream of talk in which, unlike that of other artists, a strong religious feeling appeared and was lost, only to reappear again like the white streaks which tinge a river below the cataract.

Daffodil Lamp

1899.
Height: 96.5 cm.
Courtesy McCelland & Lars Rachen, Ltd.

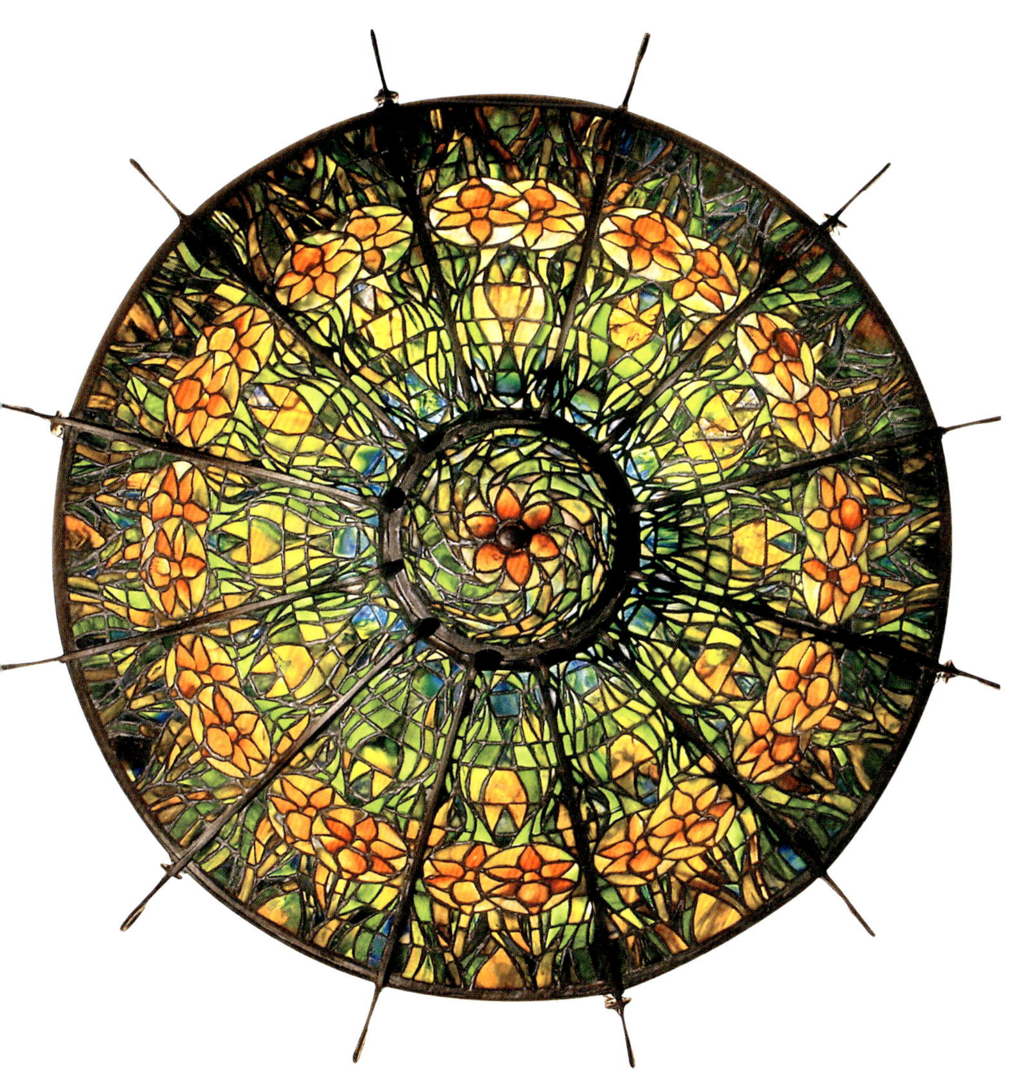

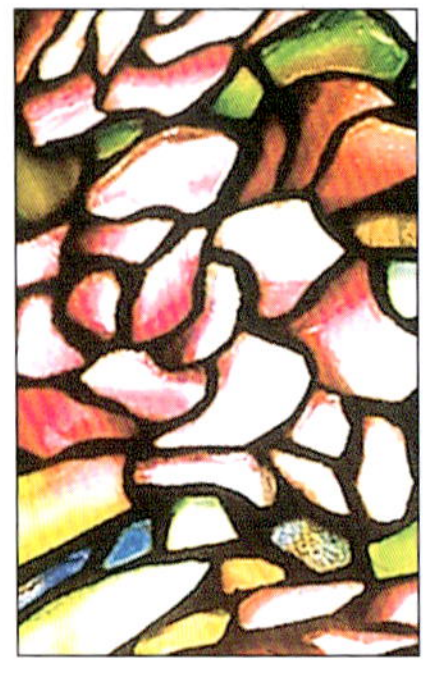

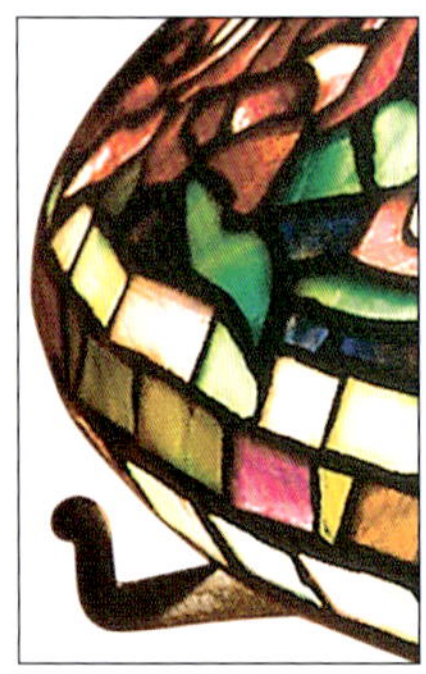

Inness in 1878 attempted to fix some of these fleeting ideas in Harper's Monthly when he wrote:

"The true use of art is, first, to cultivate the artist's own spiritual nature and, secondly, to enter as a factor in general civilization. And the increase of these efforts depends on the purity of the artist's motives in the pursuit of art. Every artist who, without reference to external circumstances, aims truly to represent the ideas

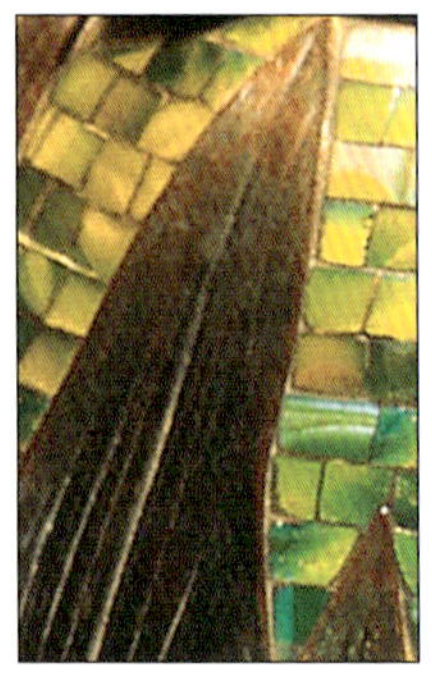

Mosaic Arrowhead Base Nº. 145 with Rose Shade

Leaded favrile glass and bronze.

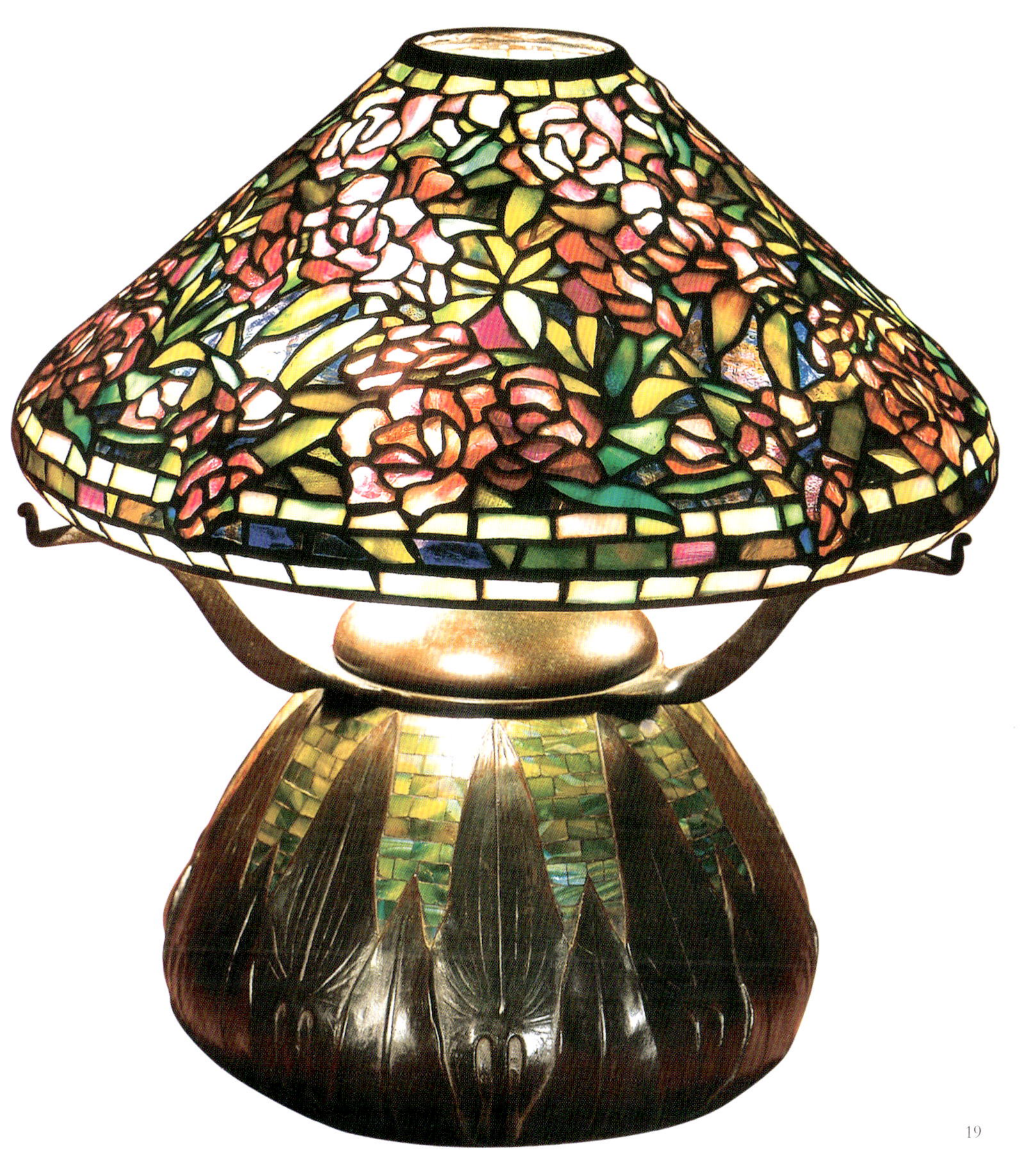

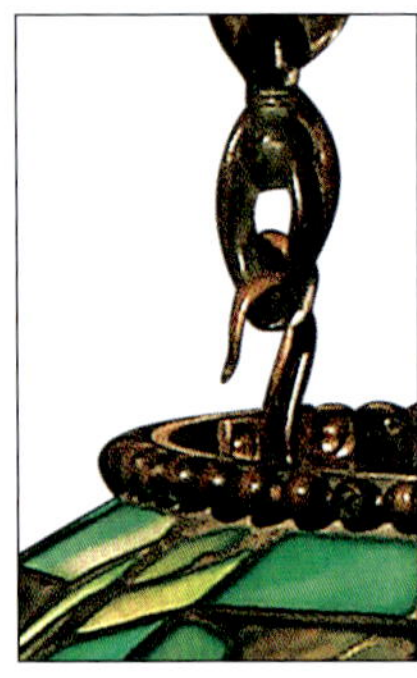

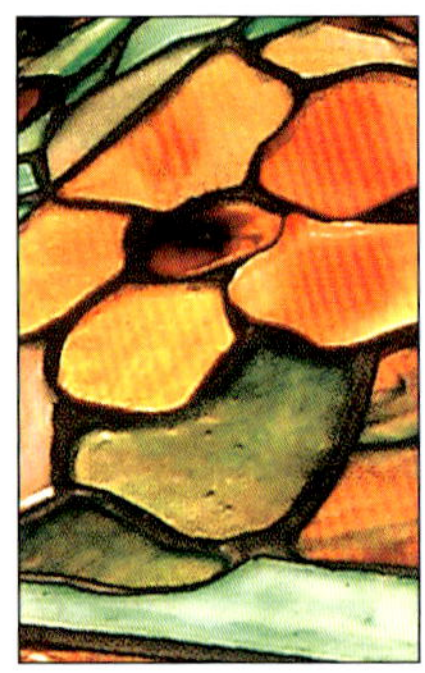

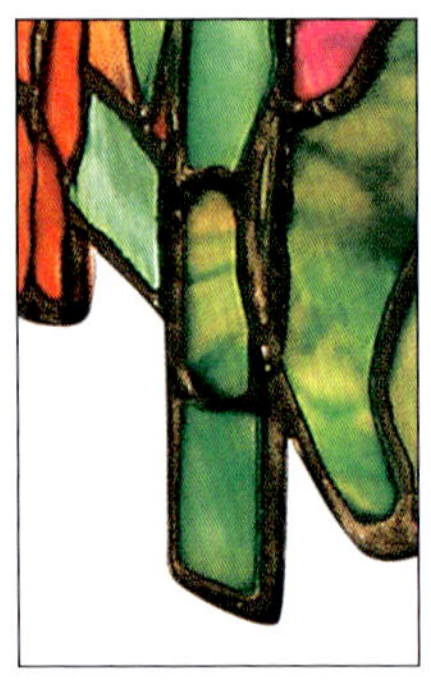

and emotions which come to him when in the presence of nature is in process of his own spiritual development and is a benefactor of his race. No man can attempt the reproduction of any idea within him from a pure motive or love of the idea itself without being in the course of his own regeneration. The difficulties necessary to be overcome in communicating the substance of his idea (which in this case, is feeling or emotion) to the end that

Nasturtium Lamp, Model Nº. 607

Height: 57 cm.
Courtesy McCelland & Lars Rachen, Ltd.

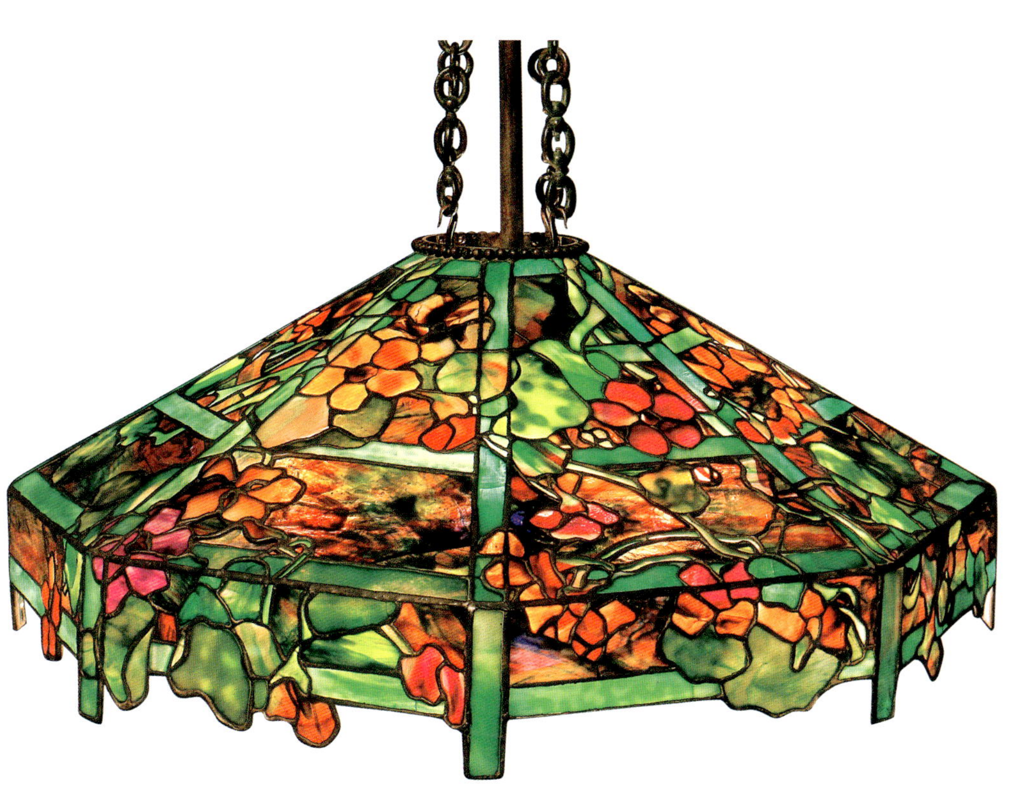

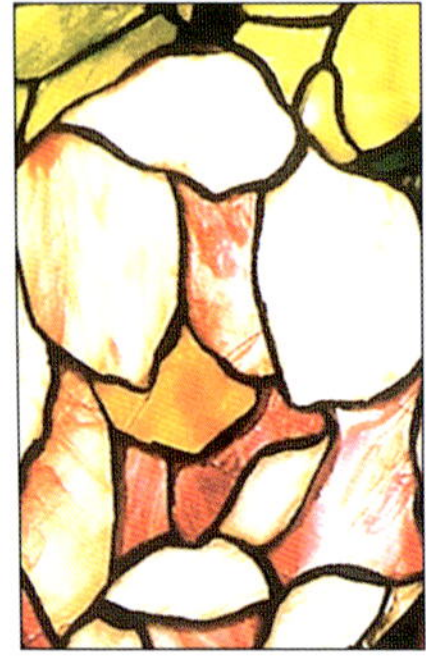

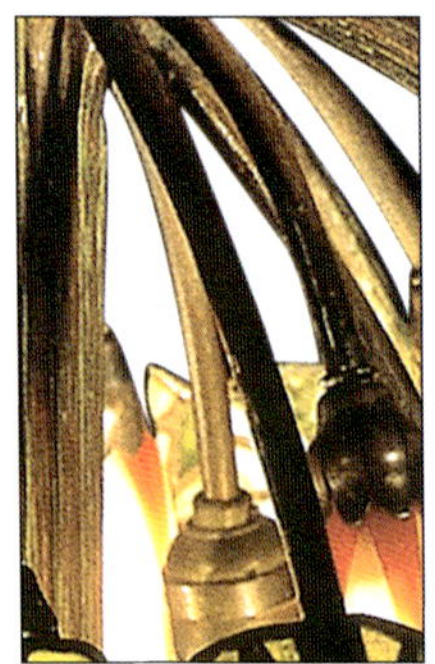

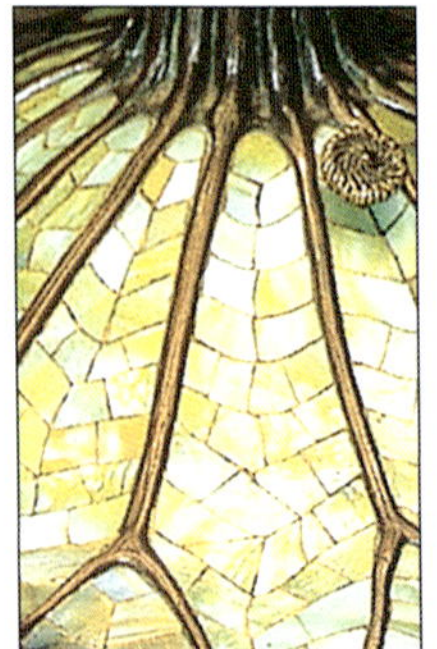

the idea may be more and more perfectly conveyed to others, involve the exercise of his intellectual faculties; and soon the discovery is made that the moral element underlies all, that unless the moral also is brought into play the intellectual faculties are not in condition for conveying the artistic impulse or inspiration. The mind may, indeed, be convinced of the means of operation,

Tree Lamp, Trunk and Root-Shaped Base, Floral Shade

Favrile leaded glass, bronze.

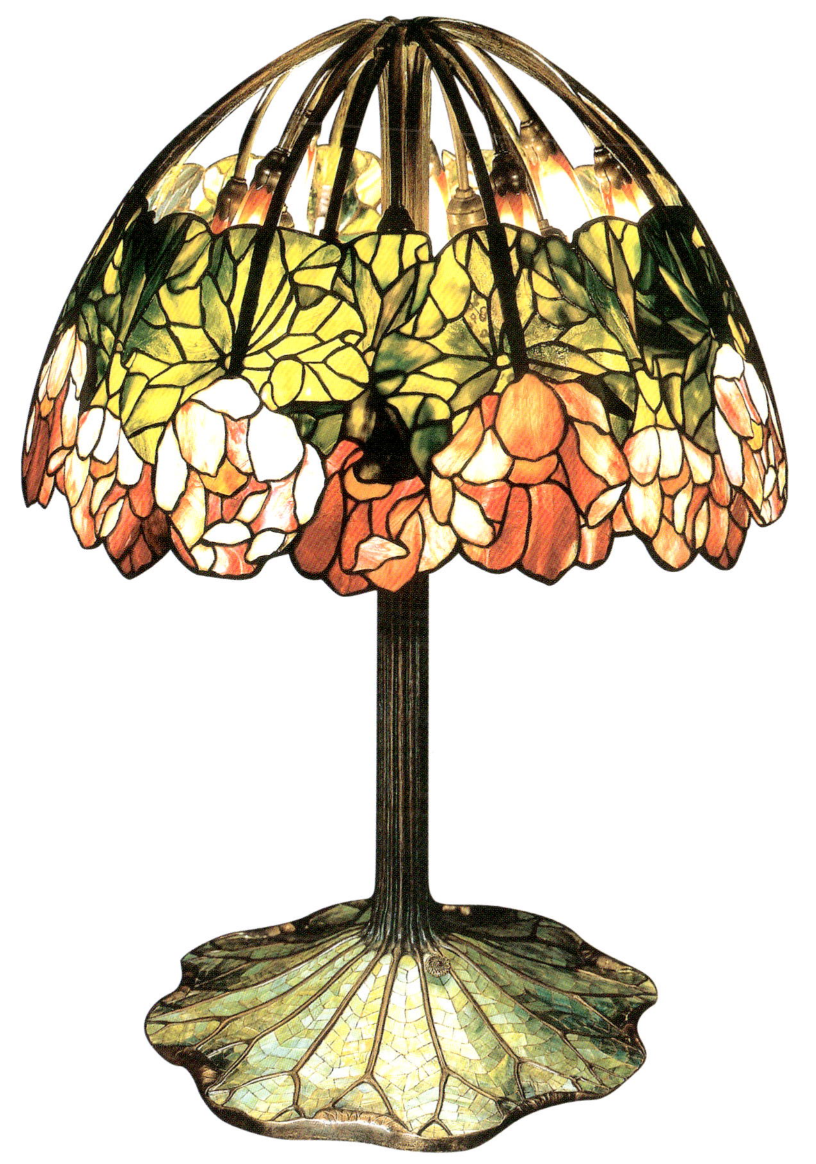

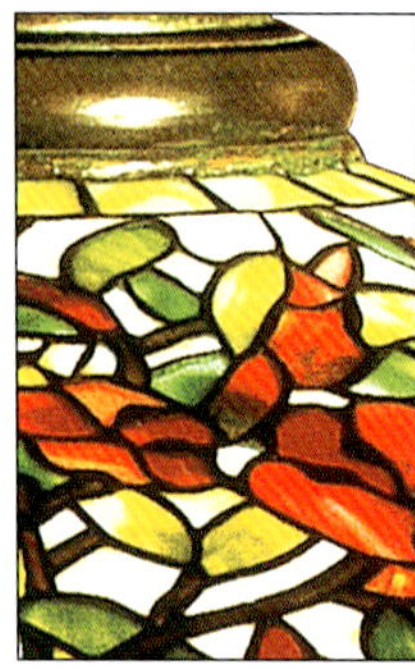

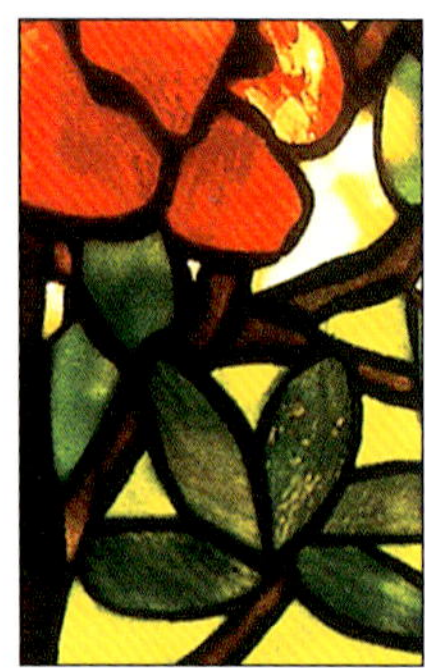

but only when the moral powers have been cultivated do the conditions exist, necessary to the transmission of the artistic inspiration which is from truth and goodness itself. Of course no man's motive can be absolutely pure and divine."

The pupil must have shared this master's love of watercolor. Indeed Isham, an excellent judge of his fellow artists, has written concerning him.

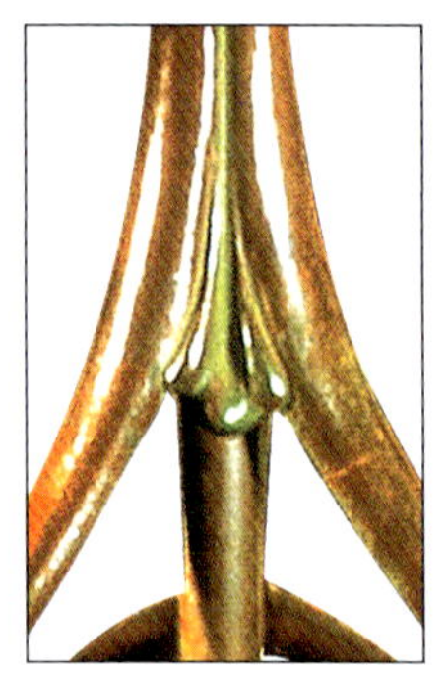

Azalea Table Lamp

Leaded glass and bronze, shade: 55.9 cm.

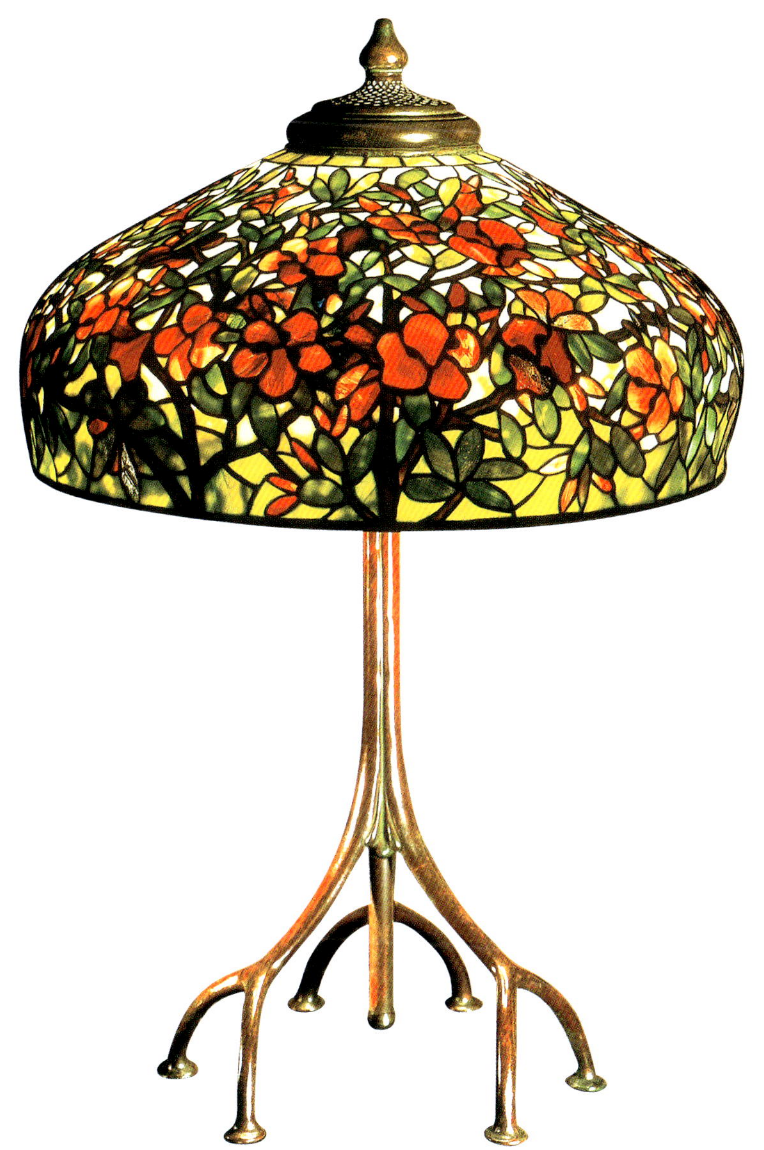

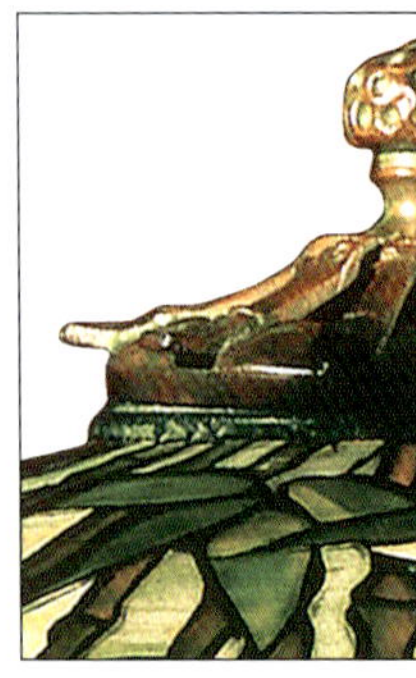

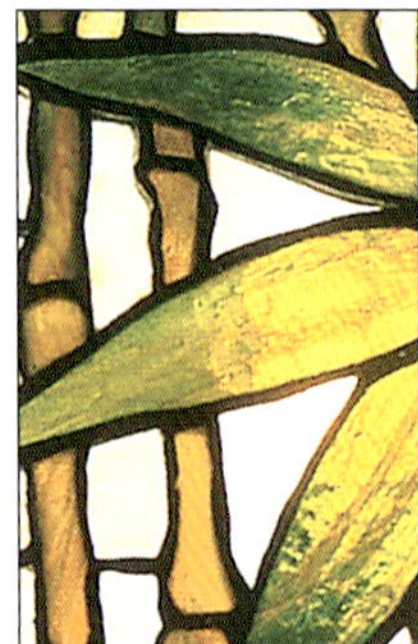

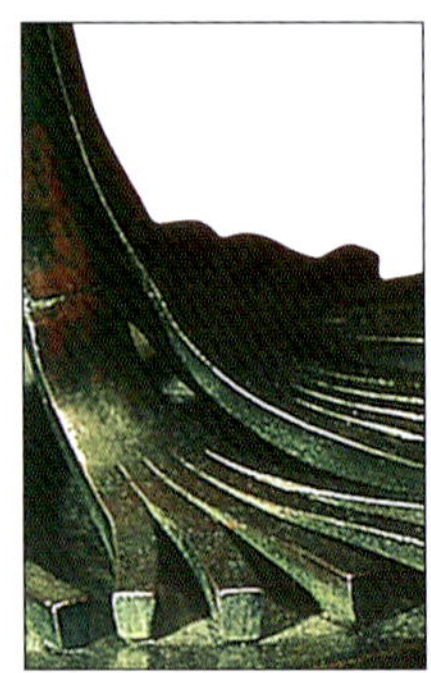

"There was much of Colman's love of warm, pure color in his paintings in transparent wash or in gouache on rough straw-board, of Italian or Mexican scenes, that used to light up the early exhibitions the Water Color Society, the firmness of outline and energy of drawing being probably the result of French training."

These last words refer to a third artist whom Tiffany admired an visited, Leon Belly of Paris, who,

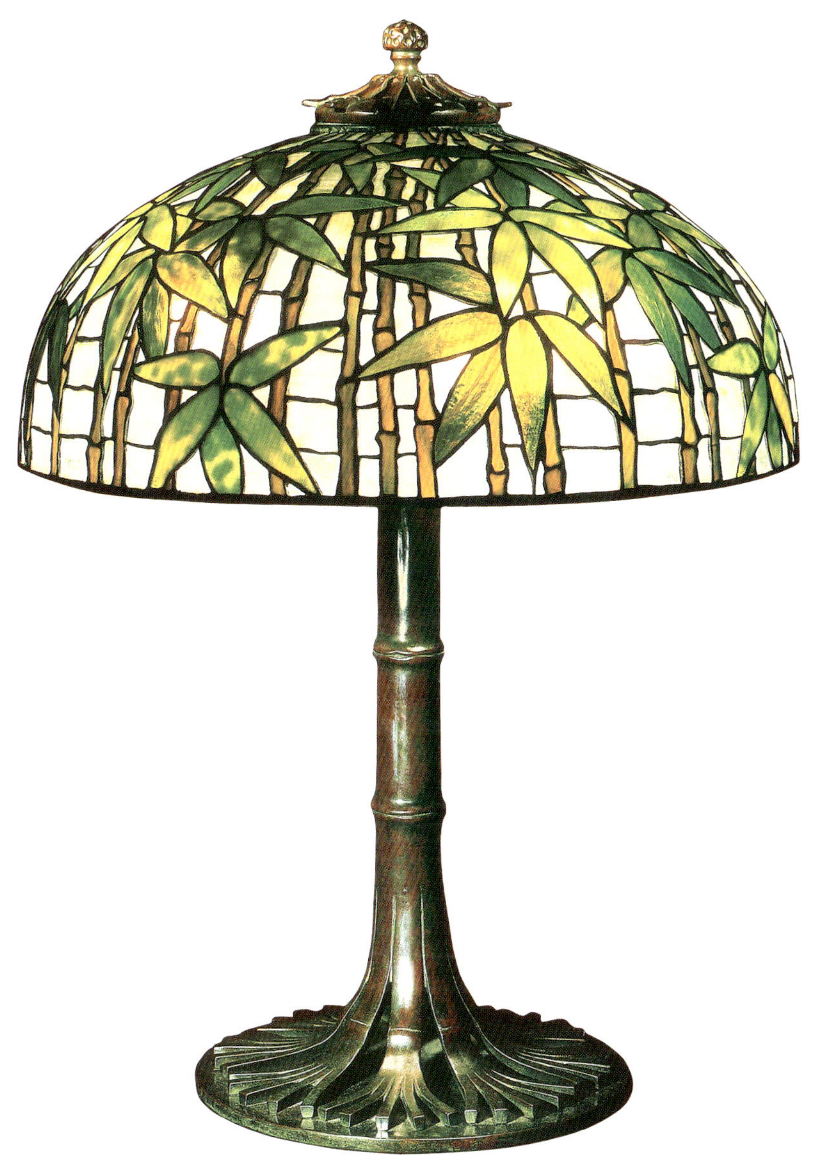

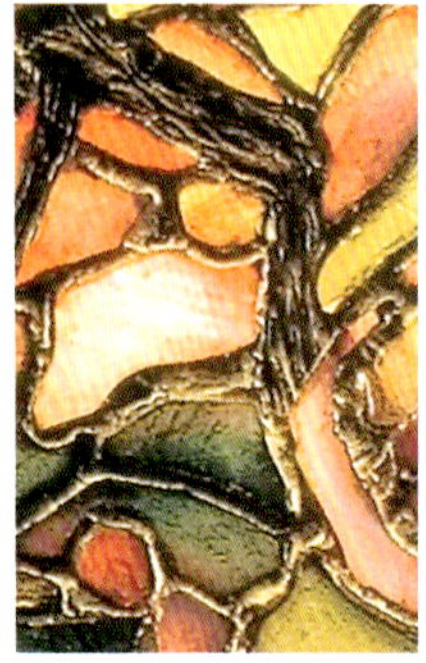

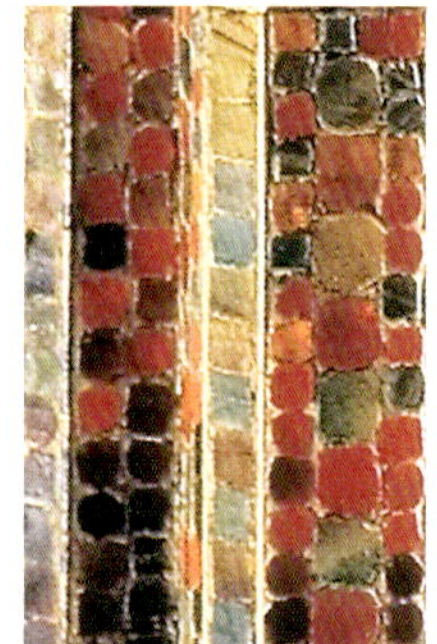

like Samuel Colman, was a landscape artist who traveled in northern Africa, Egypt, and Palestine and made his mark. Jules Breton in *Nos Peintres du siècle* says he painted Egyptian scenes "of an exact sort in which, however, one wished for more emotion. His pictures of Palestine impressed me more favorably, particularly his impressive canvas representing the Dead Sea." And in the Salon of 1867 he notes his

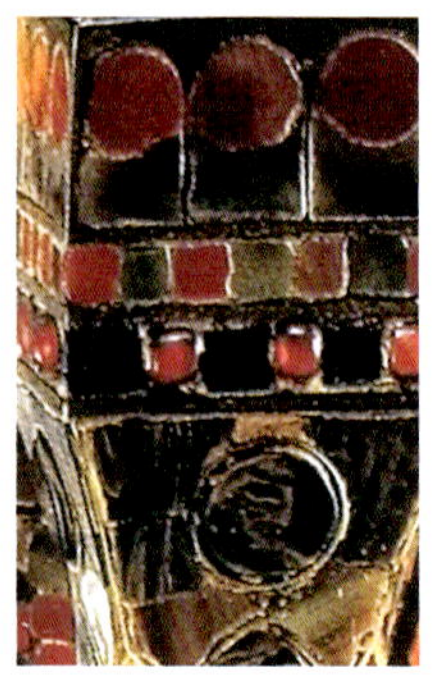

Favrile glass and bronze.

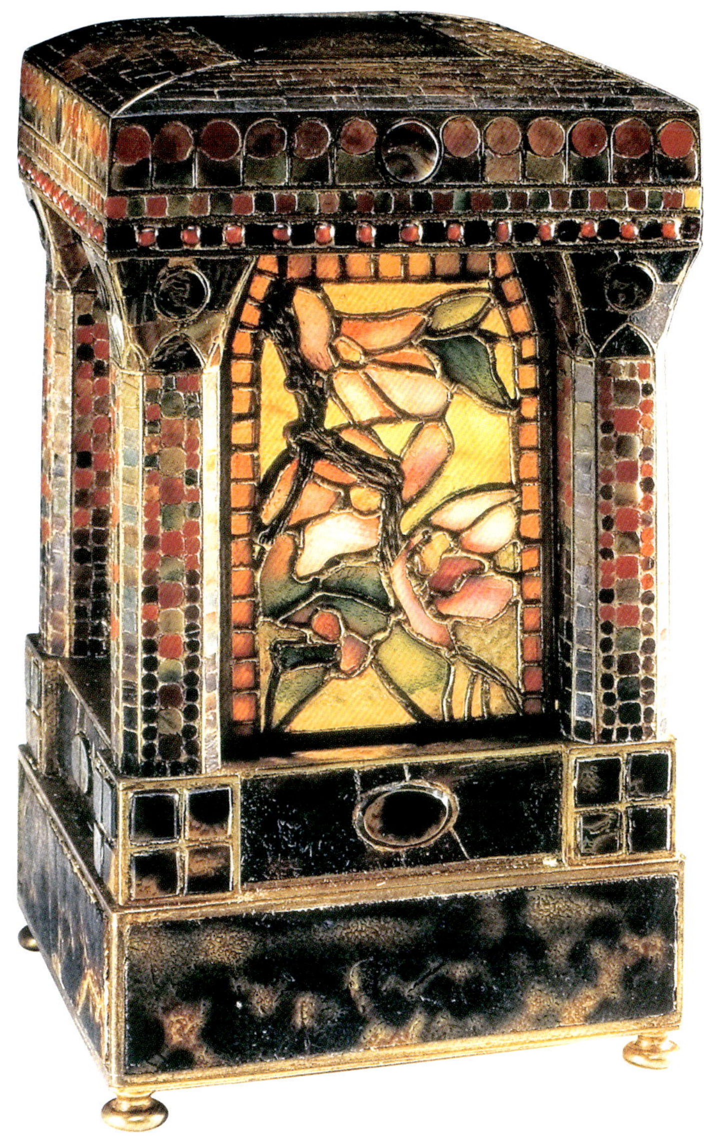

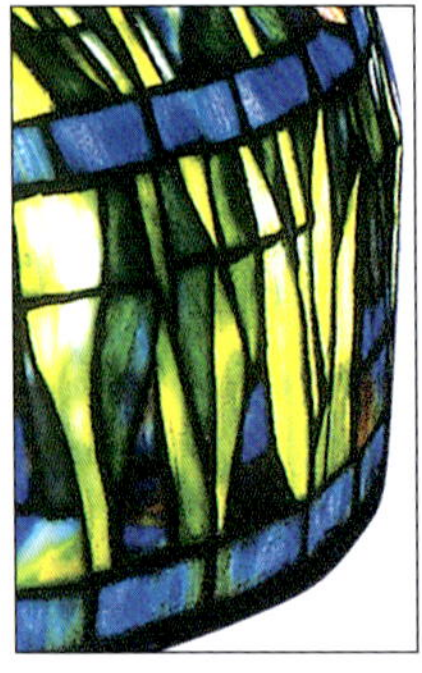

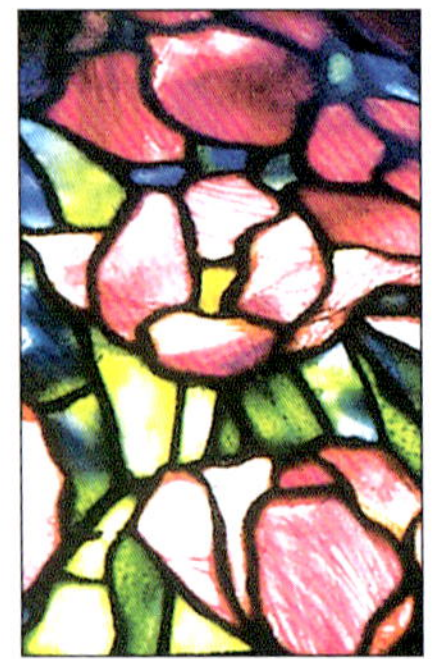

"superb views from Africa." Like Colman, the arts of the Orient appealed to him very strongly and this agreed with Tiffany's nature. Though he did not work with L. Belly, he did study hard under Bailly, a thorough teacher of drawing who lived at Passy and took particular pains with the young American. It may be remarked, however, that neither Belly's, Inness's, nor Colman's work was reflected in that of Tiffany.

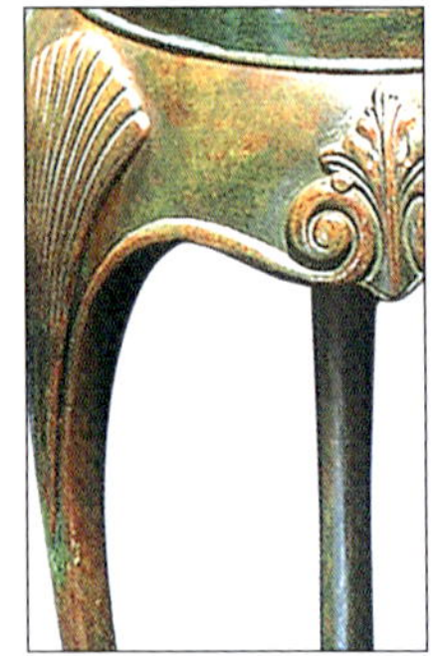

Tripod Standard Base with Tulip Shade

Favrile glass, bronze, lead.

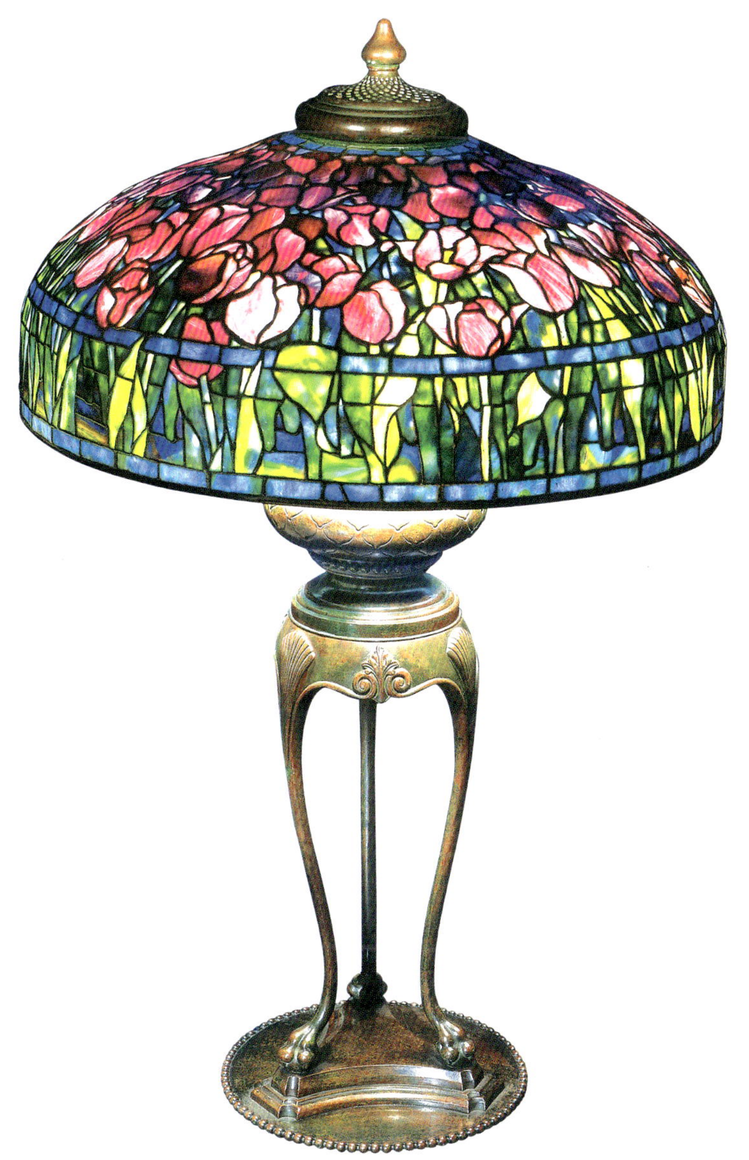

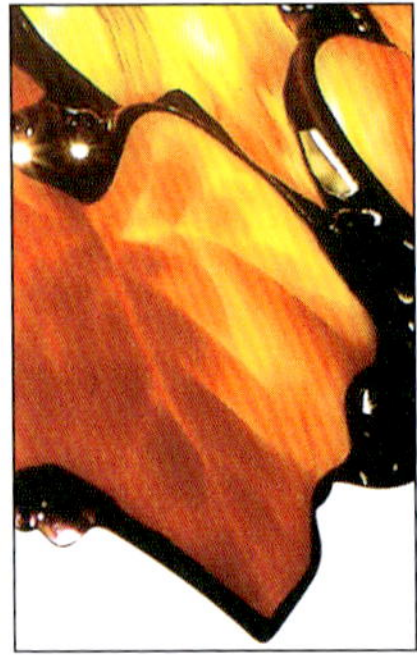

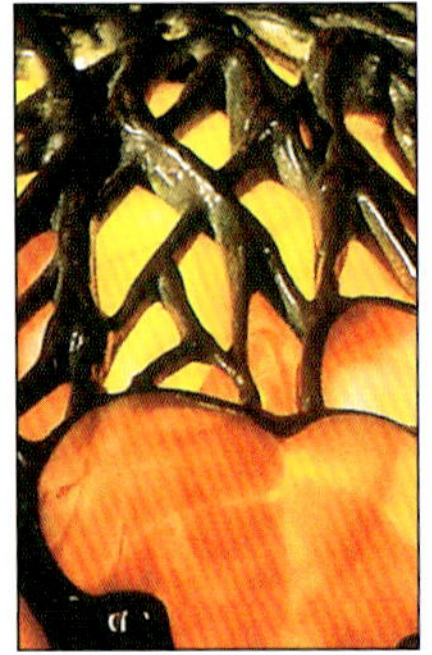

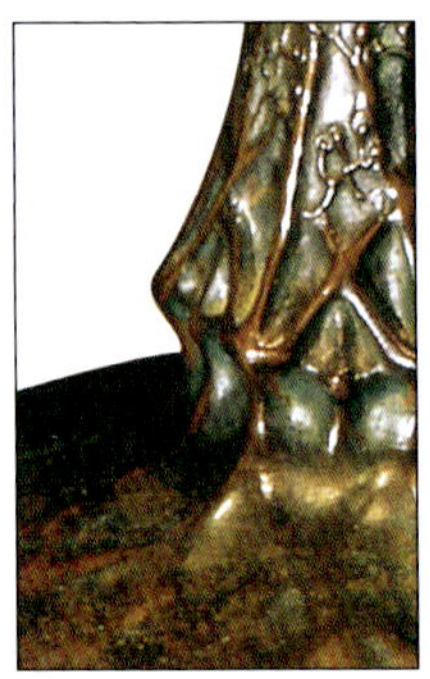

He went his own way after the modern fashion in art which seeks to encourage individuality, unlike the earlier traditions of schools and gilds which made for uniformity.

In 1870 Tiffany was elected to the Century Club. In 1871 he was accepted as Associate of the National Academy of Design and in the following year he married Miss Mary Woodbridge Goddard.

Maple Leaf Table Lamp

Leaded glass and bronze.

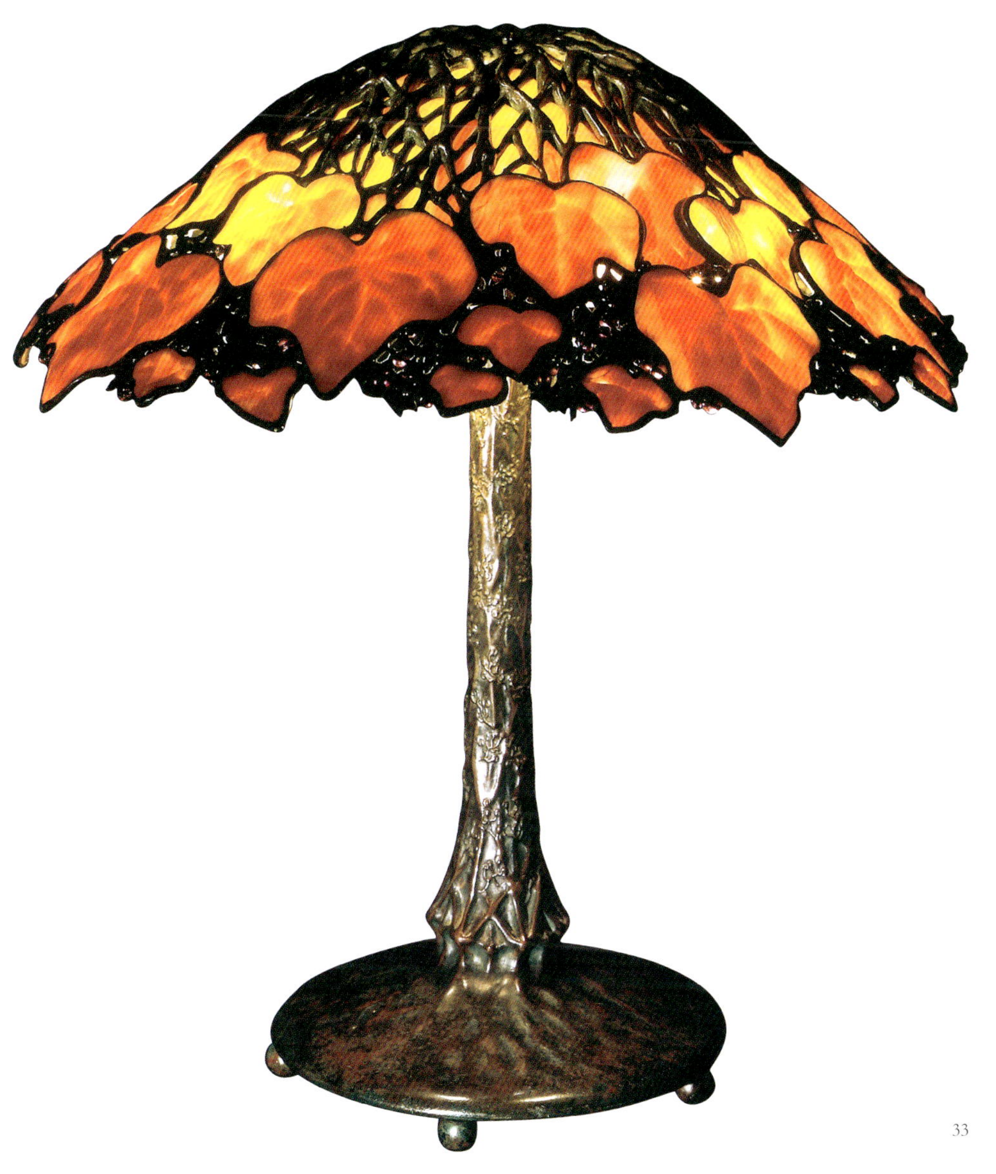

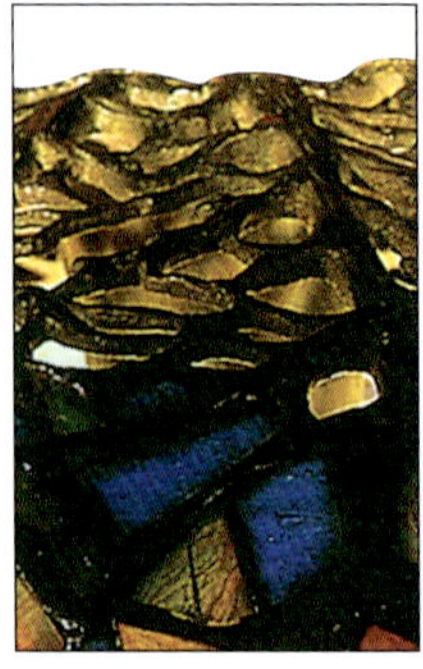

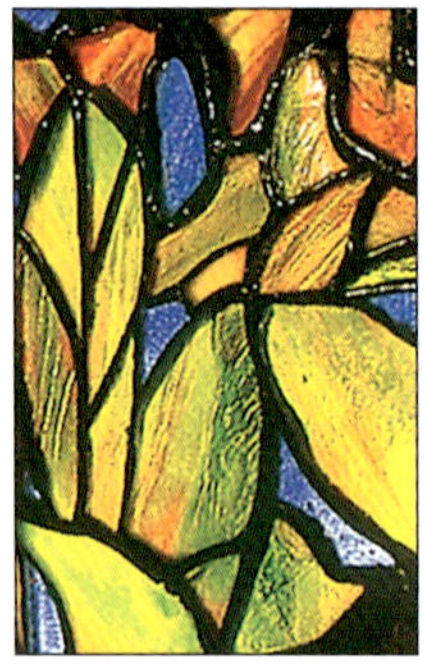

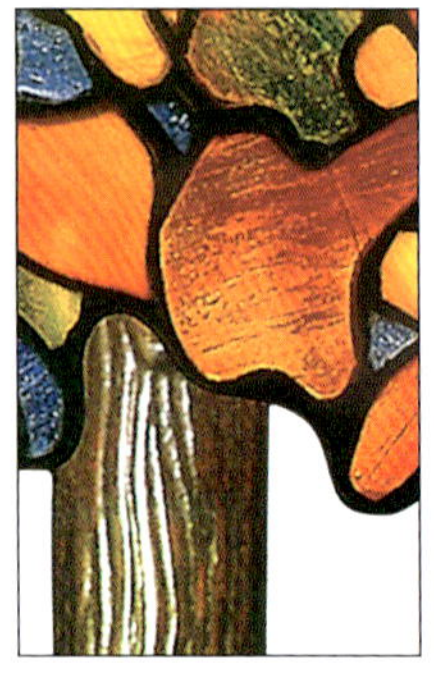

He was a member of the American Water Color Society and for many years a constant contributor. It was about this time that Tiffany enraged the "legitimate" watercolorists or sticklers for "wash" by using body color freely. Acrimonious were the remarks in the press and the studios over this audacity. Body color was a crime! This narrowness exists today, although it is shown in other ways. Not only must you pray like your neighbor,

Tree in Bloom Lamp

Leaded glass and bronze.

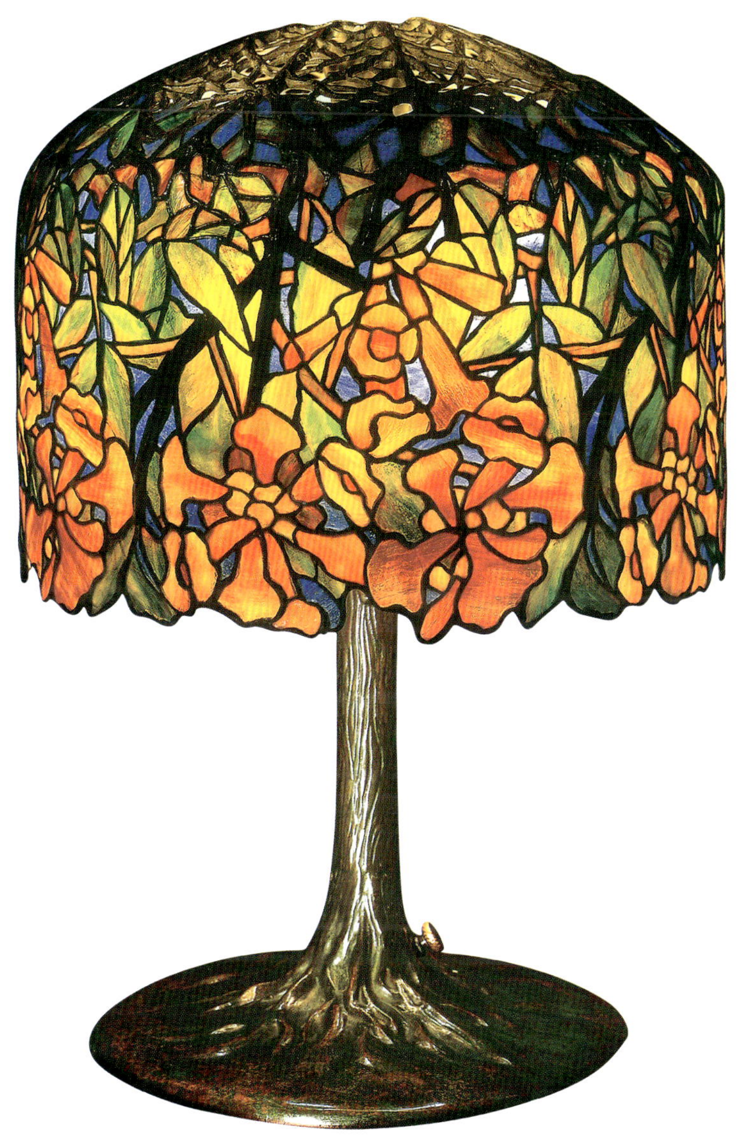

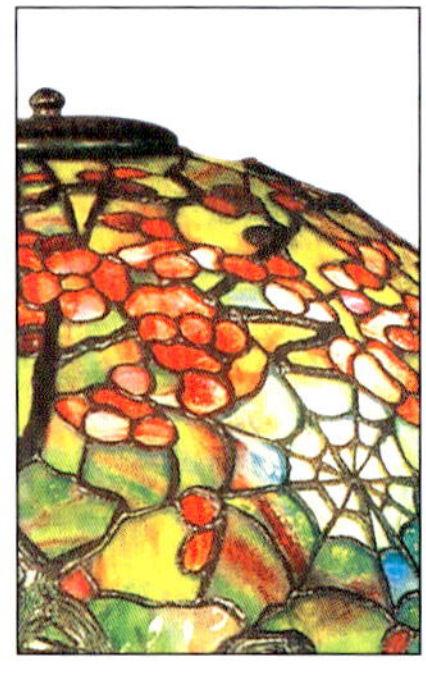

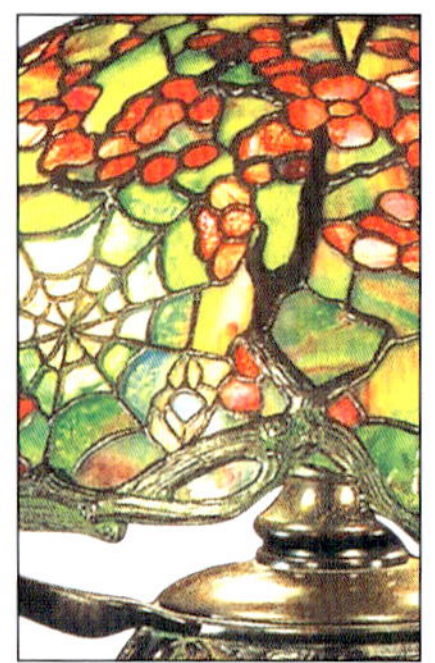

but you must use the same pigments in the same way. If not—out you go! In 1877, when the Society of American Artists was established by artists who felt that the leaders of the National Academy were too narrow in their views, he was one of the founders along with Inness, Colman, Wyatt Eaton, La Farge, Martin, and Saint Gaudens. Three years later his election as National Academician did not make him any the less a

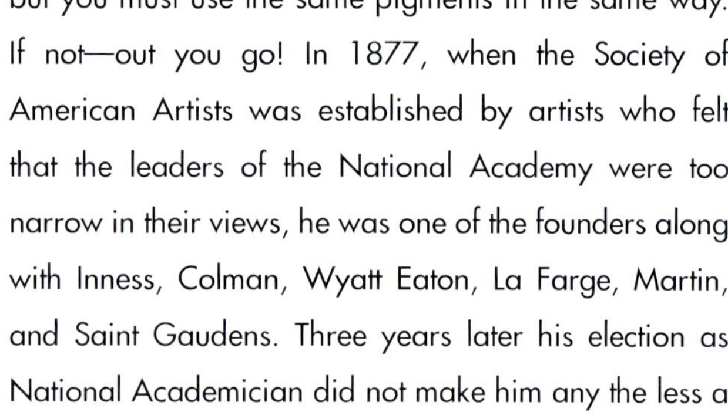

Favrile glass and bronze.

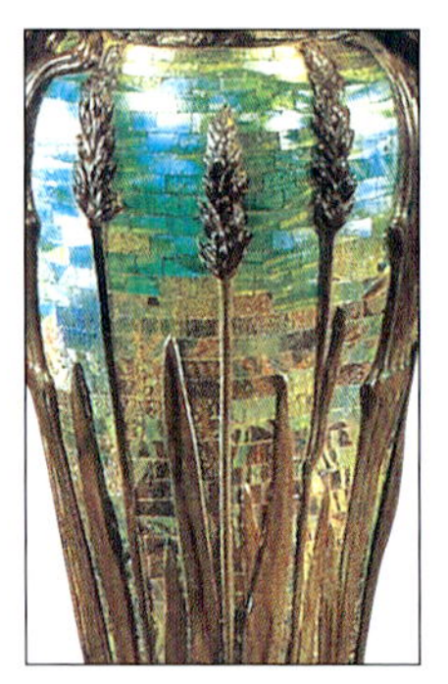

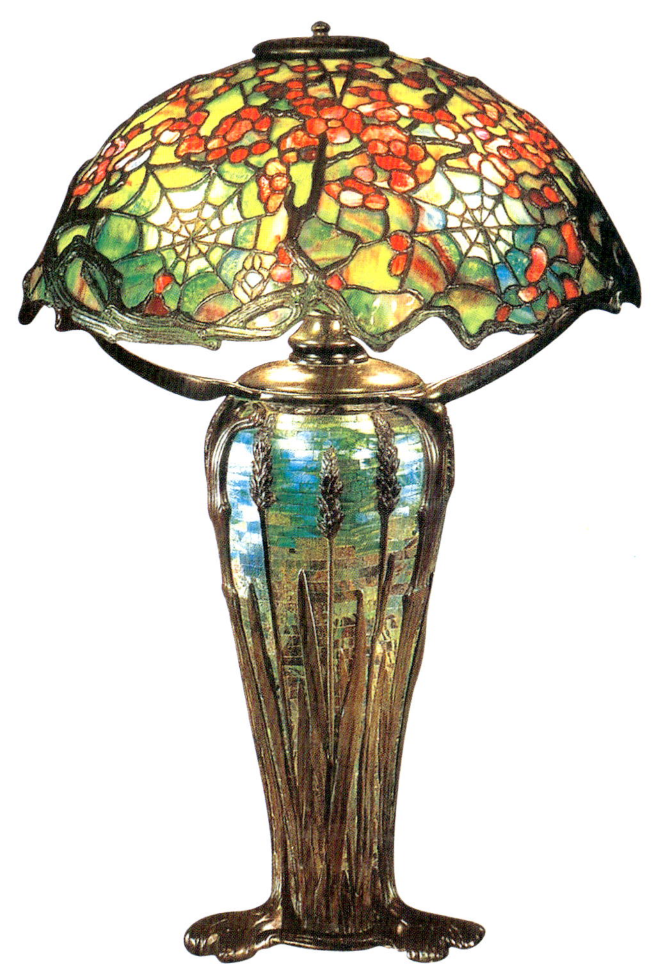

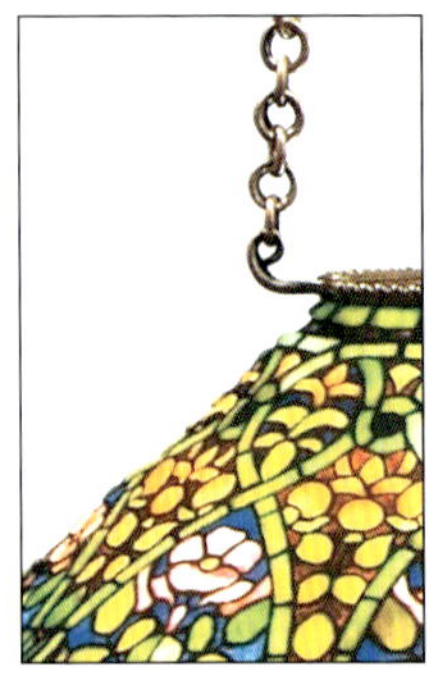

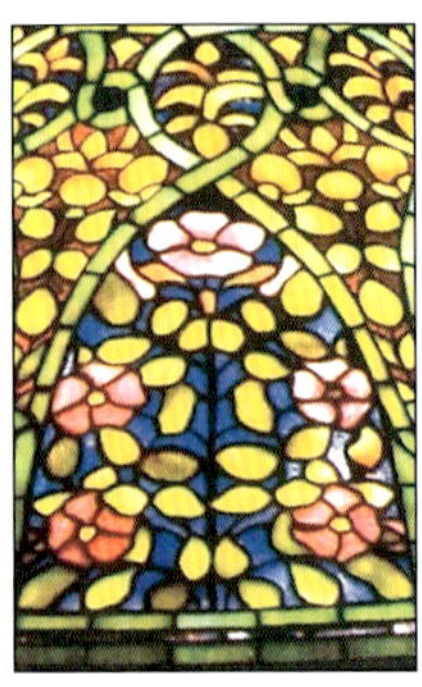

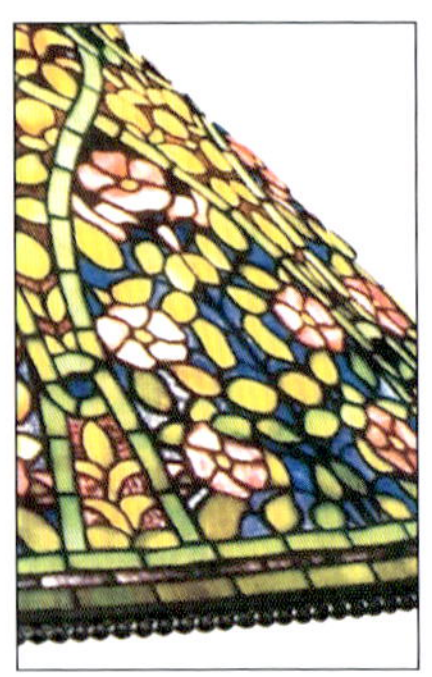

friend of the new Society. The establishment of the Architectural League found him equally receptive.

The period of 1870 to 1890 was characterized by an unusual movement in art matters by no means confined to New York, a movement that showed itself by the foundation of societies and organizations through which it was hoped to enlist the interest of the public. The National Sculpture Society, which still flourishes,

Rosette Hanging Lamp

Leaded glass and bronze.

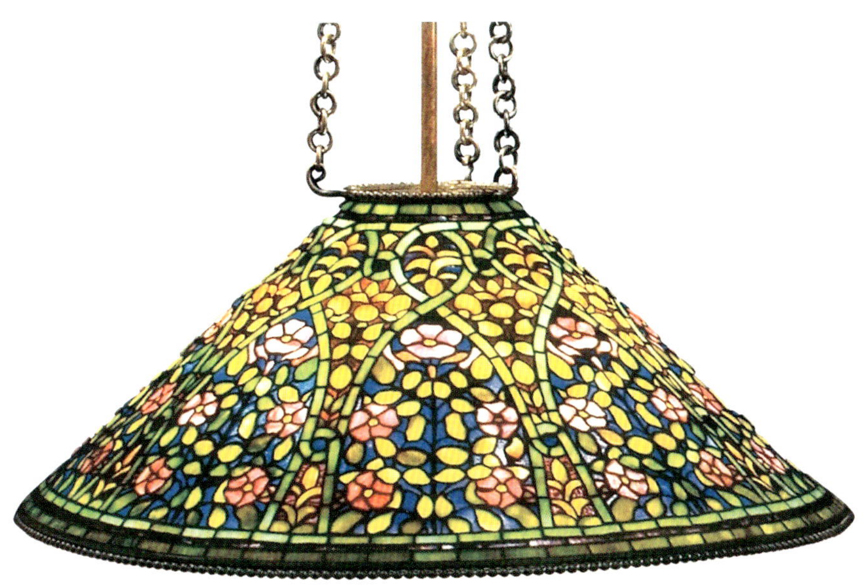

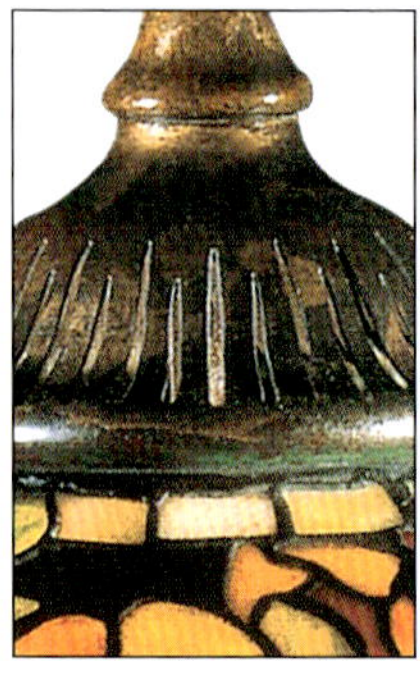

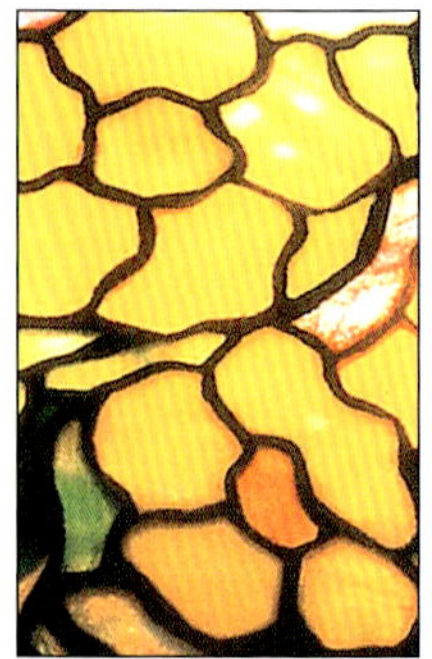

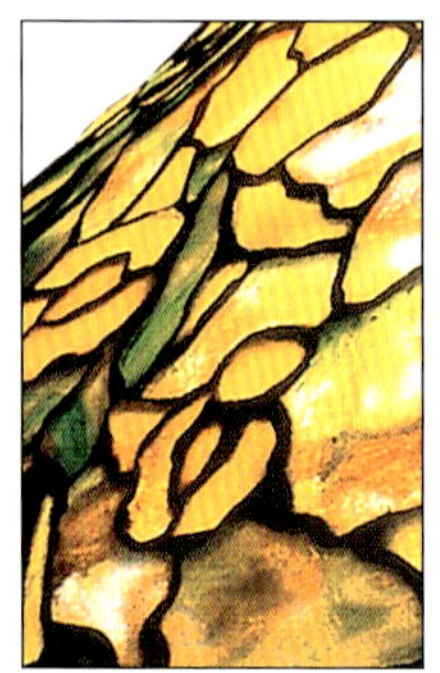

the New York Etching Club, a band of gallant but perhaps premature pastellists, and the New York Society of Fine Arts, these last no longer of this world, were started at that time. Tiffany was working out some of his ideas in other mediums than oils and watercolors even then, but he was guided by movements indicated by such organizations for the encouragement of the narrower "fine arts."

Allamander Straight Side Circular Hanging Vase

1910.
Leaded glass and bronze, shade: 71.12 cm.

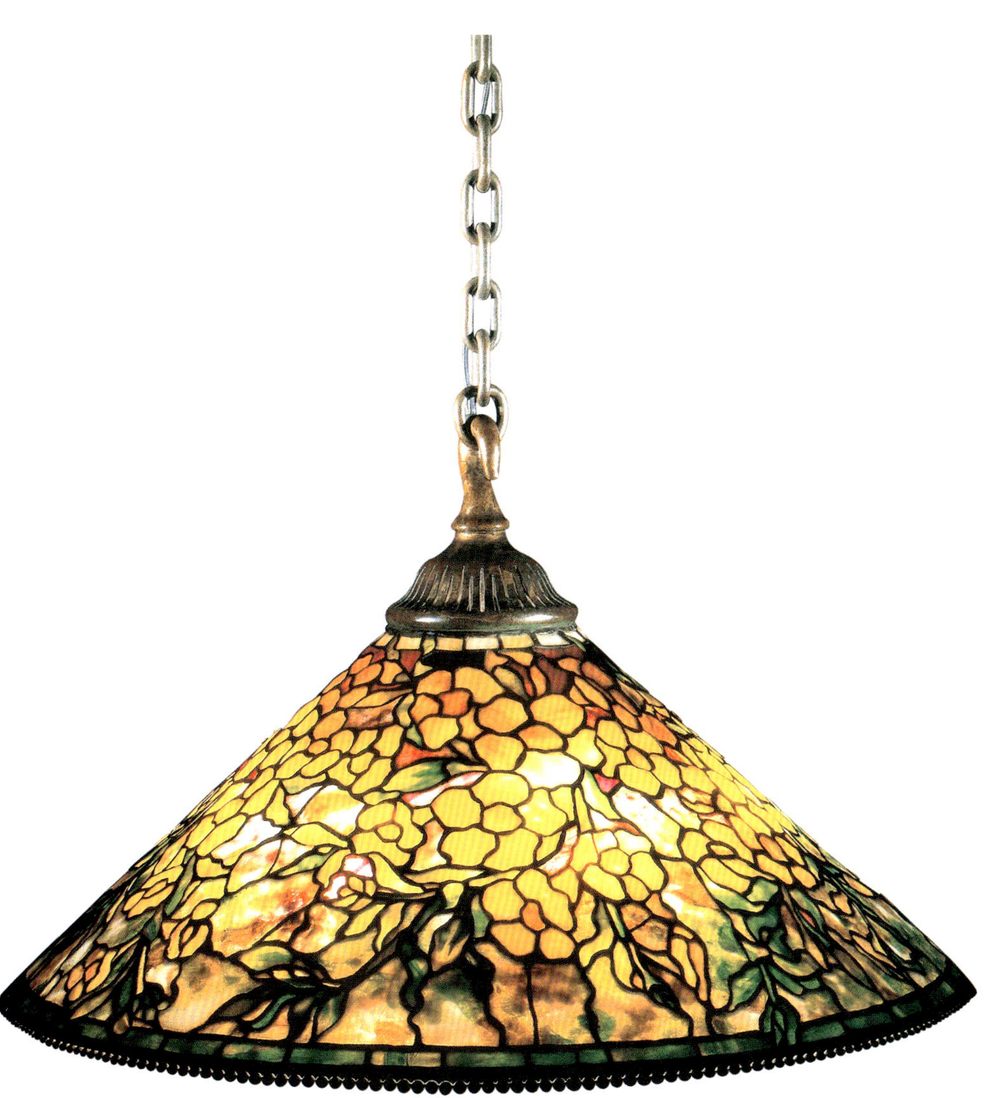

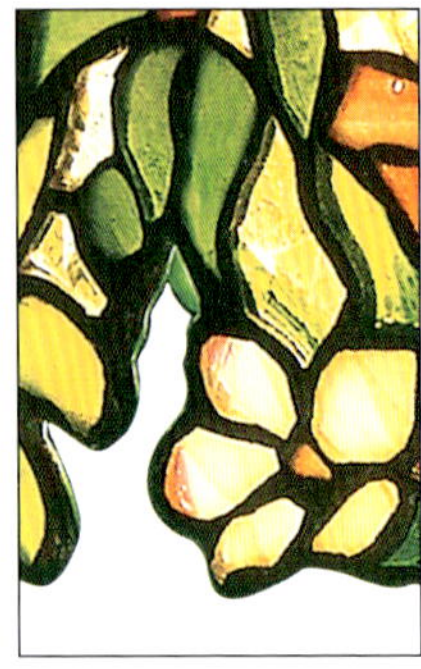

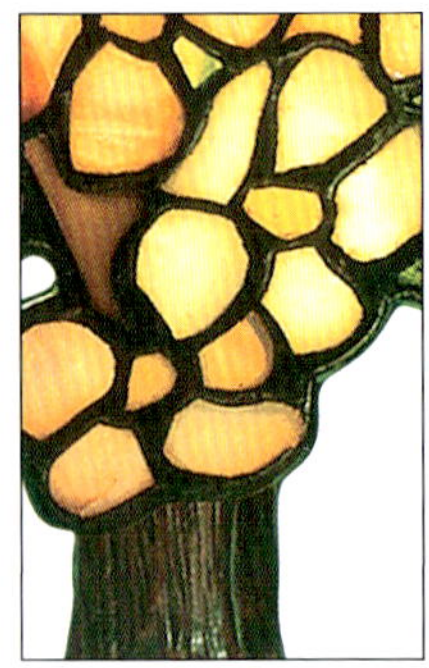

In the early seventies we find Tiffany in Algiers enchanted with the broad masses of Muslim architecture, the long level lines of mosques and their surrounding buildings cut by the trunks and shadows of palms. Here is a view in 1874 called "The Pool" which is typical of the strong sunlight, the color, the contrasts that Decamps loved to reproduce. At the same time we find him catching the character of individuals

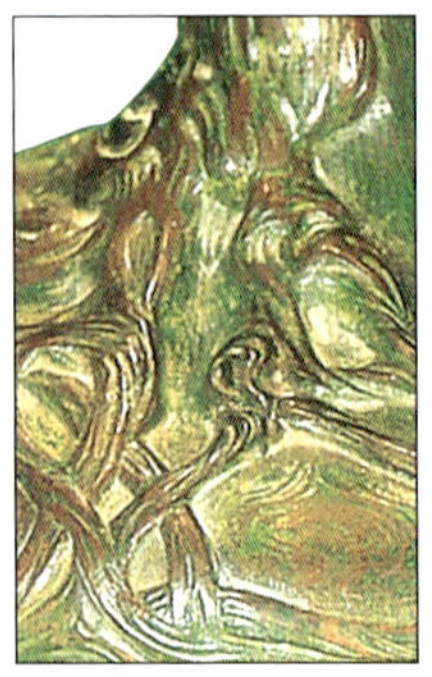

Peony Apple Blossom Lamp and Shade

Favrile glass, bronze and lead.

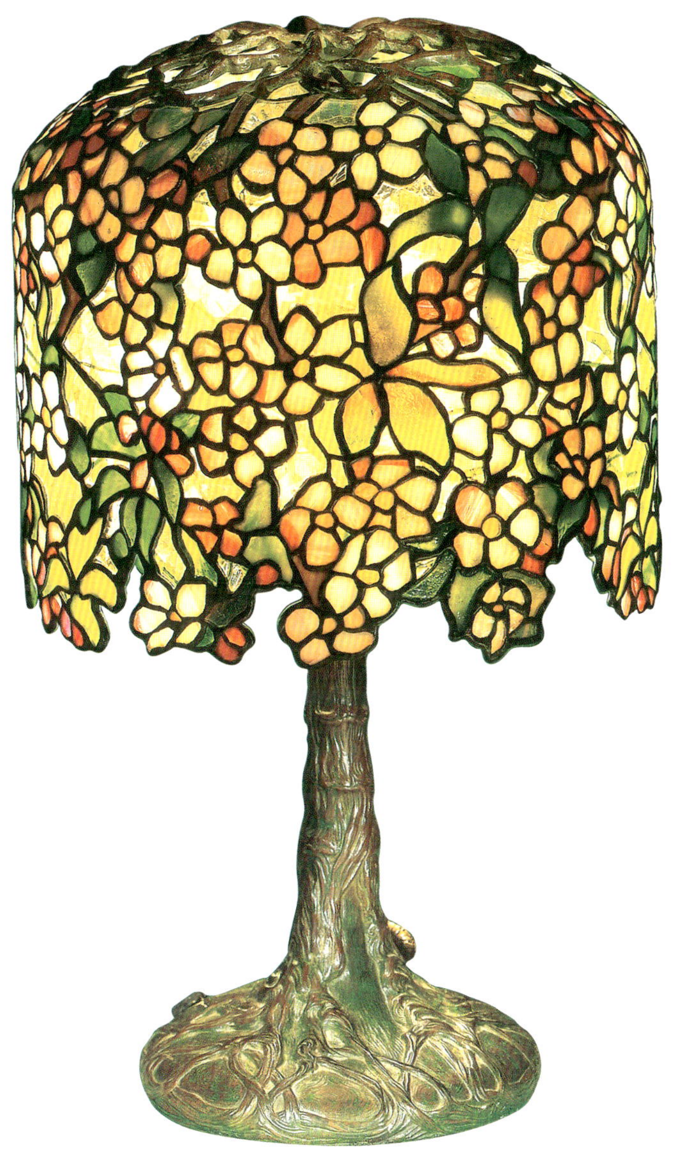

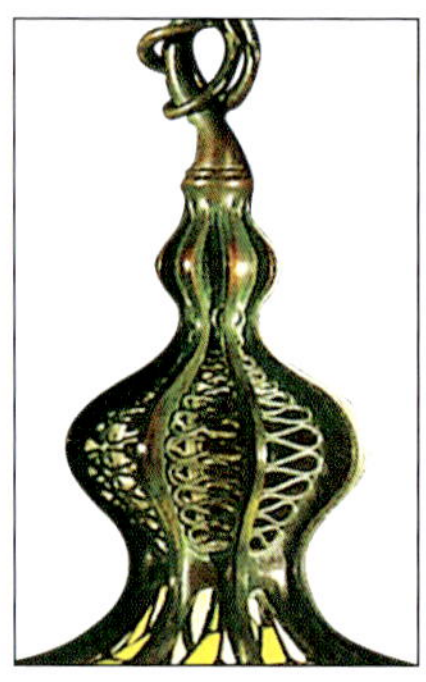

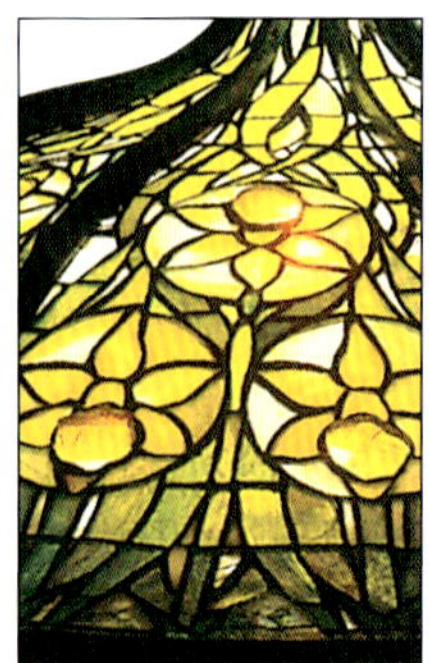

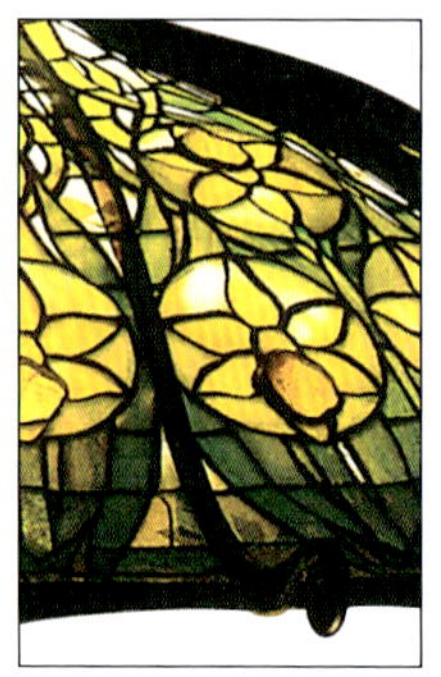

as in "Cobblers at Boufarik" (1888) and "Street Scene in Algiers," genre pictures from the Orient in which one feels the colorist as well as the painter of figures, a feeling for masses of light and shade as well as a sense of proportion in the grouping of human figures with relation to the background of architecture or landscape. On the other hand he did not, for all his experience of Europe and Algiers, disdain the home field or domestic genre.

Daffodil Flared Hanging Lamp

Leaded glass, bronze.

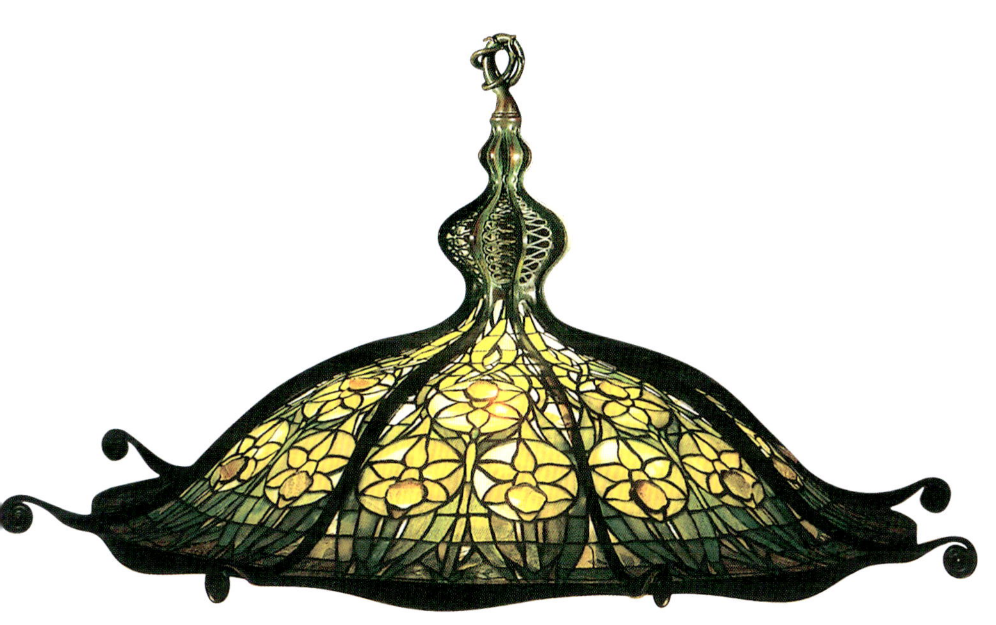

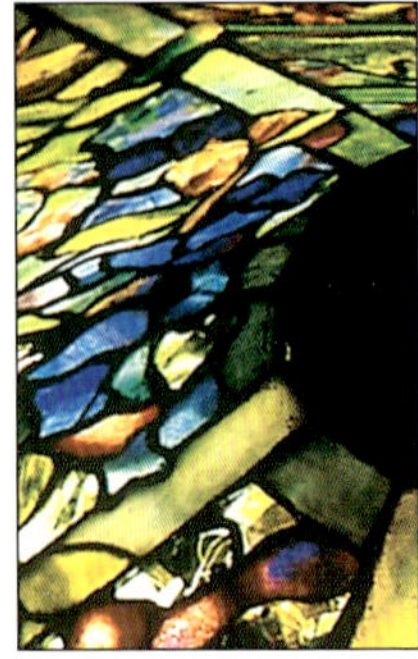

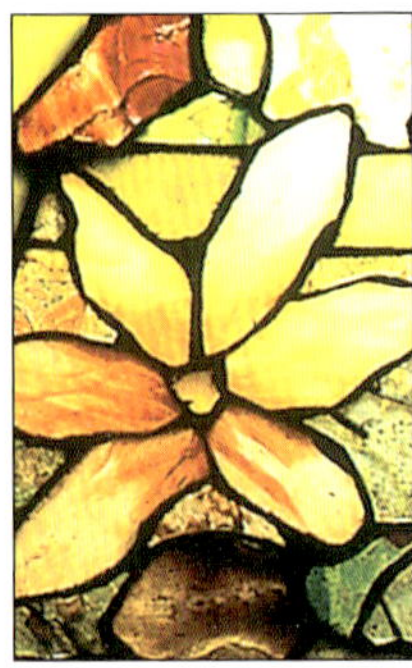

"Peacock" is a stronger and clearer presentation of the same sweeping curves, where the nude model, seated, offers through the lines of legs, torso, neck and lifted left arm the harmonious upward waves which culminate in the neck and head of Juno's bird. In this we have more distinctly enunciated a bit of symbolism. The seated figure may be called Psyche. With the peacock as

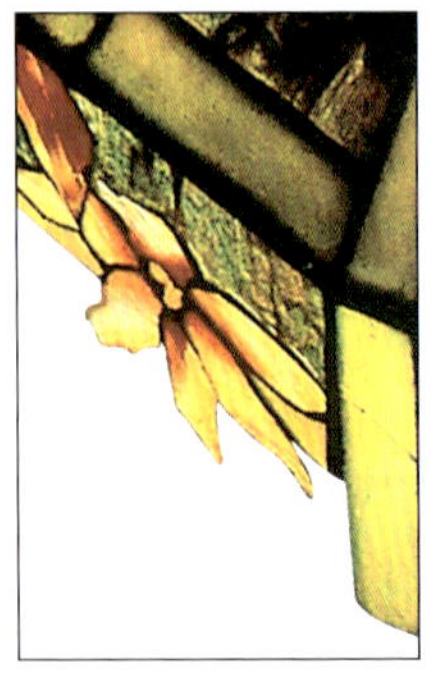

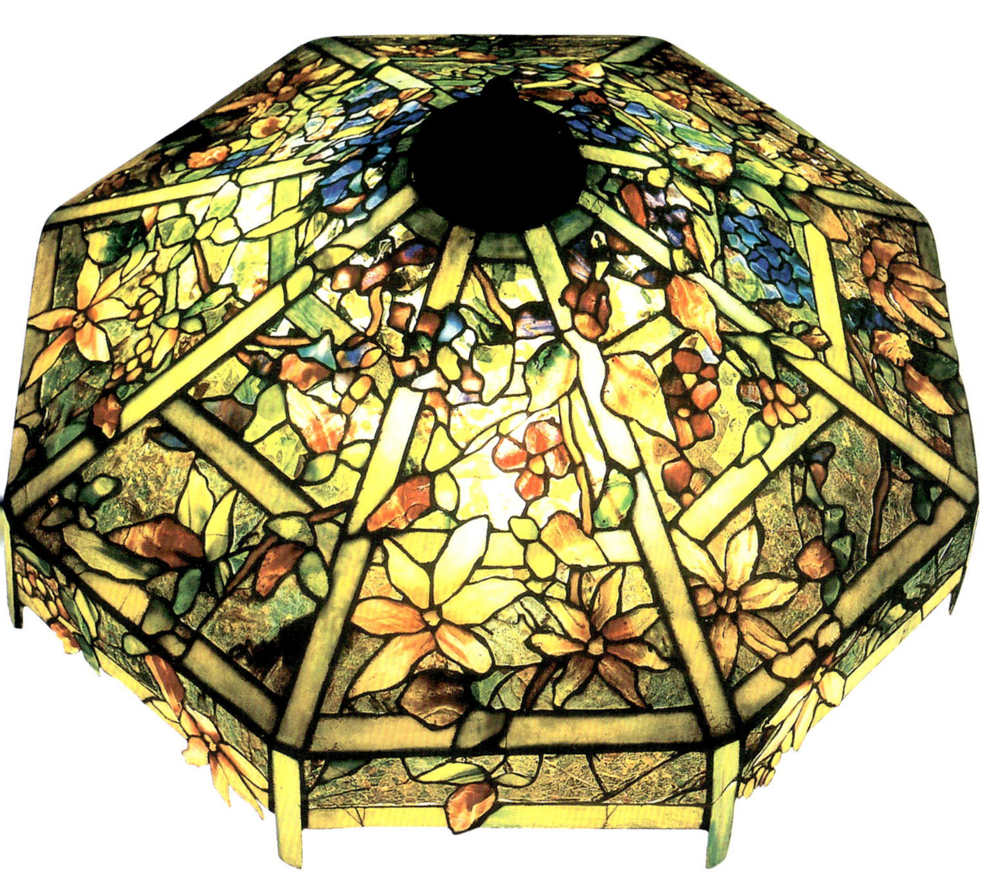

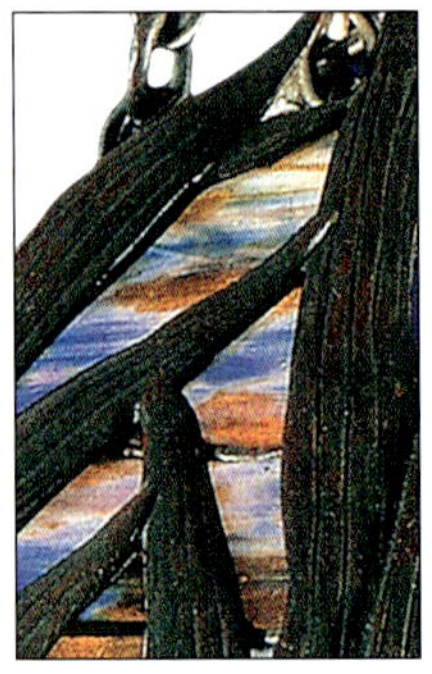

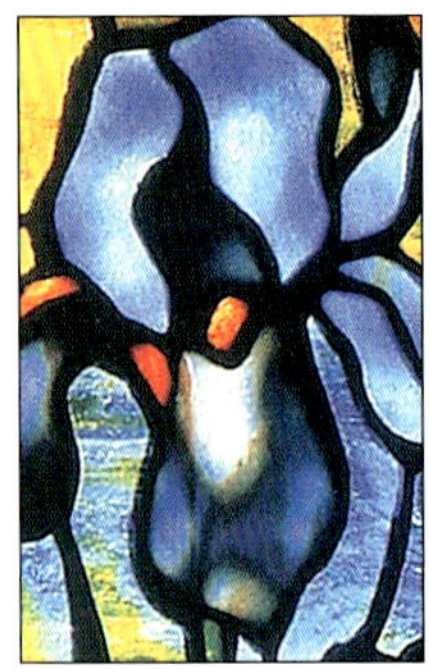

the symbol of worldliness and sensuous beauty, being a bird of pride supposed to lack intellect and soul, we may contrast the butterfly which Psyche holds out with the peacock as the traditional symbol of immortality. Psyche's face accentuates the contrast between the superior and inferior. Above the bird's head the fruit-laden branches continue the sweeping lines and carry

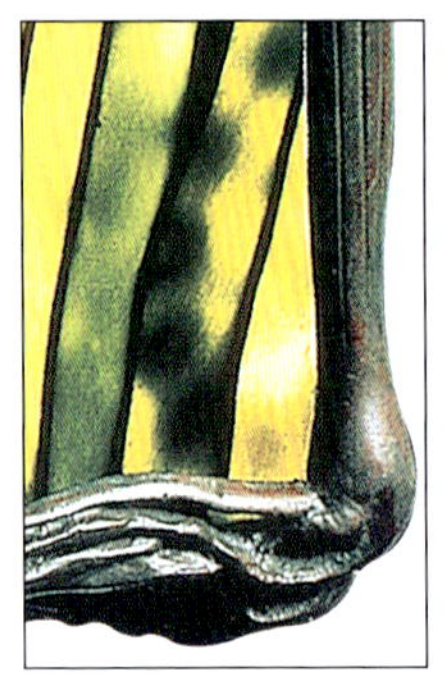

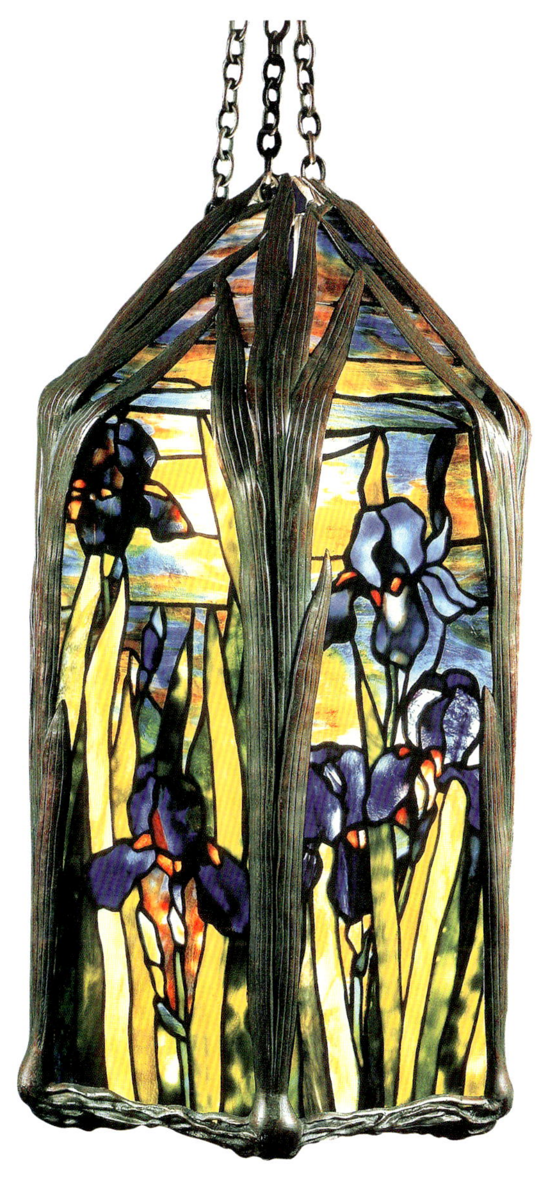

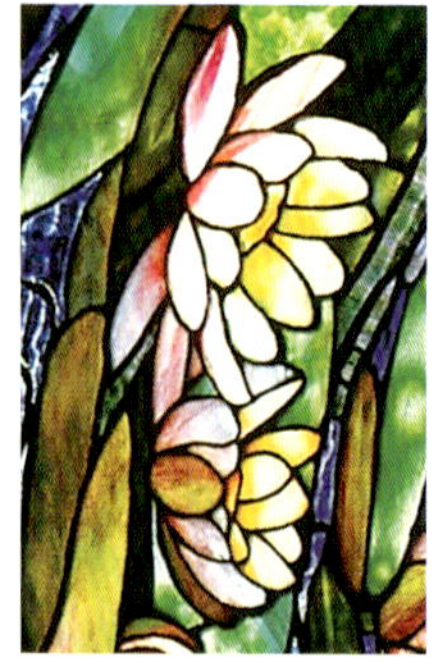

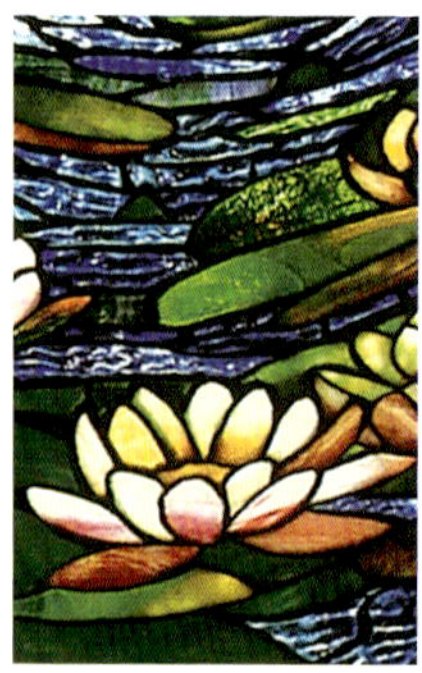

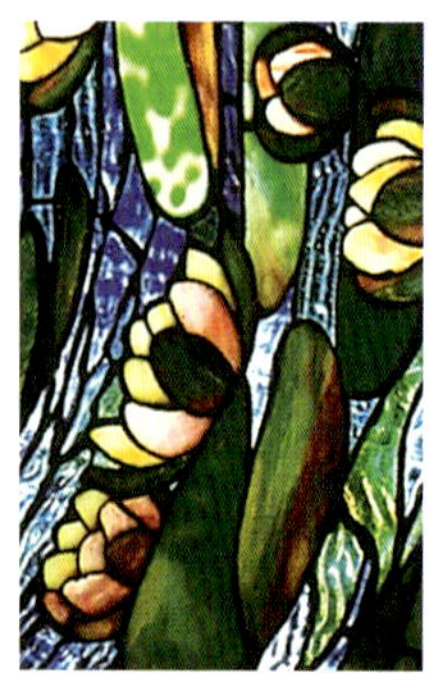

the eye back again to the seated figure. "Peonies" is an example of Tiffany's power of painting flowers with an admirable combination of arrangement and orderly disorder, at the same time that full justice is done to the beautiful rich colors of blossoms and vase. It would be easy to add to these examples, but the singular variety of his work compels one to call a halt.

Lotus Flower Sconce

Leaded glass and bronze.

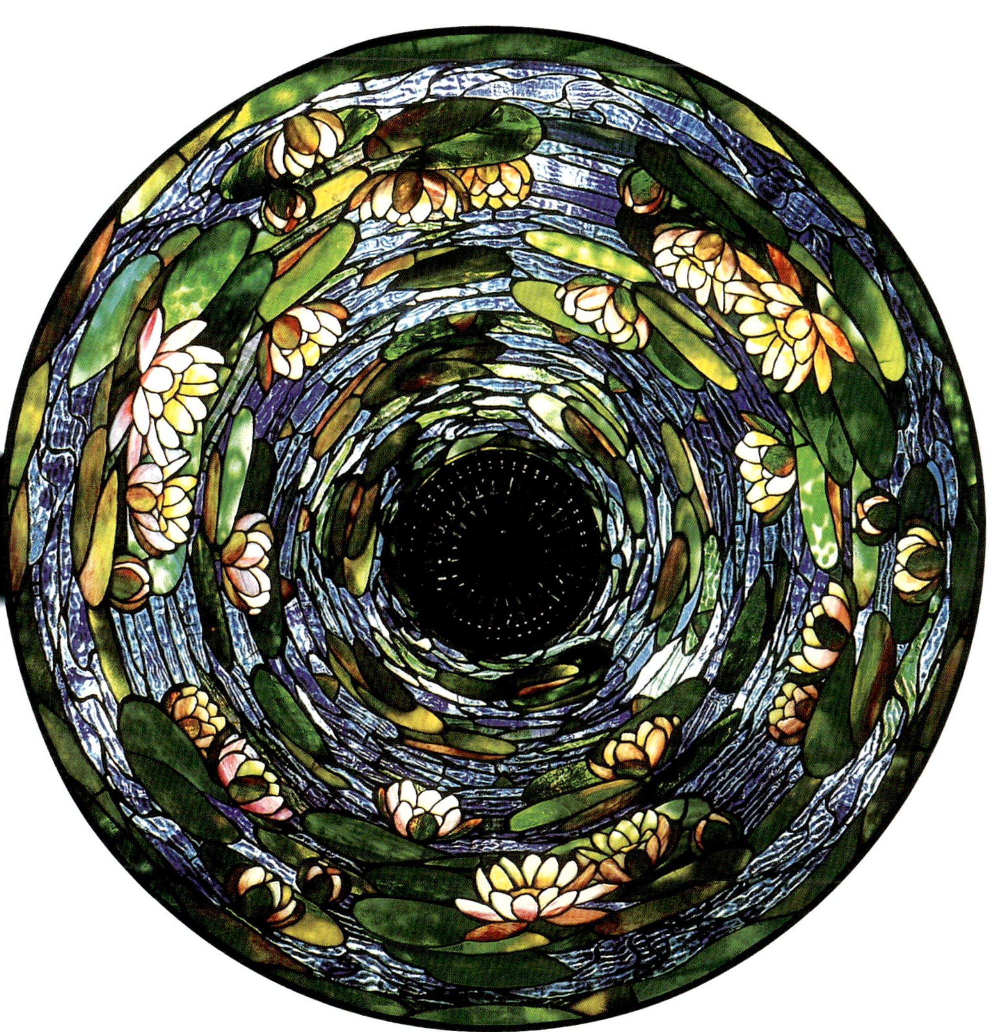

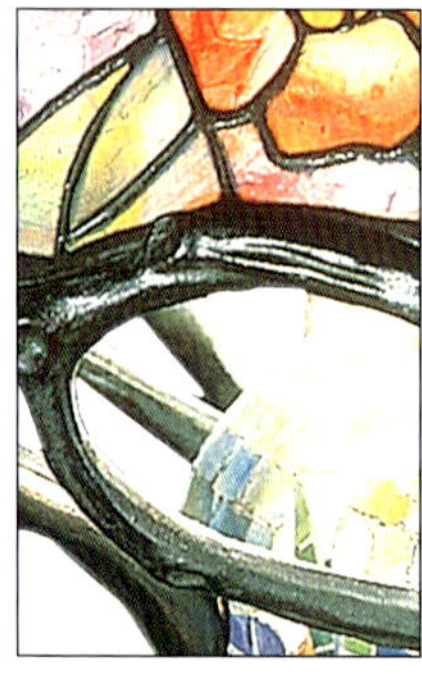

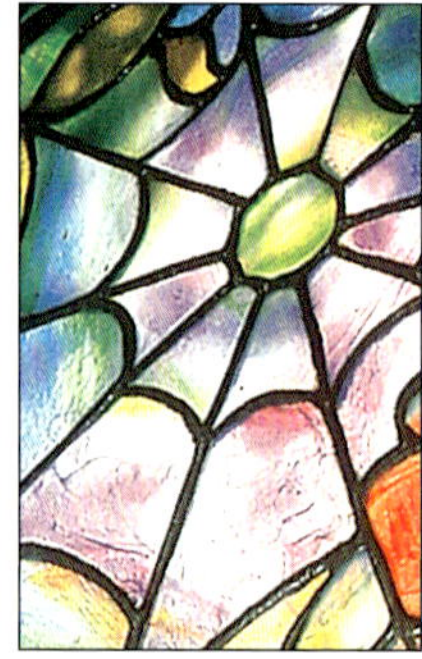

Tiffany's leaning toward the Orient was recognized by his election to the Imperial Society of Fine Arts in Tokyo; he became also a member of the Societe Nationale des Beaux Arts in Paris, while his exhibits at the Exposition Internationale at Paris in 1900 won a gold medal and the title of Chevalier of the Legion of Honor. In 1903 Yale University gave him the honorary degree of Master of Arts.

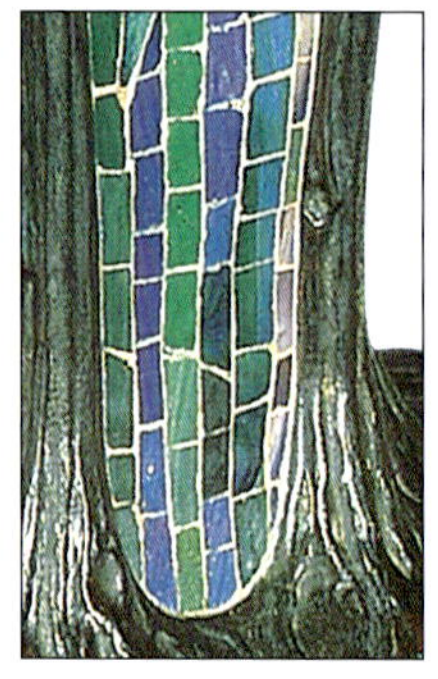

Mosaic Floral Base with Cobweb Shade

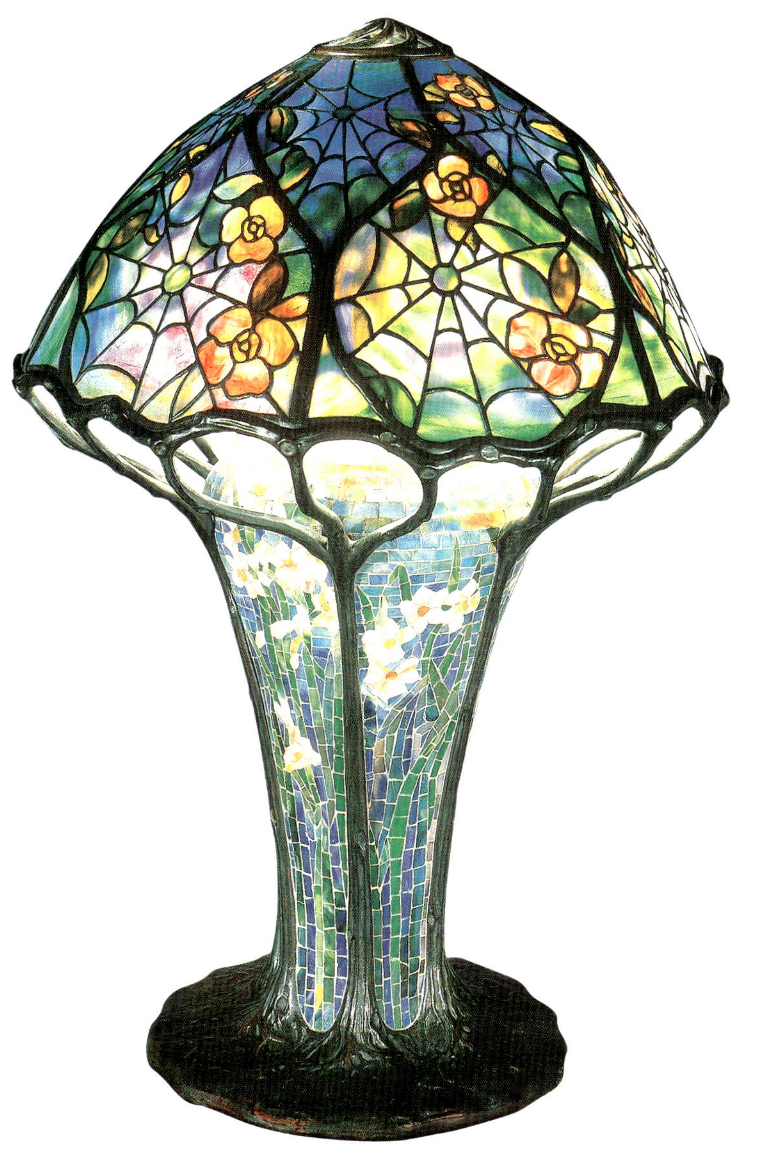

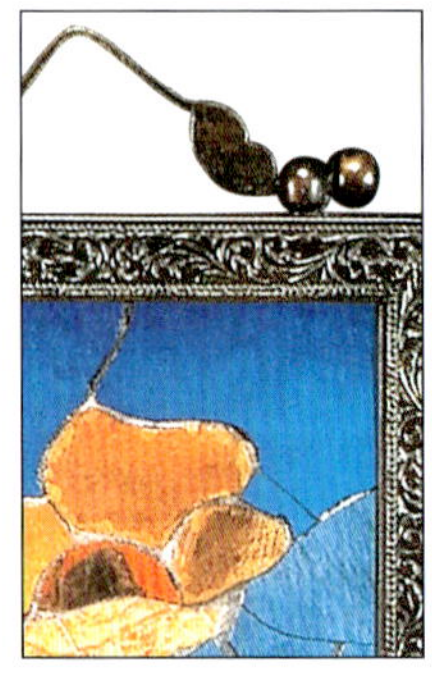

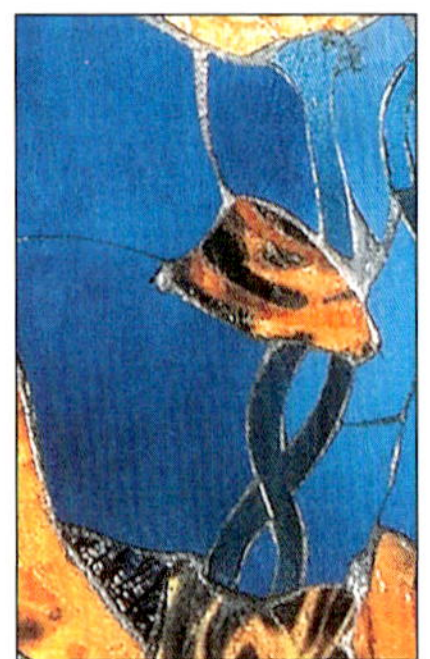

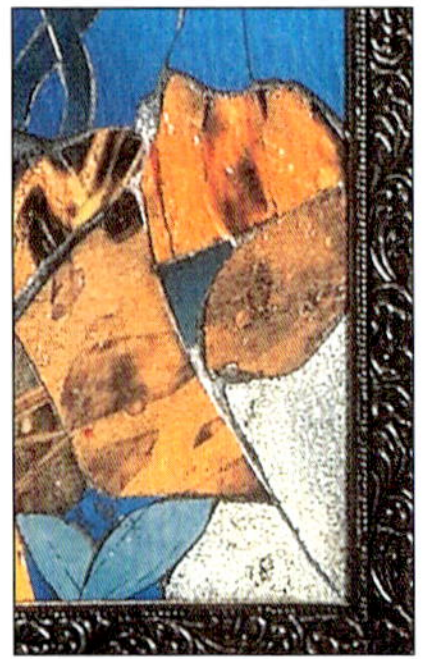

During the earlier period of his life we find Tiffany a student with masters of landscape but extending his scope into landscape with figures, thence to pictures in which the figure is everything, finally to larger decorative work where figures are employed with flowers and still-life to express emotions of a poetic or musical kind in paint. The colorist in him becomes an

Floral Frame
____
Leaded glass.

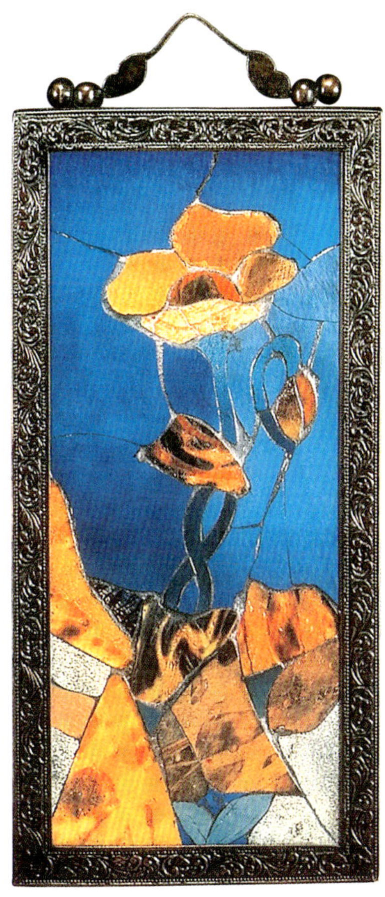

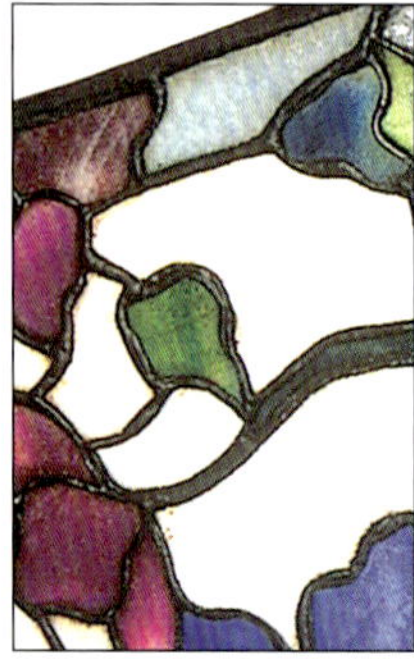

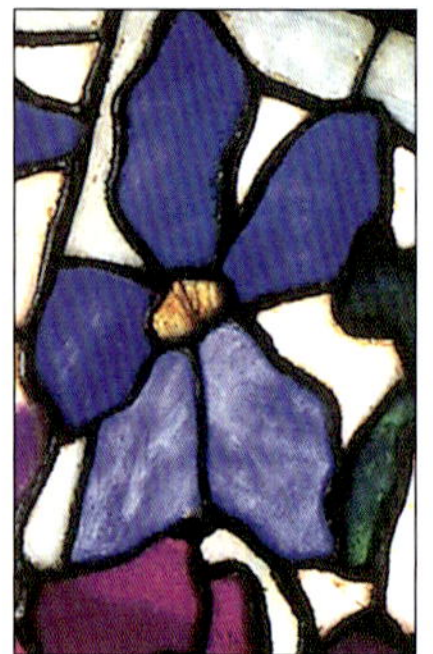

ever more important element and prepares the way for those creations in stained glass through which he has become known far beyond the borders of his own land. And though the multiplicity of demands on his time occasioned by his labors as a craftsman tended gradually to limit his work in painting and watercolors, he has never renounced easel work but continues to give such time as he can spare to his brush and palette.

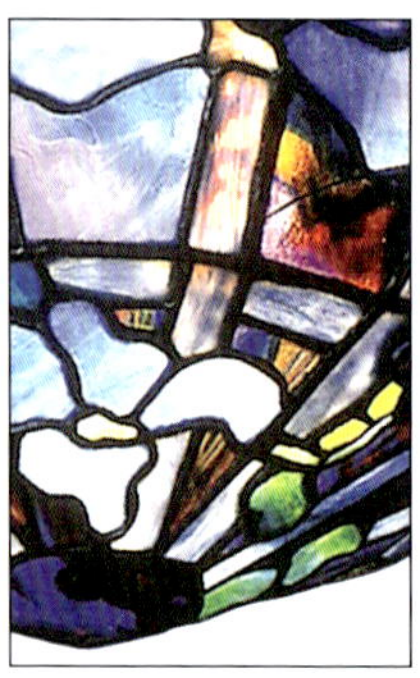

Floral Ceiling Light

Leaded glass and bronze.

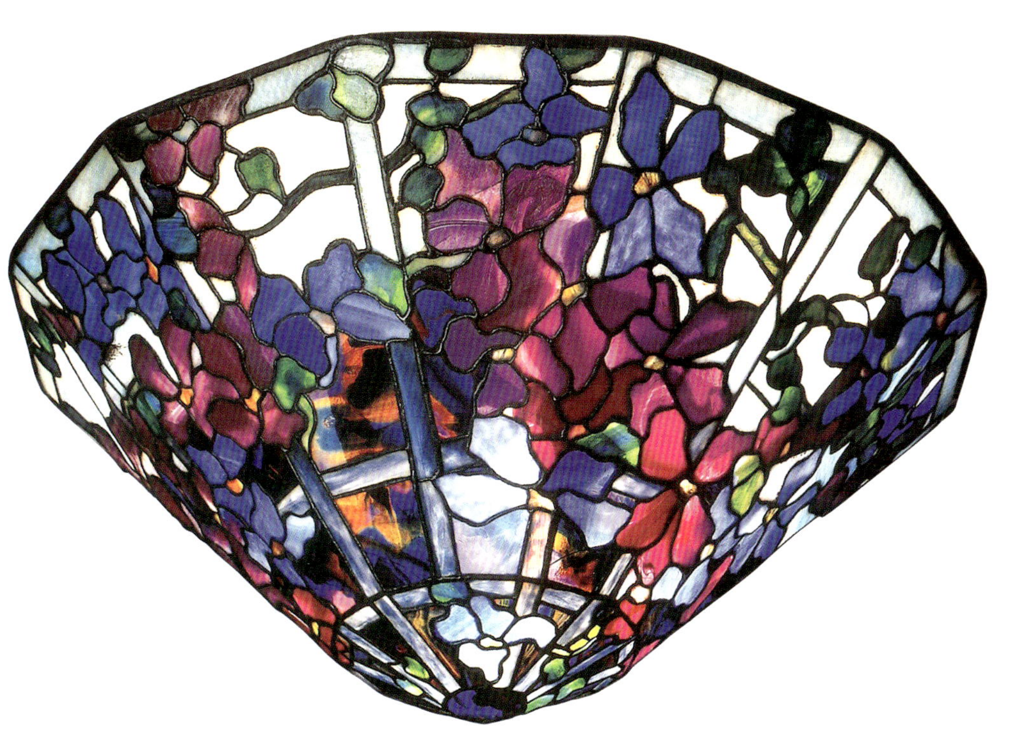

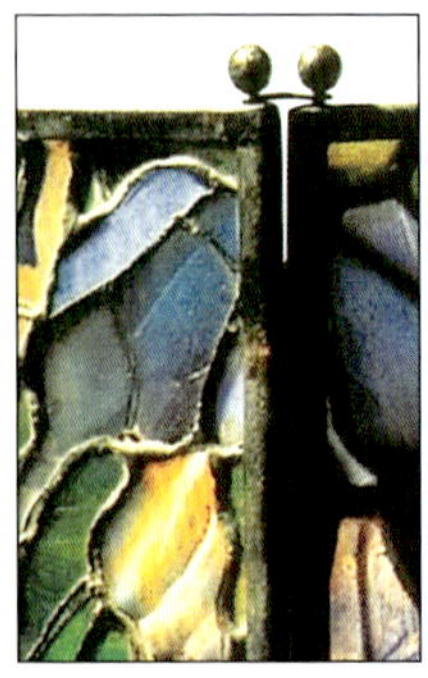

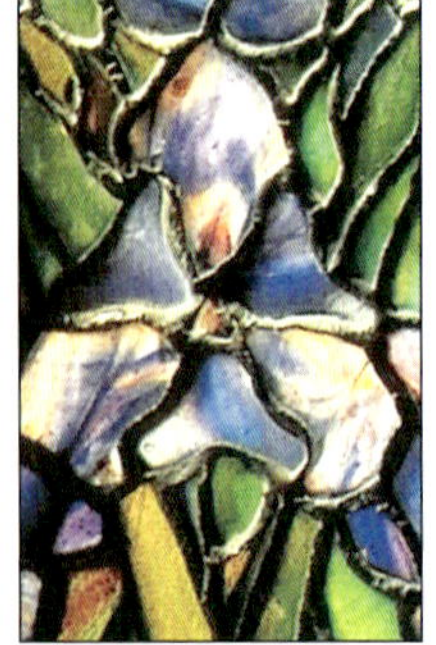

TIFFANY THE MAKER OF STAINED GLASS

During his travels in England, France, Germany, and Italy it could not fail to strike a painter possessed of a feeling for color that modern stained glass as produced in Europe lacks the fundamental quality which separates the colored glass window from mosaic, or painting on the wall, that quality, without which the stained glass window may be said scarcely to have a

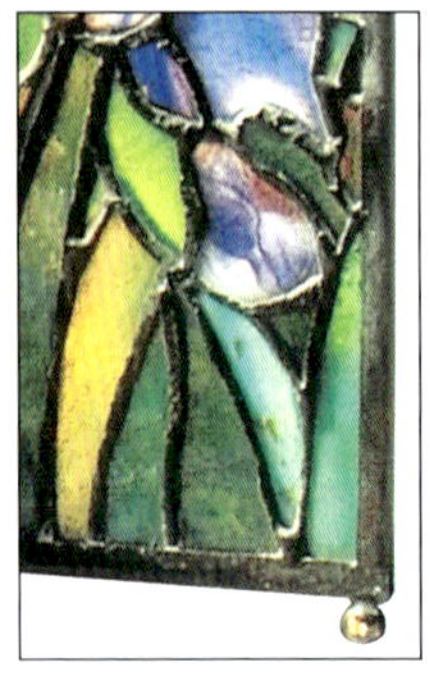

Iris Tea Screen
————————————
Leaded glass.

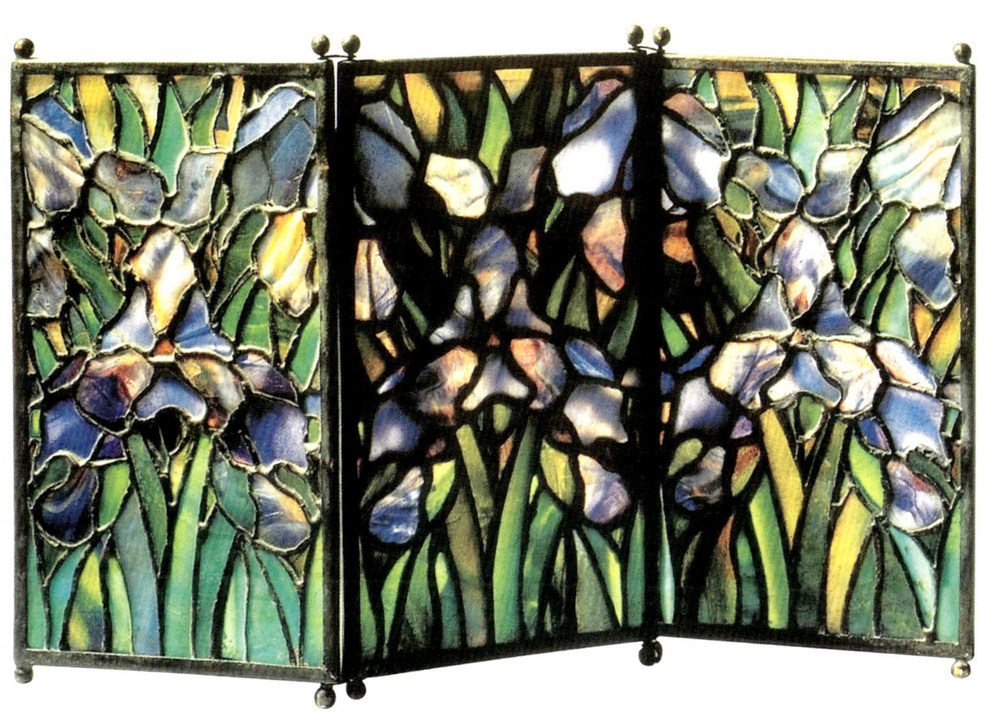

59

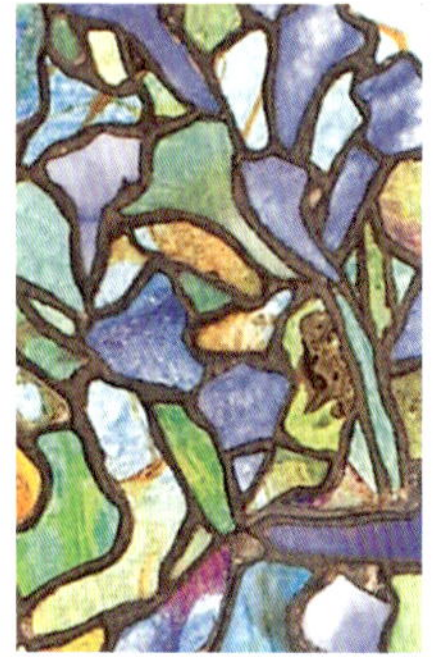

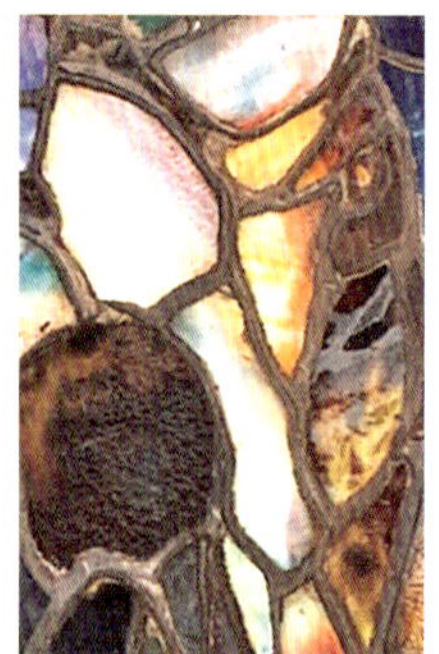

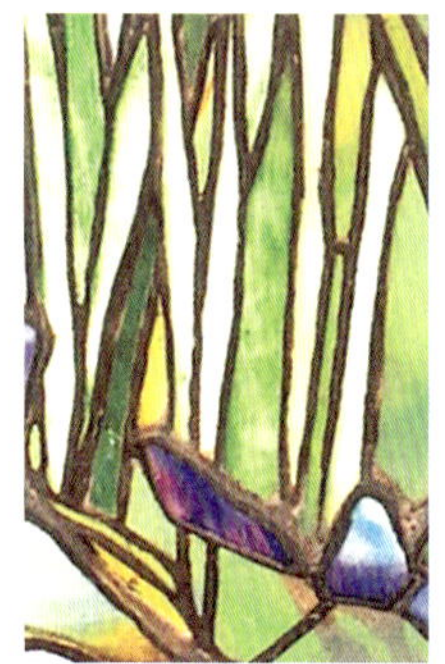

reason for existence. It may be argued in extenuation of the deplorable coldness of this glass that the cloudy skies of northern Europe, the dark atmosphere of great cities, lead people away from such "dim religious light" as the cathedrals favored in the age of the splendor of Gothic architecture.

Practical reasons may well have caused the gradual introduction of lighter tones, especially in palaces,

1900.
Collection of Allen Michaan, Michaan's Auction

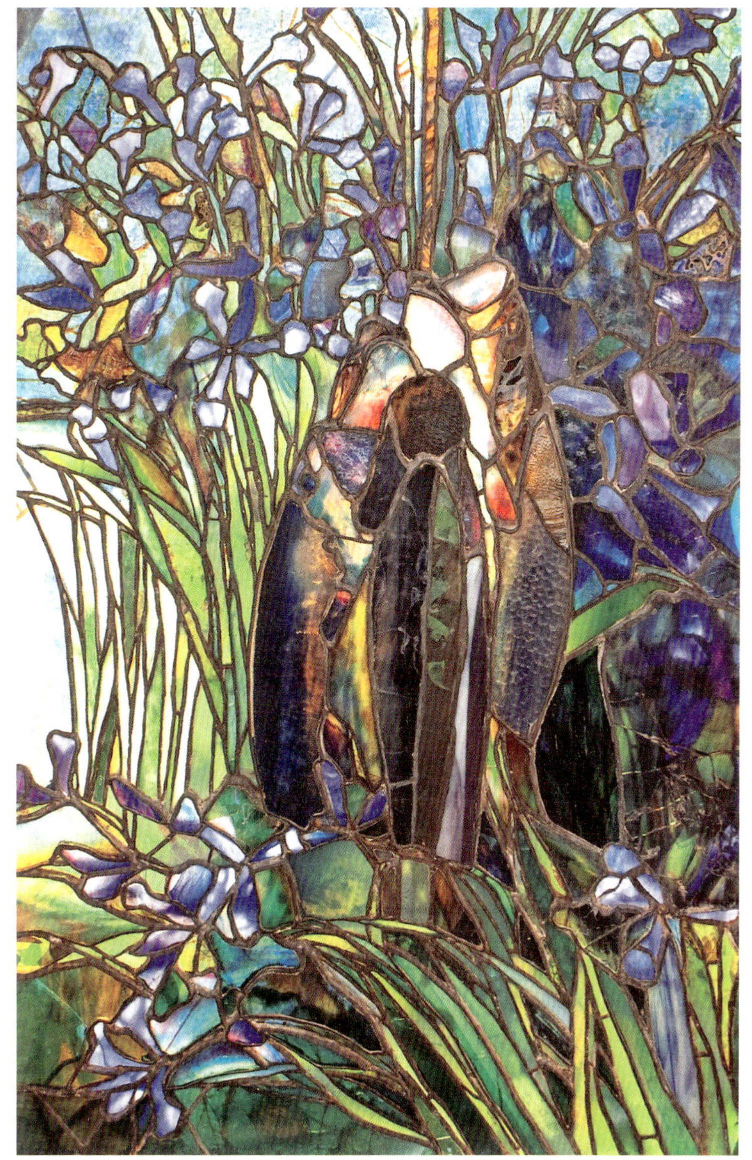

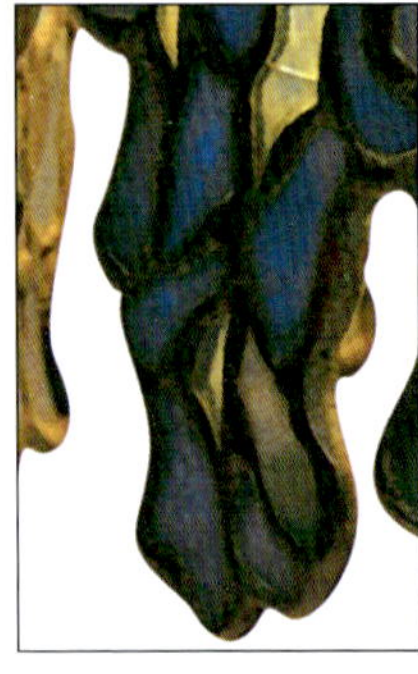

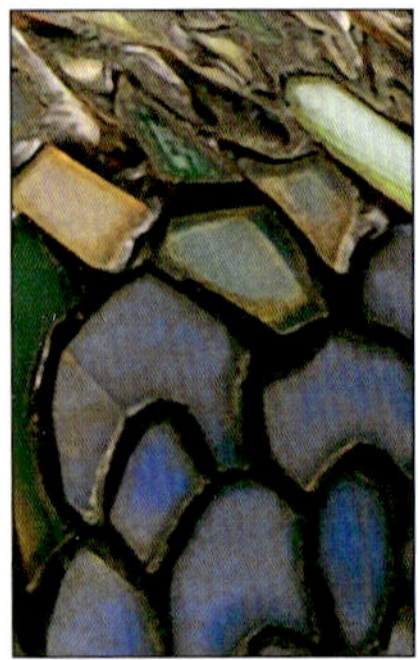

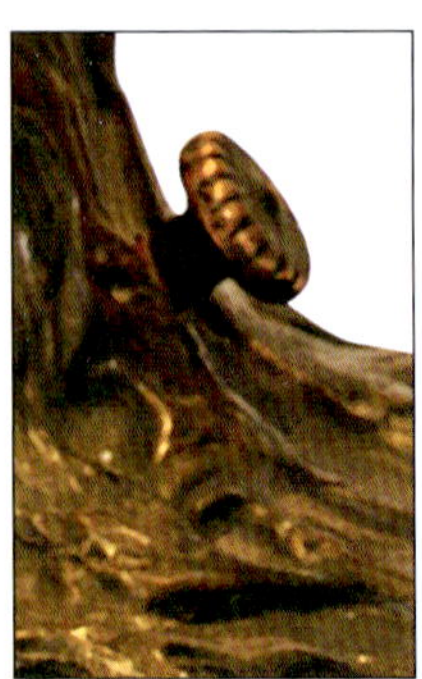

gild halls, town halls, libraries, and other places where it was necessary to have light enough for reading. But this was only one reason. A deeper-going cause was the rarity among artists of the appearance of the color-sense, something that exists or does not exist in a man, something that seems to inhere in the eye or optic nerves, something that no amount of teaching and experience in painting can do more than approximate.

Wisteria Lamp

———————

1902.
Leaded glass and bronze.
Private collection.

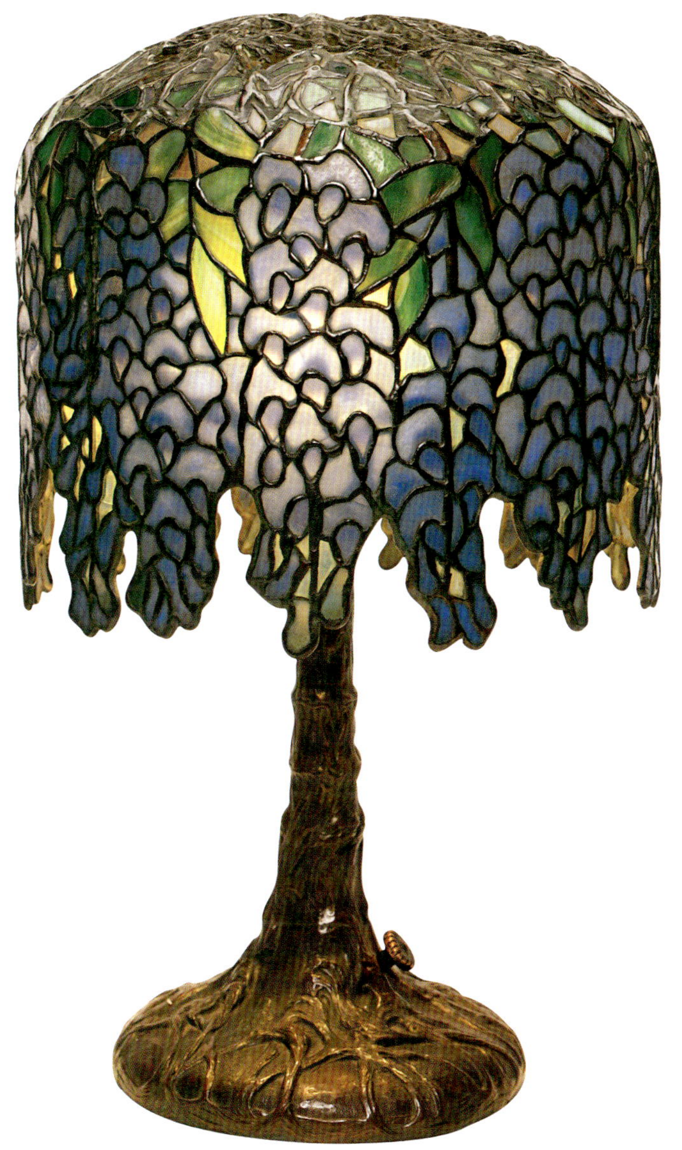

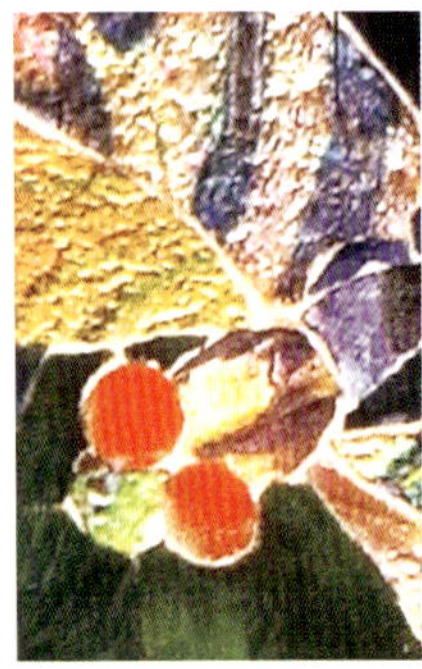

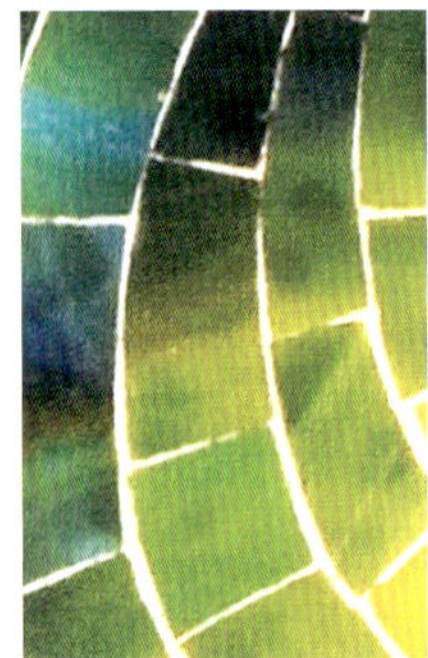

Colorists are men apart. At one period they suddenly start up in Holland and form a great art epoch. In the middle of the nineteenth century they appear with Delacroix and the Barbizon men in France. But always they are antagonized and decried by artists and critics who lack the gift, and see nature in outline rather than in color. Being in the majority, the latter persuade the public that color des not count for much when weighted

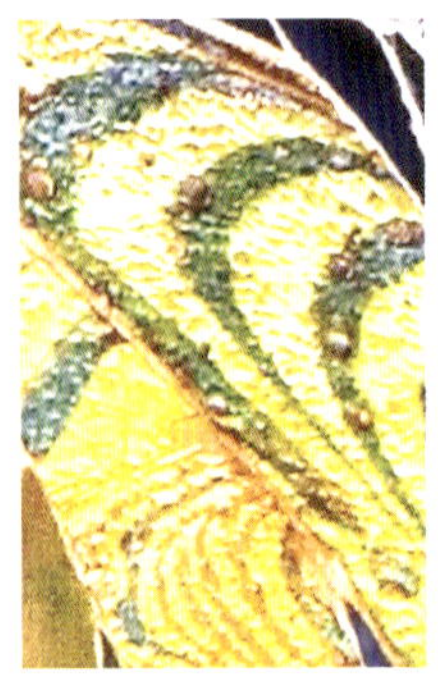

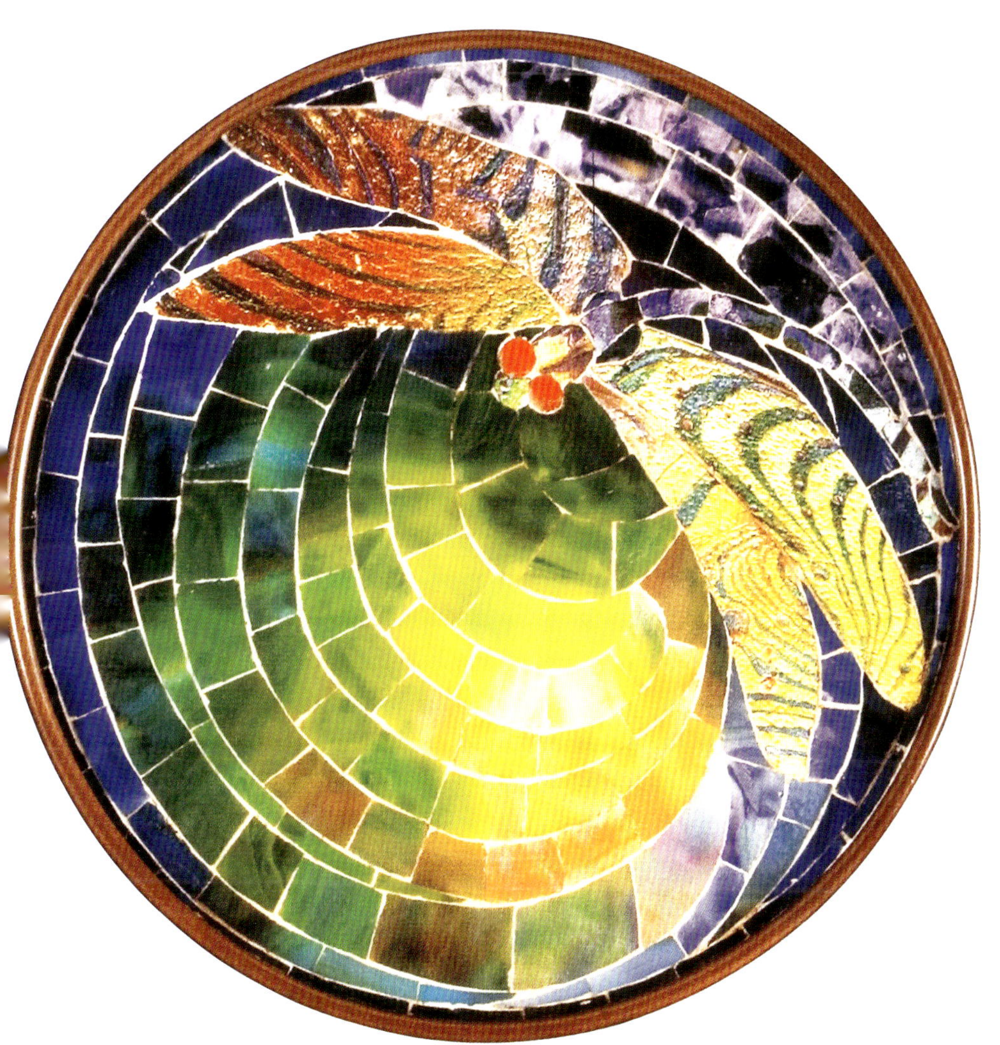

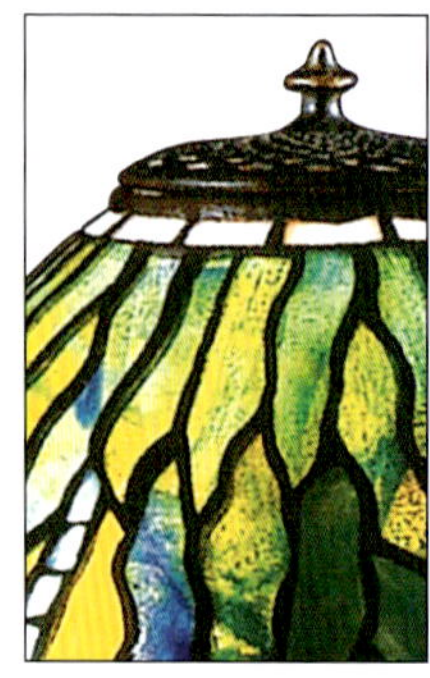

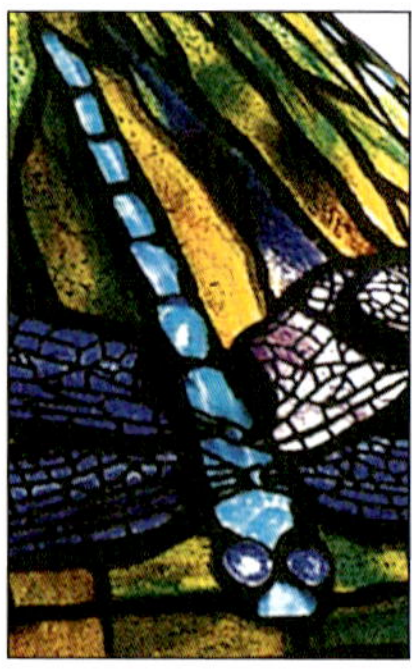

in the scale against form. And they are entirely honest and convinced of in this opinion. Slowly, however, the public comes to see that for such art-products as painting the most important ingredient is color, and in time the colorist is exalted.

Consider a moment the difference between looking at a painting on a solid surface darkened still further by the paint, and looking into a material in which color is fused, this material so placed that light falls through it!

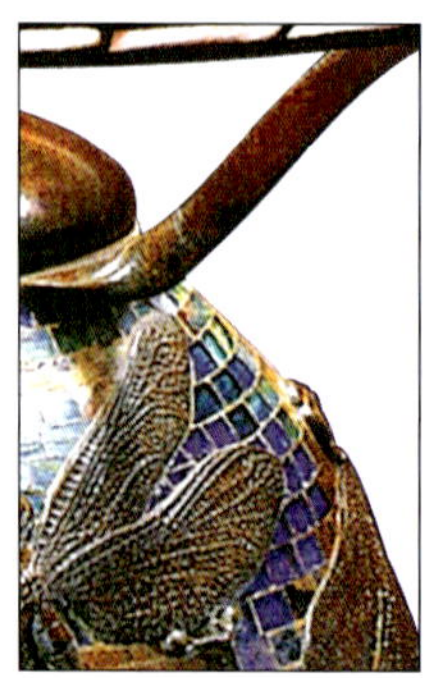

Mosaic Dragonfly Base Nº. 147

Favrile glass, bronze.

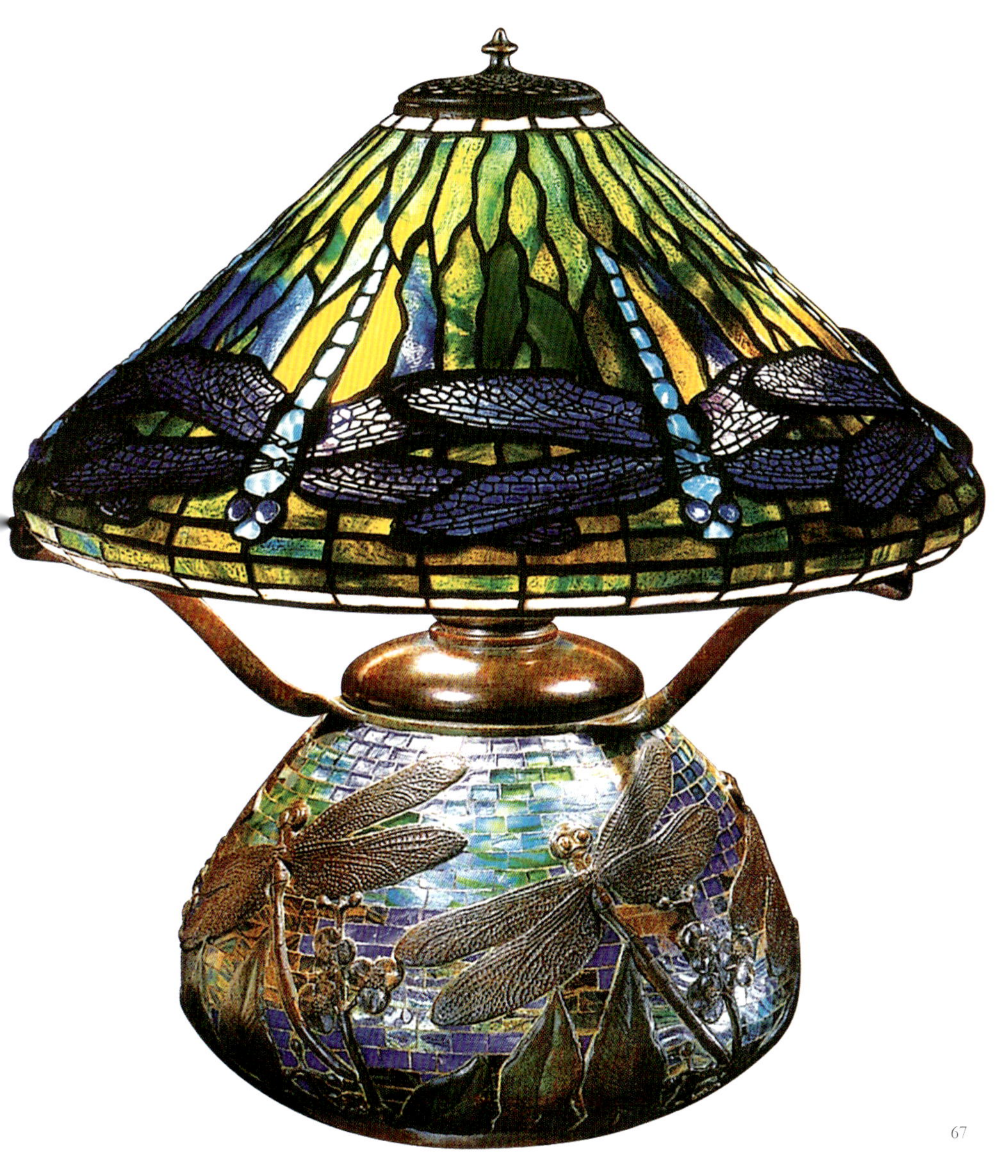

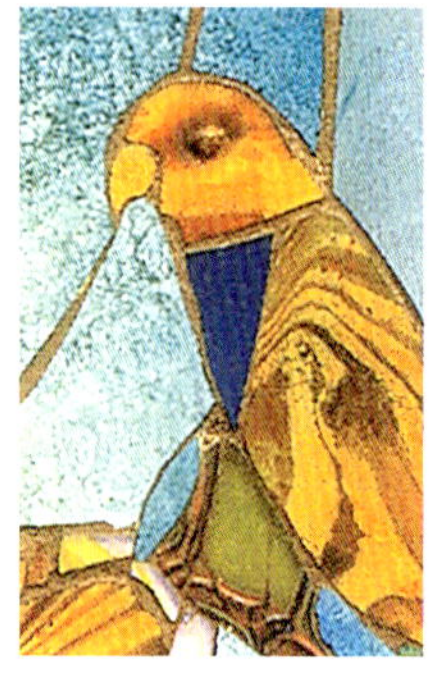

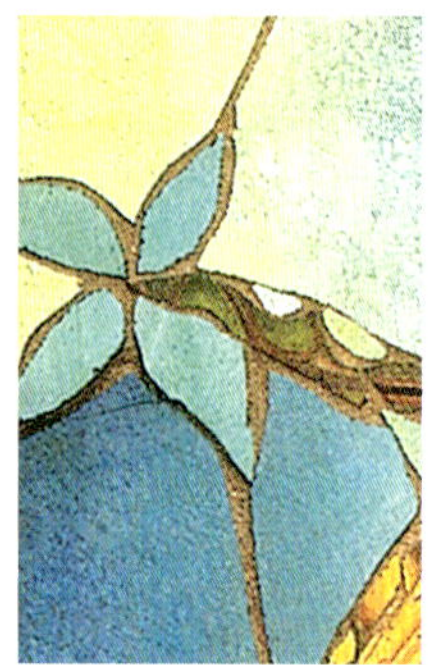

Coming back to America where the skies and atmosphere, summer and winter, seem to ask for interiors and sheltering the eyes from an excess of brilliancy, Tiffany could not but realize that here was a branch of art neglected, or rather badly served, in Europe, which might offer new fields of delightful work to the new world.

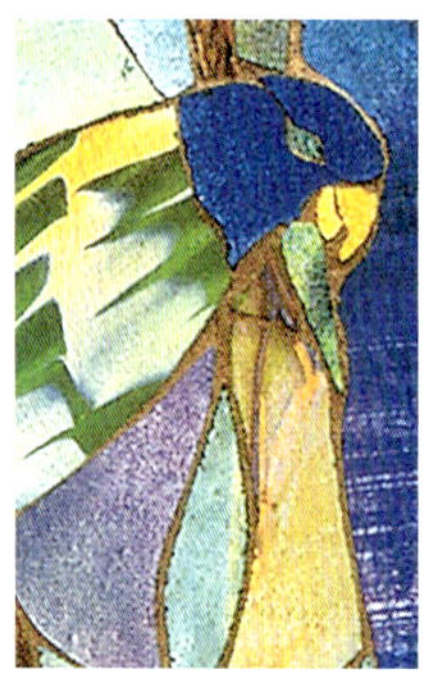

Birds on a Branch

Leaded glass.

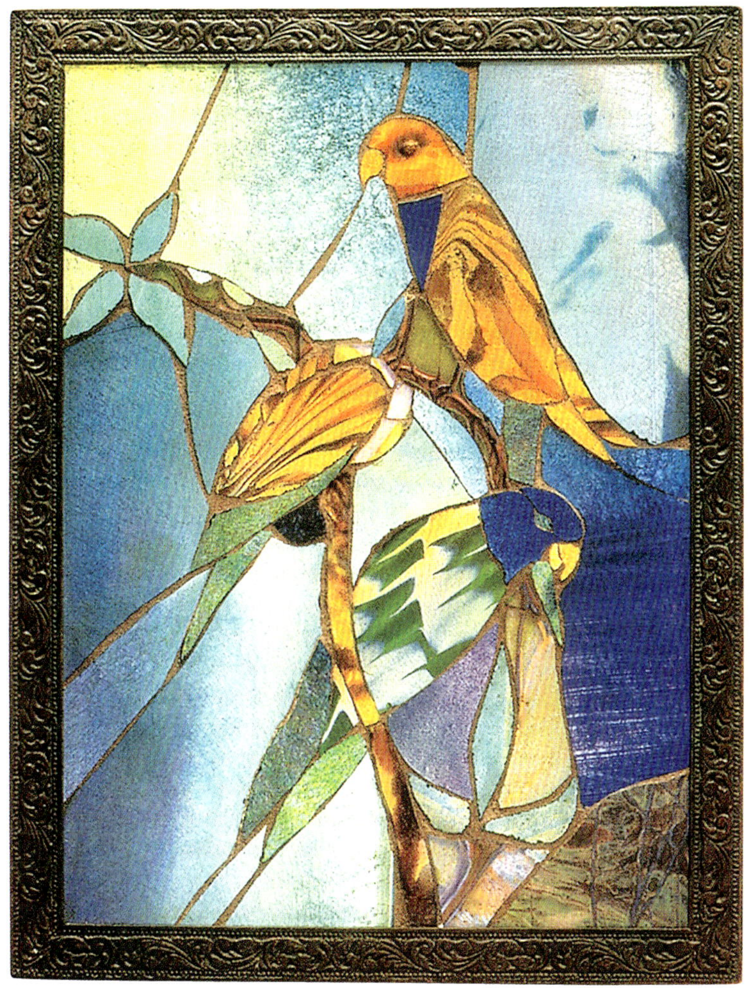

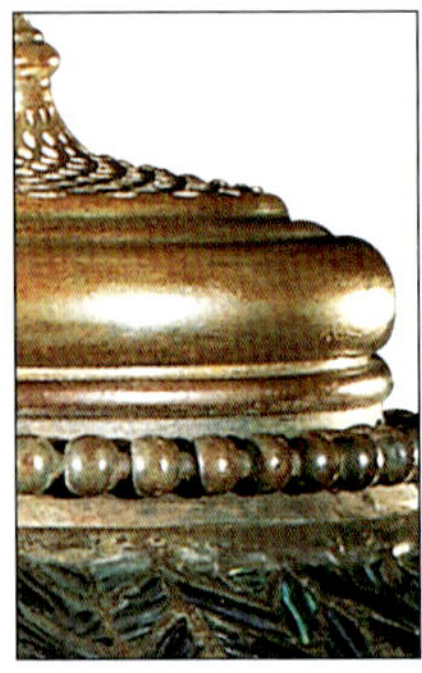

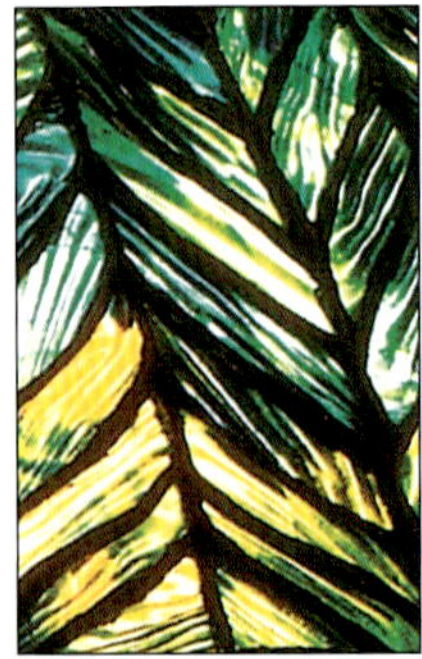

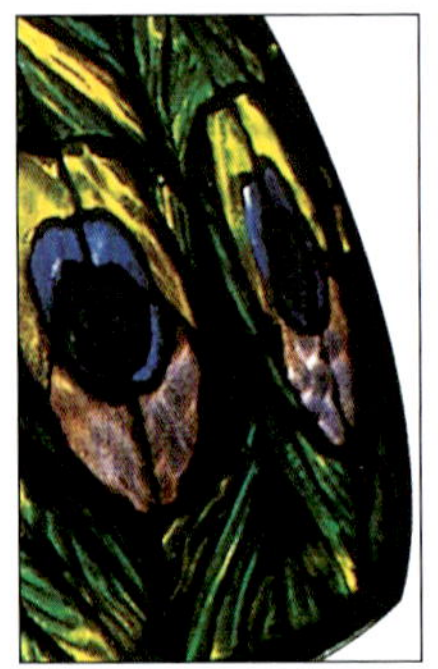

The first windows were mattings, lattices of wood or open-work stone, skins or slabs of ice (under the Arctic Circle), horn, thinly wrought alabaster, and at last glass. And the first glass we may imagine as a material discovered by potters in search of glazing to make their pots impervious to water, which glaze, build up by hand in shapes just like clay, and then subjected to the heat of the kiln, formed the earliest vessels of glass.

Peacock Hanging Lamp

Leaded glass, bronze.

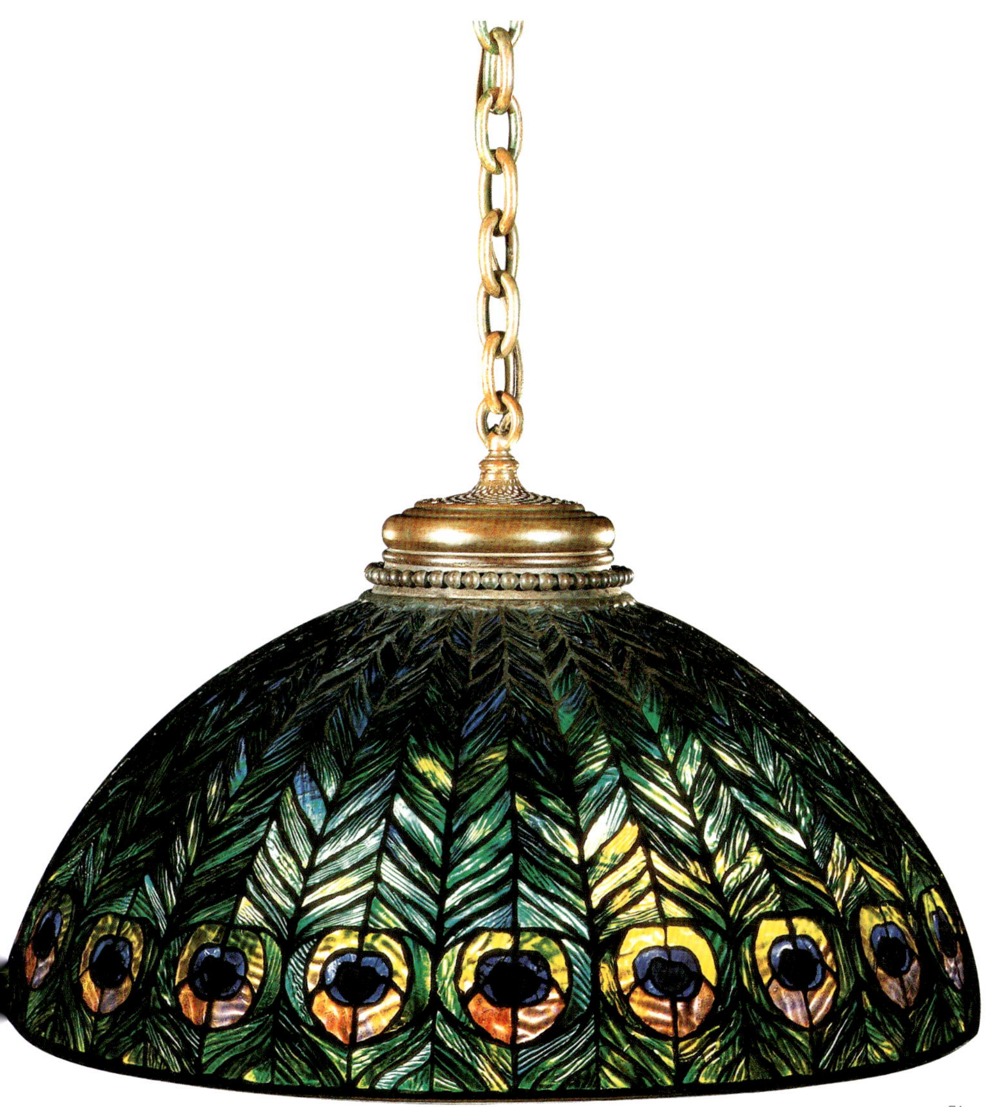

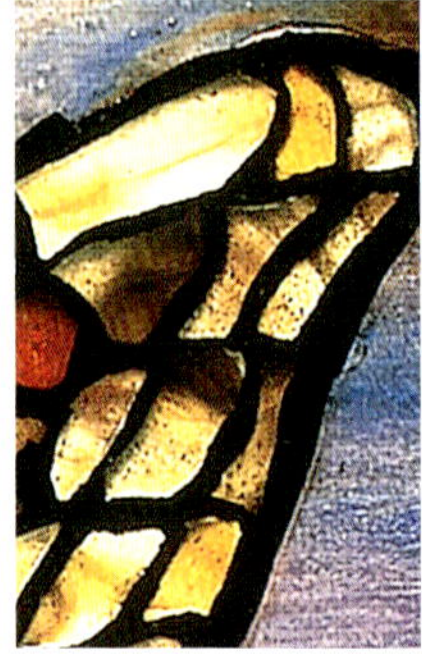

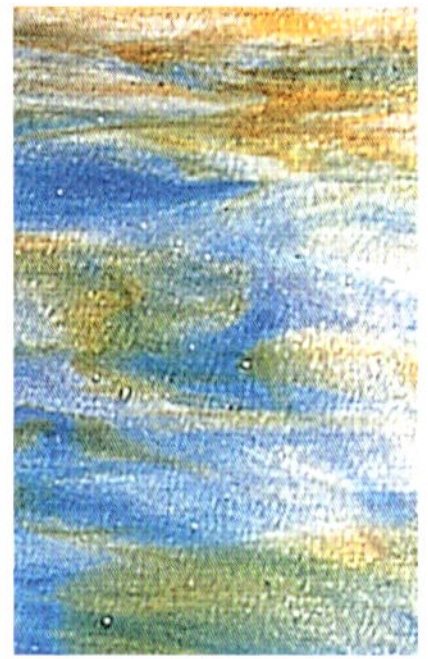

That the Byzantines had glass windows on the small scale is pretty certain, but window glass as we know it must be credited, not to the people of the Mediterranean, but to those of northern Europe. If they did not invent the use of colored or stained ecclesiastical glass, which apparently they took after the Crusades from the expert glass mosaic artists of the late Greek empire, it is probable that they did begin the use of

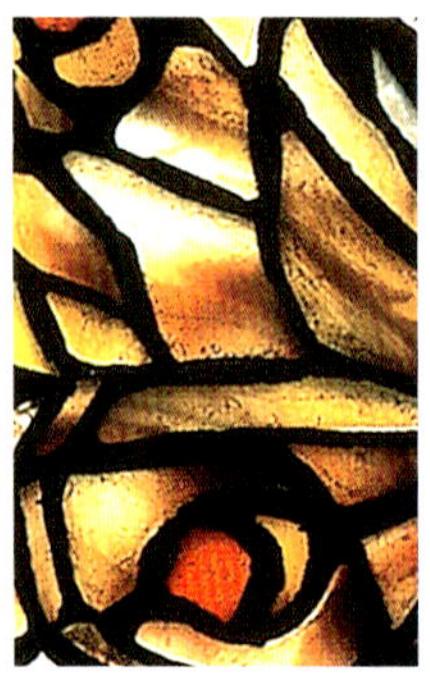

Butterfly Plate

Leaded glass.

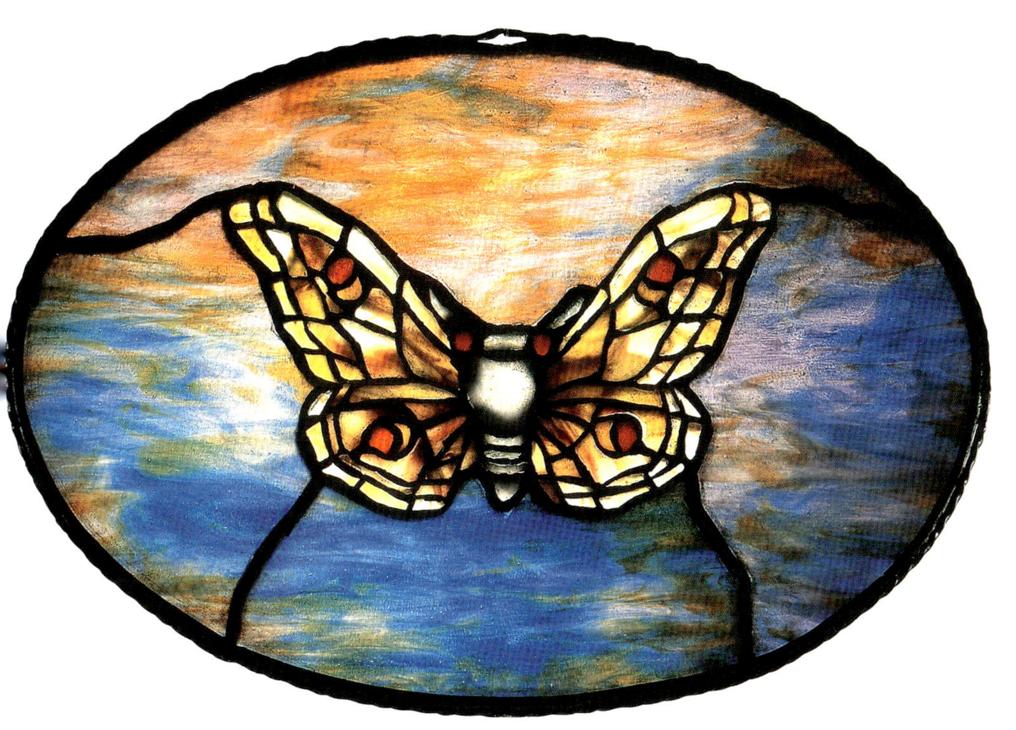

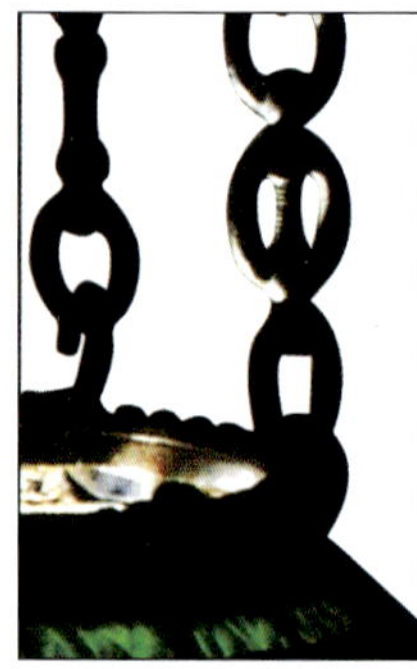

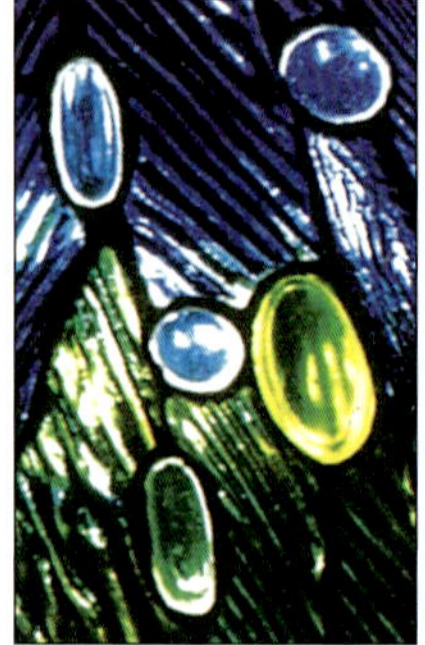

glass for ordinary windows, pushed by the climate which, in winter at least, exacted a closed room lit from outside.

Language gives us a clue.

The word *glass* belongs to the Teutonic languages and has been allied to glow and glare, as if it meant the "shining" thing. But the Celts, who preceded the Teutons in Europe, have the same word for a color.

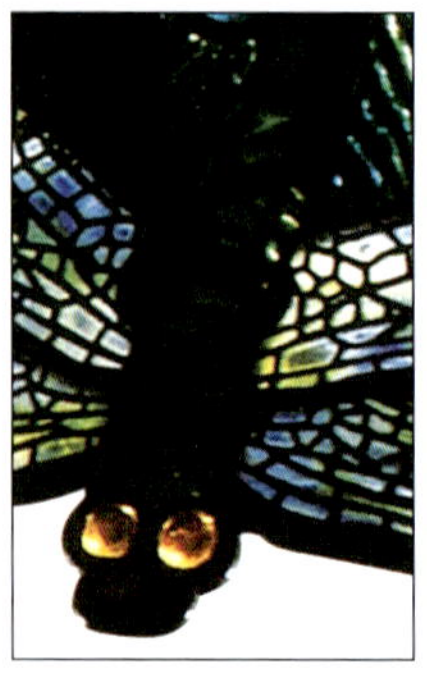

Dragonfly Hanging Lamp

Leaded glass, bronze.

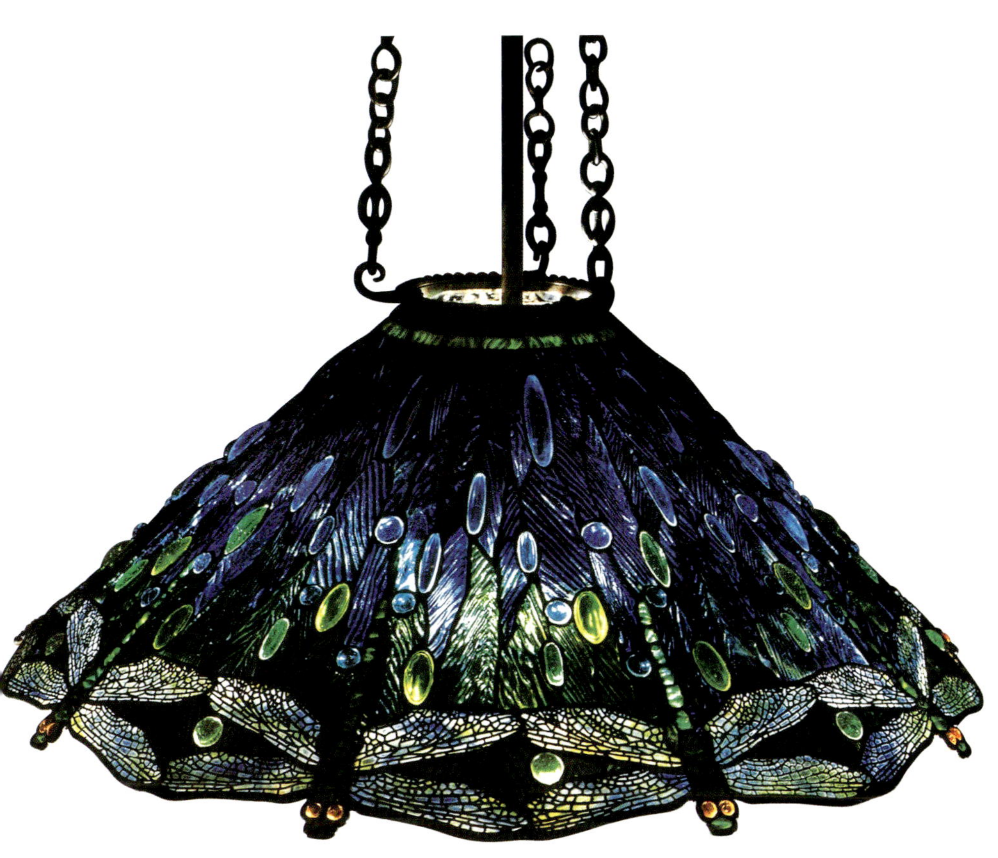

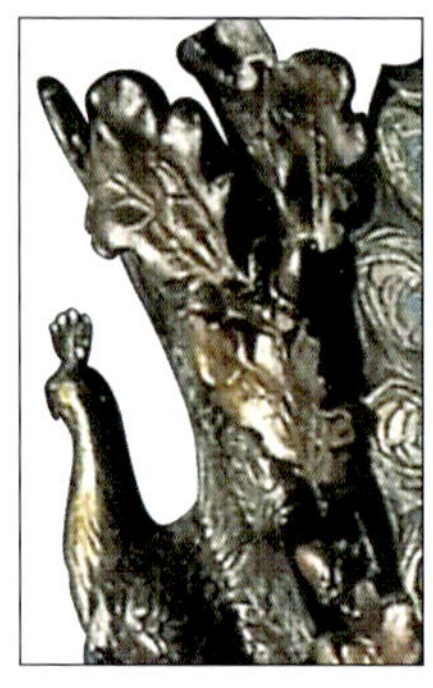

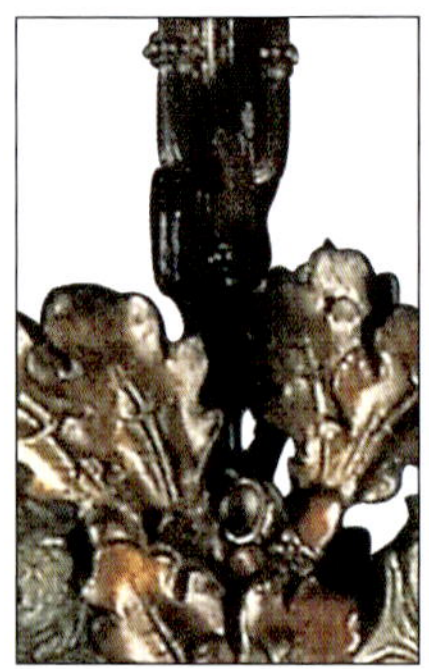

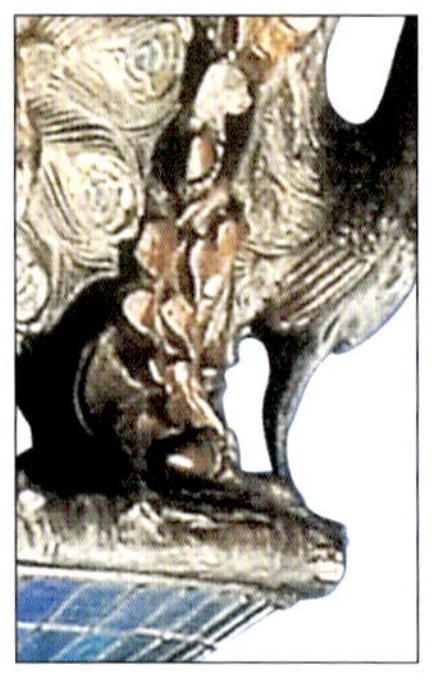

Irish *glas* means gray or bluish gray, like steel. Welsh glass means "blue, greenish gray." *Glaukos,* "shining" is a close parallel in Greek. A similar word for amber among the Teutons got into late Latin as "glesum." We may imagine that the earliest glass imported by the Phoenicians into northern Europe was a kind of bottle glass in gray and blue tones and was called the "blue-gray" stuff by the Celts, who gave the word to the

Sculpted Bronze Hanging Lamp

Leaded glass, bronze.

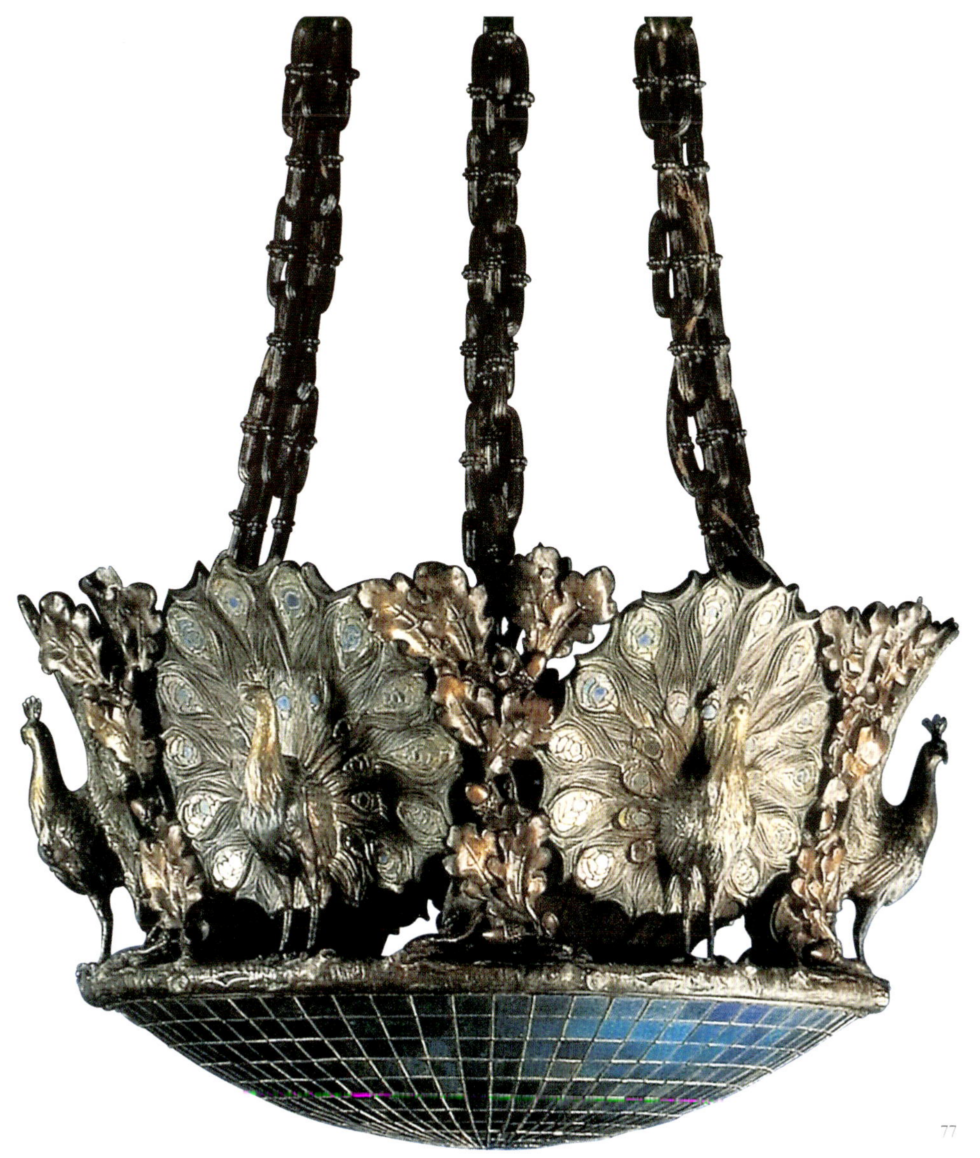

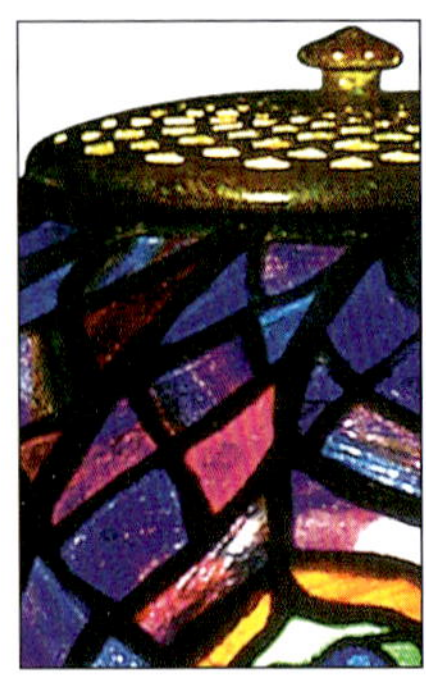

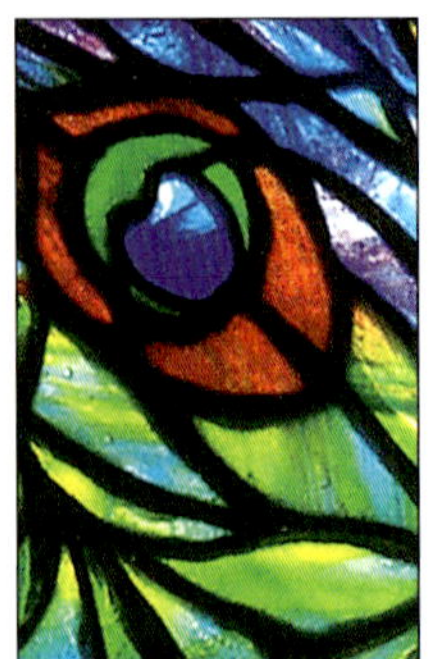

Teutonic tribes, alternately conquered by them or their conquerors in turn. As soon as glass was made in Europe it would be natural that those who could afford the luxury would substitute this material for the parchment or horn used by primitive races of the north in their narrow window openings to let in the light and exclude the cold.

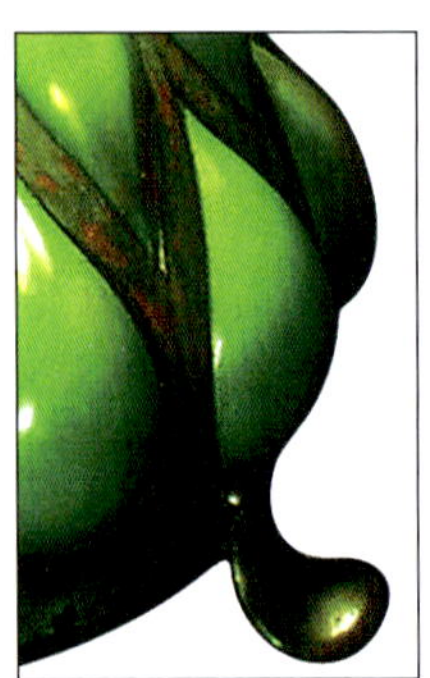

Library Standard Blown Glass Base with Peacock Dome Shade

Favrile glass, bronze, lead, shade: 40.6 cm.

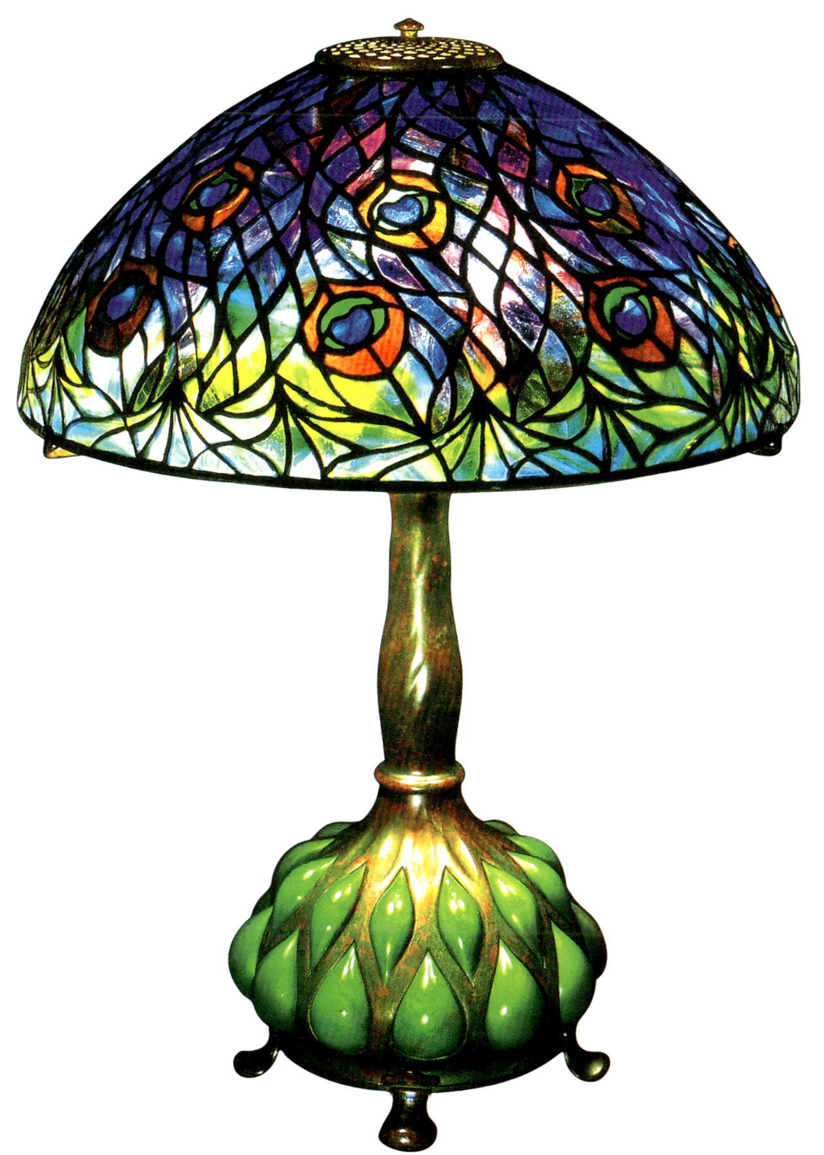

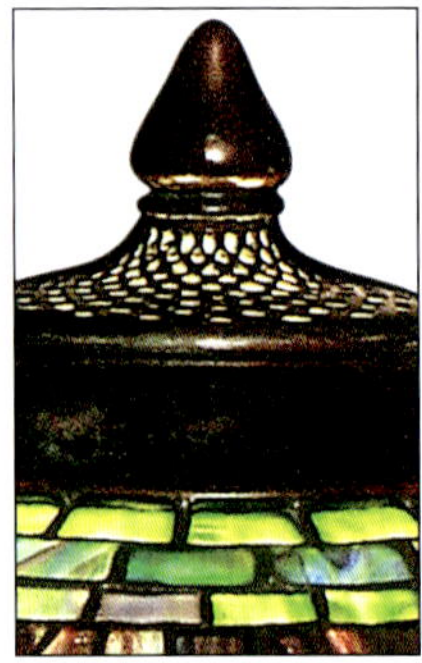

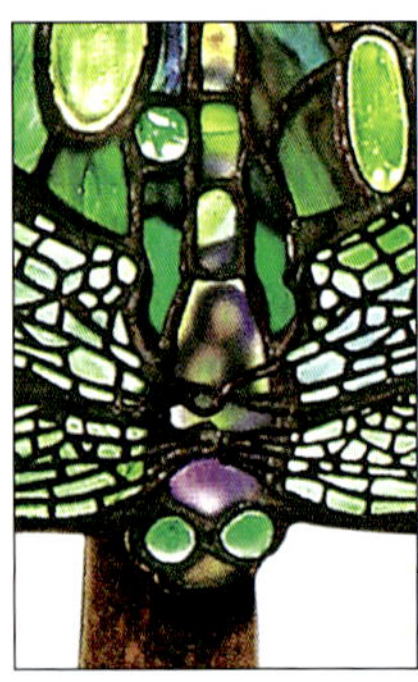

Originally, we must argue by analogy, windows or the gratings in the window were stopped by materials which allowed some light to filter through, but did not permit those inside to see out. Transparent glass is a comparatively late invention. When stained windows, therefore, came up in Europe it found people indifferent because unused to the convenience of transparent panes. The heavy leads and thick, dark-toned panes in

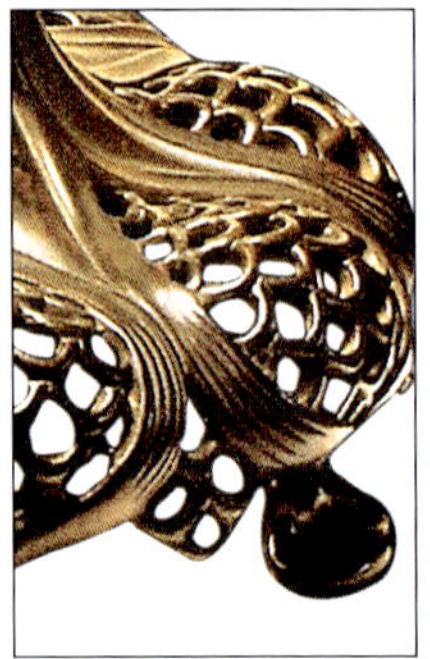

"Dragonfly" Lamp, Model N°. 1507

before 1906.
Leaded glass, bronze, height: 57 cm.
Courtesy McCelland & Lars Rachen, Ltd.

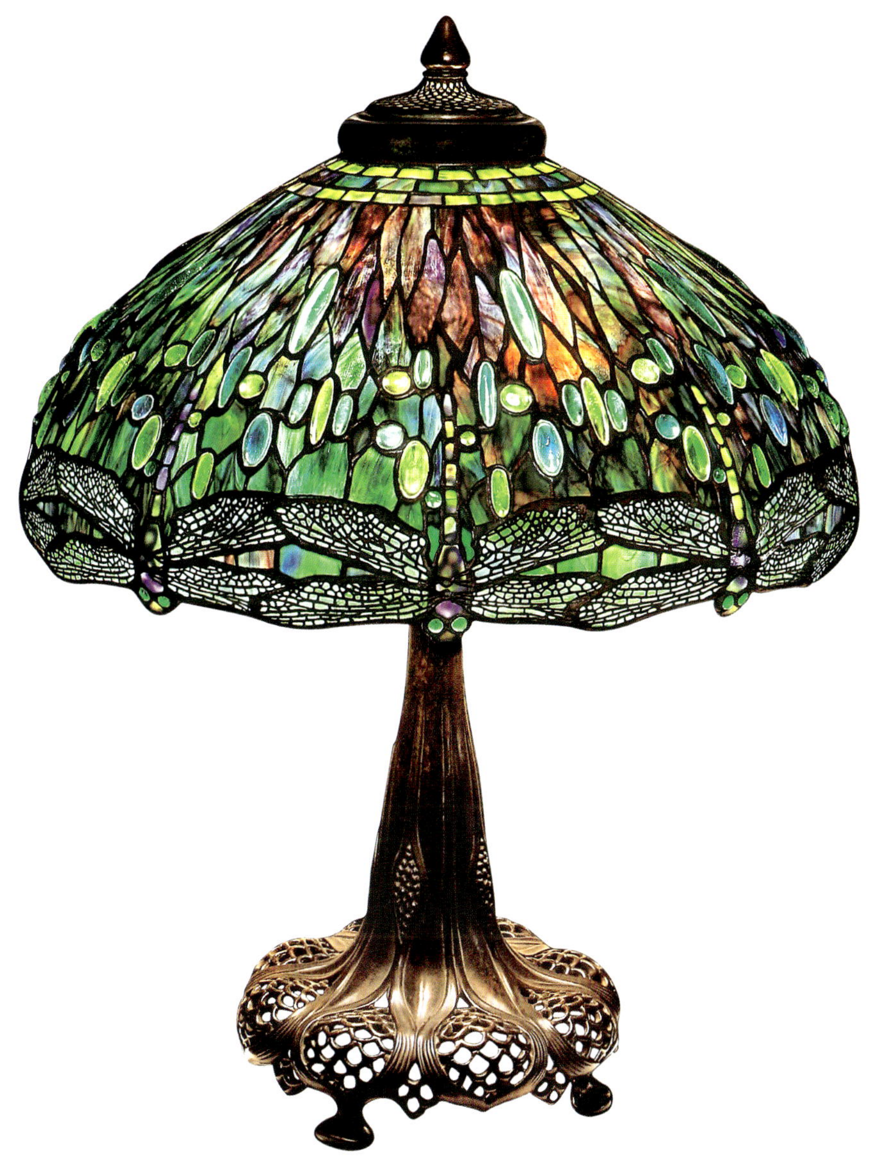

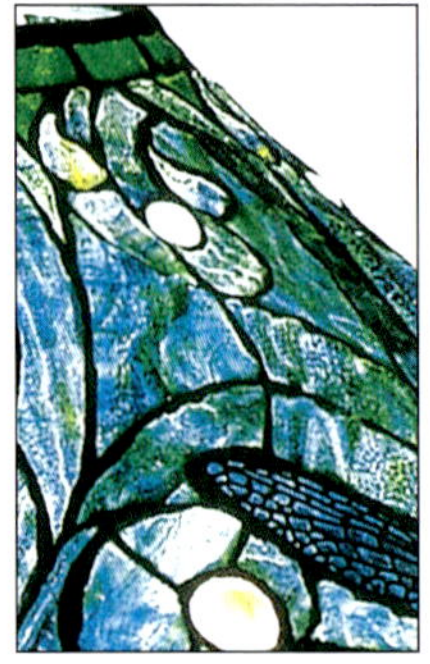

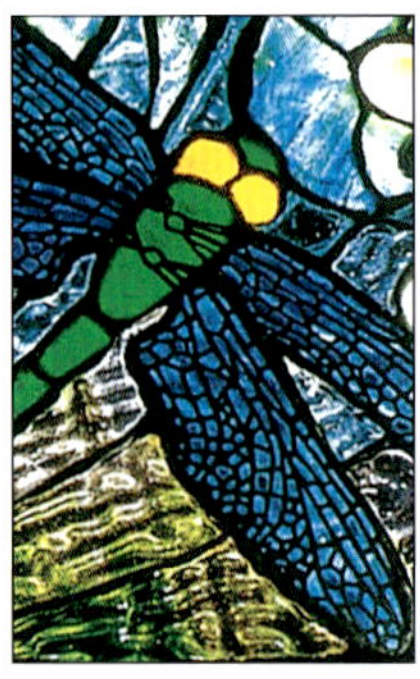

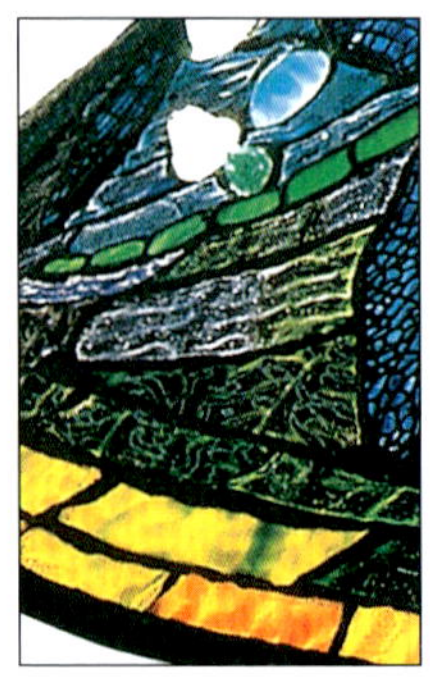

old cathedrals, like those of Chartres, Beauvais, York, etc., delighted their eyes and did not bother them by reason of the dimness of the light that fell through. This is a point which should be remembered by those who study old and modern glass windows. There was beauty of color in windows before clear glass panes, transparent as air so much as existed in Europe.

"Dragonfly" Shade

1899-1905.
Glass set by lead.
Private collection, New York.

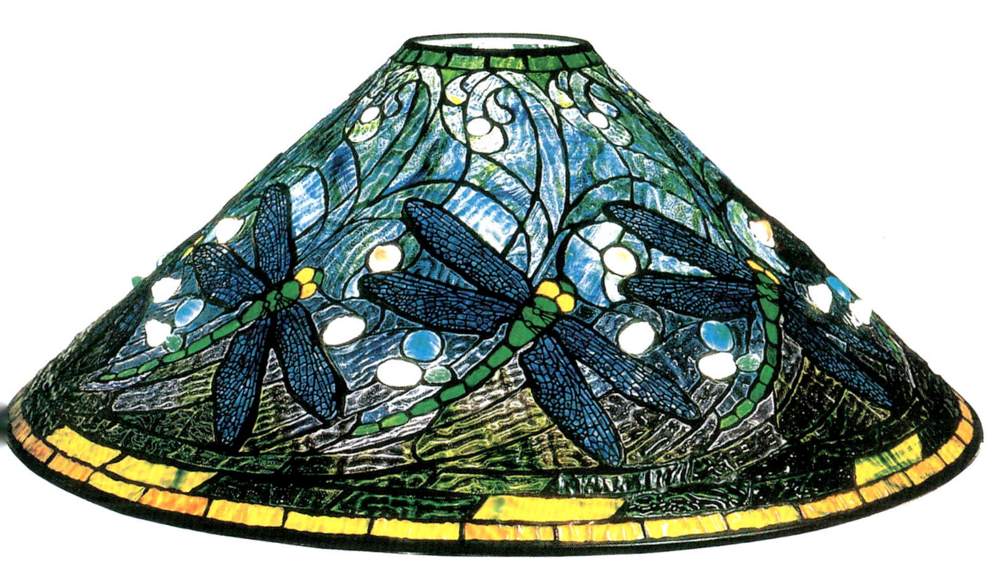

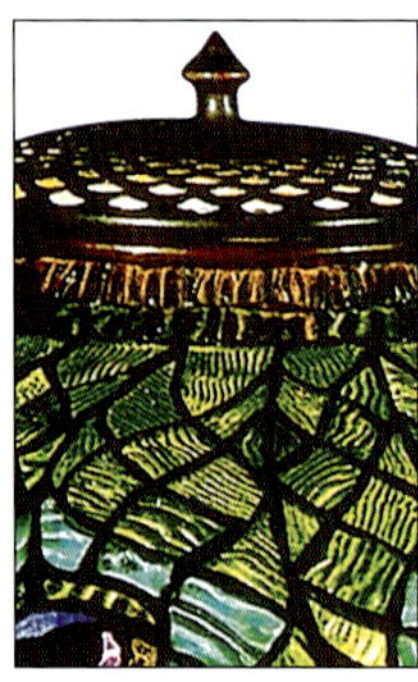

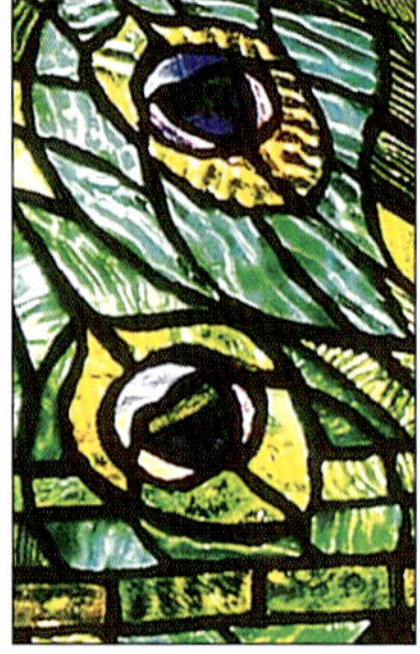

Cennino Cennini, who was living in Padua about 1400, gives in his *Trattato della Pittura* directions how to glue sheets of paper together to obtain a piece as large as the window, "draw your figure first with charcoal, then you will fix it with ink, your figure being completely shaded as if you were drawing it on a panel. Then your master glass-worker takes this drawing and spreads it on a table or board, large and flat,

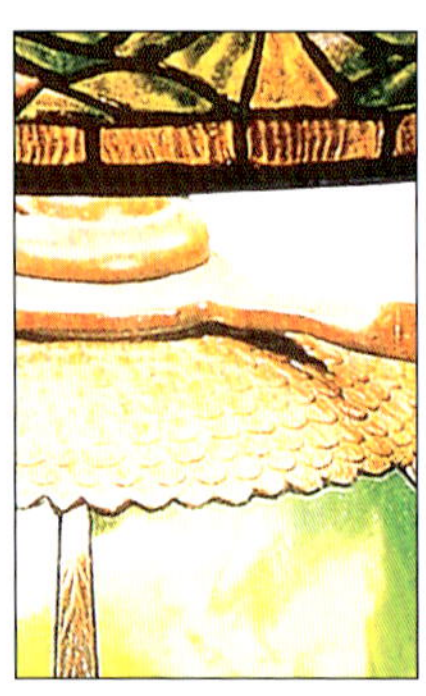

Peacock Oil Lamp

Leaded glass, favrile glass, bronze.

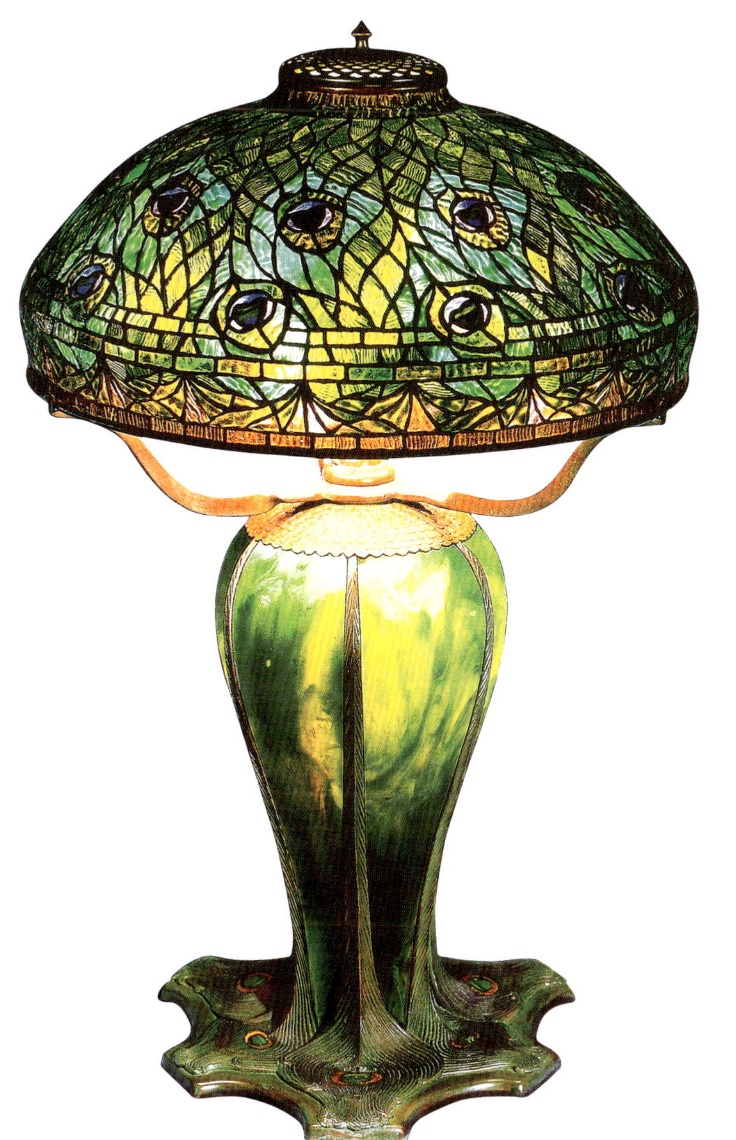

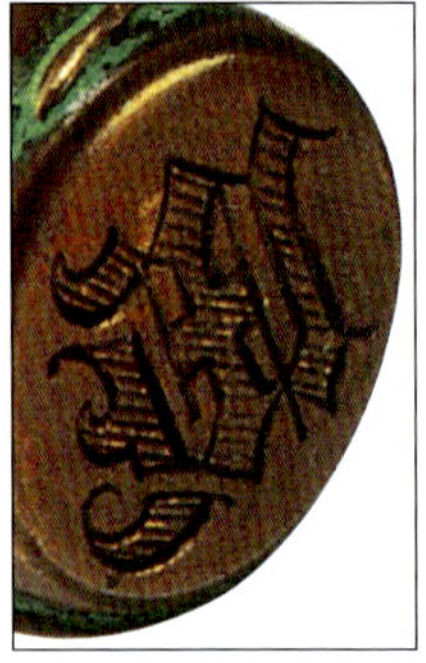

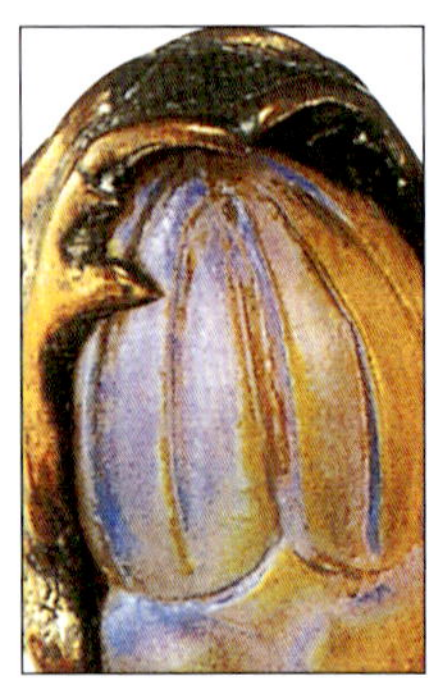

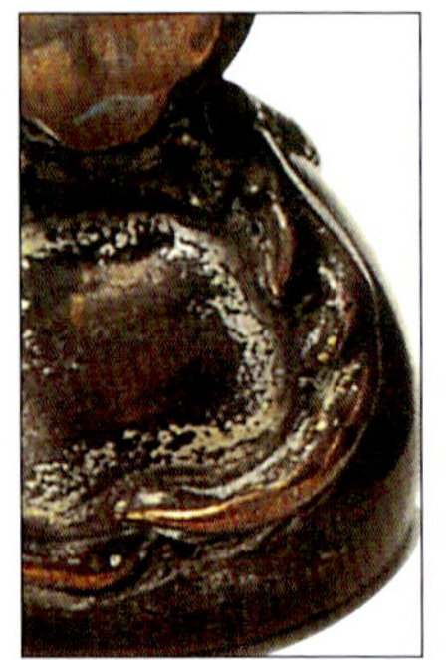

and according as he wishes to the color the draperies, so bit by bit he cuts the glasses and gives you a paint which is made of well-ground cuttings of copper and with this paint with a small minever brush piece by piece, you paint the shadows on the glass, matching the folds together and the other parts of the figure according to how the master has cut the pieces and laid them together; and with this paint you can always

Scarab Seals

———————

Favrile glass and bronze.

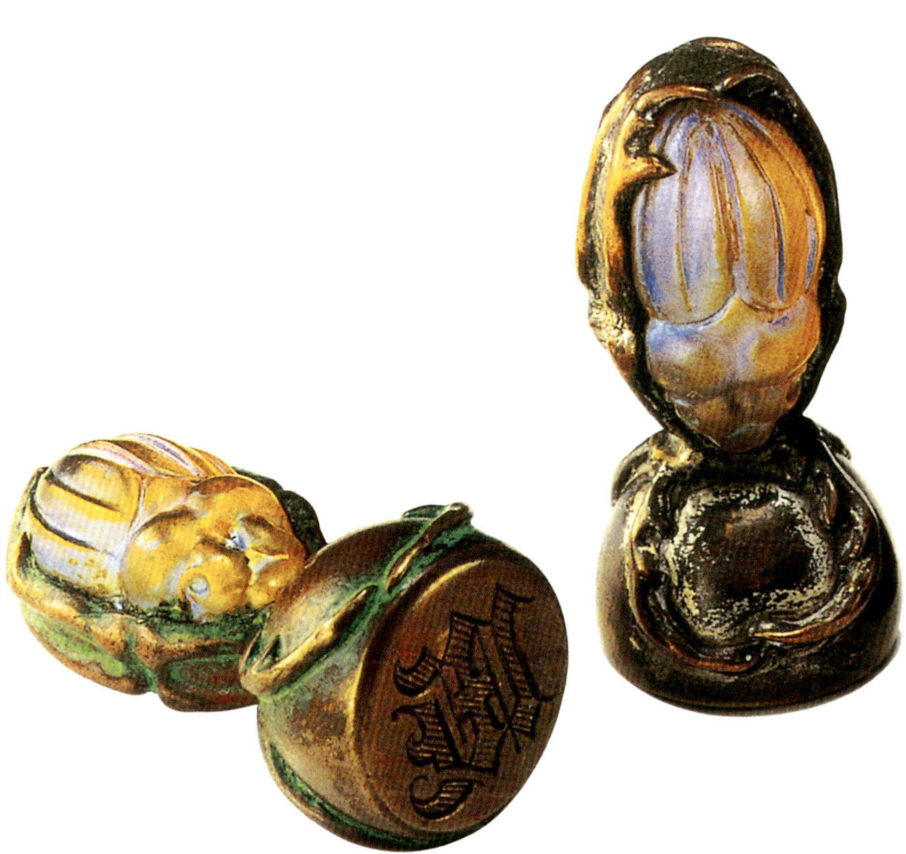

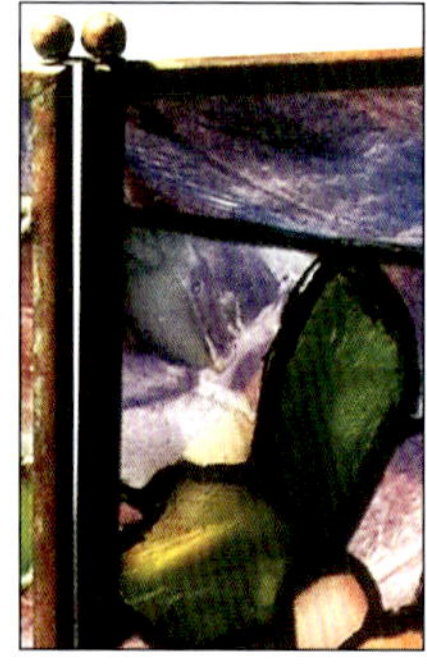

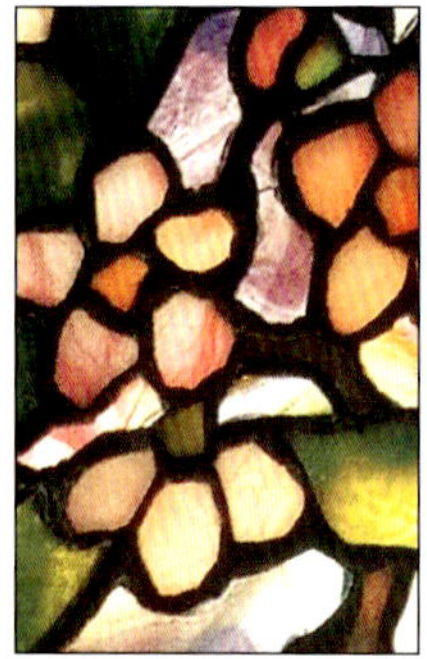

shade – on every kind of glass. Then the master, before joining the pieces together, as is the custom, bakes them moderately in iron cases on hot coals and then joins them together. There is this advantage, that it is not necessary to paint the ground color, as glass can be had in every color."

Nowadays, in America at least, much greater care goes in to the preparations for a window. A color sketch

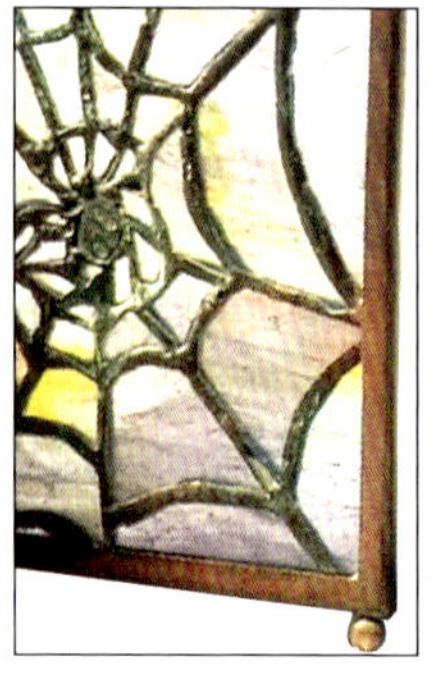

Leaded Tea Screen
Leaded glass.

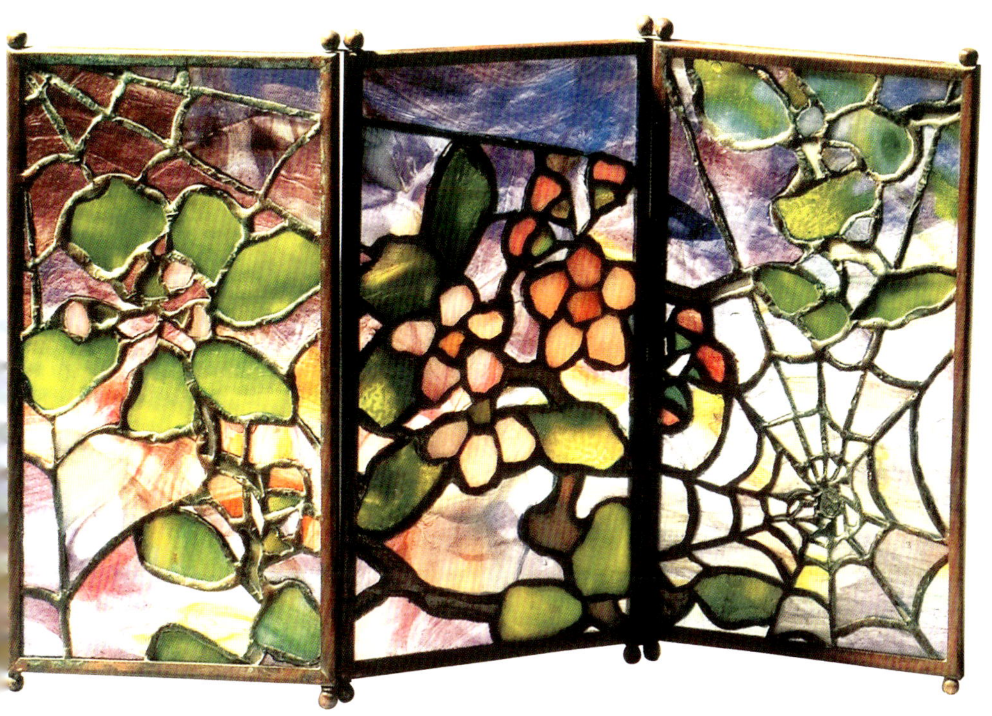

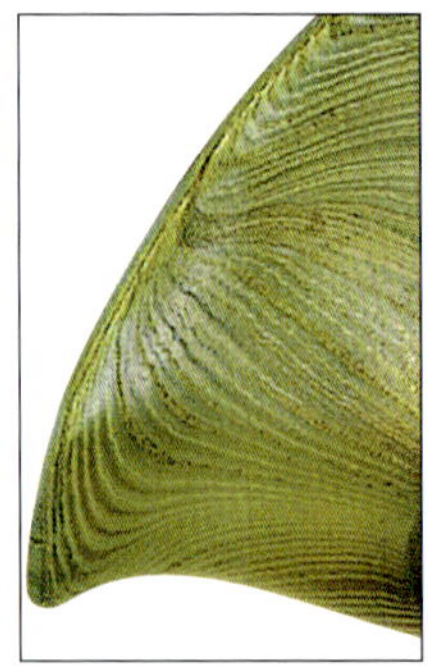

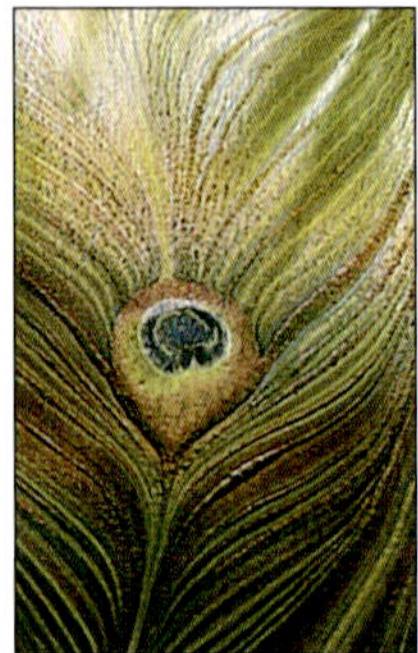

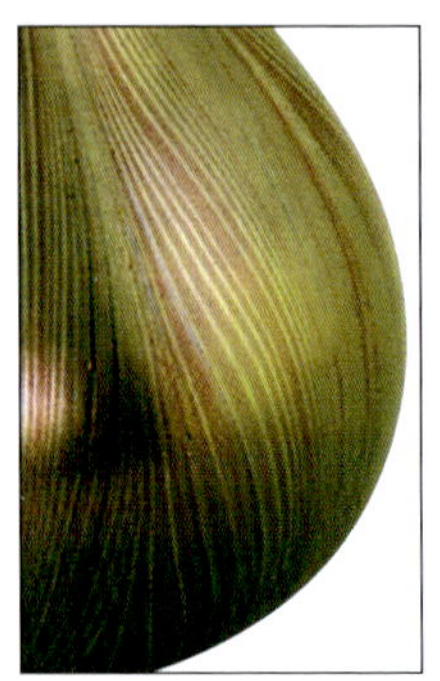

for composition and the distribution of colors leads to the grand cartoon. From this, two transfers are made on paper. One is kept as a guide for the artist who arranges the leads and puts the glass pieces together. The other is divided on the lines of the leads, being cut into separate patters which are arranged on a glass easel; this is placed against a strong light. The patterns are easily removable. Selecting the sheet of glass which

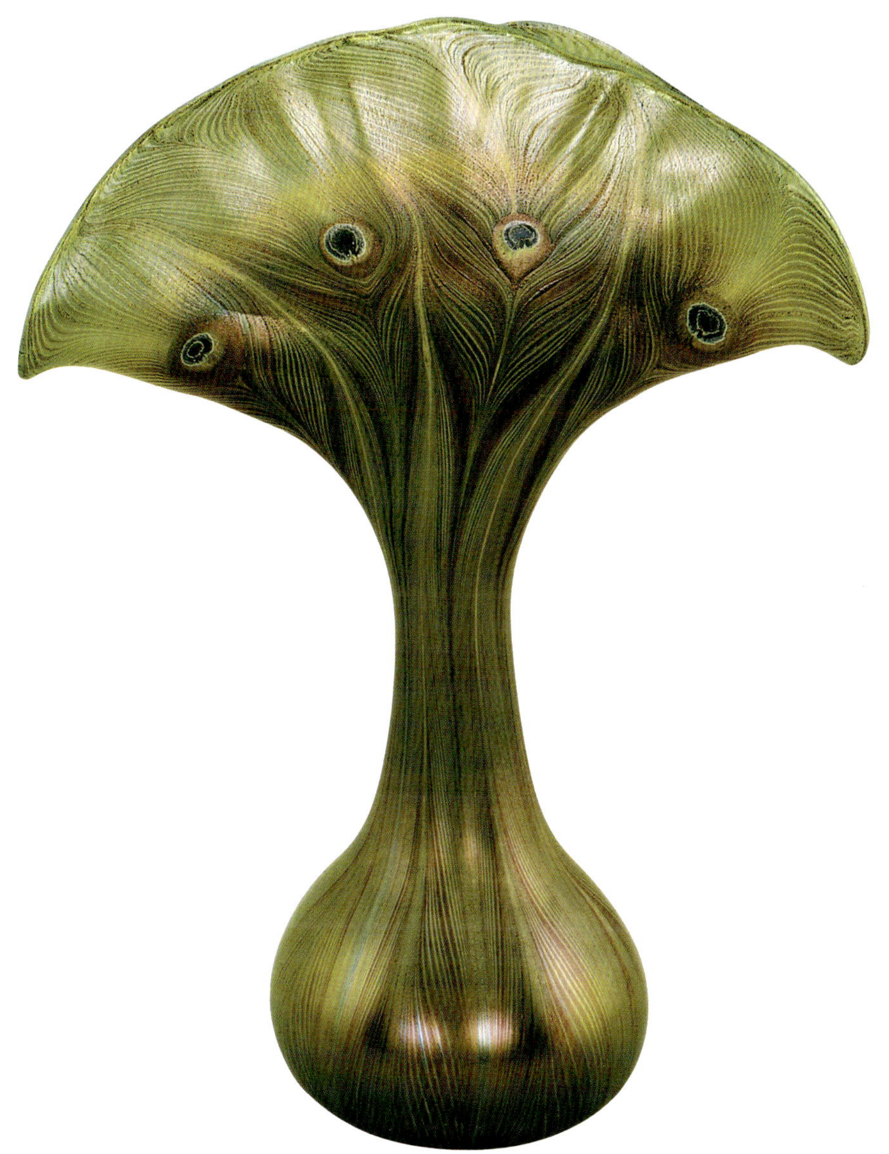

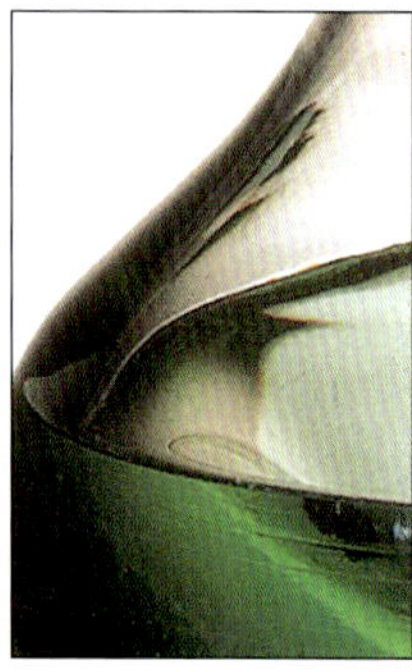

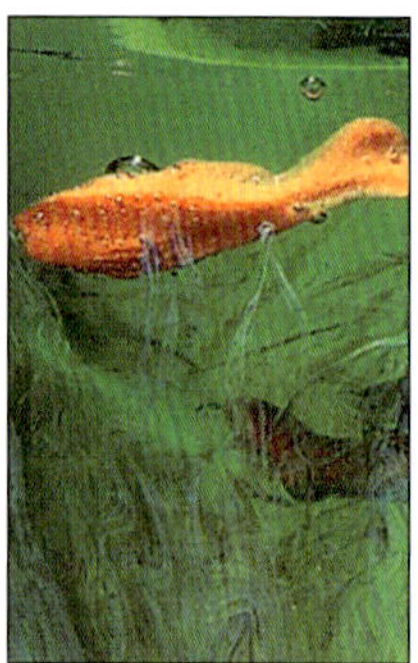

seems to hit the right color for a given section of the design, the artist removes the paper pattern at that point from the easel and passes the sheet of colored glass between his eyes and the opening left by the pattern he has removed. Making that part of the colored sheet which has been selected, the glassman then places the paper pattern upon it and cuts round its edges with a diamond. The piece thus shaped is then fixed with wax to the glass easel whence the paper pattern has come.

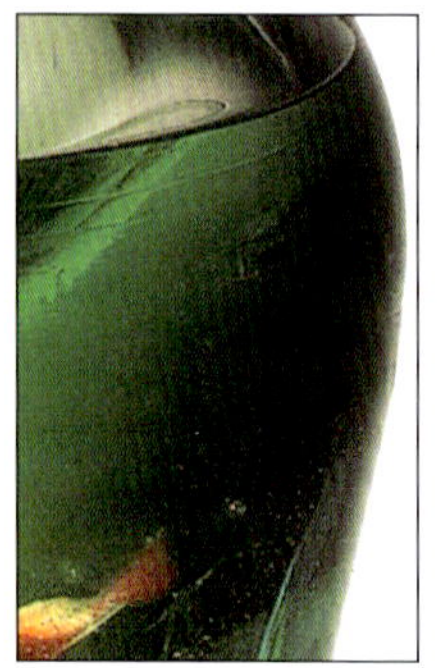

Aquamarine Vase with Goldfish

1913.
Collection of Mary Beth and Walter Buck.

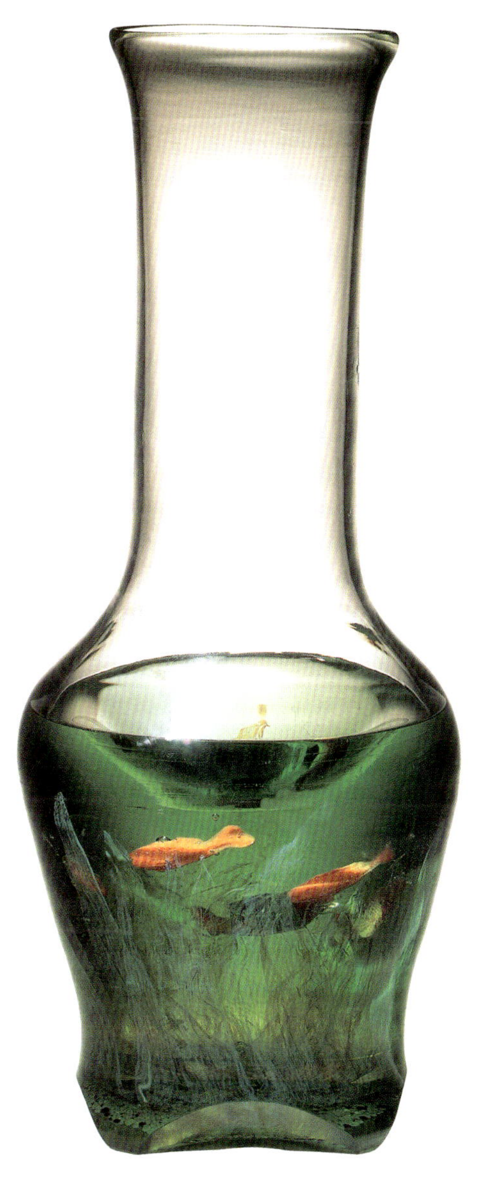

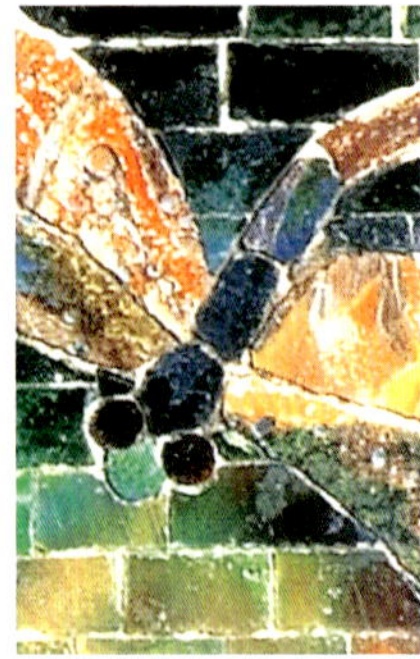

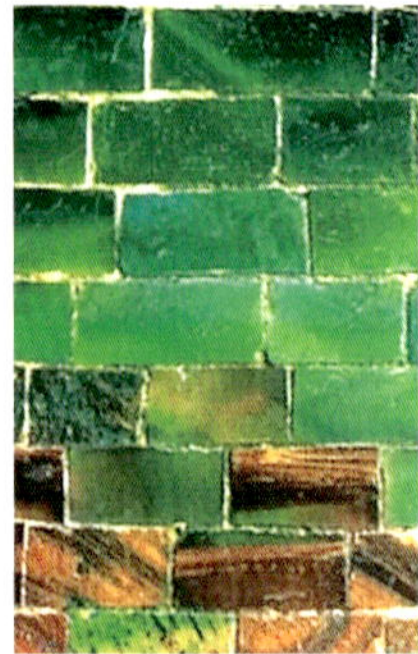

Thus piece by piece, glass in various colors and shades takes the place of the paper. Changes are often made. If a color will not come otherwise, a second colored piece is placed over or under the first in order to obtain the required tint or tone; this is called plating or "cased" glass.

The leads are also different from mediaeval leads. They are not so heavy, and they are used so as to aid

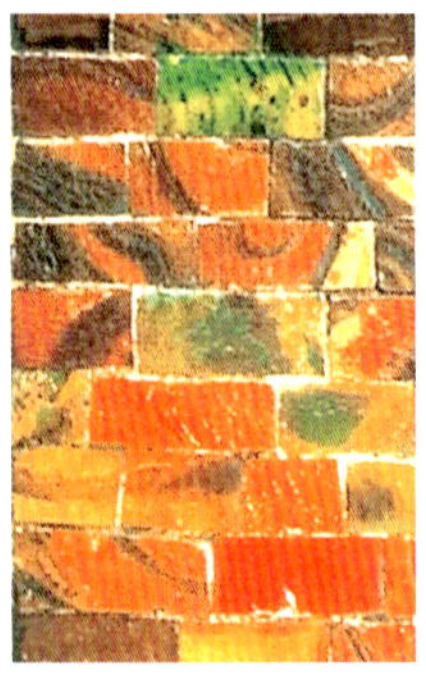

Dragonfly Mosaic

Leaded glass and bronze.

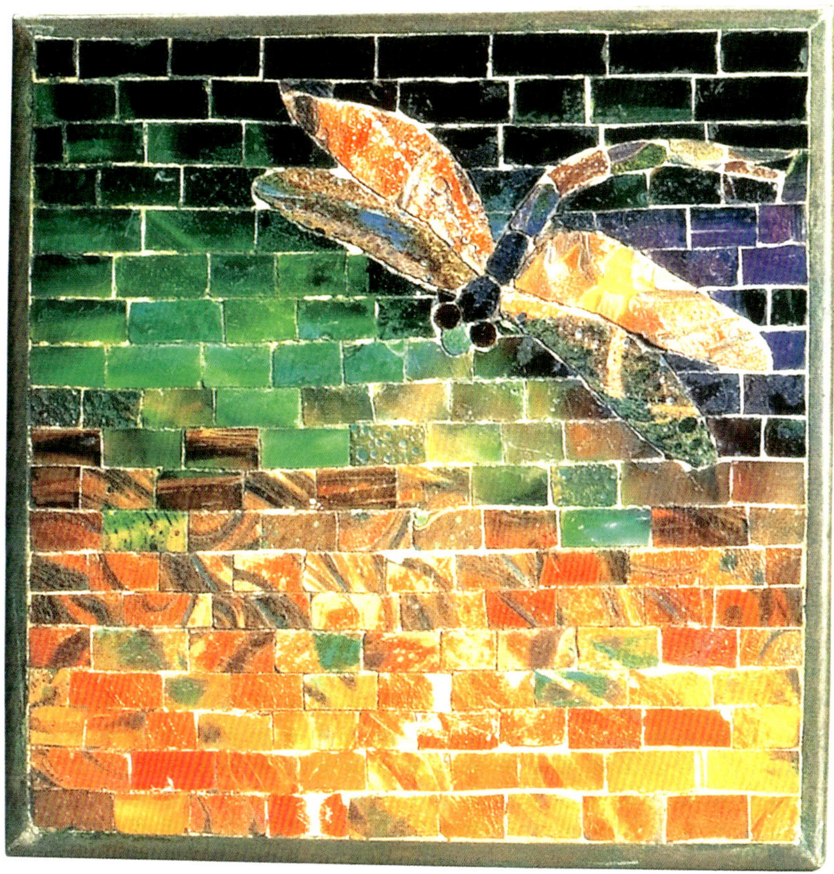

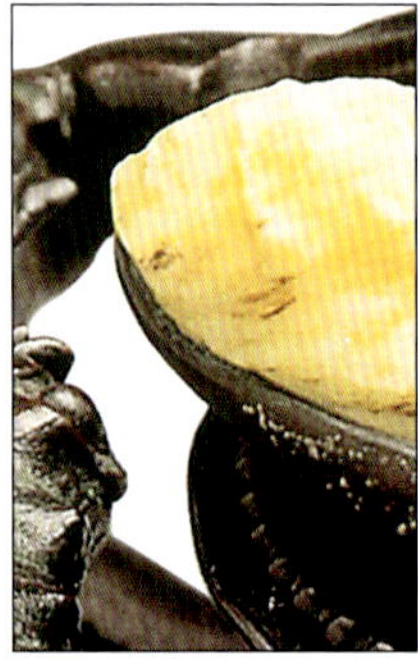

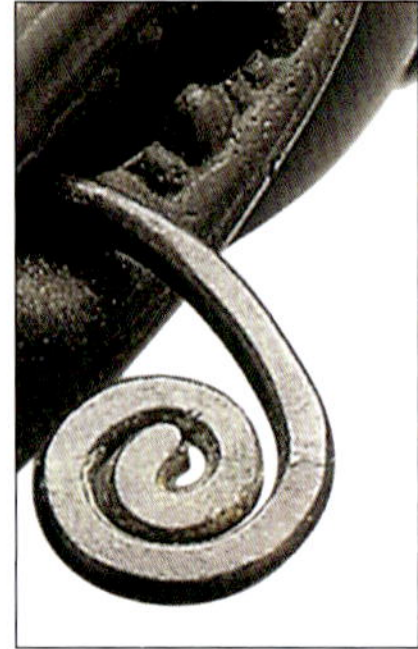

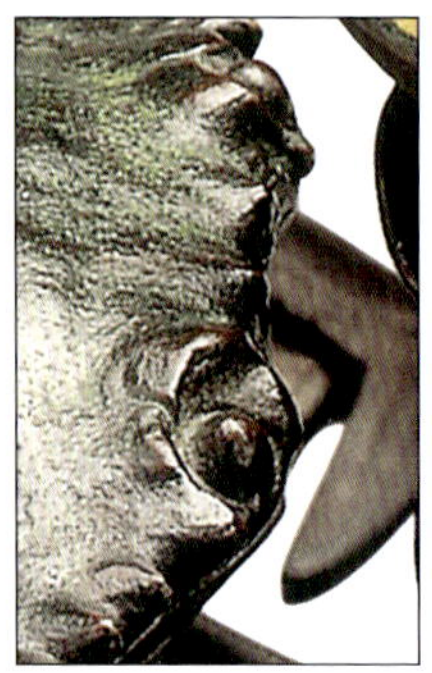

rather than interfere with the picture. Attempts have been made successfully to suppress the leads, sometimes by fusing together adjacent edges of glass patterns or even by arranging the patterns between two great sheets of plate glass, the transparent sheets acting as supports to keep the window from buckling and the Pieces from shifting from their proper order. Beside and beyond all these and other mechanical contrivances,

Crab Inkstand

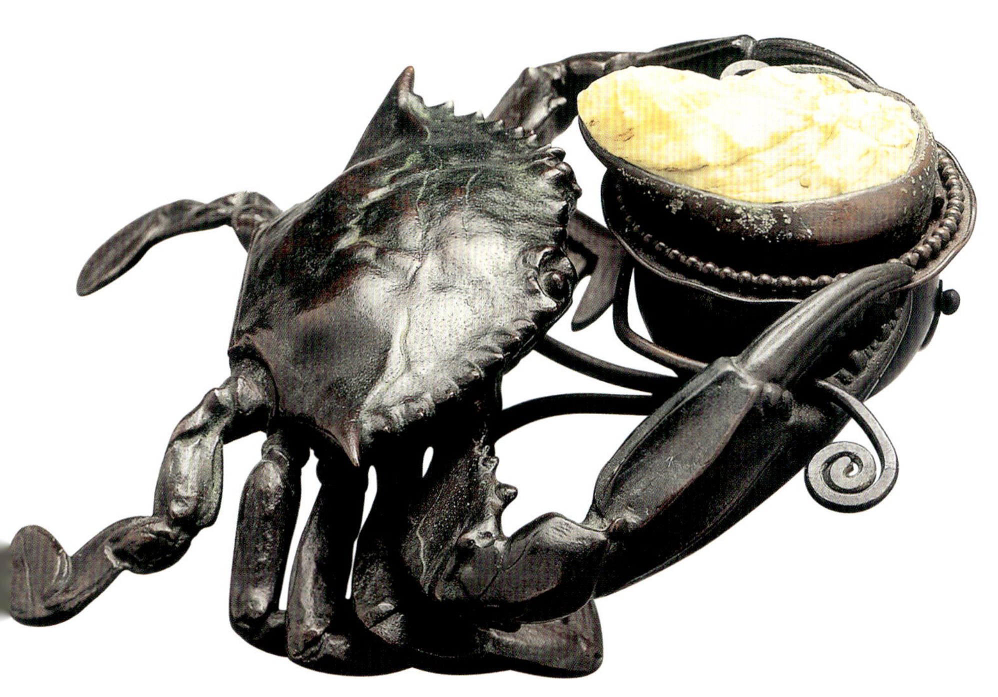

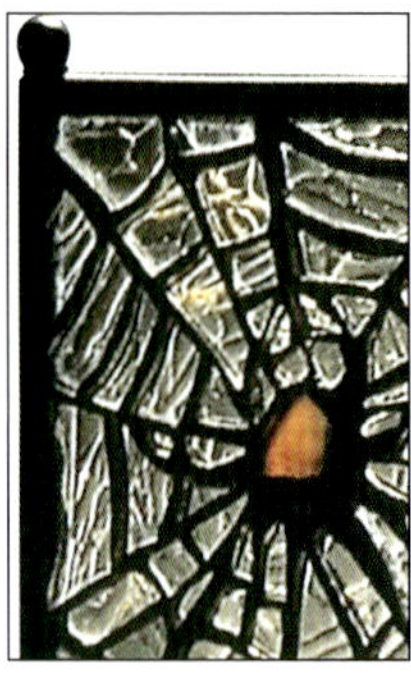

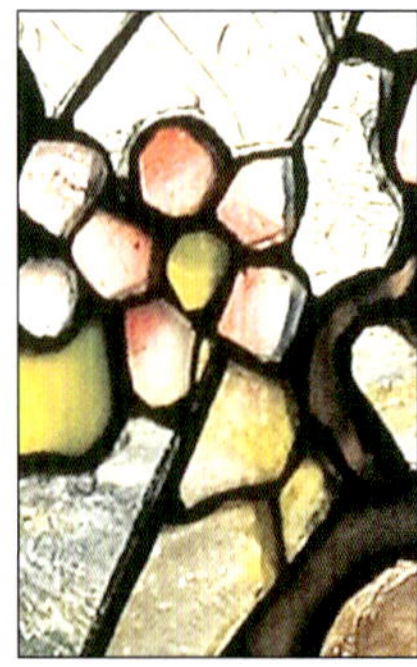

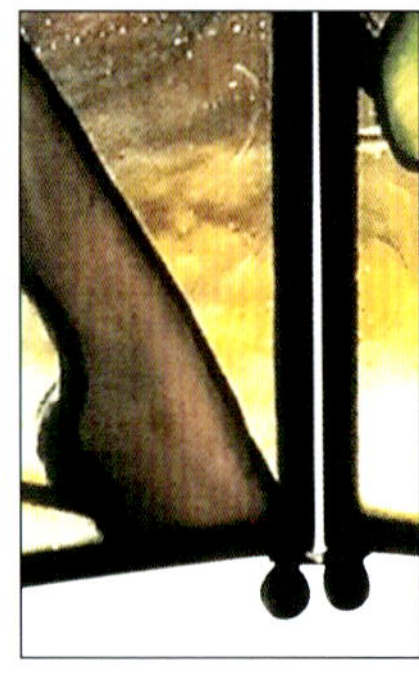

more important than these, is the fact that we have a far wider range of color in glass than did the mediaeval workmen.

The result of all these experiments and inventions may be summed up in the statement that modern American window painters can use glass as a painter uses his colors, lightening or darkening his work at will.

Cobweb Leaded Tea Screen

Leaded glass.

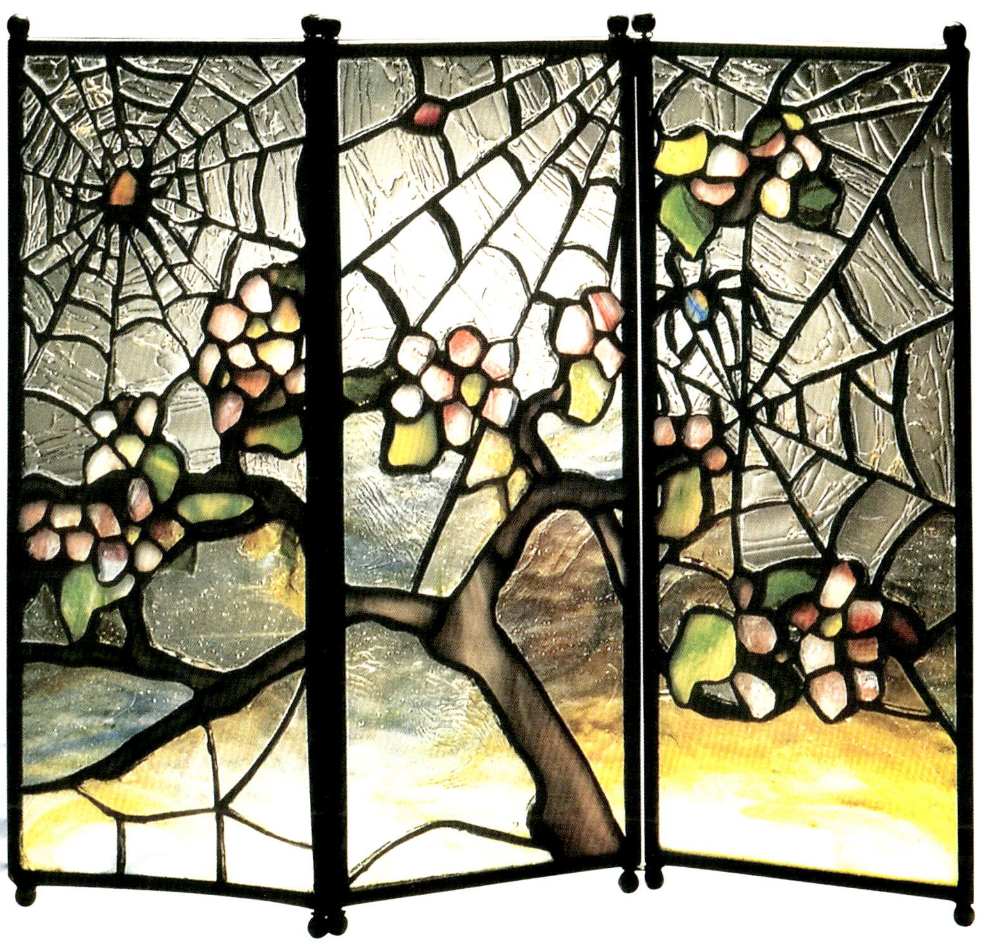

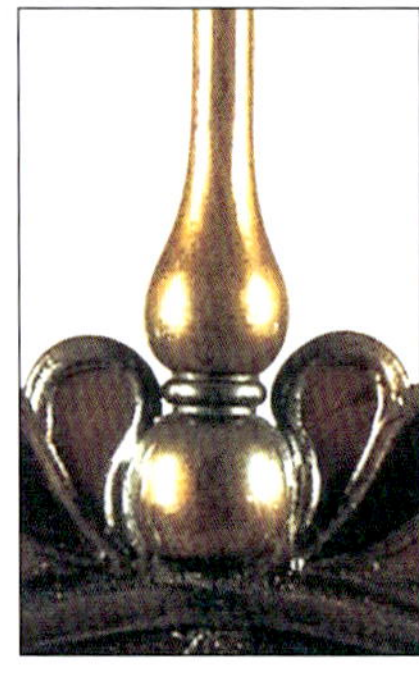

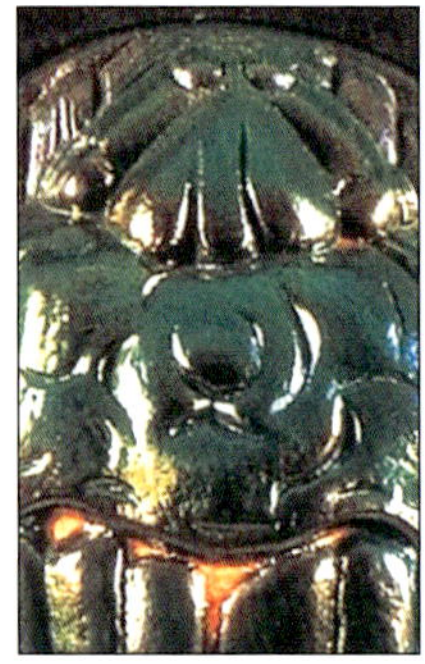

By the employment of opalescent glass they can produce such effects of marvelous delicacy as Corot achieved beyond all other oil painters in his treatment of white clouds shot with tender rosy tints.

As early as 1875 Mr. Tiffany was at work on inventions which tend to minimize the use of enamels not only for draperies but for flesh tones. At Thill's glasshouse in Brooklyn he succeeded in obtaining some glass which

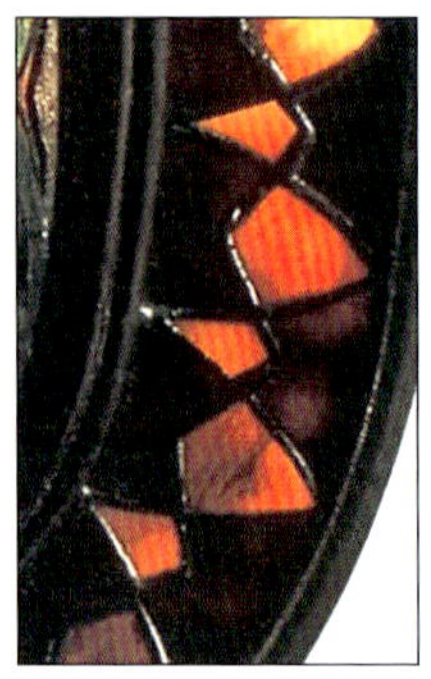

Favrile Glass Scarab

Favrile glass, leaded glass, bronze.

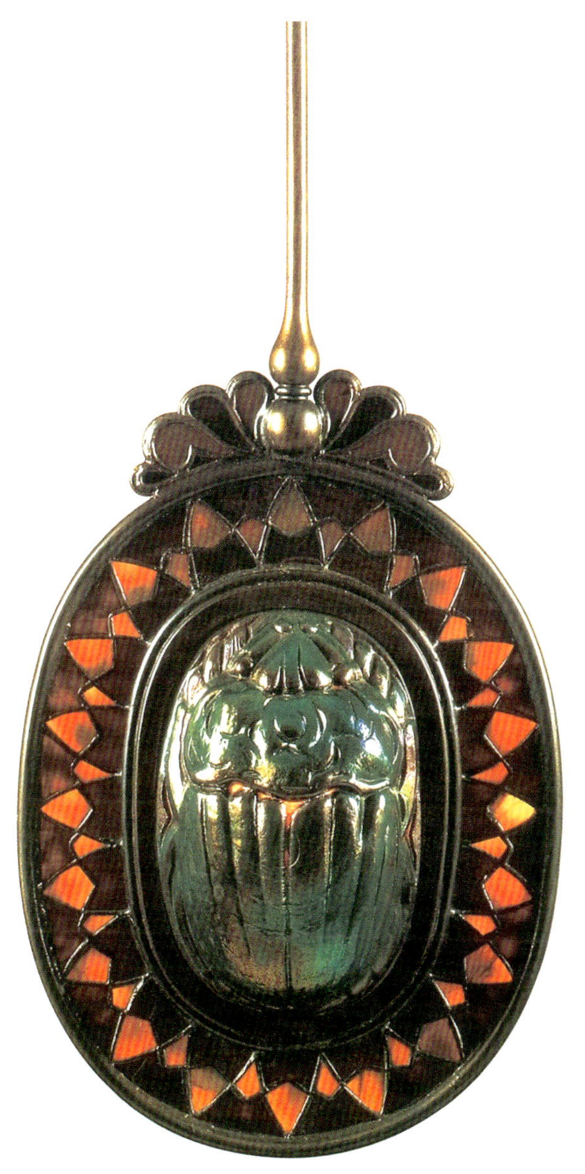

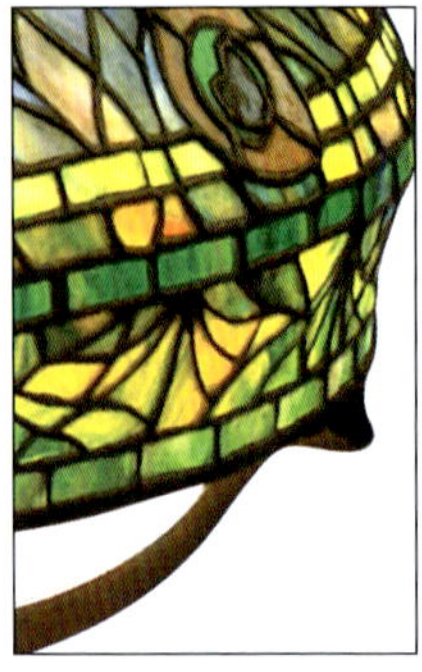

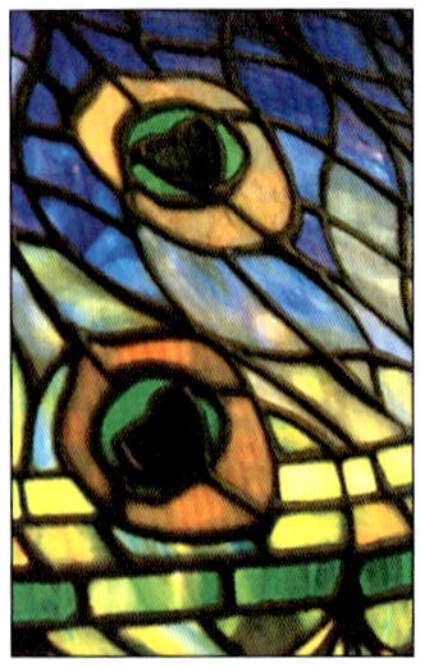

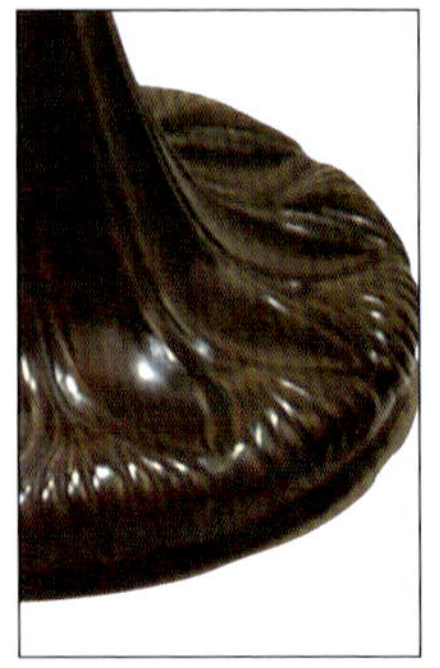

could be used for draperies without further painting and firing. But it was not till 1878 that he established a glass-making house of his own. Andrea Boldini, of Venice, who represented himself as one of the workers in the Murano factory under Dr. Salviati, was in charge of the furnaces. This house burned down, as did a second. From about 1880 to 1893 Mr. Tiffany experimented at the Heidi glasshouse in Brooklyn,

Peacock Lamp

1905.
Leaded glass and bronze, height: 69.85 cm.
Private collection.

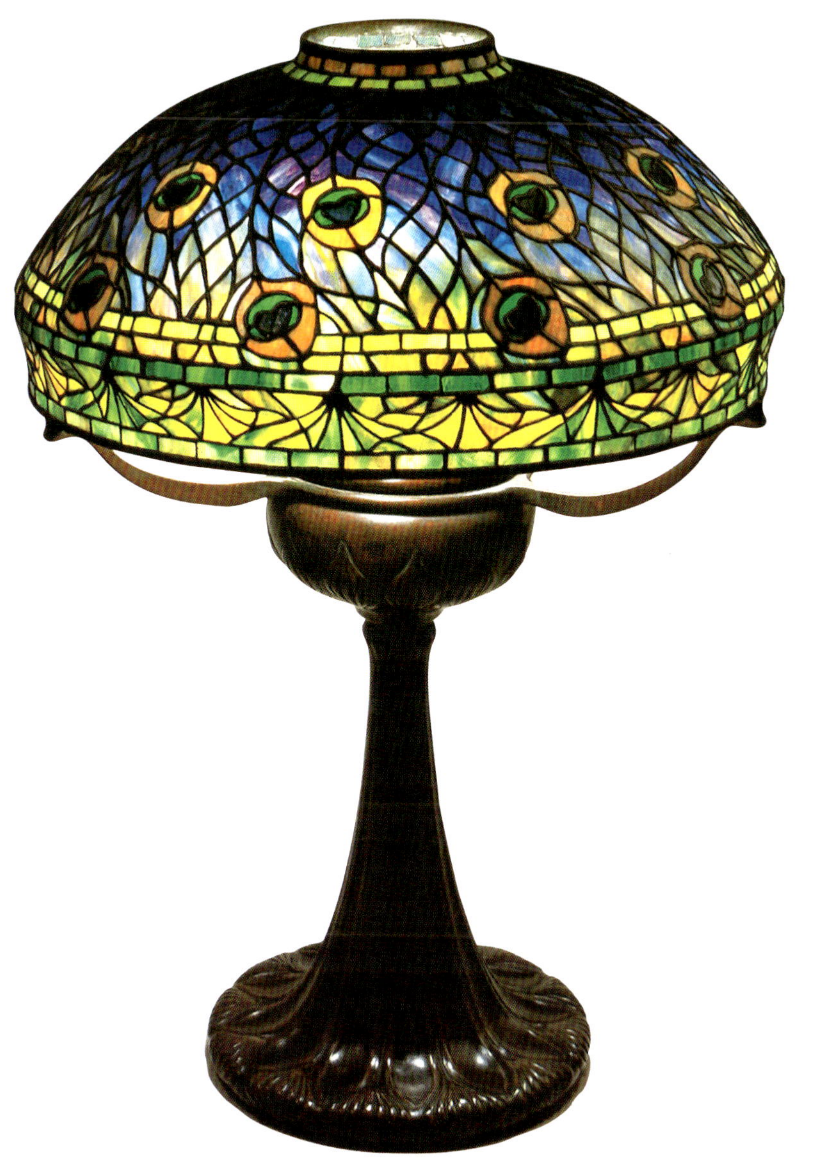

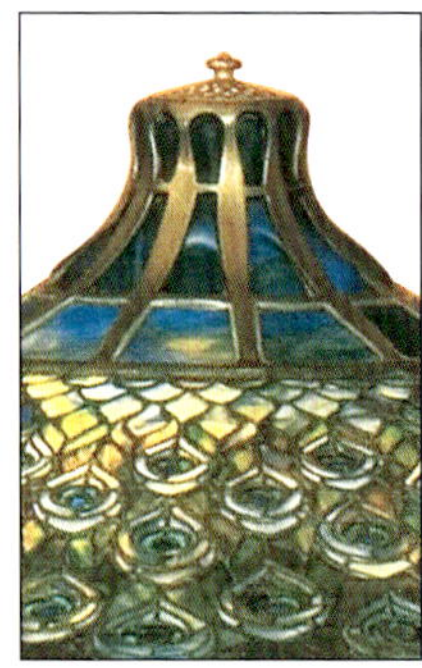

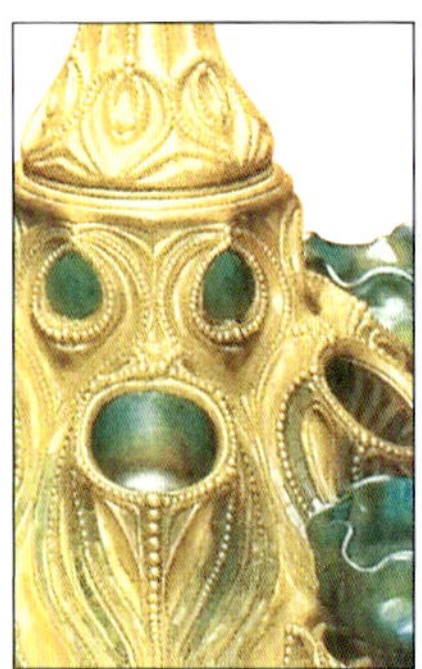

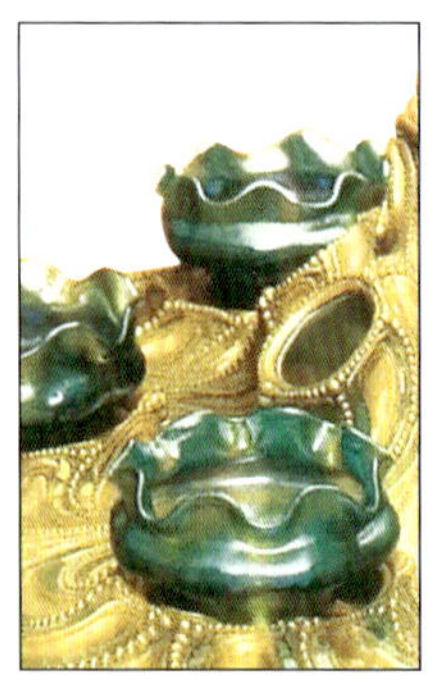

constantly improving upon his original ideas and learning to his cost that it would be useless to expect to make really beautiful windows unless he could control furnaces of his own where his ideas would be carried out without interference from those who either could not or would not understand.

Finally, in 1893 a glasshouse was established at Corona, Long Island, and put in charge of Mr. Arthur J. Nash, a practical glass manufacturer from Stourbridge,

Favrile glass, leaded glass, bronze.

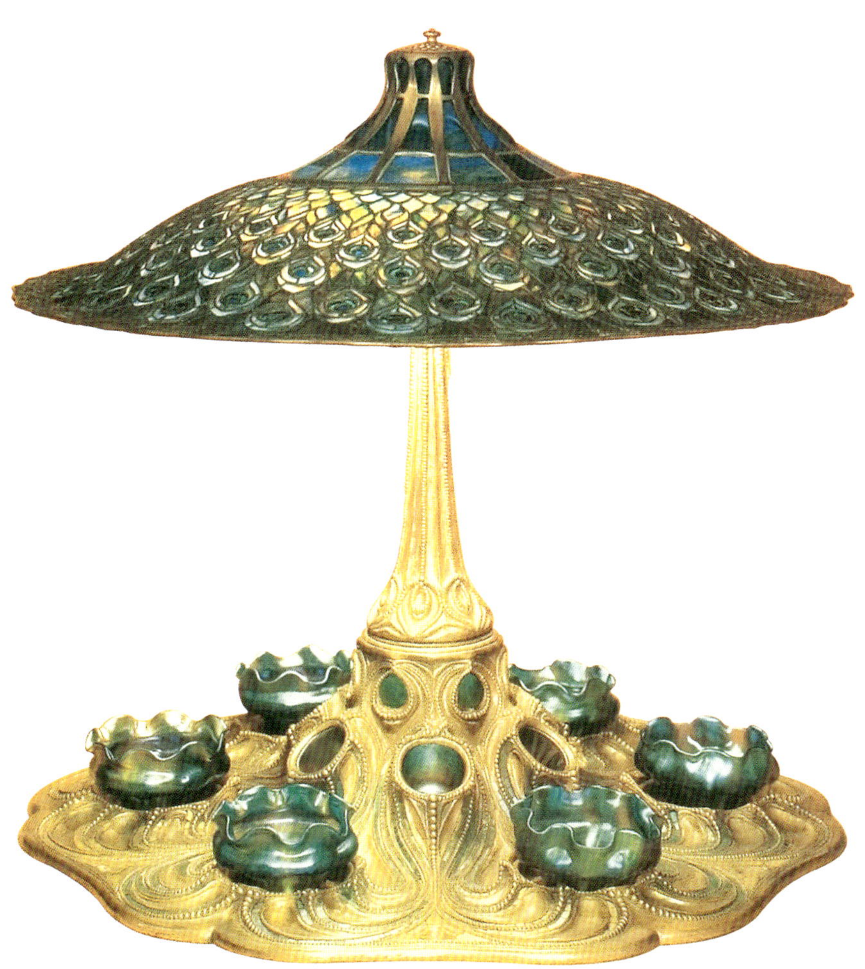

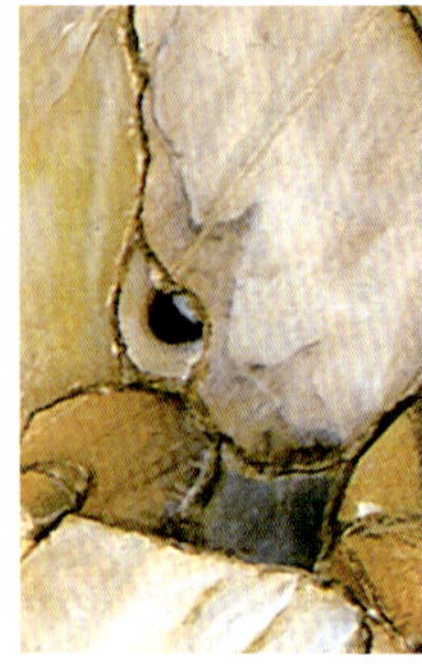

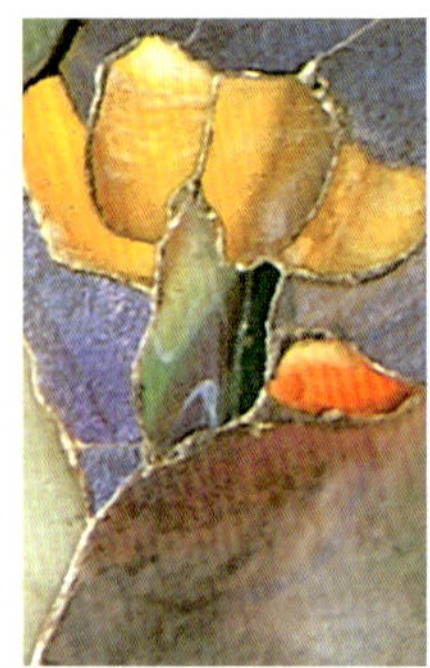

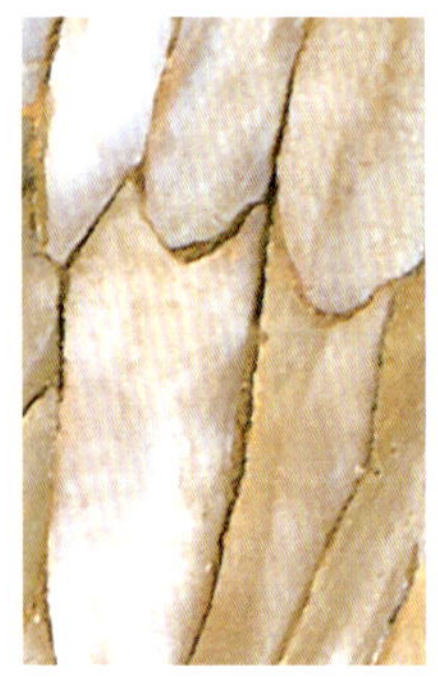

England, who superintended the building of the factory. In 1902 the title of the factory became the Tiffany Furnaces. Although once destroyed by fire this establishment remains and flourishes.

It was in 1878 that Mr. Tiffany had an opportunity to put his ideas of a church window into operation. English and Continental glass relied for effects of perspective, light and shade and details on surface

Mosaic Panel with Sulfur-crested Cockatoos

1916.
Glass tesserae, 78.7 x 58.4 cm.
Haworth Art Gallery, Accrington.

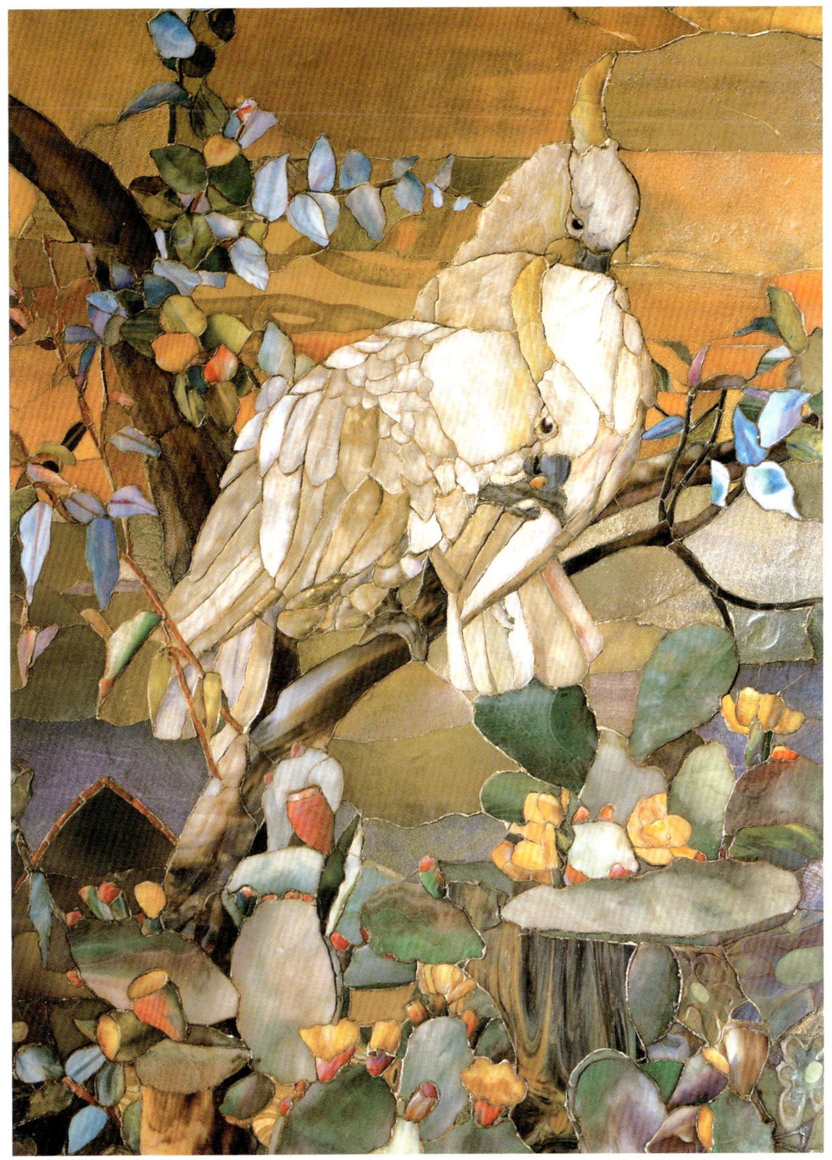

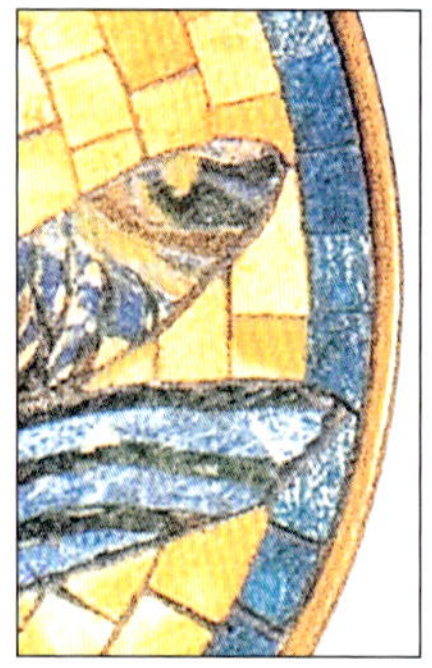

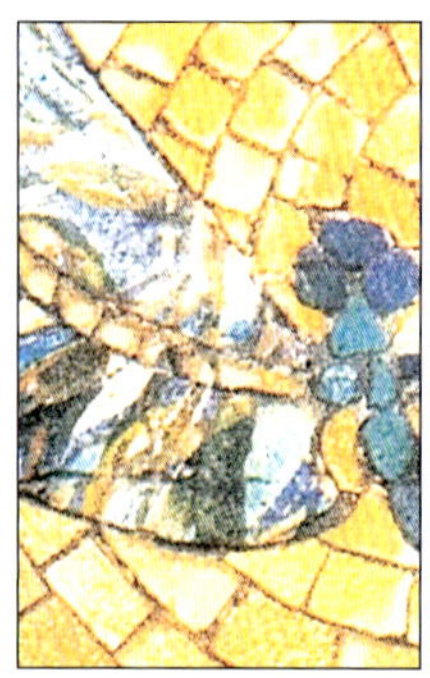

paints or pigments burned or fused upon the glass, after the fashion Cennino Cennini described six hundred years ago. Starting from the principle that these effects ought to be expressed in the substance of the glass itself, he sought to make a material in which colors and combinations of color, hues, shades, tints and tones should there without surface treatment, so far as possible.

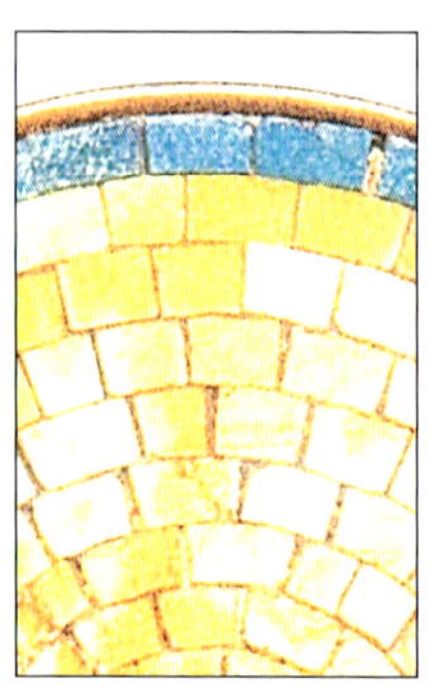

Mosaic Dragonfly Sconce

Leaded glass and bronze.

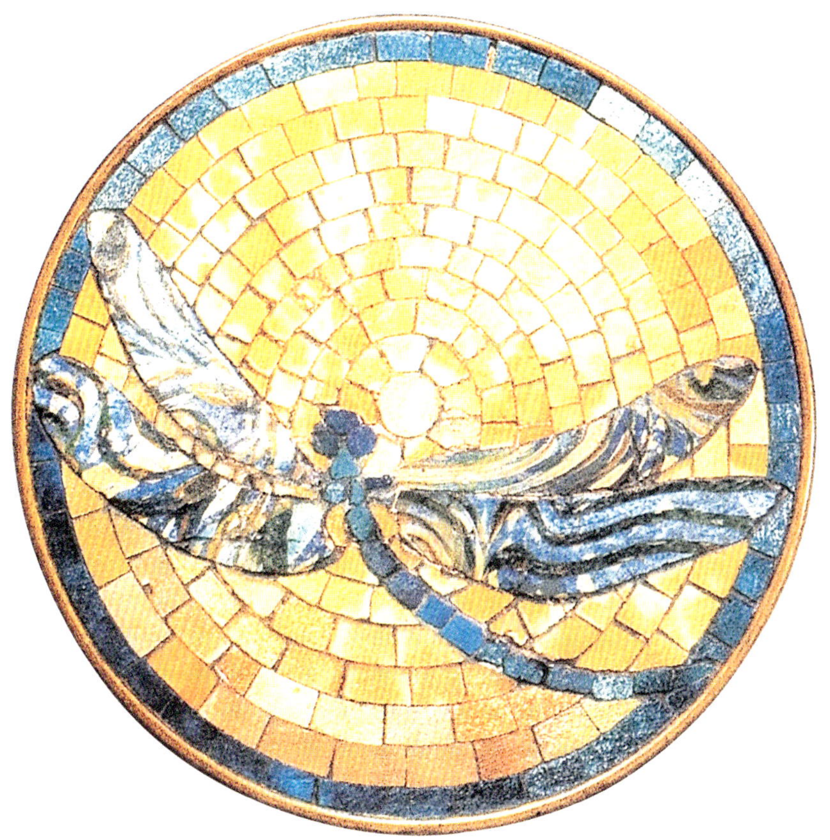

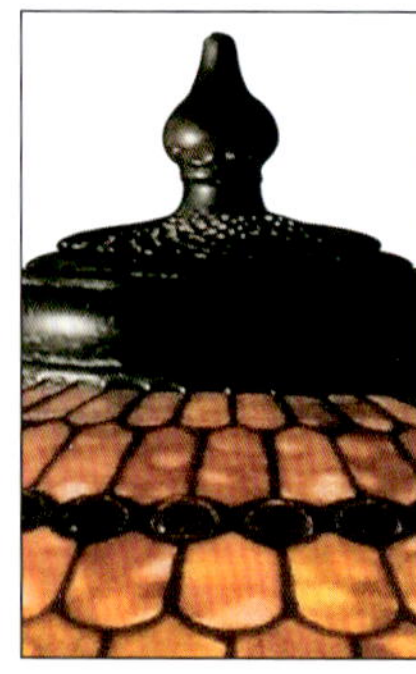

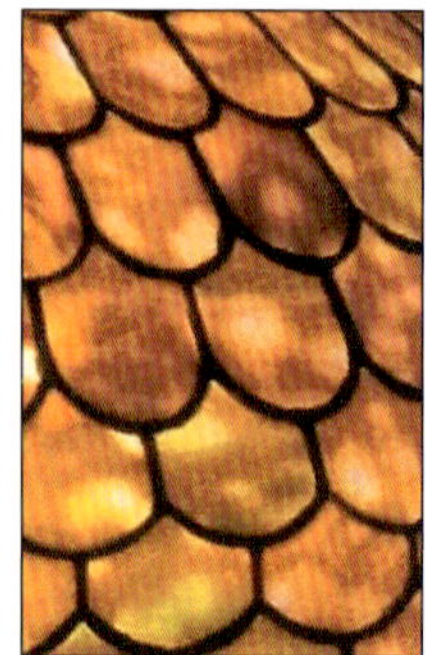

The Four Seasons, a domestic window exhibited in Paris and London was wrought in glass without the employment of any pigments.

The Valiant Woman was executed in the same fashion in 1902 for Mr. T. E. Stillmann and placed in the Church of the Pilgrims, Brooklyn Borough, New York City. It is a double window in which architectural and tree motifs are used to balance the composition,

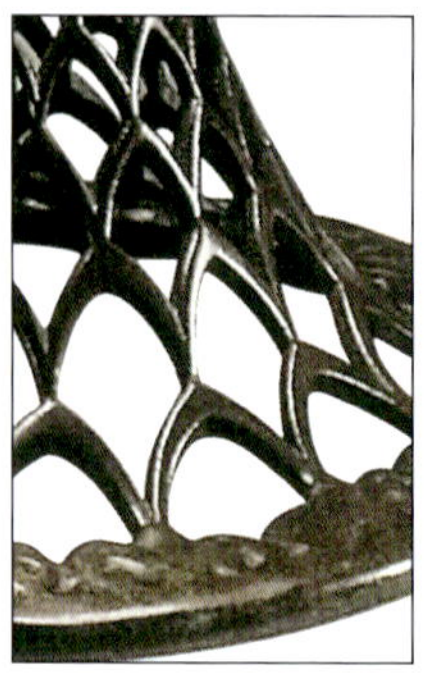

Fishscale Table Lamp

Leaded glass, bronze.

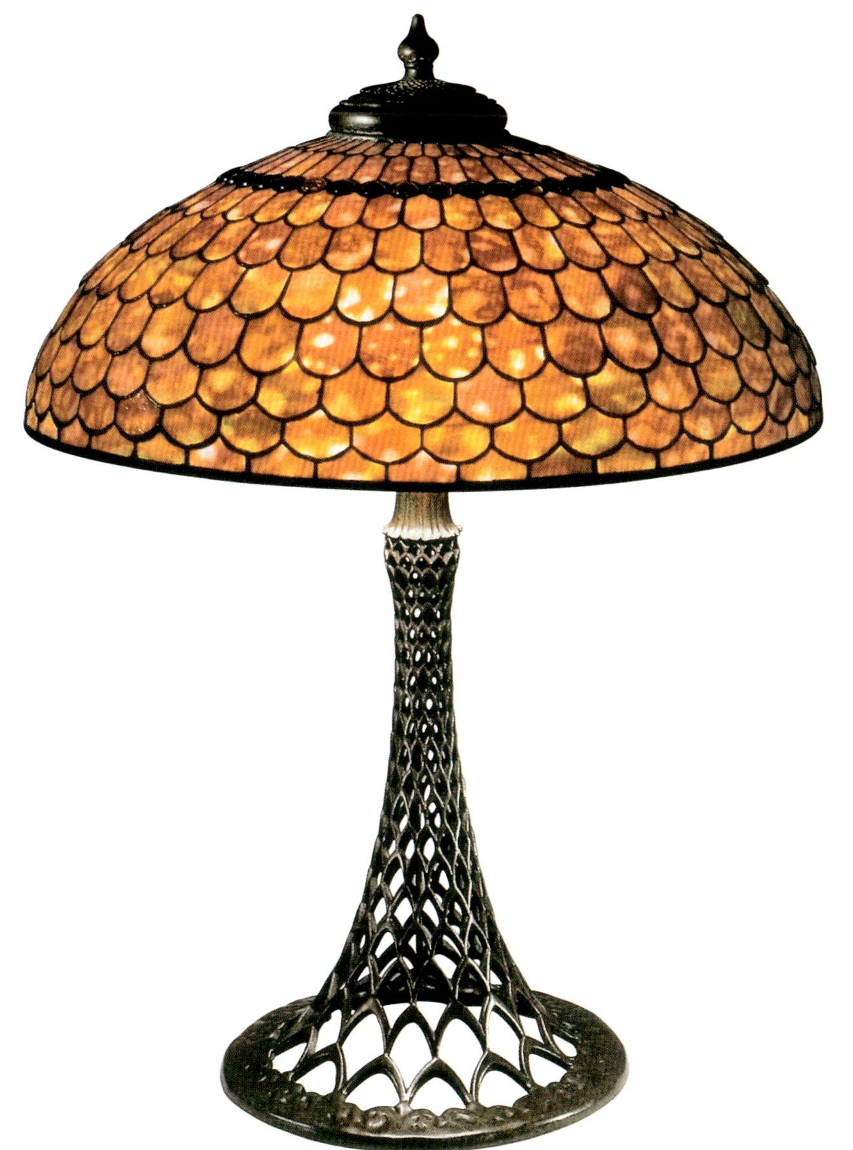

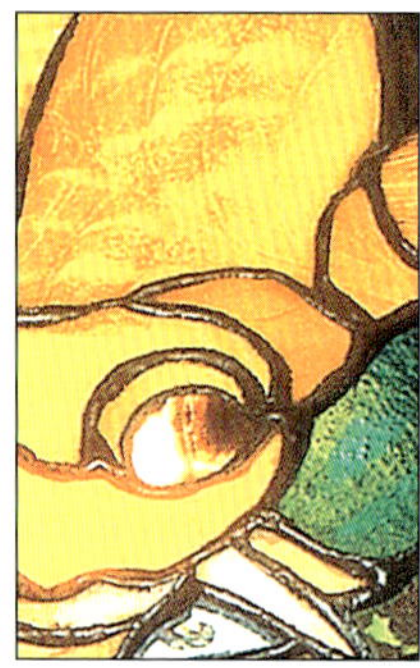

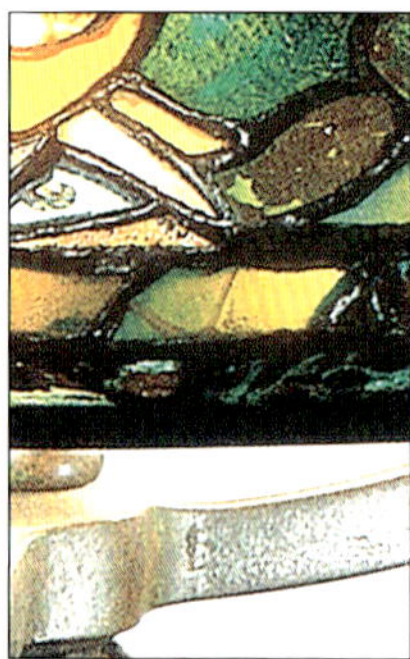

and the lead lines reinforce the main outlines of the figures. The only concession to enameling is found in the faces of the valiant woman and the people gathered in admiration before the terrace on which she stands. The lower squares of this double window are richly colored with marble tones and flower decorations. They carry inscriptions:

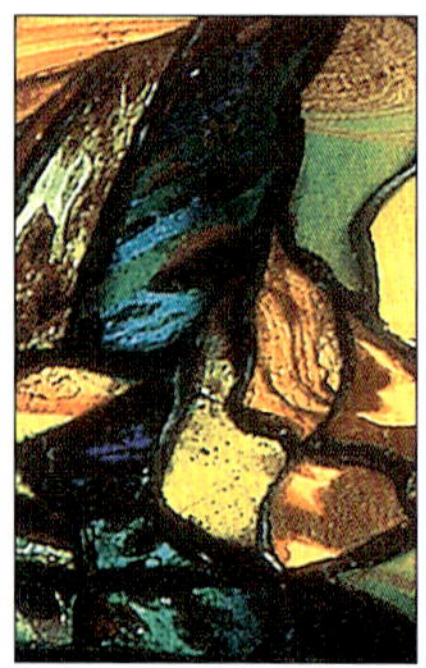

Fish and Water Cone Shade

Diameter: 40.6 cm

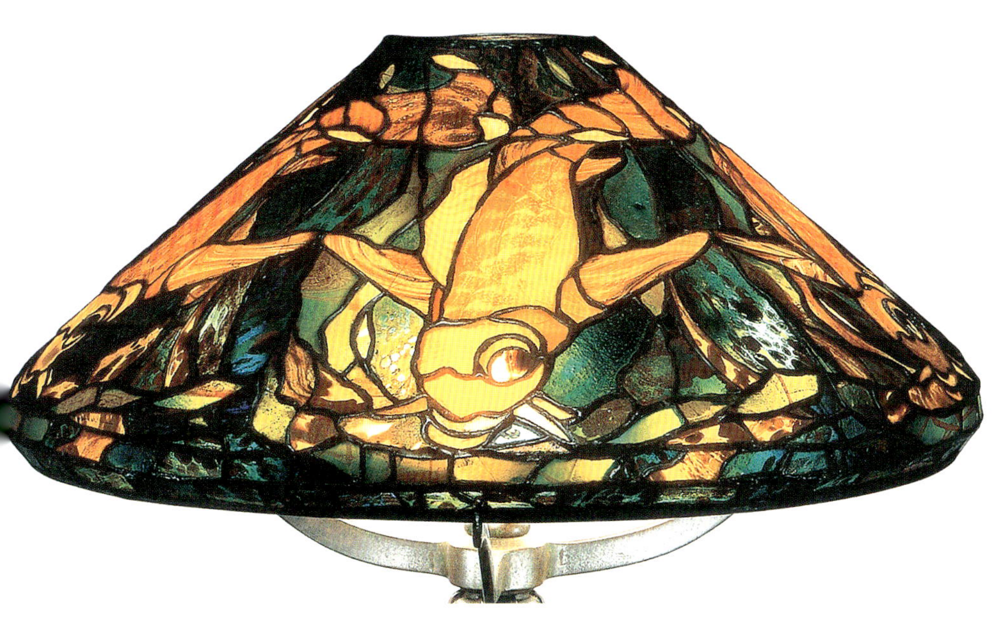

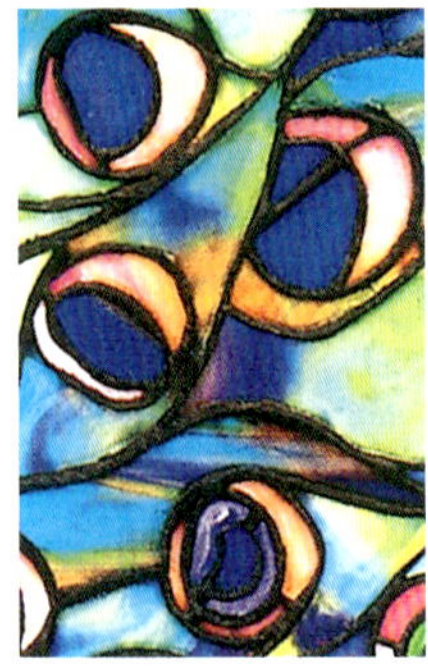

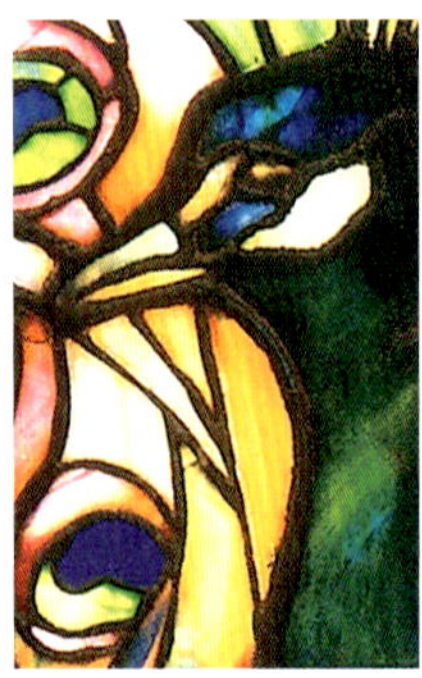

THE WOMAN THAT FEARETH THE LORD, SHE SHALL BE PRAISED. GIVE HER OF THE FRUIT OF HER HANDS AND LET HER OWN WORKS PRAISE HER IN THE GATES.

In an article called "American Art Supreme in Colored Glass," contributed to the *Forum* in 1893, Mr. Tiffany deplores the fact that while "today this country

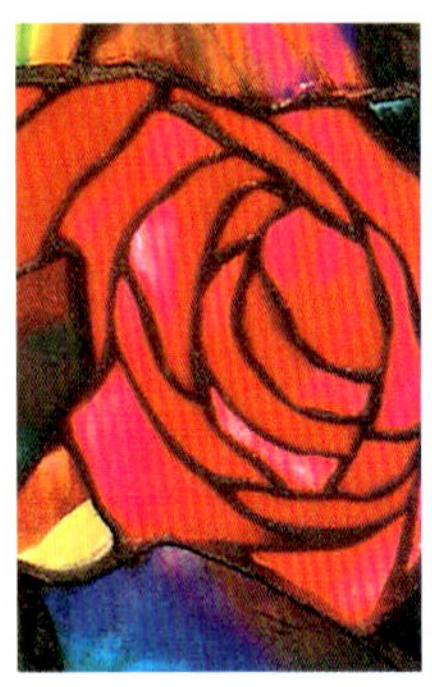

Window
———
Leaded glass.

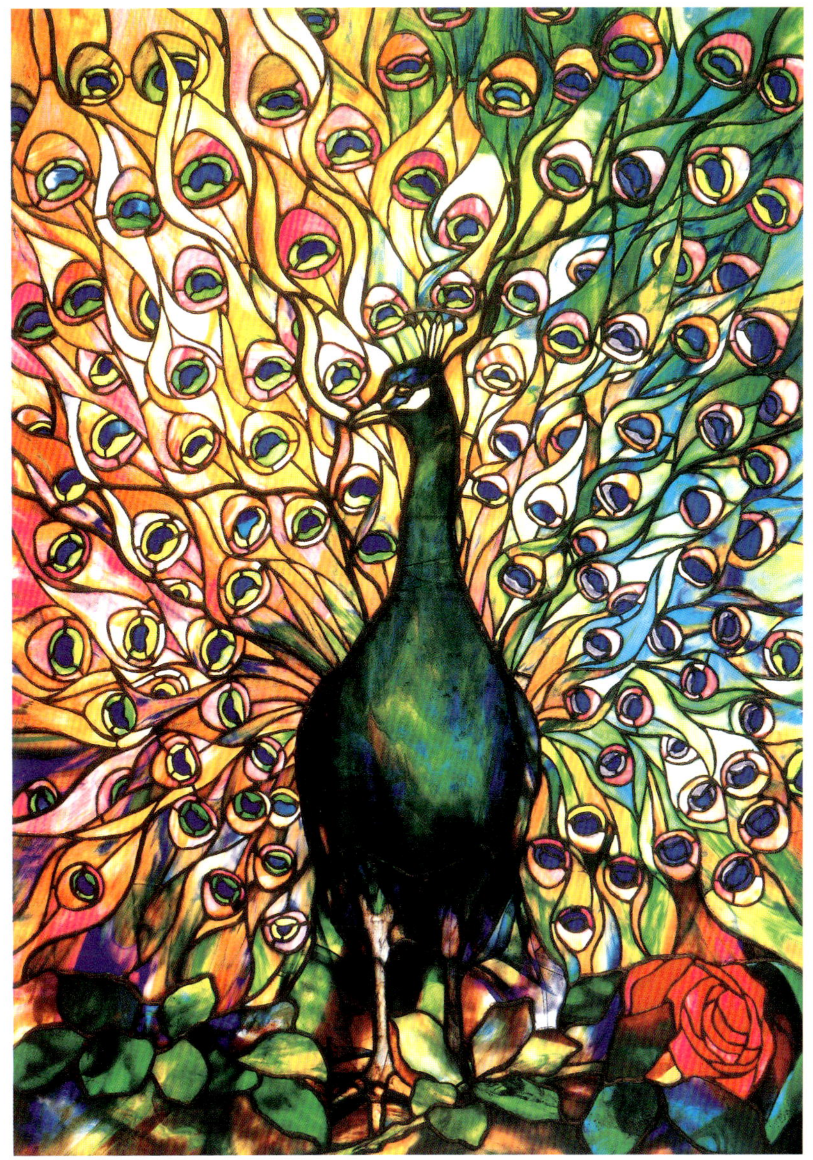

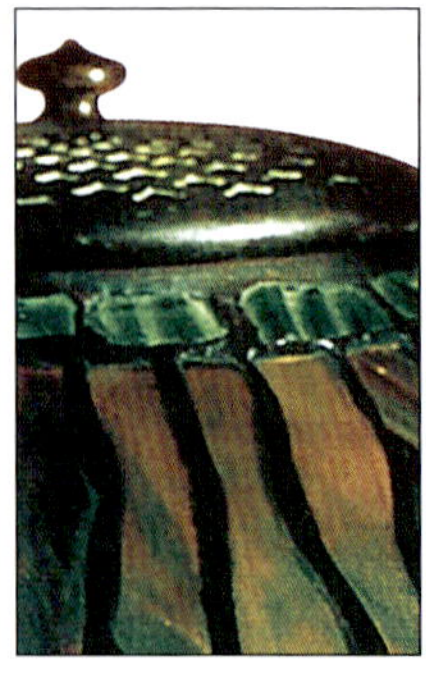

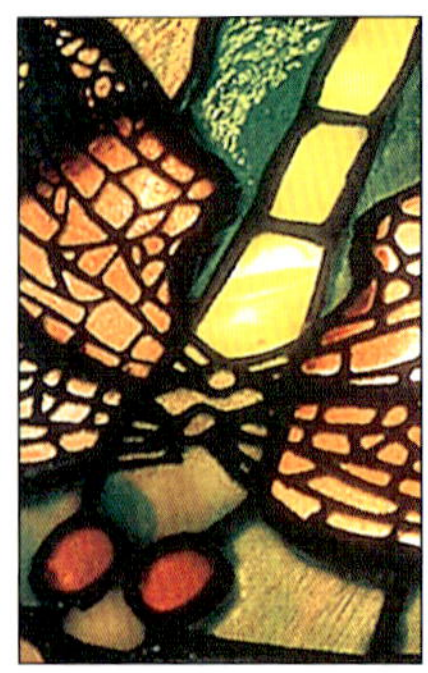

unquestionably leads the world in the production of colored glass windows of artistic value and decorative importance," yet the managers of the World's Fair at Chicago had not made provision for showing American windows. "An intelligent exhibition would have aided greatly in crushing out the purely commercial spirit which too often invades this field."

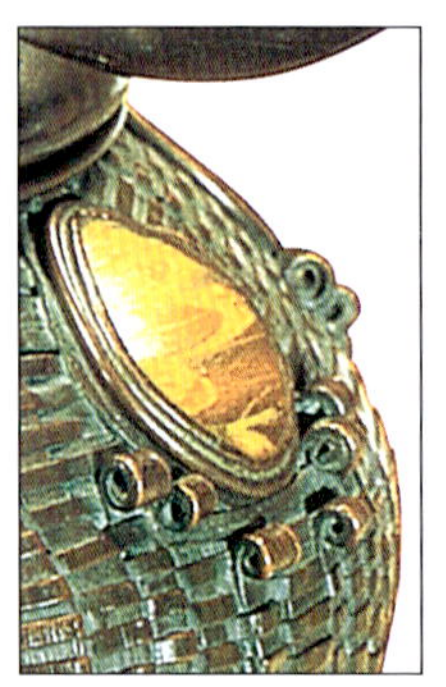

Oil Lamp, Base Nº. 140, Shade Nº. 1462

Leaded favrile glass and bronze.

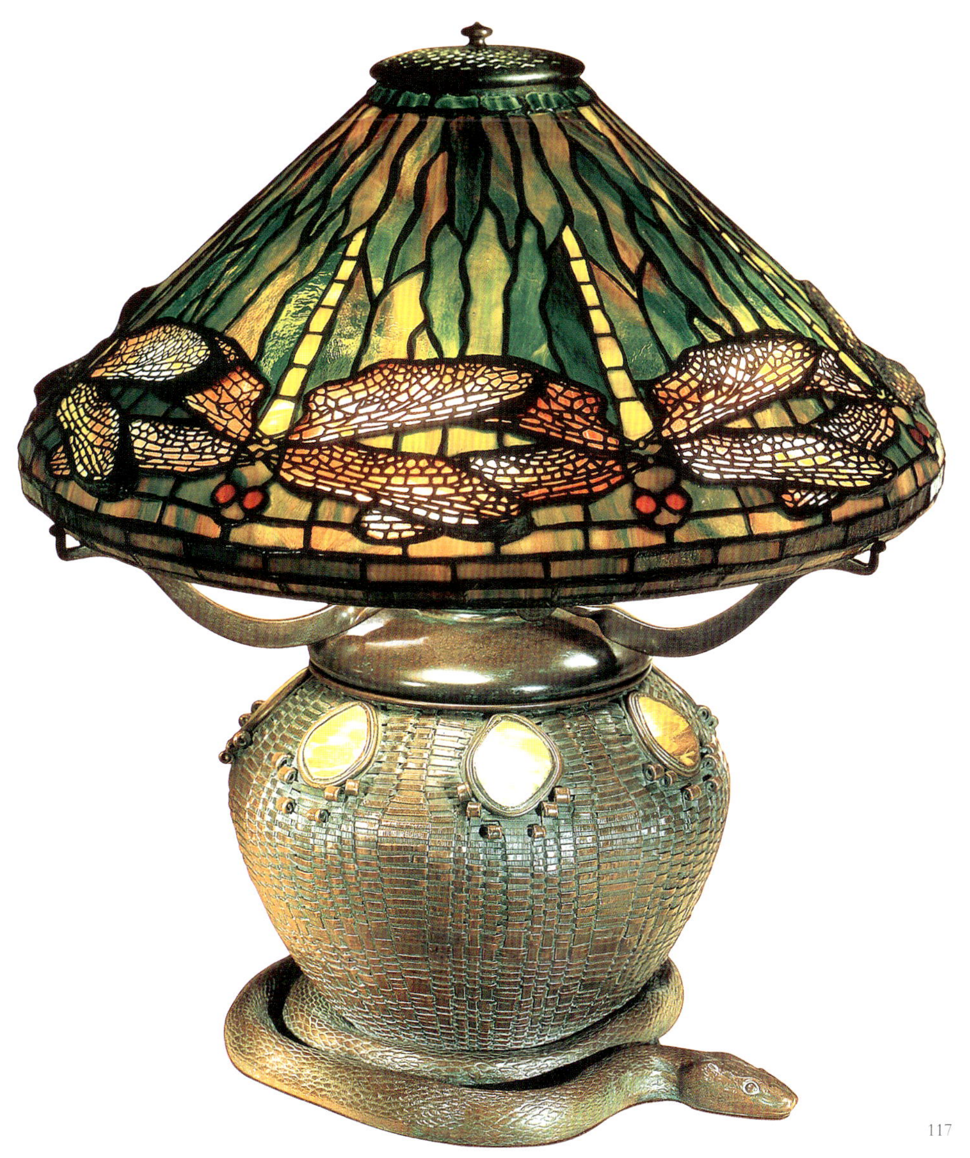

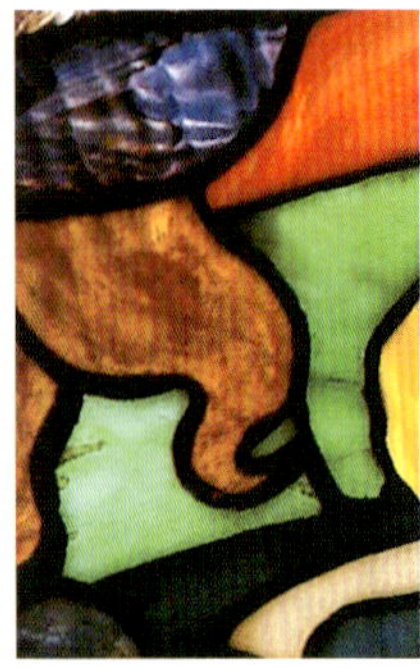

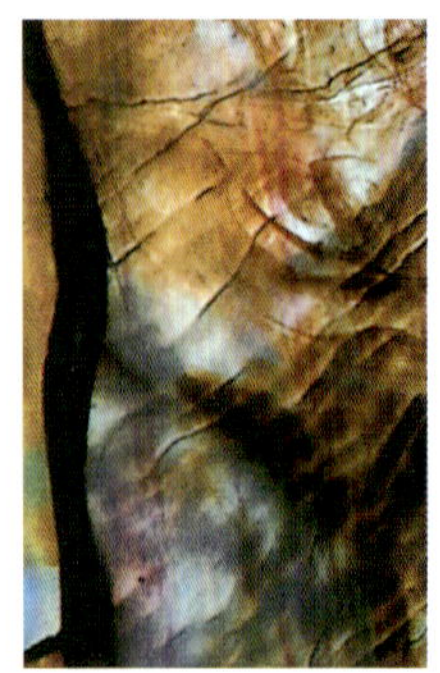

In this paper Mr. Tiffany had the boldness to compare modern American glass with mediaeval and to its advantage. "I maintain that the best American colored windows are superior to the best mediaeval windows."

In the old windows the folds in the draperies were obtained by placing pieces of glass of the same color

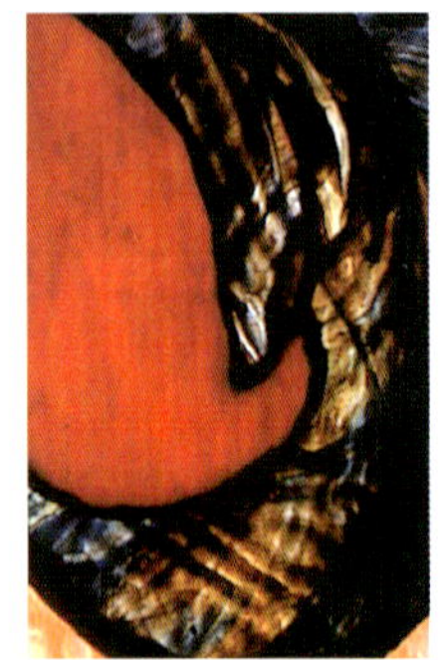

At the New Circus, Father Chrysanthemum

Henri de Toulouse-Lautrec, Louis Comfort Tiffany, 1894.
Mottled, printed and superimposed glass, 120 x 85 cm.
Musée d'Orsay, Paris.

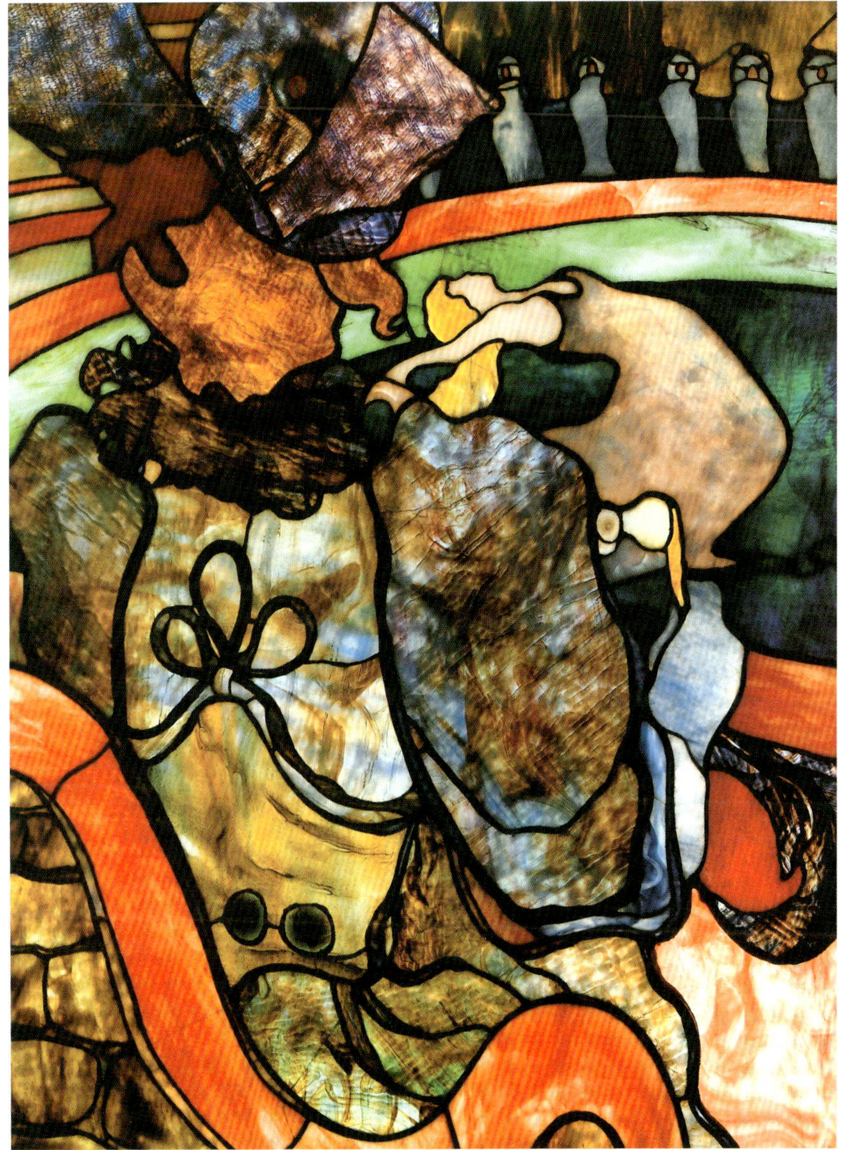

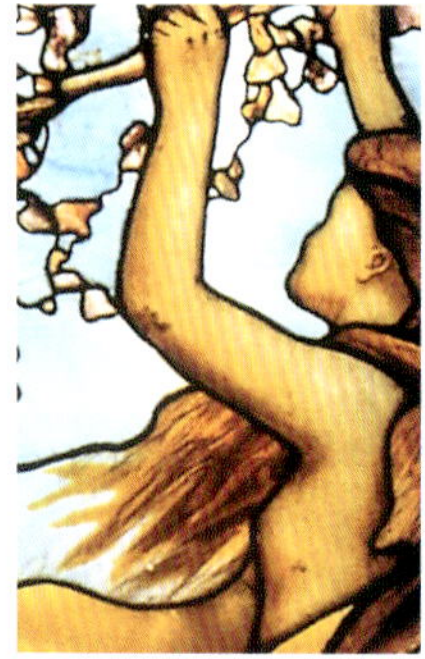

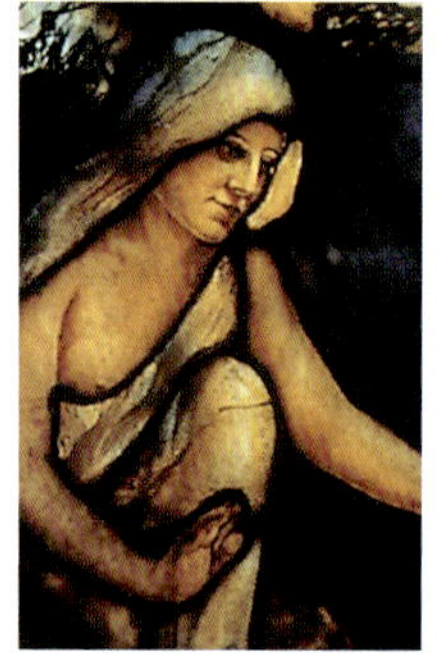

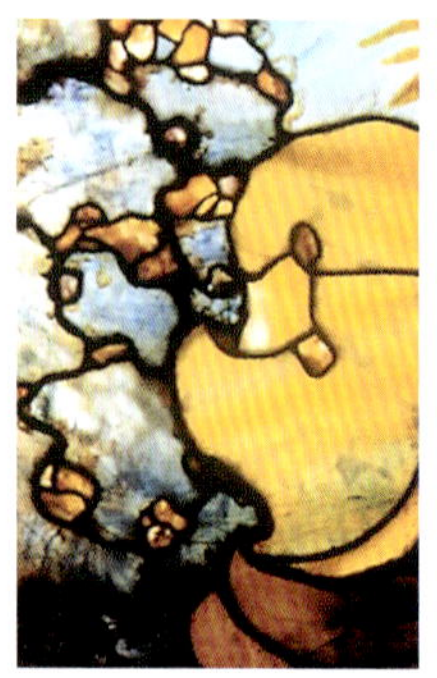

but of various shades side by side, or by painting the shadows upon a sheet of glass with a brown enamel. In America a pot-metal glass is forced into folds and wrinkles while in a molten condition; these folds are adaptable to many forms of drapery. Such glass gives the effect of light and shade in draperies without using so many lead-lines and doing away altogether with paints and enamels.

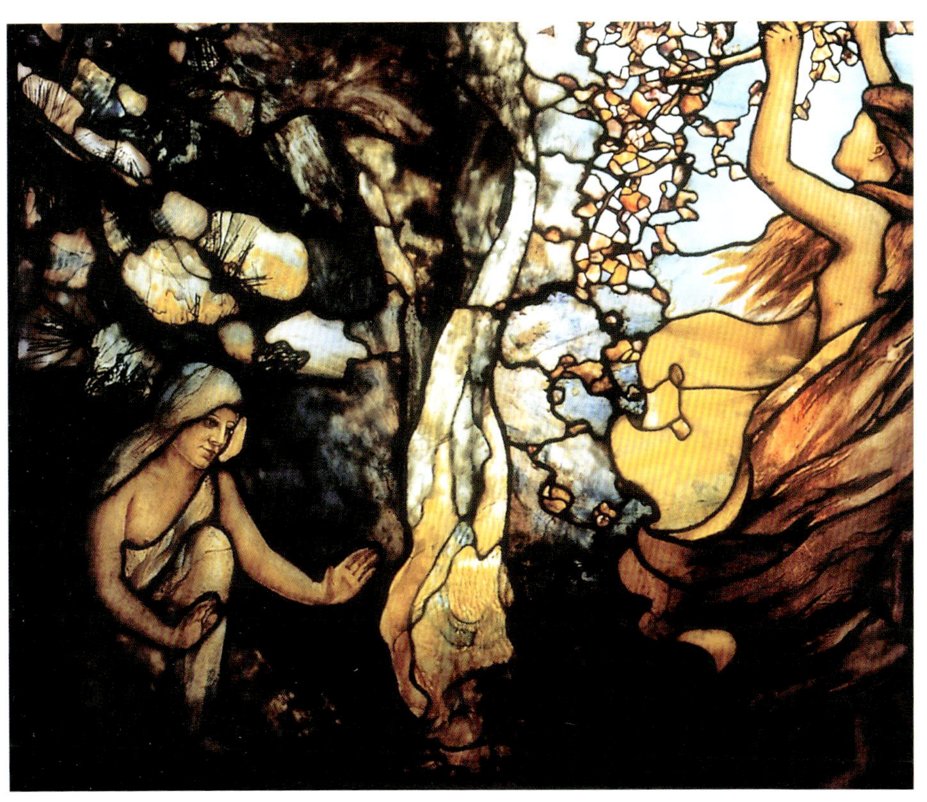

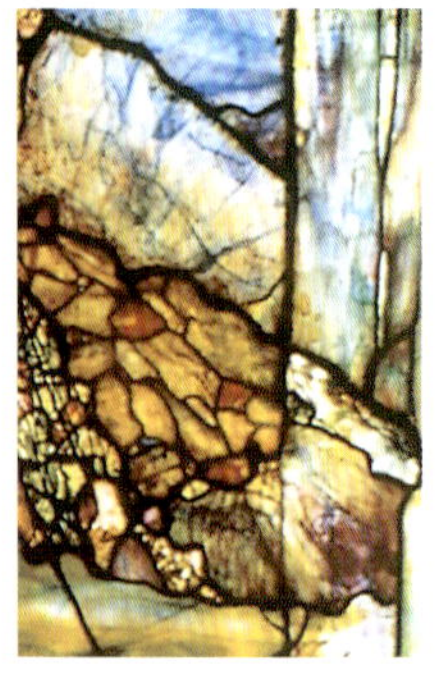

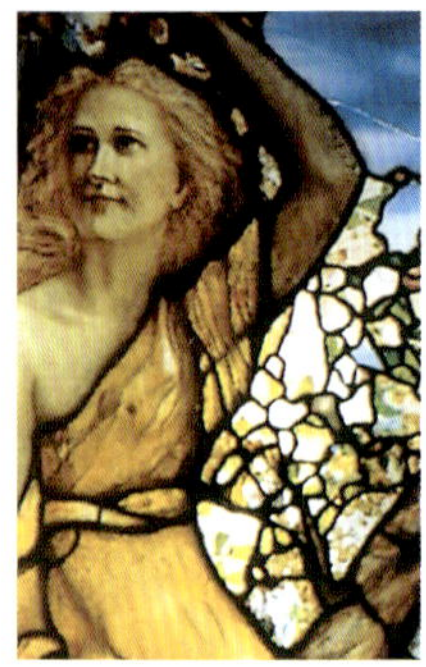

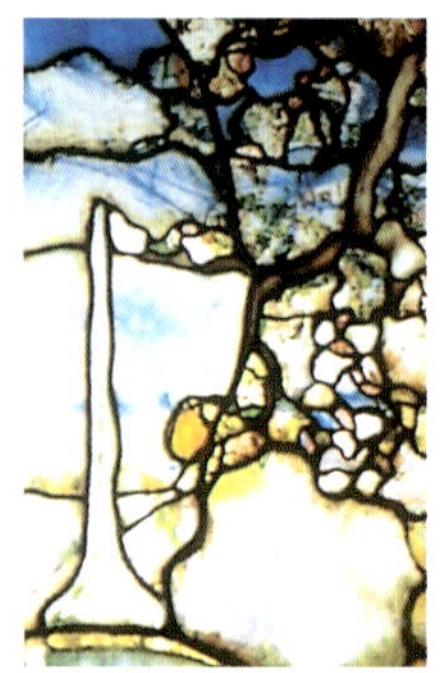

"In the windows of the thirteenth, fourteenth, and fifteenth centuries, for example, the foliage and colors were produced largely by means of stains and enamels, in this country we produce foliage by introducing into a sheet of glass while molten, other pieces of glass of the proper colors, having stems, leaf and flower forms."

Four Seasons

1897.
Favrile glass, lead. Jason Mc Coy Inc., New York.

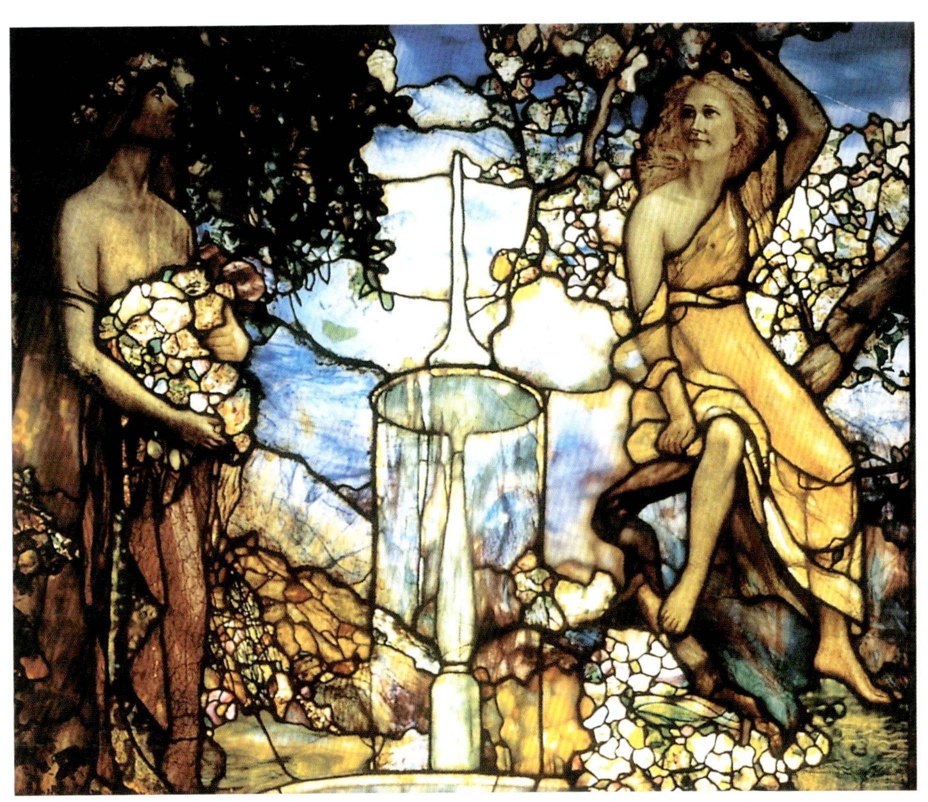

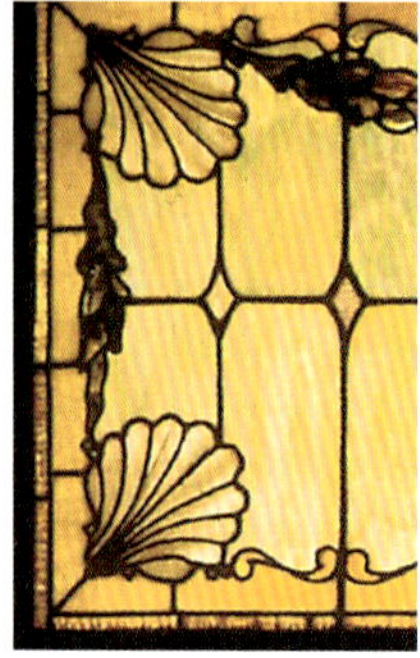

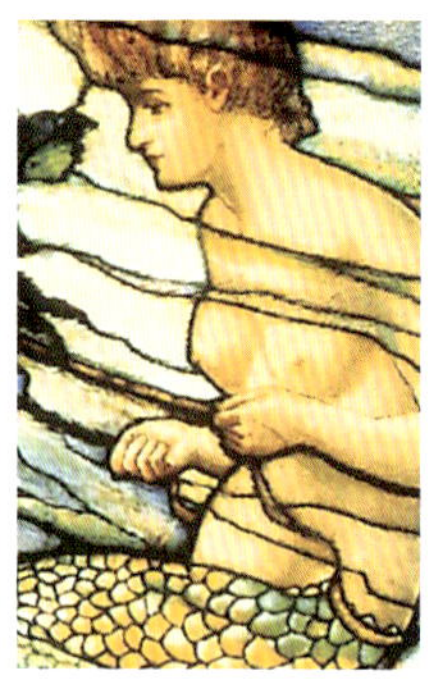

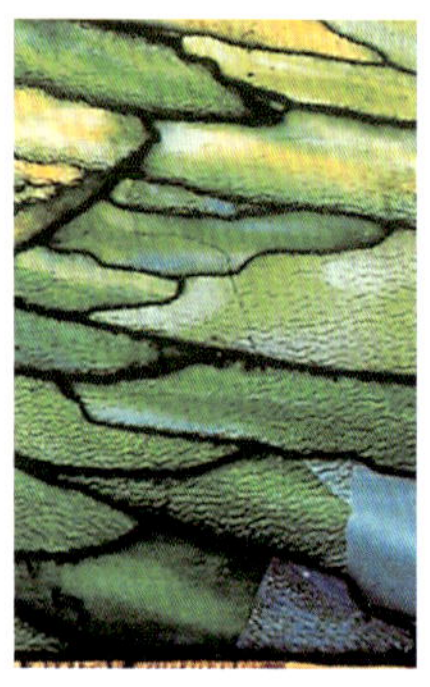

Mr. Tiffany spoke with authority, from long experience and after many disappointments in men and materials. The next seven years were crowded with interest. Success crowned the efforts which had extended crescendo for at least two decades. At the Universal Exposition of 1900 in Paris he took the Grand Prize and was decorated Chevalier of the Legion of Honor.

Siren Stained Glass

1899.
Carl Heck, Aspen.

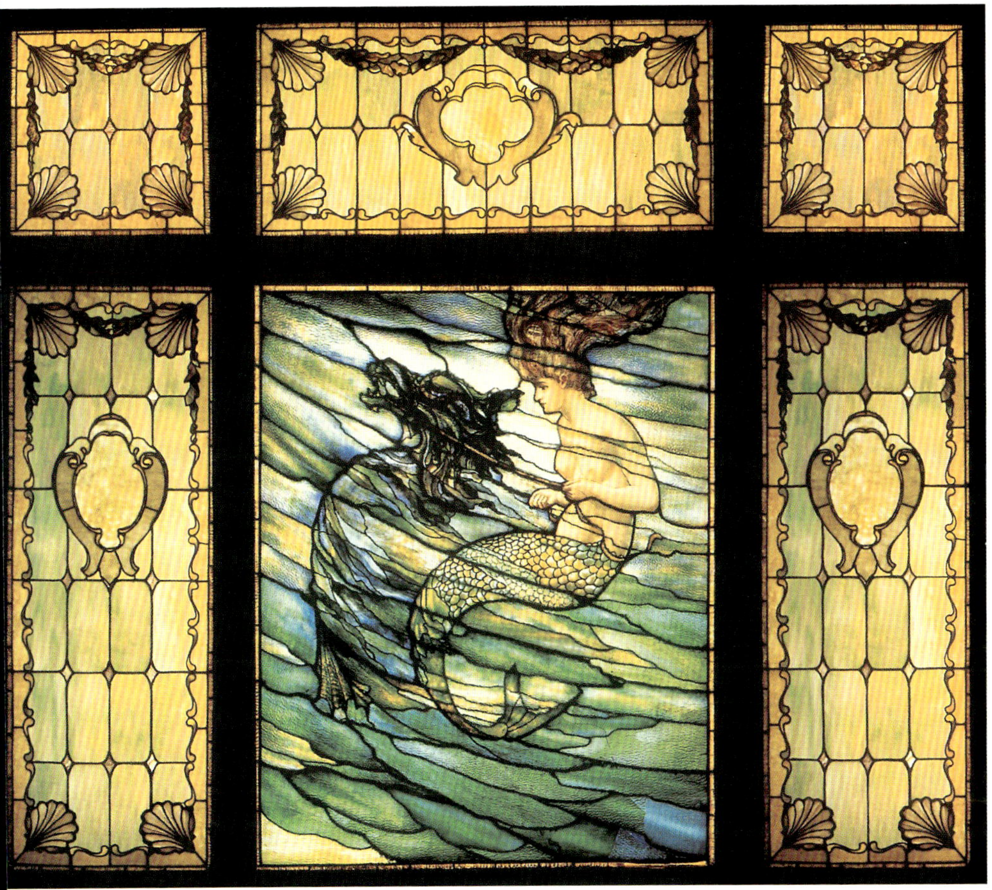

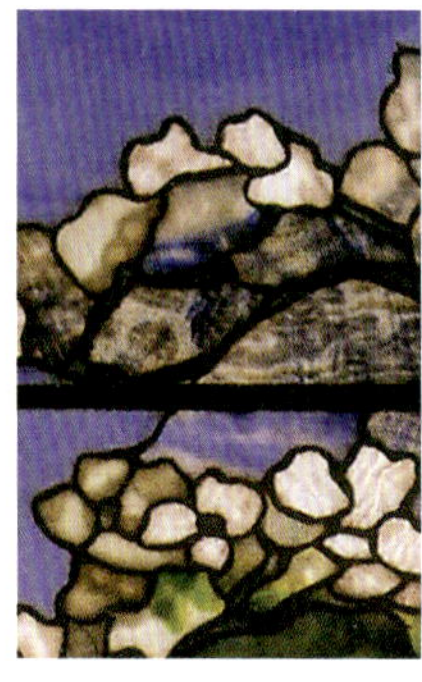

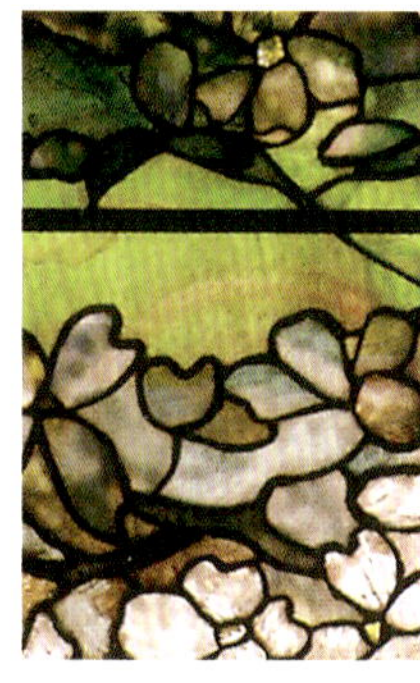

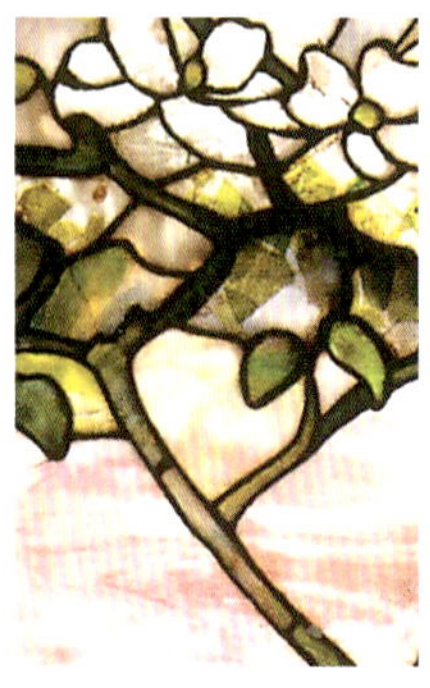

One point touched upon by Mr. Tiffany should not be overlooked. The new method demands much more thought and care on the part of the window designer. He can not turn his sketch over to the foreman and expect results worthy of his reputation. He has to superintend every stage of the work just as carefully and with the same zeal as during the evolution of an oil painting.

Dogwood

——————

1900-1915.
Glass and lead, 254 x 142.2 cm.
The Metropolitan Museum of Art, New York.

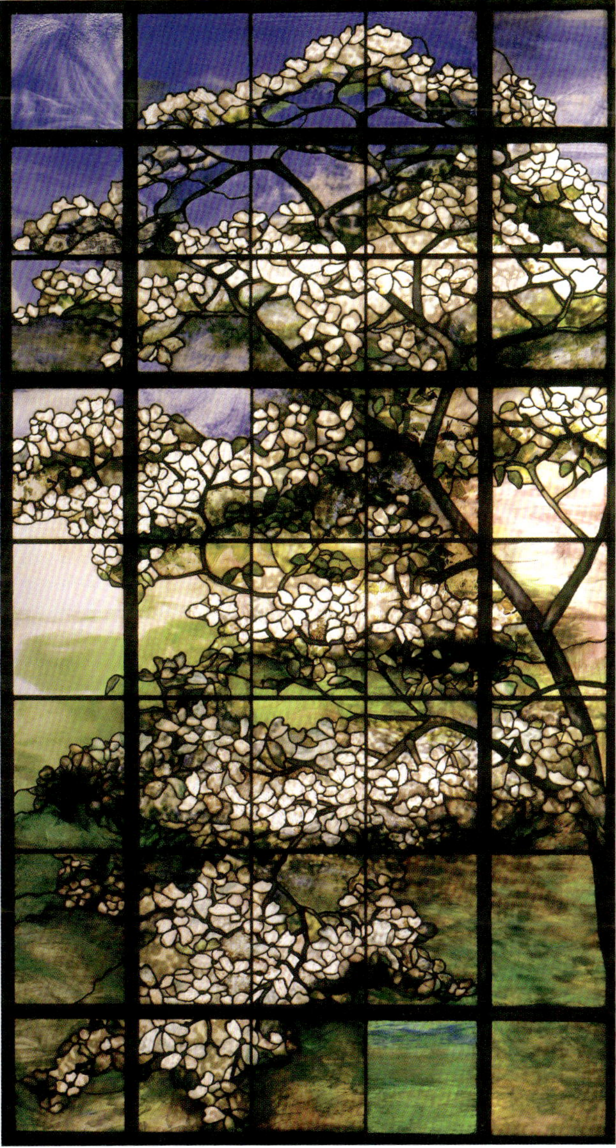

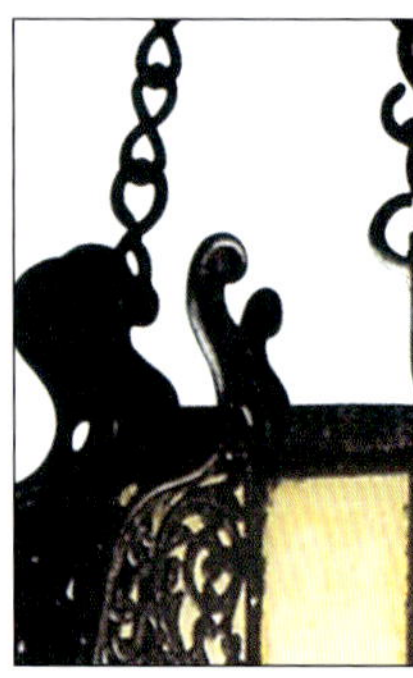

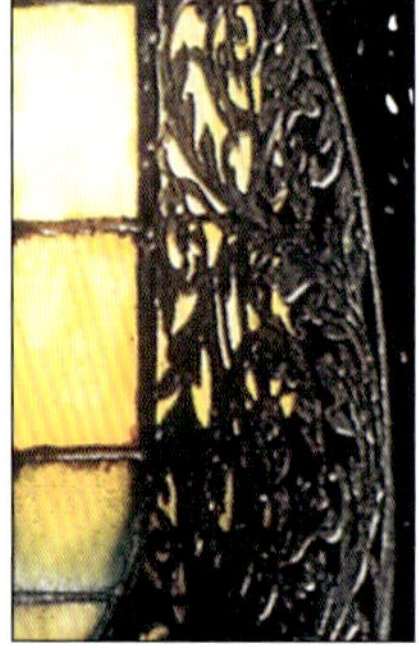

For as in painting the introduction of a color in one part of the canvas, or of a tint or tone, has its blissful or baneful effect upon all that has gone before, so with a stained glass window; no other eyes than those of the original artist can tell whether the fresh note added to the rest is the right or the wrong one. Infinite, endless labor makes the masterpiece.

Three lancet openings of a window in Christ Church, Fairfield, Connecticut, consist of medallions containing

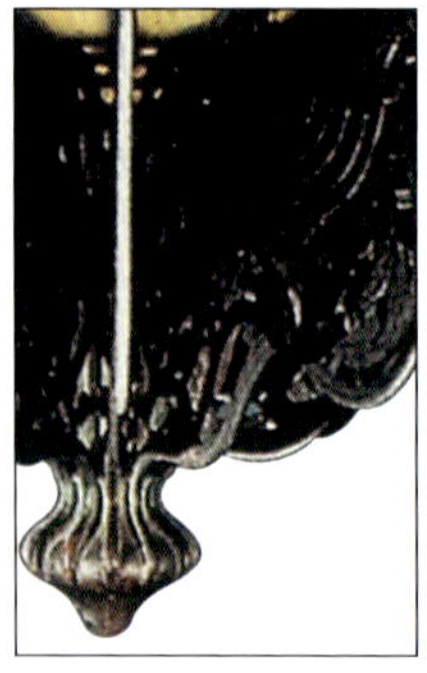

Bronze Sculpted Hanging Lamp

Leaded glass and bronze.

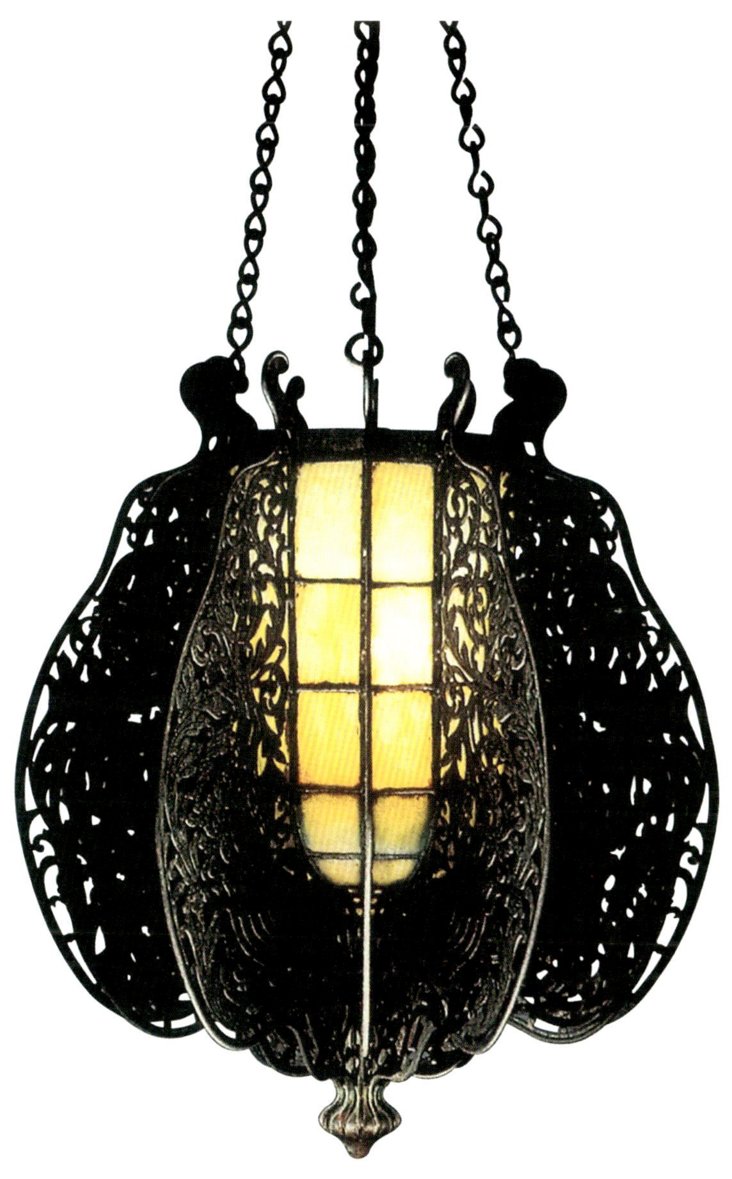

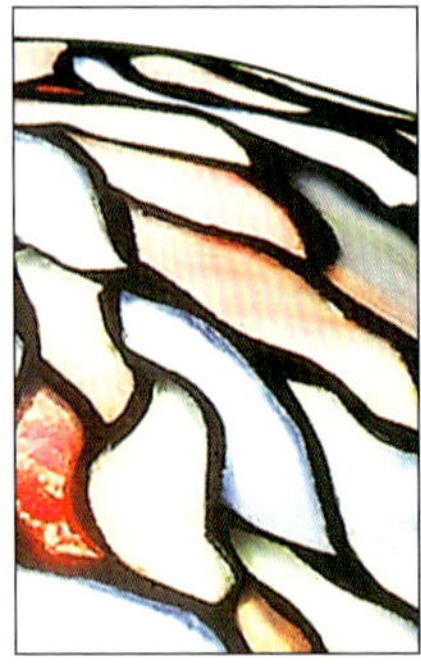

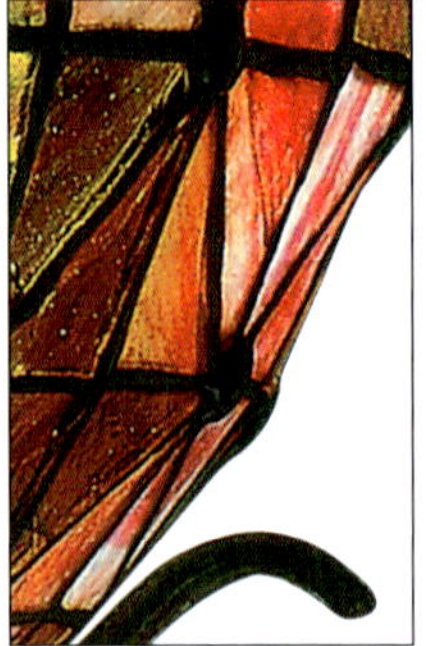

religious groups set in an elaborate system of interlaced decoration. The subjects of the medallions are Christ as an infant, with the doctors in the temple, exhorting, calling the children to him, healing the sick, raising the dead, etc.

A decorative cross of interlacing lines and ribbons set against rich tiles belongs to 1908. It is purely secular and depends for its effect on the deep and glowing tones as much as on the original design.

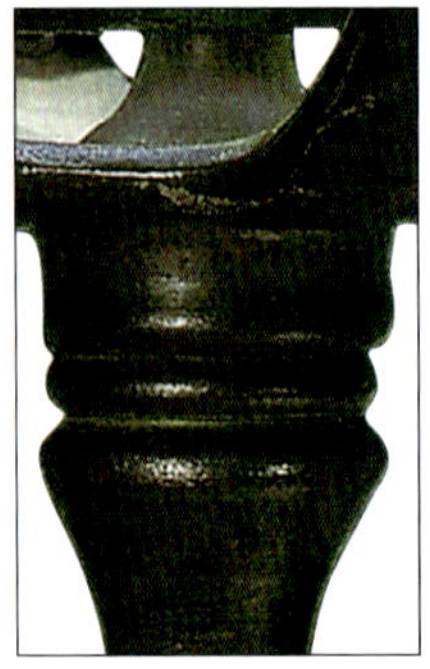

Ball Floor Lamp

Leaded glass, bronze.

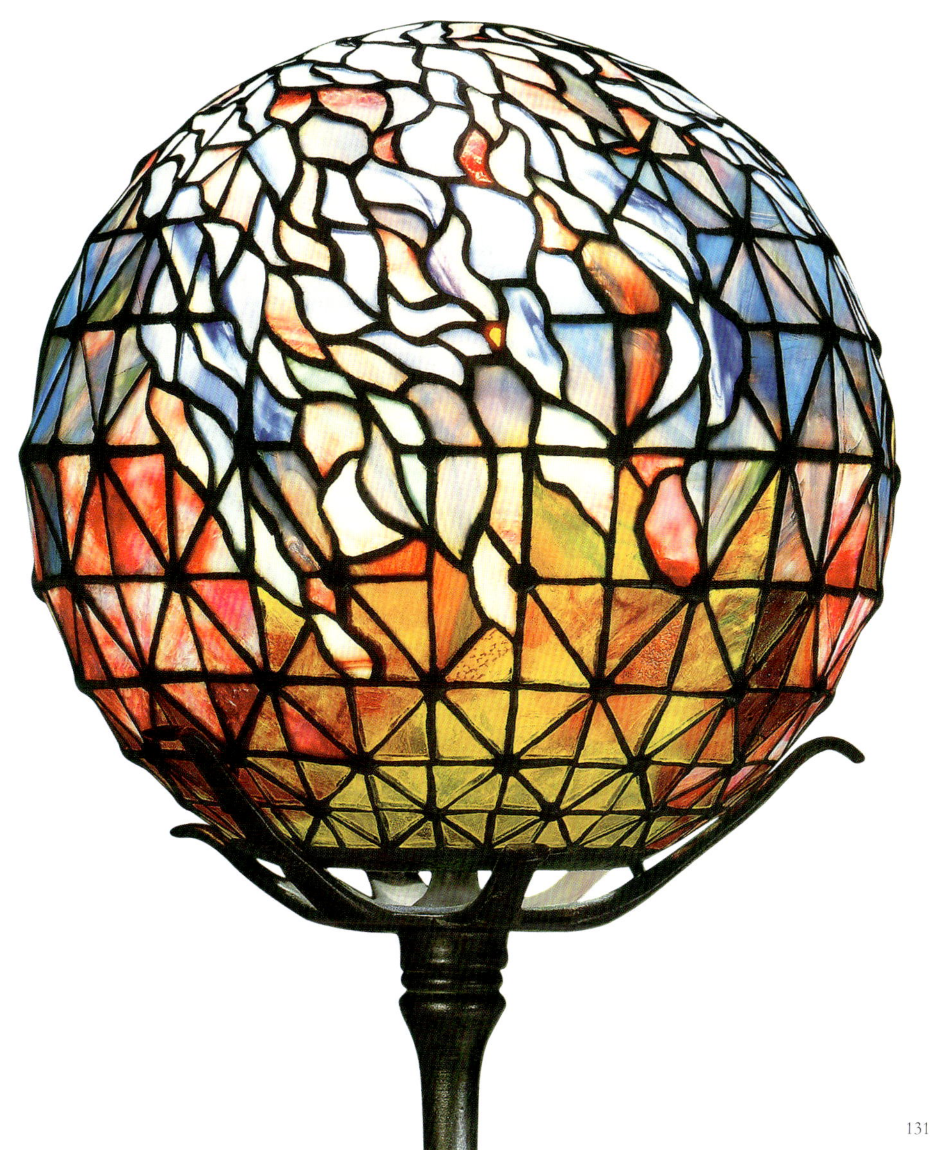

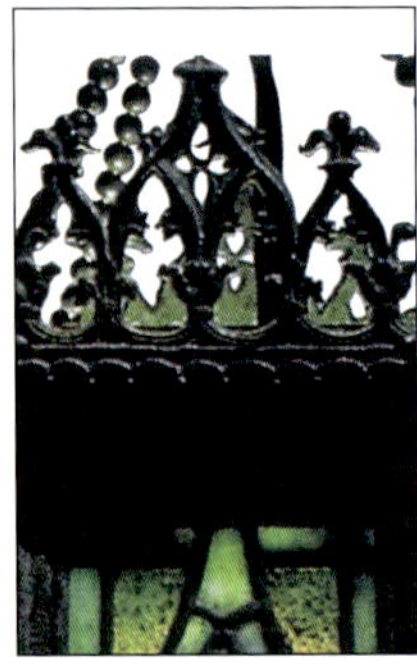

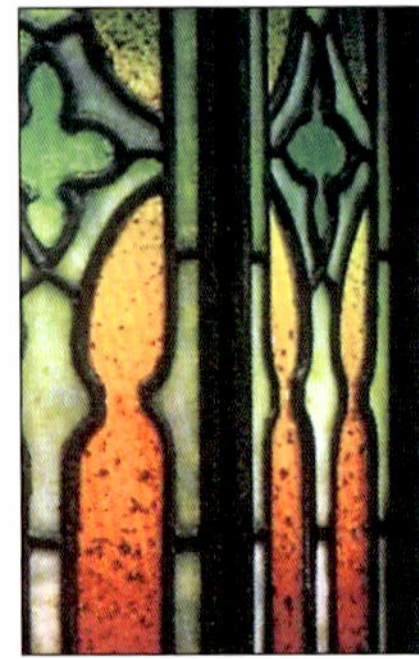

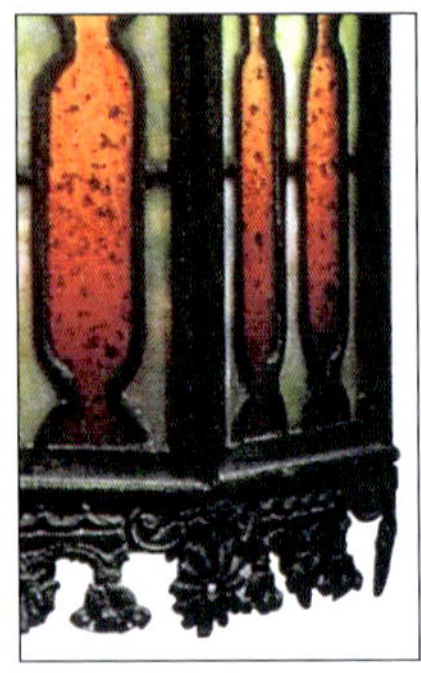

A sylvan composition of two girls in the woods plucking flowers by the brink of a stream represents windows for the home.

But it would be too long to enumerate the windows for churches, public buildings, and homes which have issued from the Tiffany Studios under the direction of Louis C. Tiffany. American glass has had a distinguished originator and forefighter in him. He has had to contend

Bronze Sculpted Table Lantern

Leaded glass and bronze.

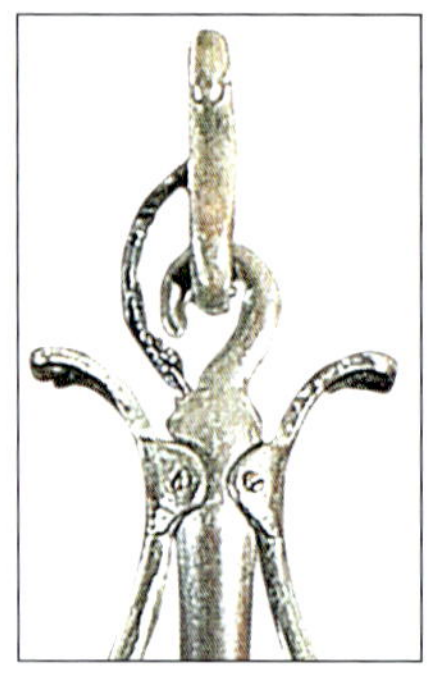

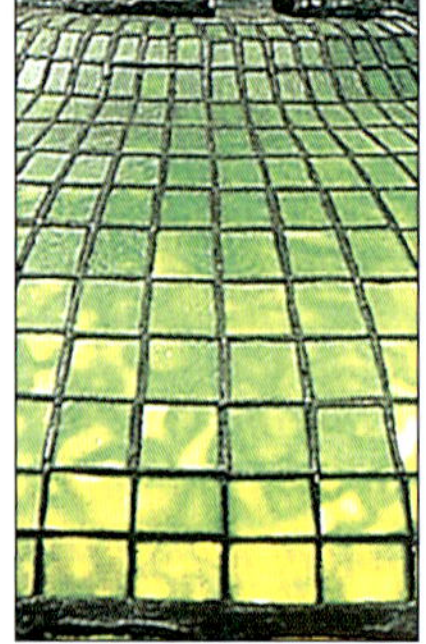

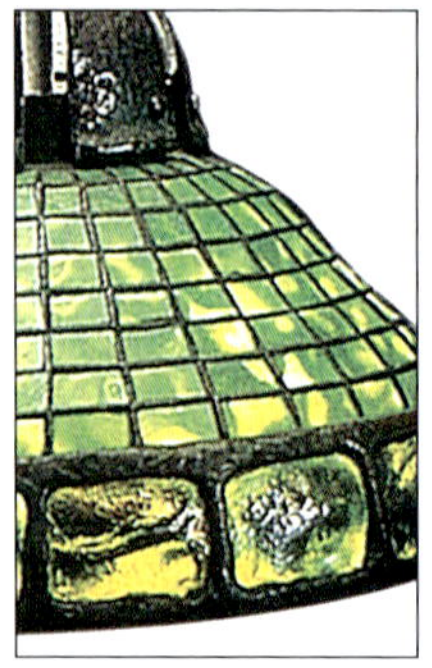

against the tradition in the Episcopal Church of the United States which looks with reverence toward the Church of England, from whence it sprang. The prejudices of clergymen and vestrymen are in favor of British glass for windows, notwithstanding its coldness and lack of character. There is no reasoning with a sentiment. It affects our church architecture in general with a sameness and a lameness truly deplorable.

Triple Lamp Chandelier

Favrile glass and bronze.

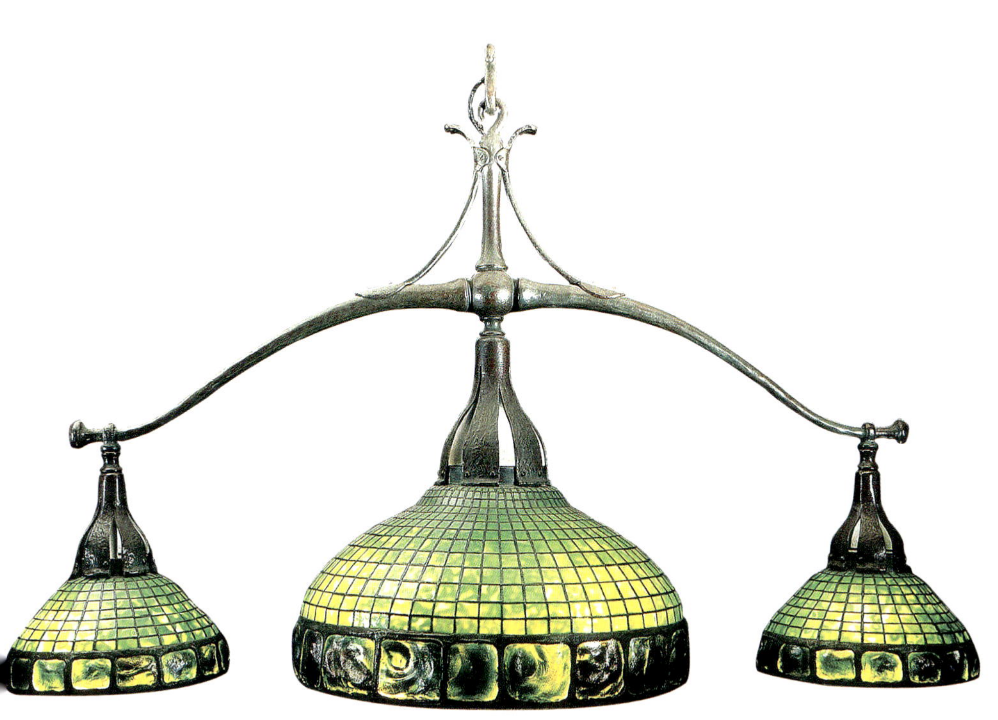

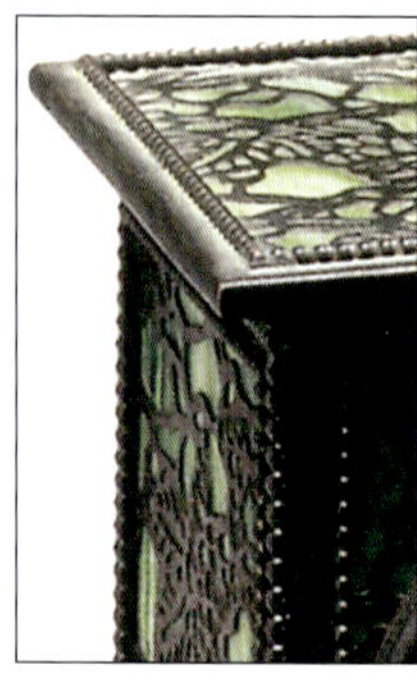

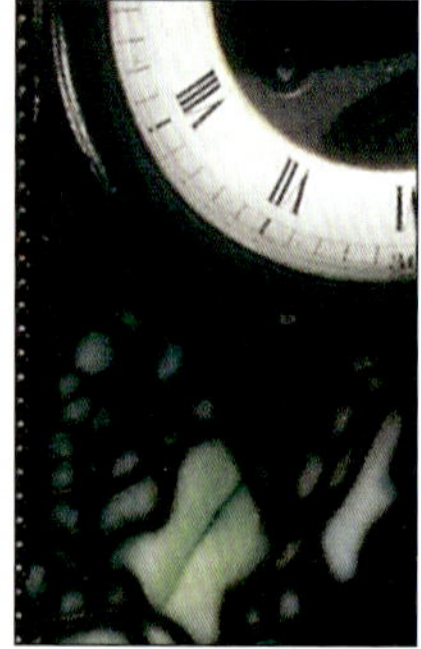

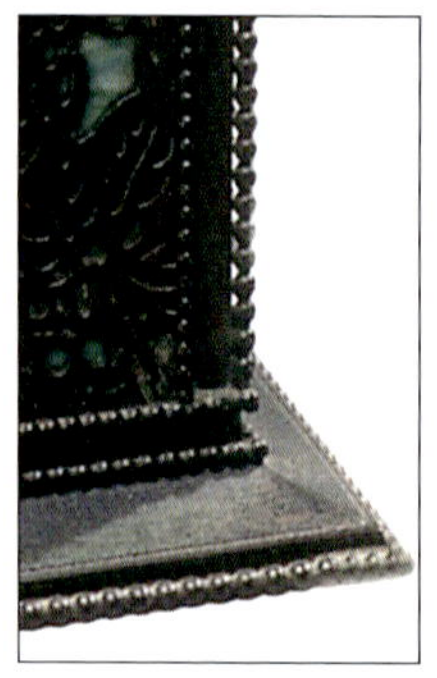

FAVRILE GLASS

However, it was not by the way of stained glass windows that Louis C. Tiffany won his widest fame. His protest against certain great American expositions for their neglect of American stained windows (published in the *Forum*) was necessary, because the managers of such fairs declined the expense of preparing suitable halls with day and night lighting such as are needed for the proper exhibition of

Finely Sculpted Bronze Clock

Favrile glass and bronze.

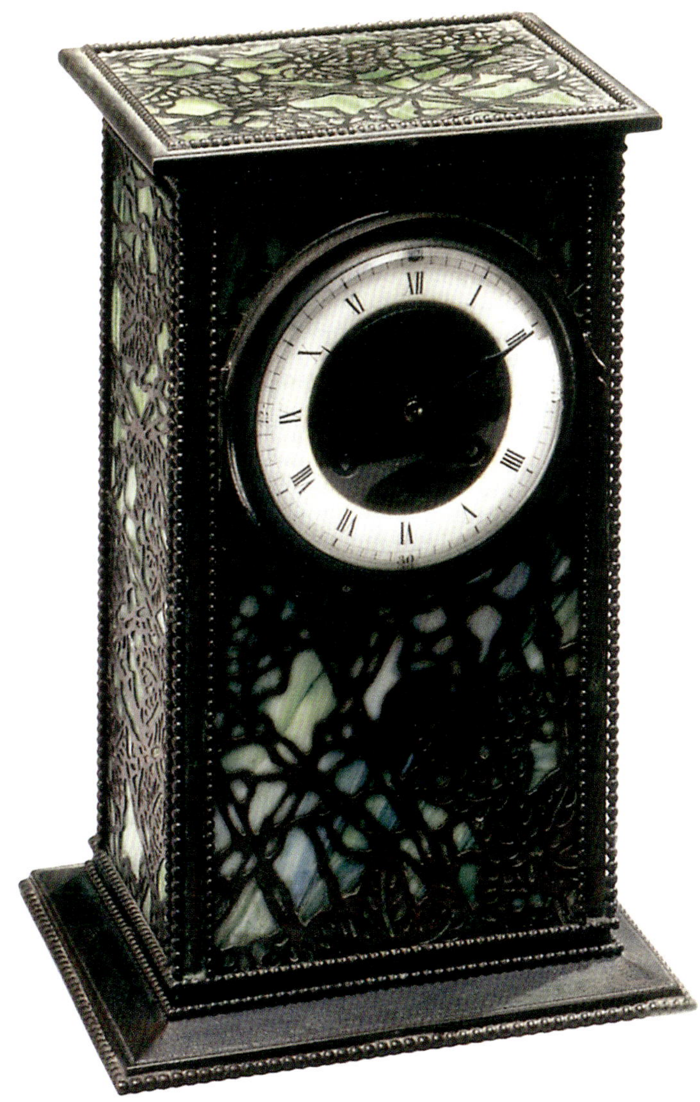

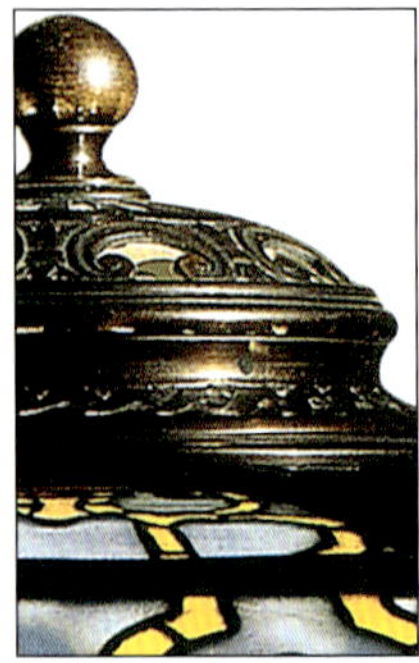

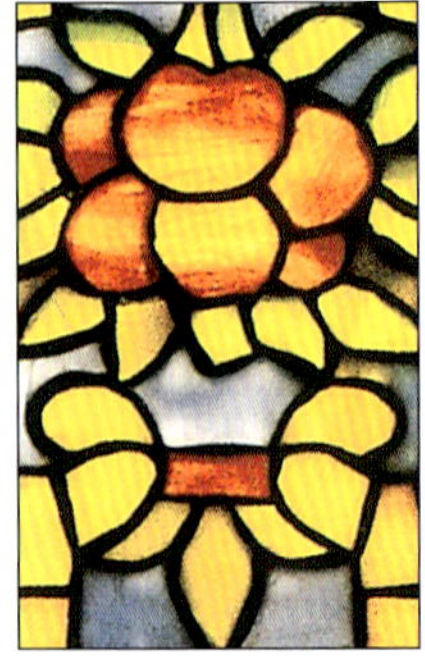

stained glass. They are indeed unwieldy objects to exhibit. Not so the small glass objects for the drawing room, the dining table, the boudoir. Ancient glass of Chinese, Venetian, Bohemian and British origin has made the circuit of the world. The somewhat mysterious but once very famous myrrhine glassware, under the Caesars, left nothing to be desired in the admiration of classical writers or the sums spent on their purchase by the collectors of the day.

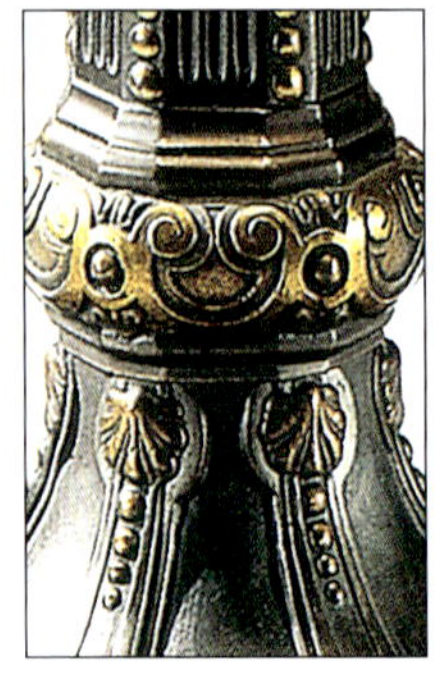

Oil Lamp, Sculpted Base

Glass and bronze.

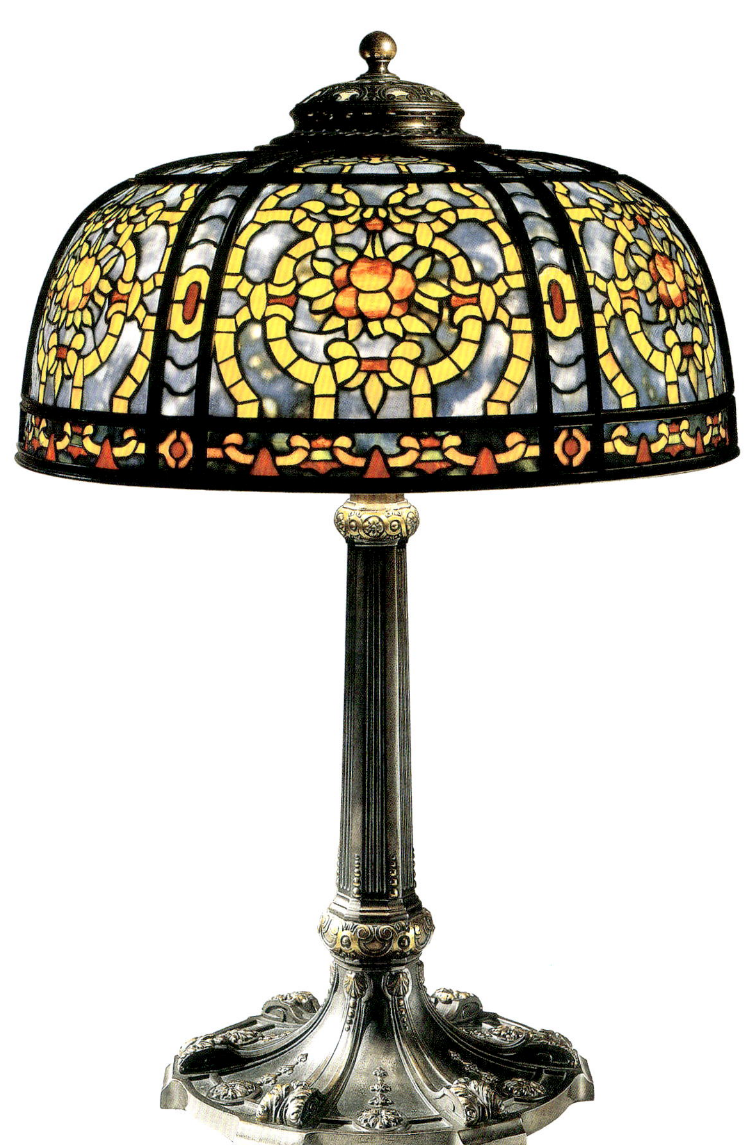

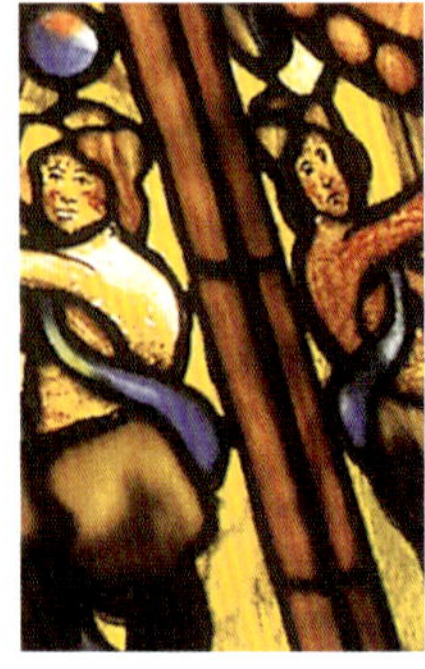

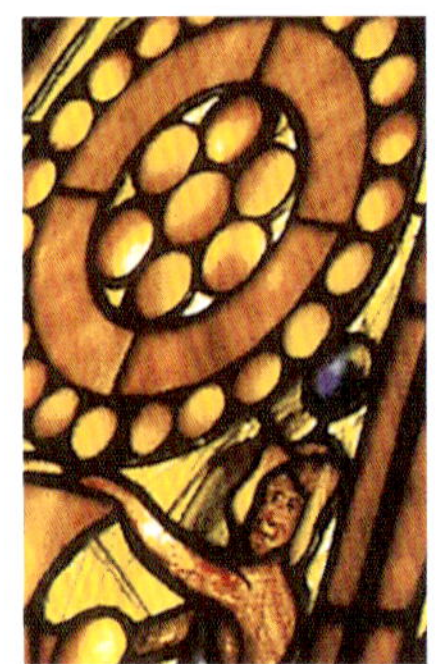

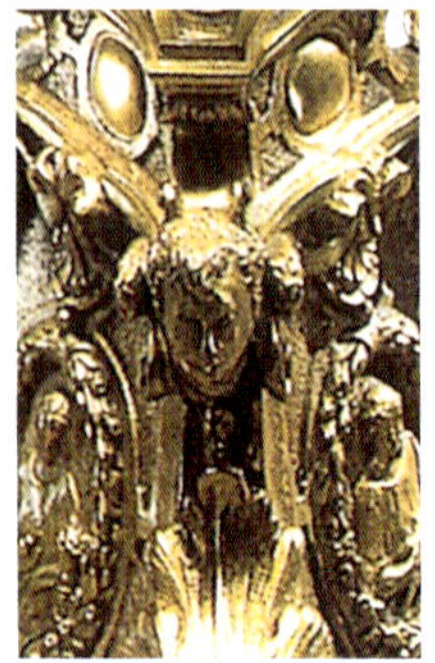

Tiffany, as we have seen, experimented upon the colored glass used in draperies and shadows in various glass furnaces, and finally in his own. Much pot-metal of a very glorious color could never find a place in windows. Stores of it accumulated; it was evident that an industry pushed so far ought to strive to lower the annual deficit by the utilization of byproducts, just like any other. This was one but by no means the only reason for the

Glass, lead.
Private collection.

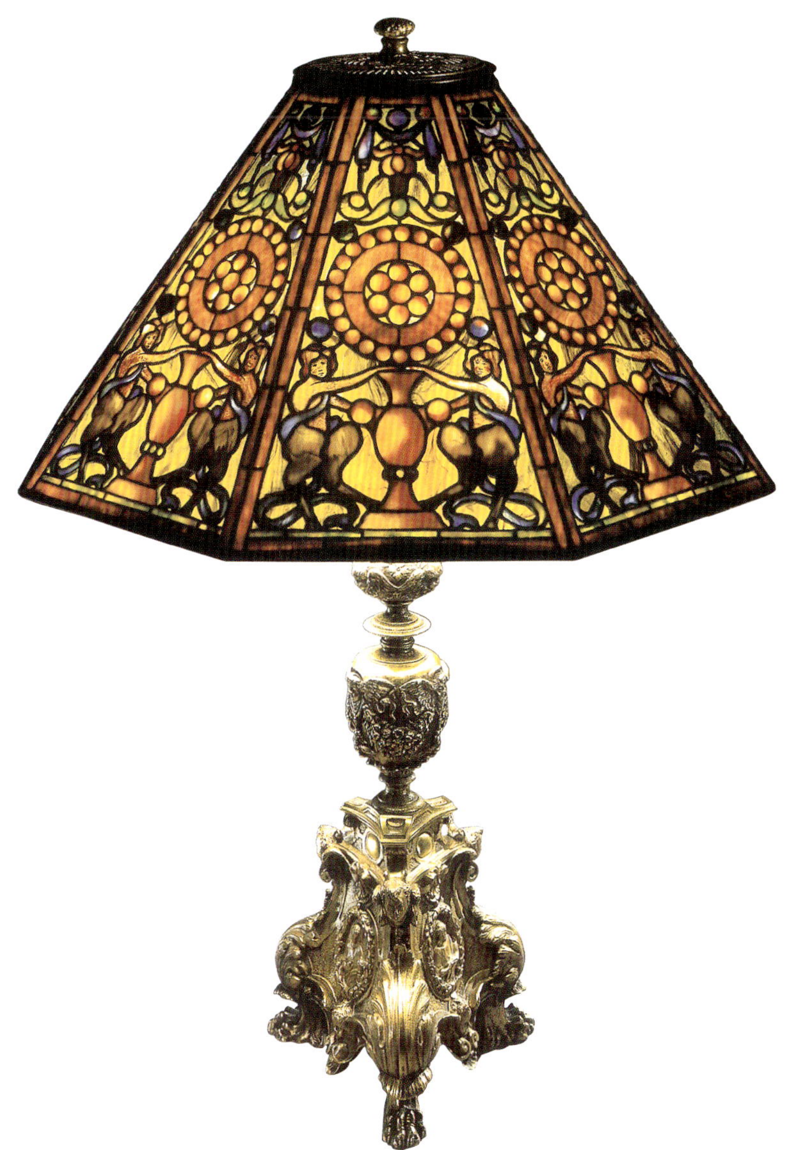

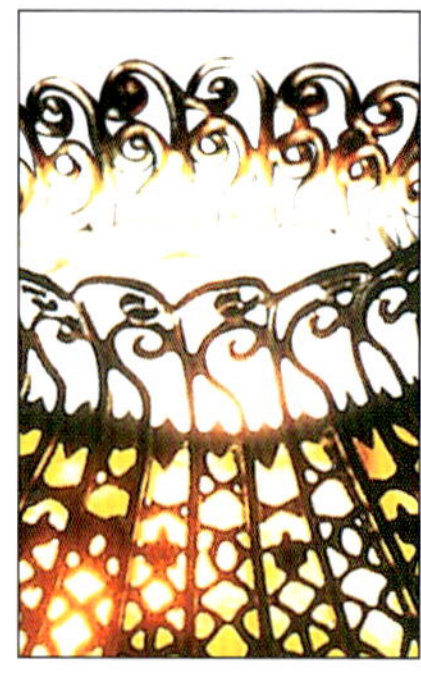

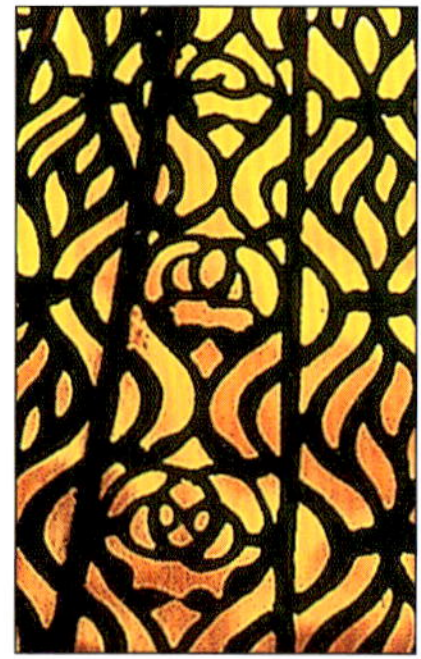

attention he turned to small glass and the production of a very popular, very varied and beautiful glass of novel quality which received the title *favrile* as a name easily spoken and readily recalled, the root being *faber*.

Favrile is distinguished by certain remarkable shapes and brilliant or deeply-toned colors, usually iridescent like the wings of certain American butterflies, the necks of pigeons and peacocks, the wing-covers of

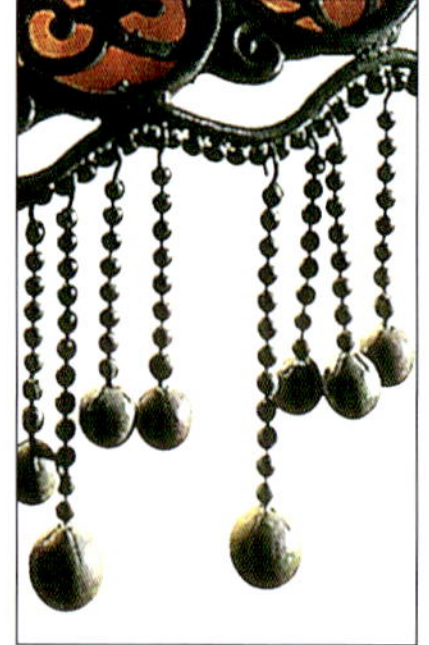

Filigree Bronze Shade with Metal Ball Fringe

Bronze, favrile glass, shade: 45.7 cm.

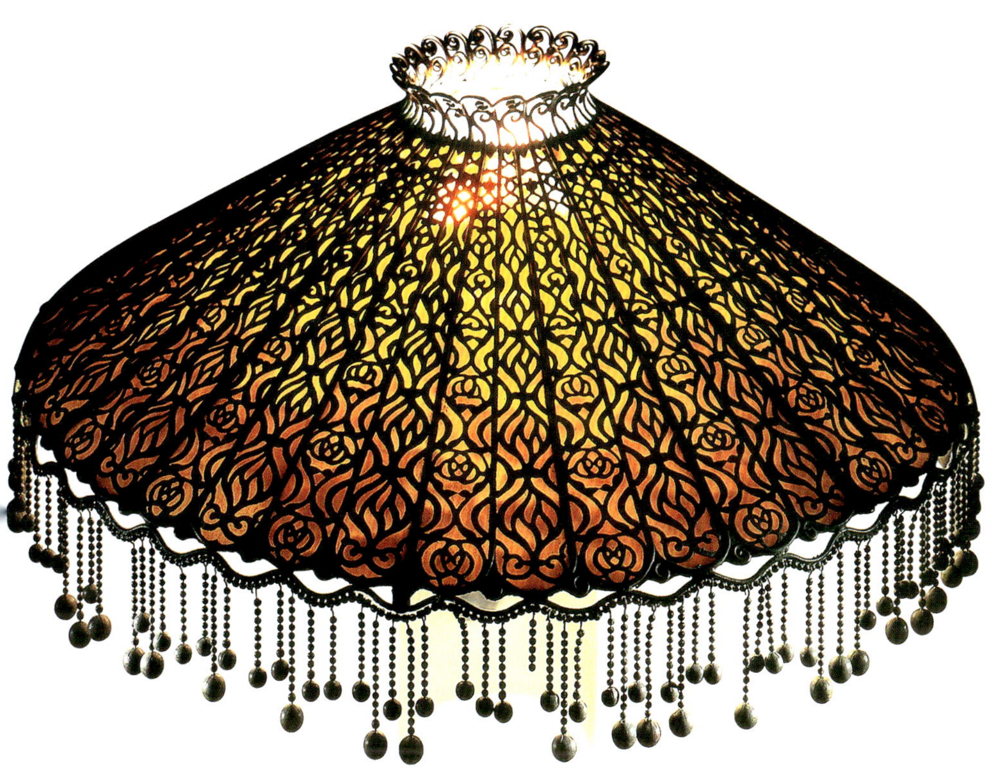

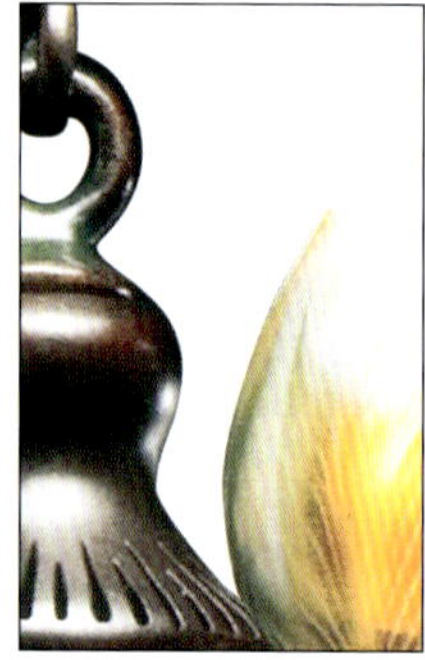

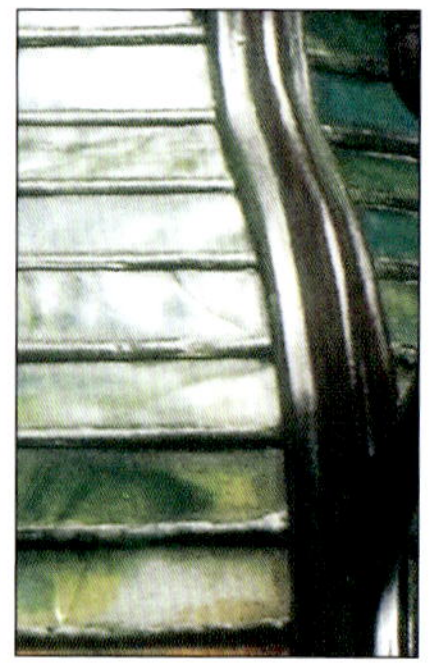

various beetles. Its commonest use is for flower vases and table decorations, but it is also employed for plaques on the wall like the decorative glass boards that Clement Massier made at Golfe-Juan, pressing them into low reliefs and charging them with flame-colored glaze. It is employed in mosaic and the tiling of floors and walls and more recently for table services to fill the role usually allotted to chinaware. Toilet boxes, trays,

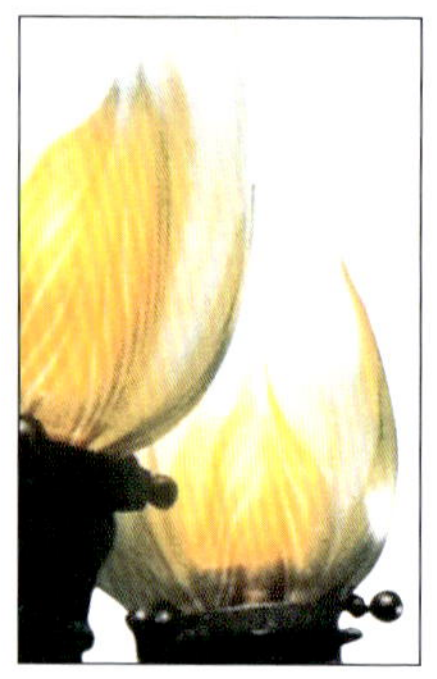

Chandelier

———

Favrile glass and bronze.

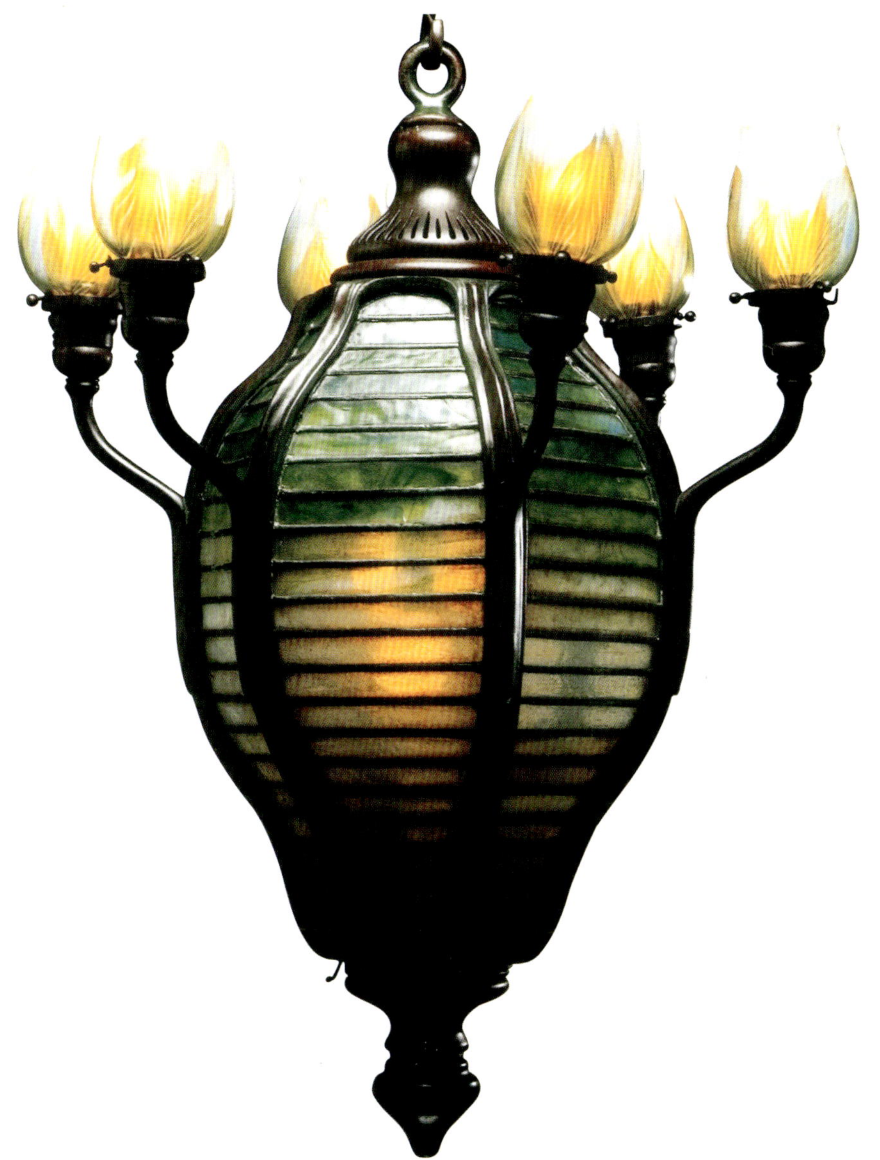

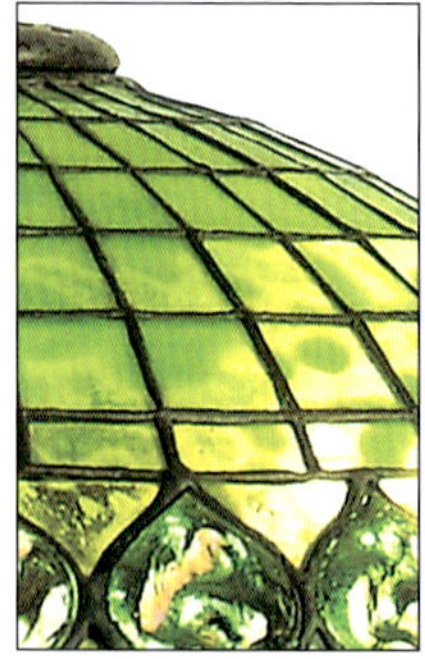

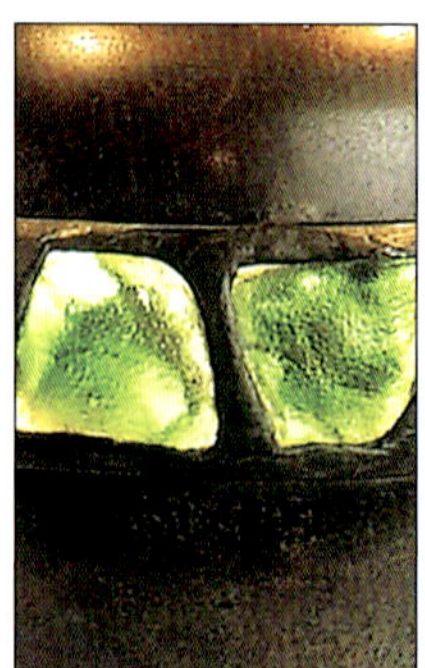

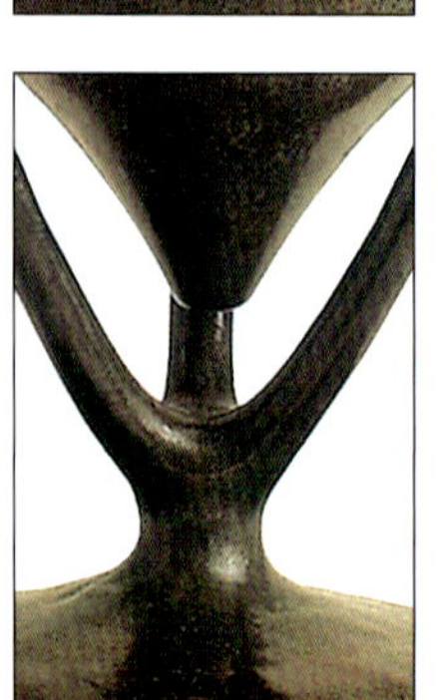

bonbonnieres, vanity, snuff and cigarette boxes, great vases, lamp shades, tea sets, whatnots—there is scarcely a field into which favrile has not entered with success. From the first it was popular. Though in the matter of stained glass windows Tiffany had to deplore a preference among the clergy for the cold and dull output of British studios, the appeal made to the people's love of color was not misunderstood when it came to small objects.

Unusual Table Lamp with a Domed Shade

1905.
Geometric panels of marbled green glass and a band of diamond-shaped turtlebacks. The urn-shaped bronze base is set with further turtleback plaques and held between three arms rising from a spreading circular foot, height: 53 cm.
Private collection.

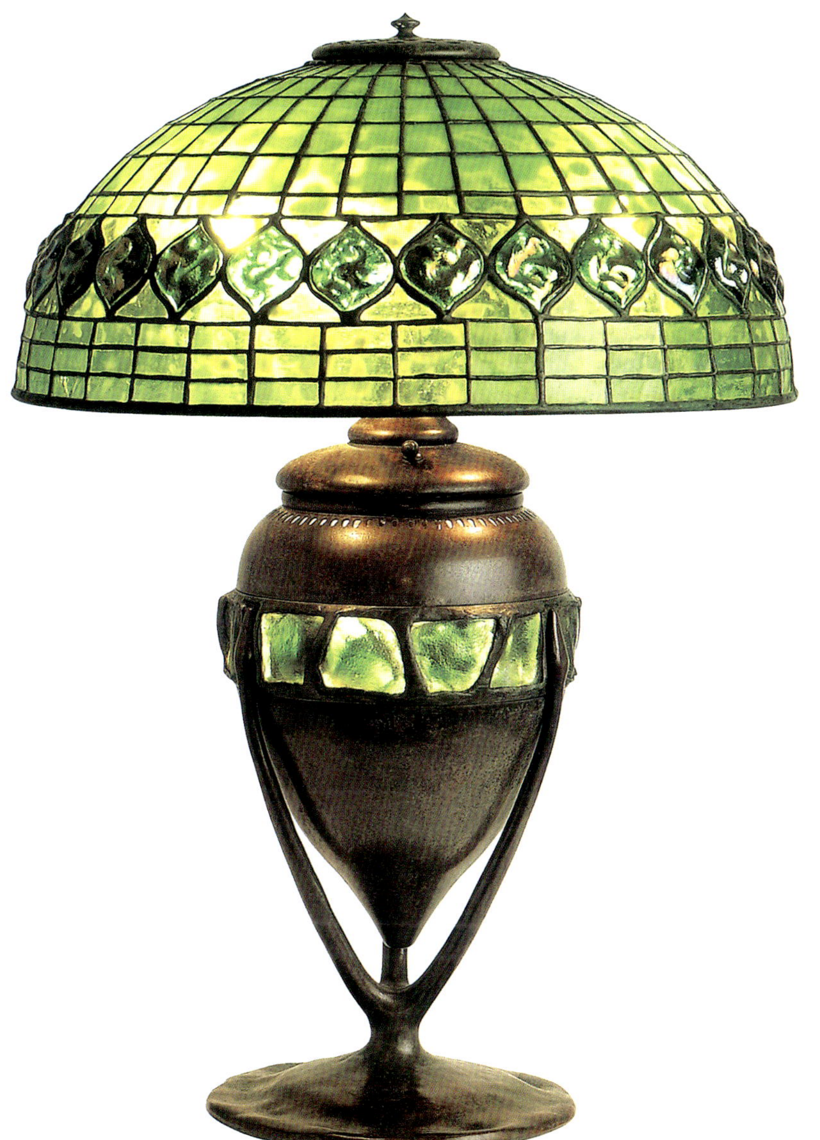

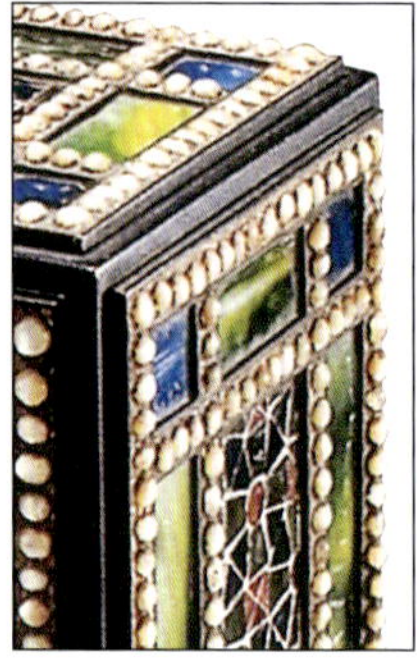

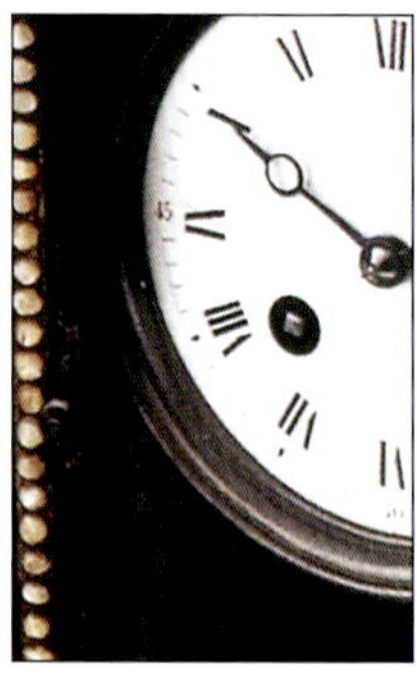

Such success demonstrated a current in popular taste on which other glass makers were eager to embark, and favrile soon received that mark of honor which is called the sincerest flattery. Bohemian glassware appeared in the American market copying some of the forms and trying to imitate some of the colors of favrile, while appealing to the multitude with low prices. The peacock-feather design was a favorite.

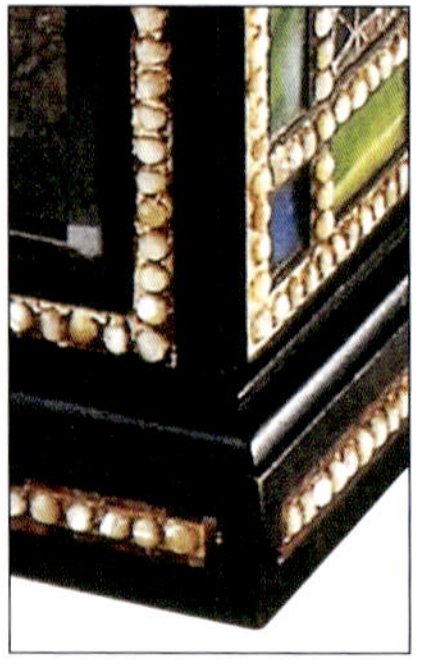

Mosaic Mantle Clock

Favrile glass, glass, bronze.

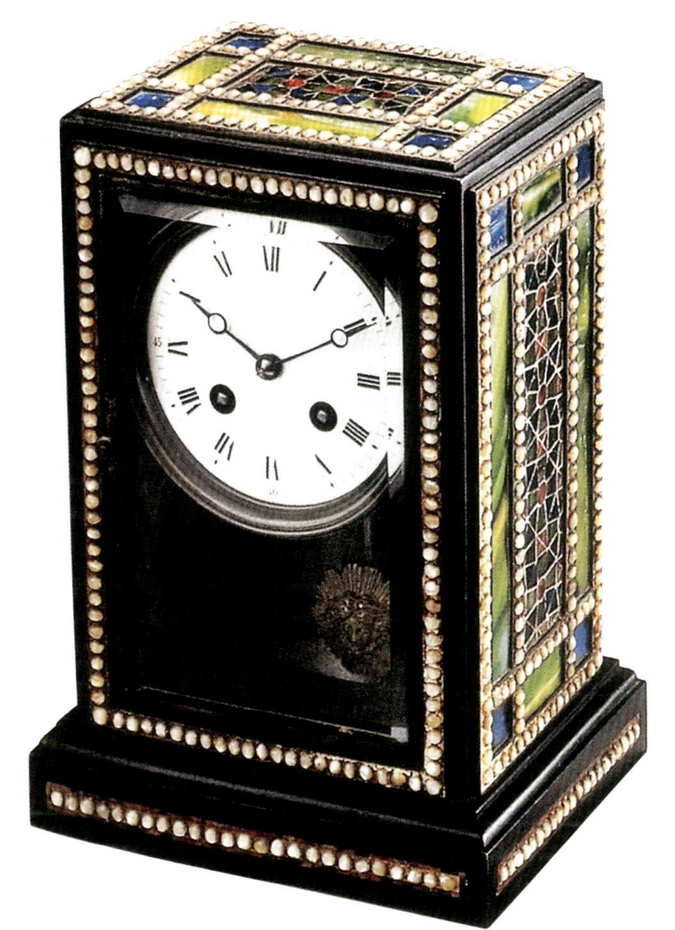

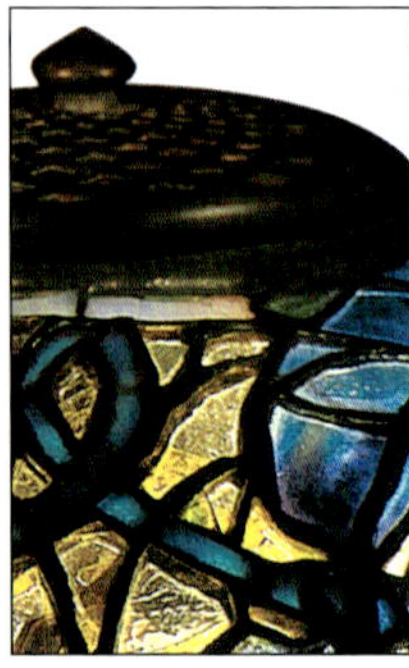

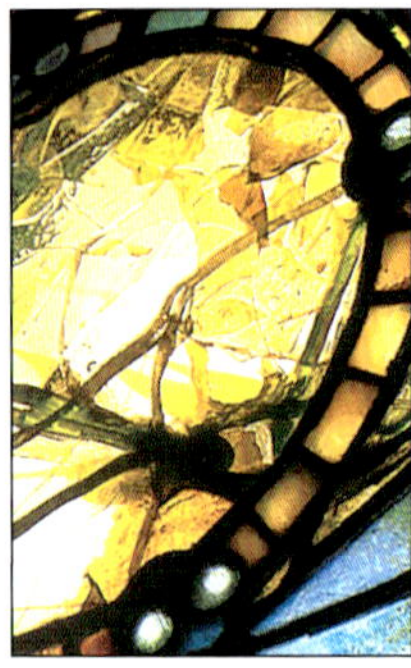

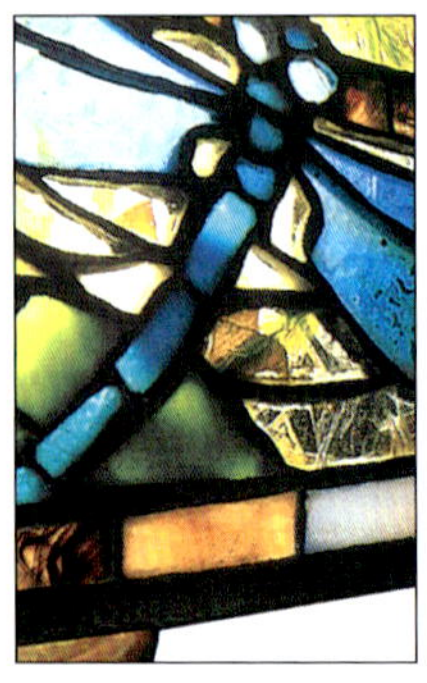

But the colors were thin and flat when compared with Tiffany pieces. Better results were obtained in Vienna where one maker, analyzing the ware and following closely Tiffany's models, produced copies of the original pieces not without success. But he found that the way was long and very difficult. What was needed was a system which would produce as brilliant results cheaply enough to overcome the costs of transportation; the copyist found it too expensive.

Spun Oval Body, Swamp Flower Base

Leaded glass and bronze.

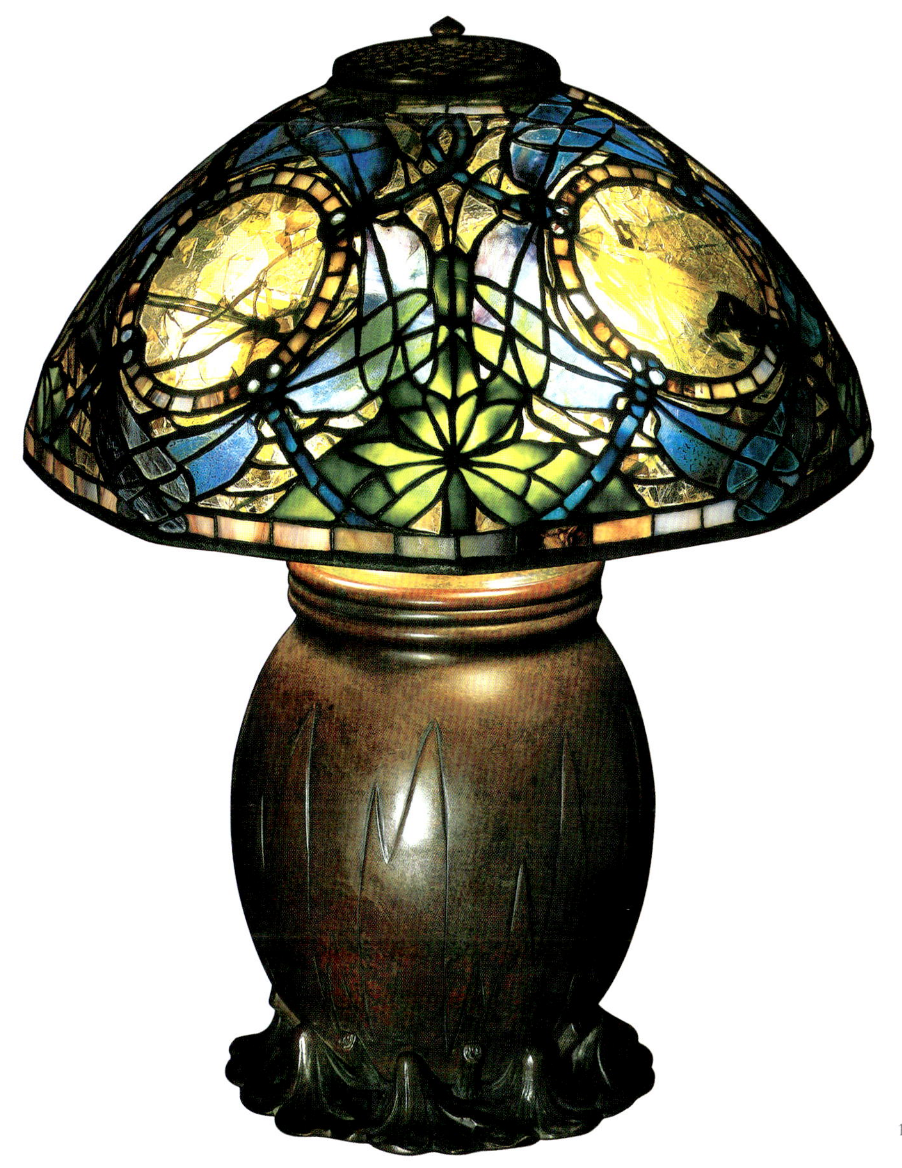

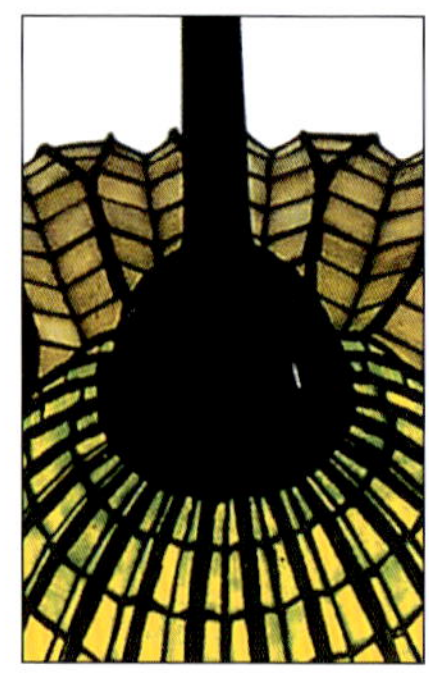

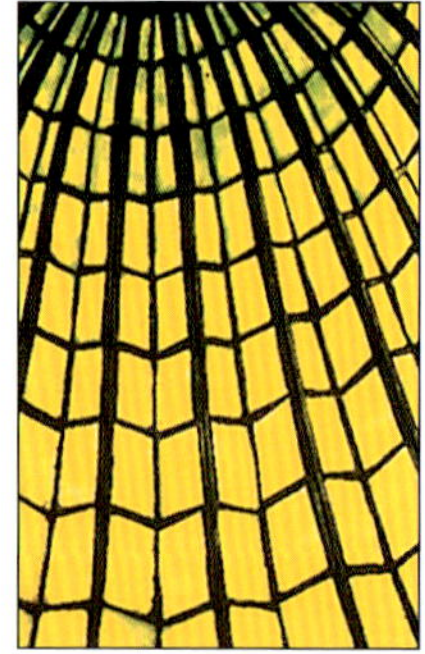

In pursuing his experiments in what is known as favrile, the artist was attracted by the effect of colored glass immersed in a solid sea of transparent crystal. The old Venetians used to imprison gold foil, forming therewith figures in the bottom of drinking cups. Figures and pictures caught in glass like flies in amber are not unknown in the past. But here again Tiffany produced something new. For a time he devoted himself to the

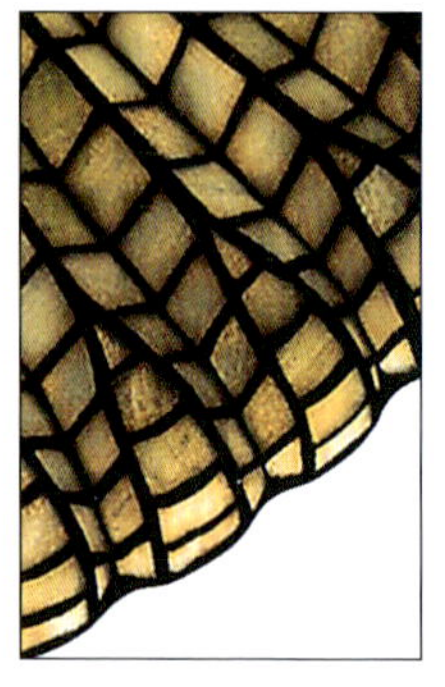

Geometric Pendant Light

Leaded glass and bronze.

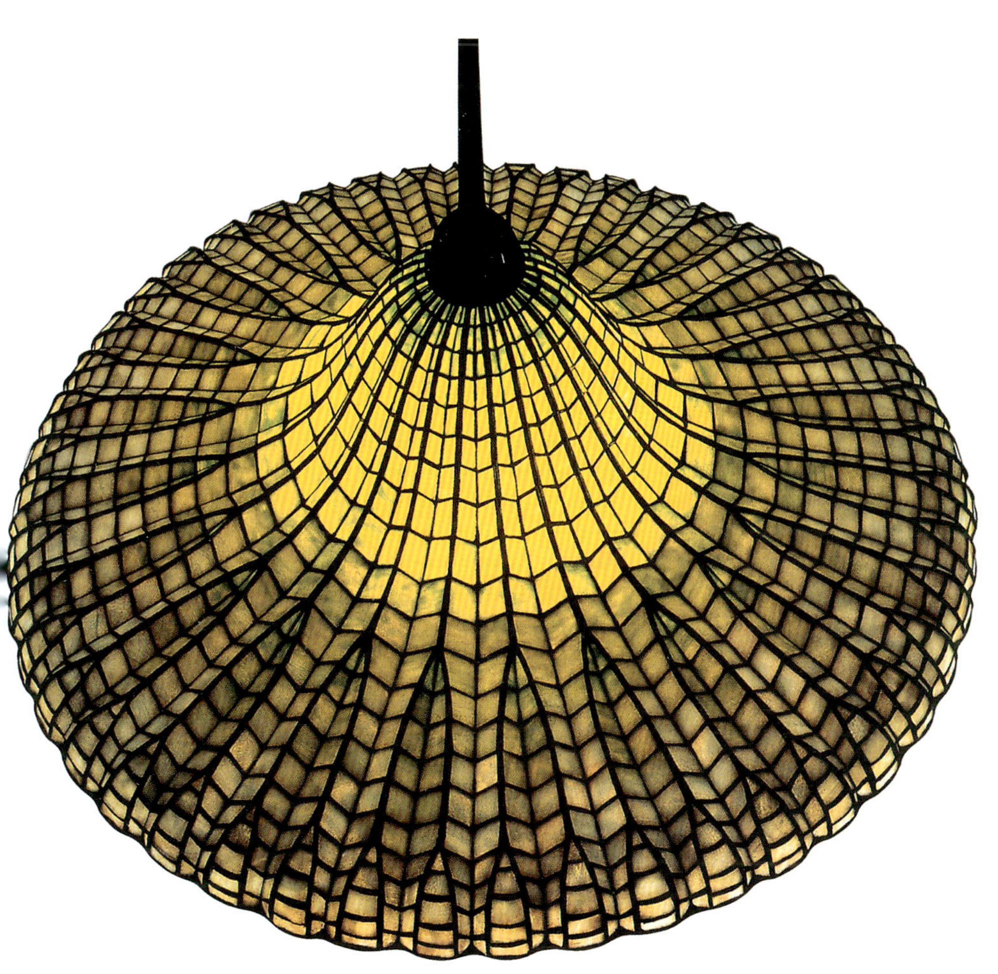

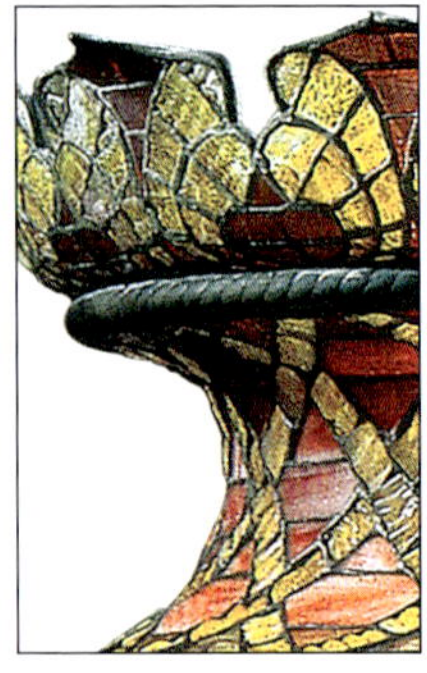

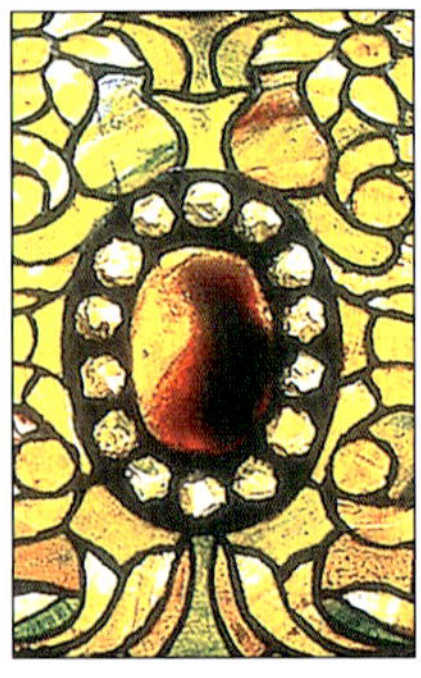

production of charming little petals, flowers, leaves in glass, which were assembled in proper natural order and then annealed all about with clear glass until gradually a vase was formed, in the solid stem of which or in its broad thick bottom the flowers hung suspended. This style of vase, however, can never become widely used because the extreme difficulty of its construction makes its cost too great. They will soon become rare.

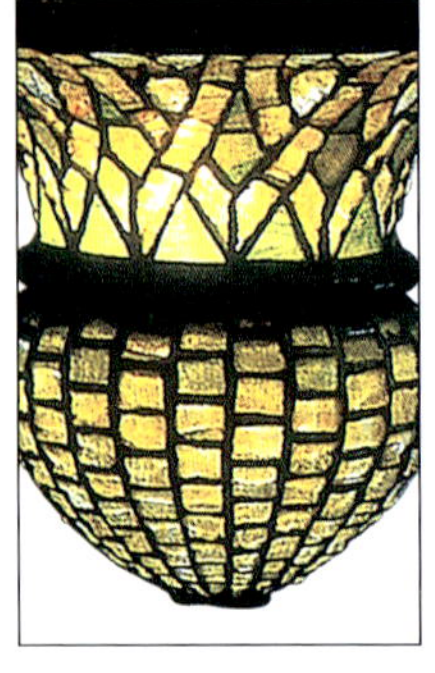

Hanging Lantern

Leaded glass, bronze.

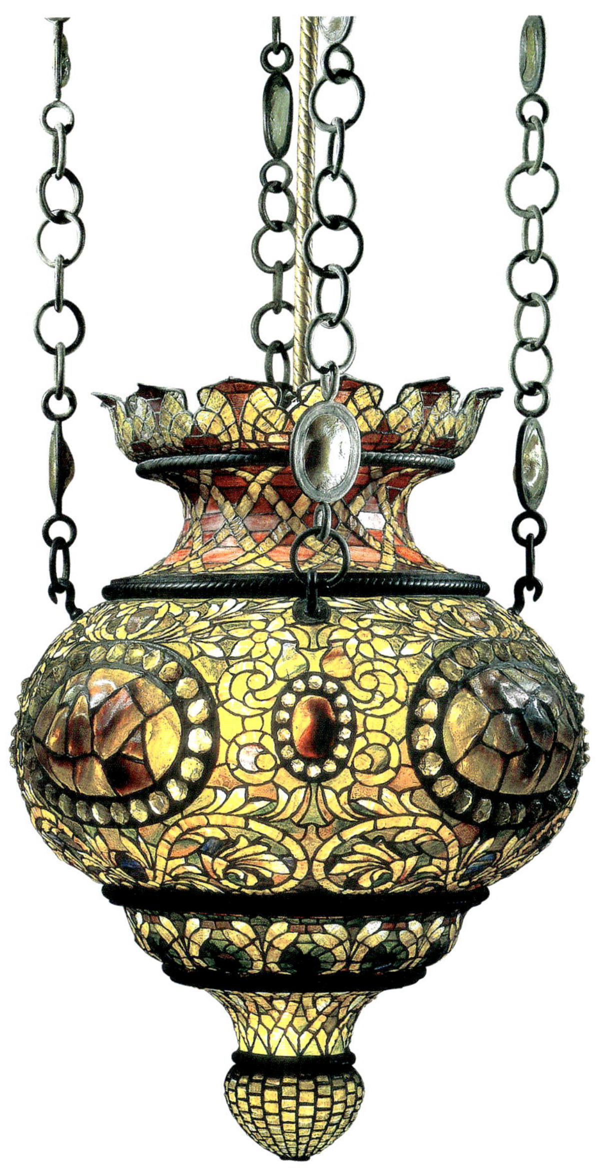

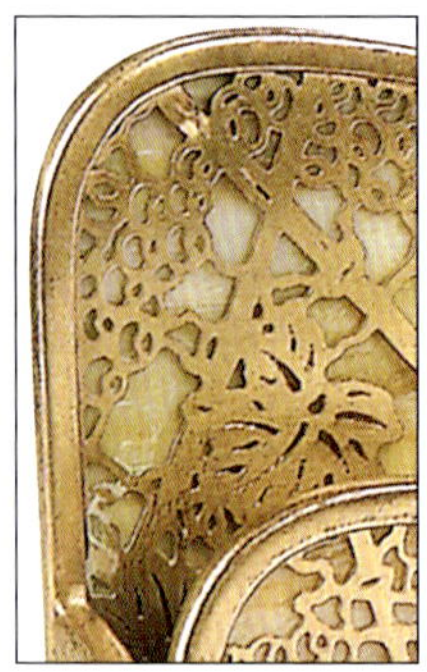

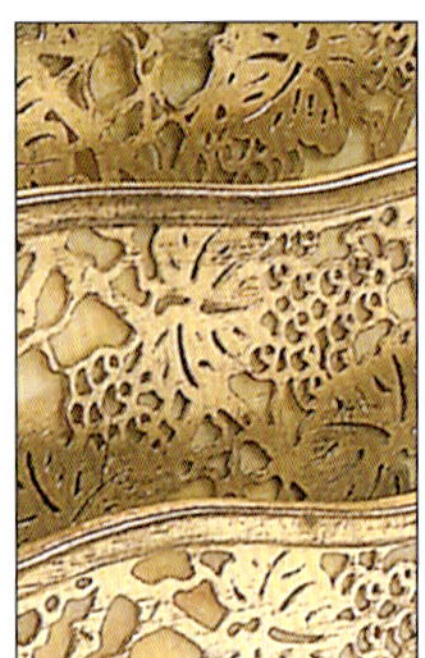

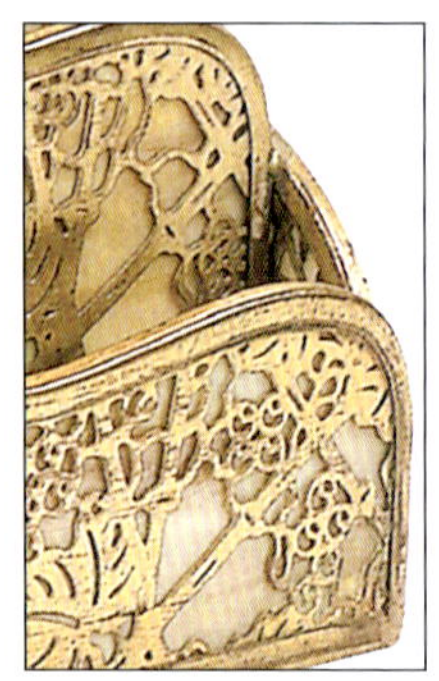

Given another artist placed in similar conditions who is intensely interested in the experiment and can devote the time to it, and similar results may be obtained.

The development of iridescent colors and all the varied hues and shades in favrile glass calls upon chemical knowledge and makes the production of new combinations a very fascinating occupation.

Stationery Rack with Three Shaped Dividers

1900.
Gilt bronze with a trellis-and-foliage pattern revealing
honey-coloured marbled-glass, height: 25 cm.
Private collection.

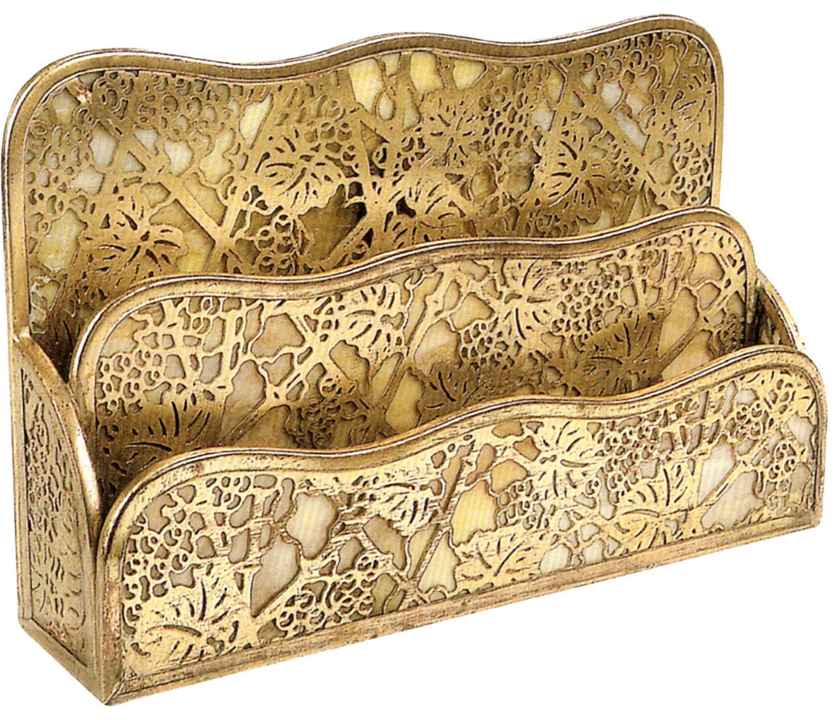

157

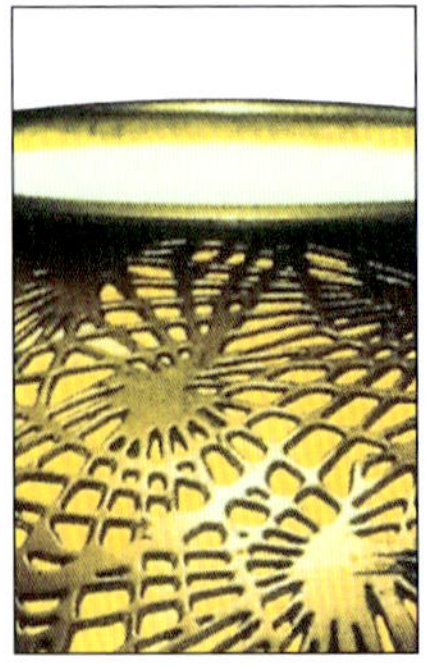

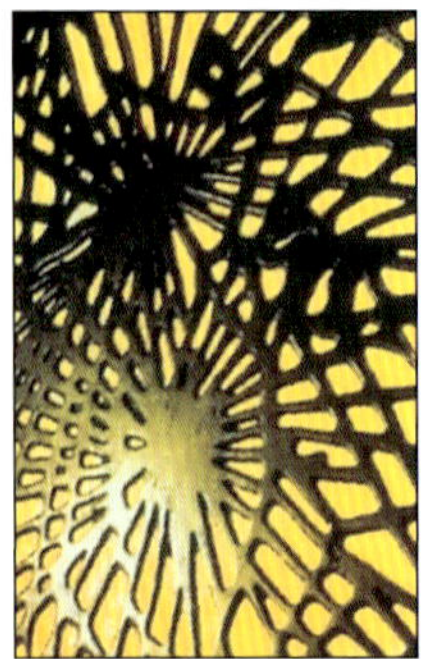

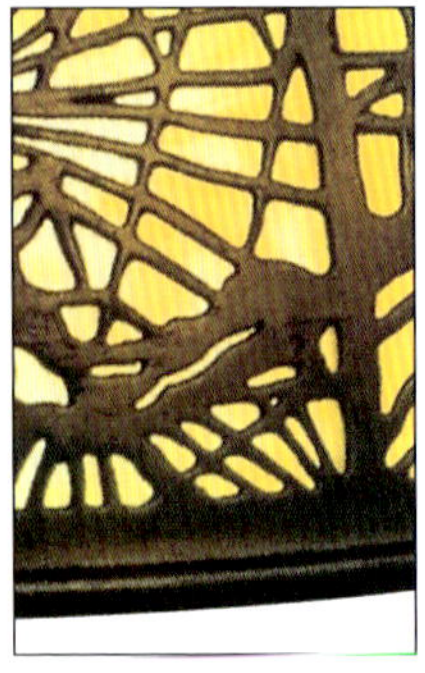

Ancient Greek and Roman glass subjected to the disintegrating effects of burial for long periods in a humid soil has produced objects of great attraction to amateurs, some of whom devote themselves to their collection. Just as modern painters have tried to rival the tones effected by age on old pictures in painting, so in his favrile glass Tiffany has vied with that beauty which has been added to antique glass by the centuries,

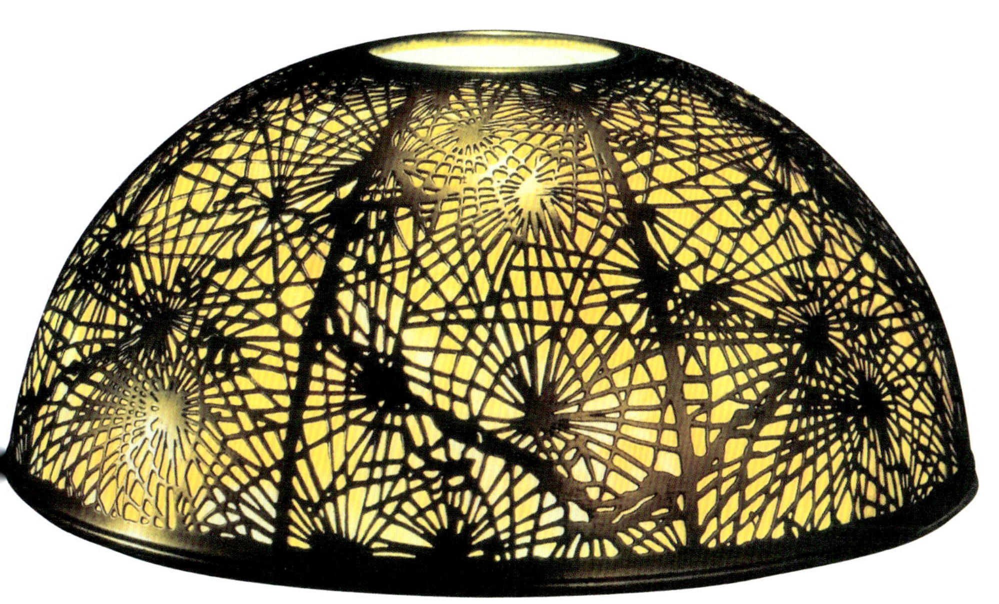

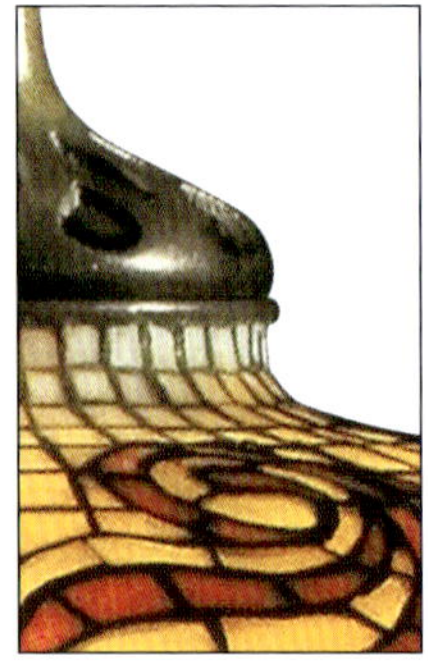

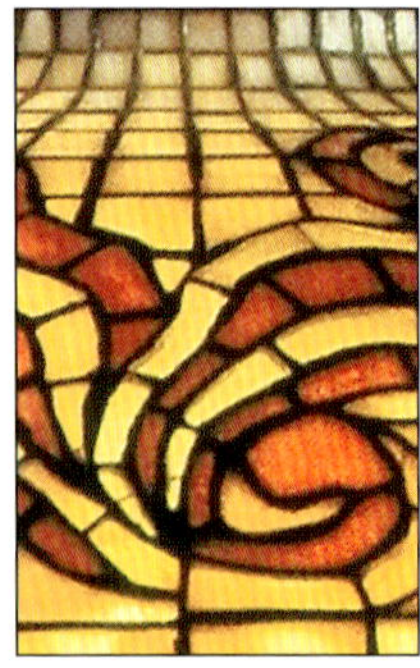

aided perhaps by the oily contents of such receptacle as were filled with cosmetics and other unguents. His taste in color has found expression in a thousand articles of applied art; these occupying prominent places in households, have exercised a happy influence on the taste of citizens. It is obvious that such influences exist and make themselves felt; but that is seldom thought of. Yet the fact that things of daily use like lamps, flower vases,

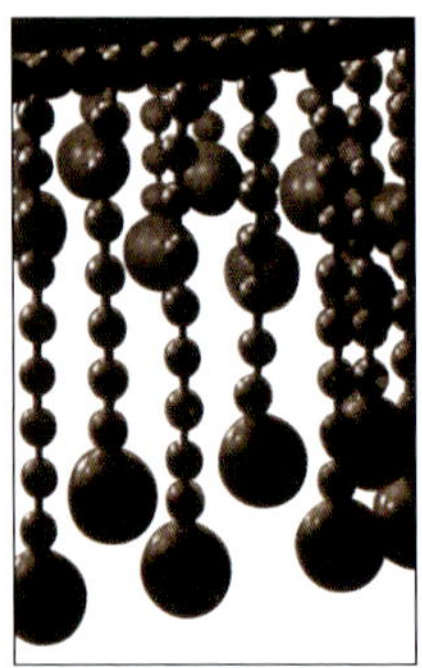

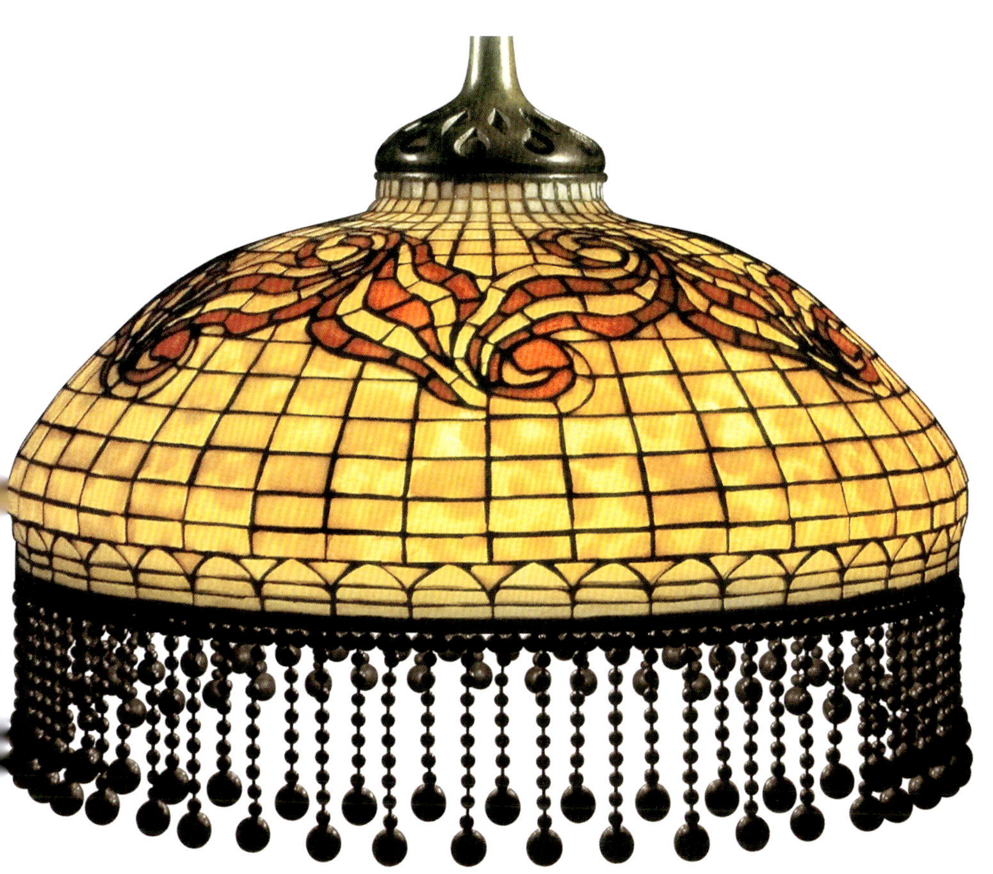

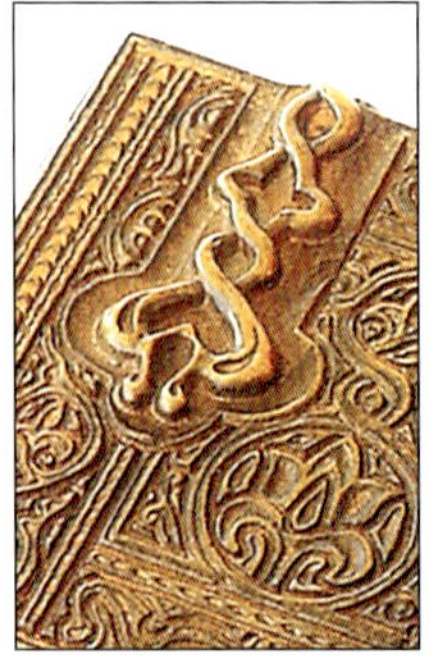

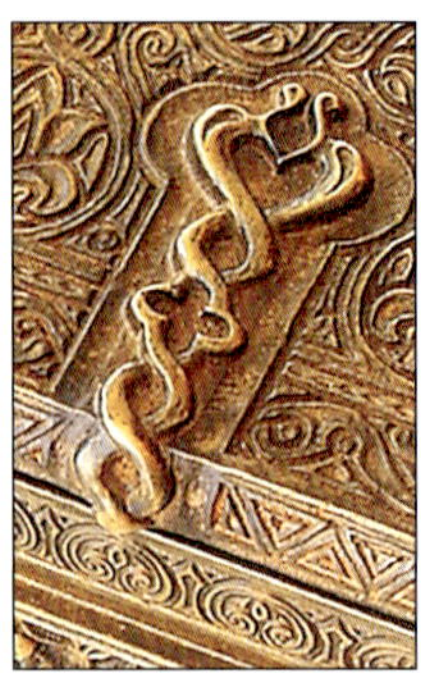

and toilet articles reach a wider public than do paintings and sculpture make the "decorative" arts more important to a nation than the "fine" arts. Hence the value to a community of artists who devote their talent to making things of use beautiful. They are educators of the people in the truest sense, not as school masters laying down the law, but as masters of art appealing to the emotions and the senses and rousing enthusiasm for beauty in one's environment.

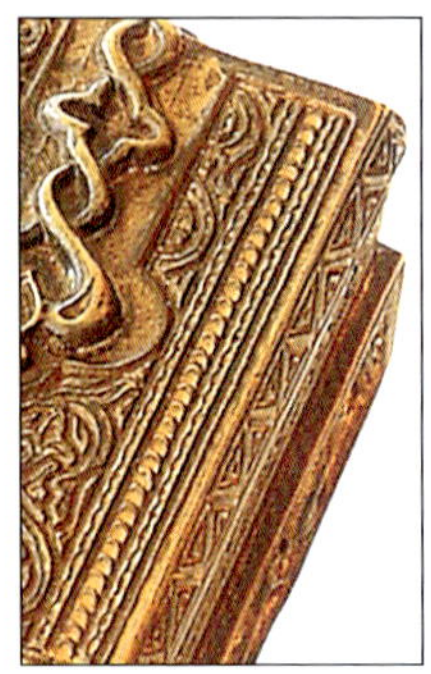

Rectangular Venetian Box

1915.
Gilt bronze with cover cast with scrolling panels, geometric banding, and roundels. Interwoven tendrils appear as hinge motifs, height: 12.5 cm.
Private collection.

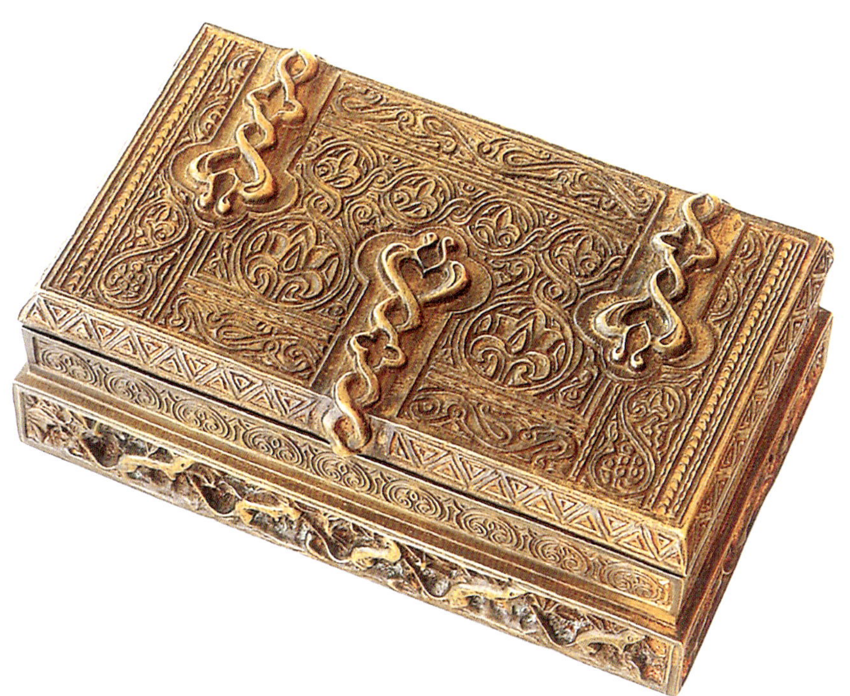

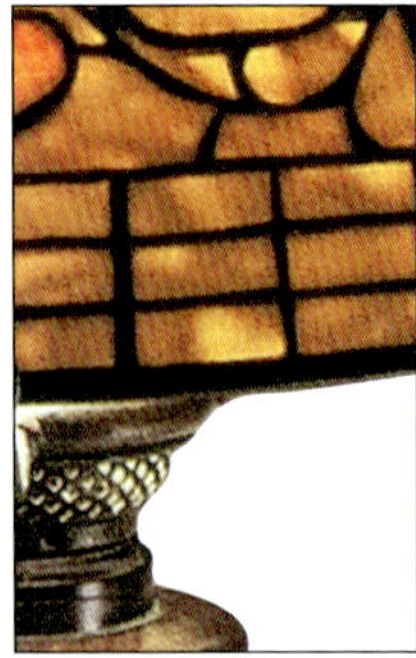

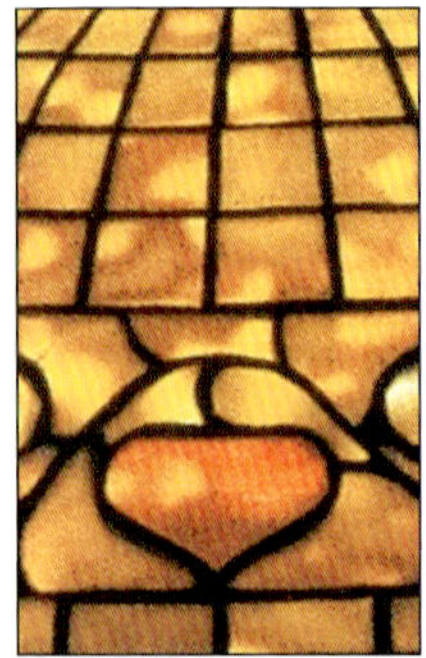

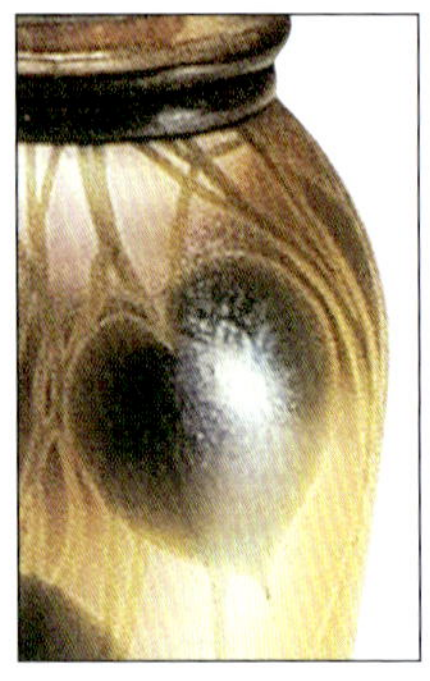

ENAMELS AND JEWELRY

The writer has met several men who made a practice of collecting unset precious and semi-precious stones and carrying about with them a large wallet filled with the choicest specimens of their hoards. One was Henry Ward Beecher. They enjoyed handling these jewels and loved to watch them sparkle in the sunlight as they shifted them from side to side. One can imagine Louis C. Tiffany also doing this.

Favrile Glass Lamp with a Domed Geometric Shade

Favrile glass, leaded glass and bronze.

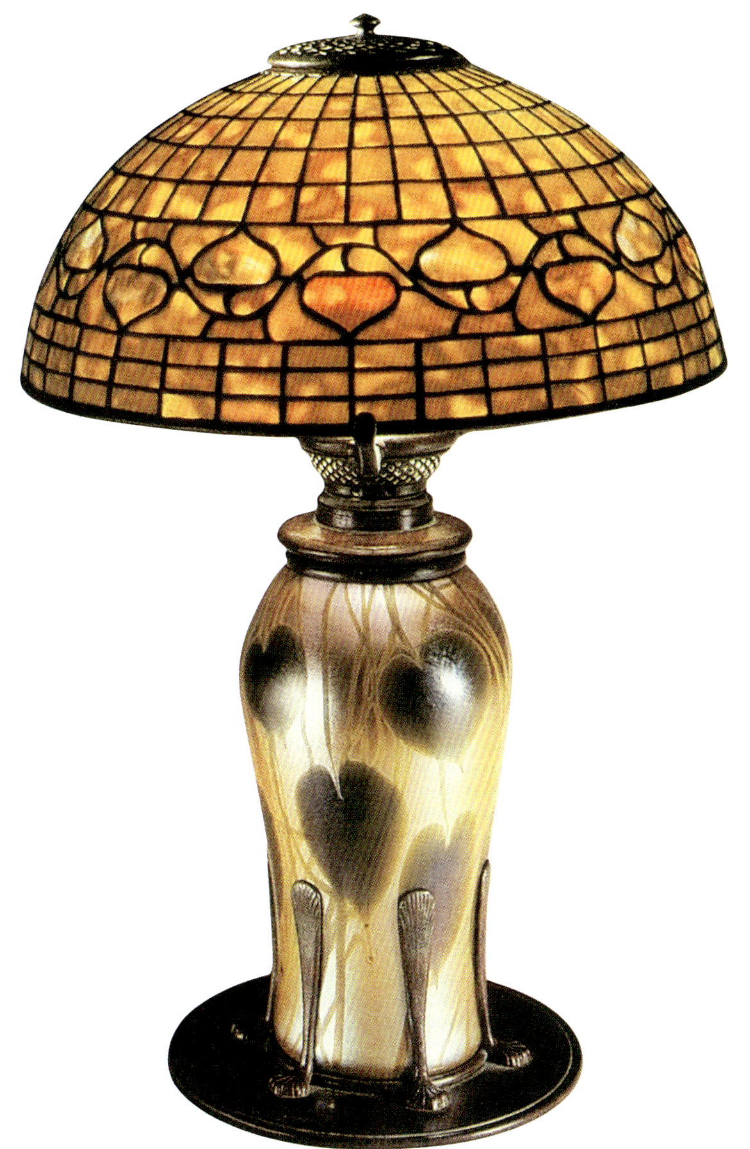

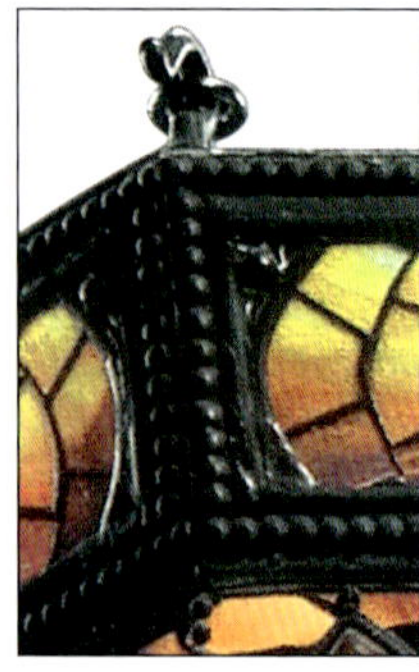

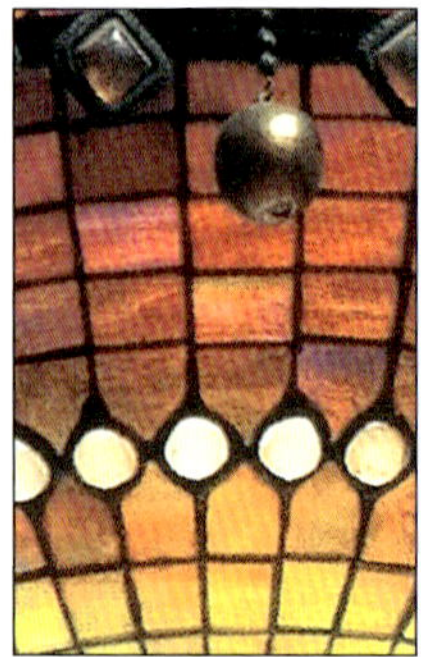

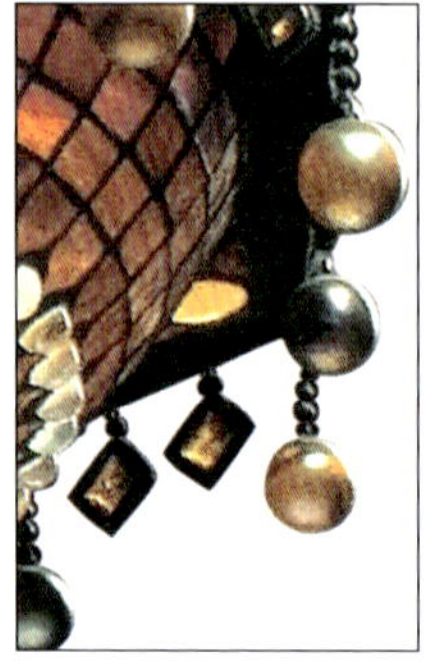

But with him, if he ever did it, the act would have been, not a purposeless one of simple enjoyment in the glow and sparkle of jewels, but a fruitful deed, the first step to the production of some little work of art.

Stained glass windows and small objects in colored glass led their designer naturally, one may say inevitably, to a synthetic treatment of enamel and precious stones. A painter who is born with a sense for color—and he,

Geometric Hanging Lamp with Metallic Pearl

Glass and bronze.

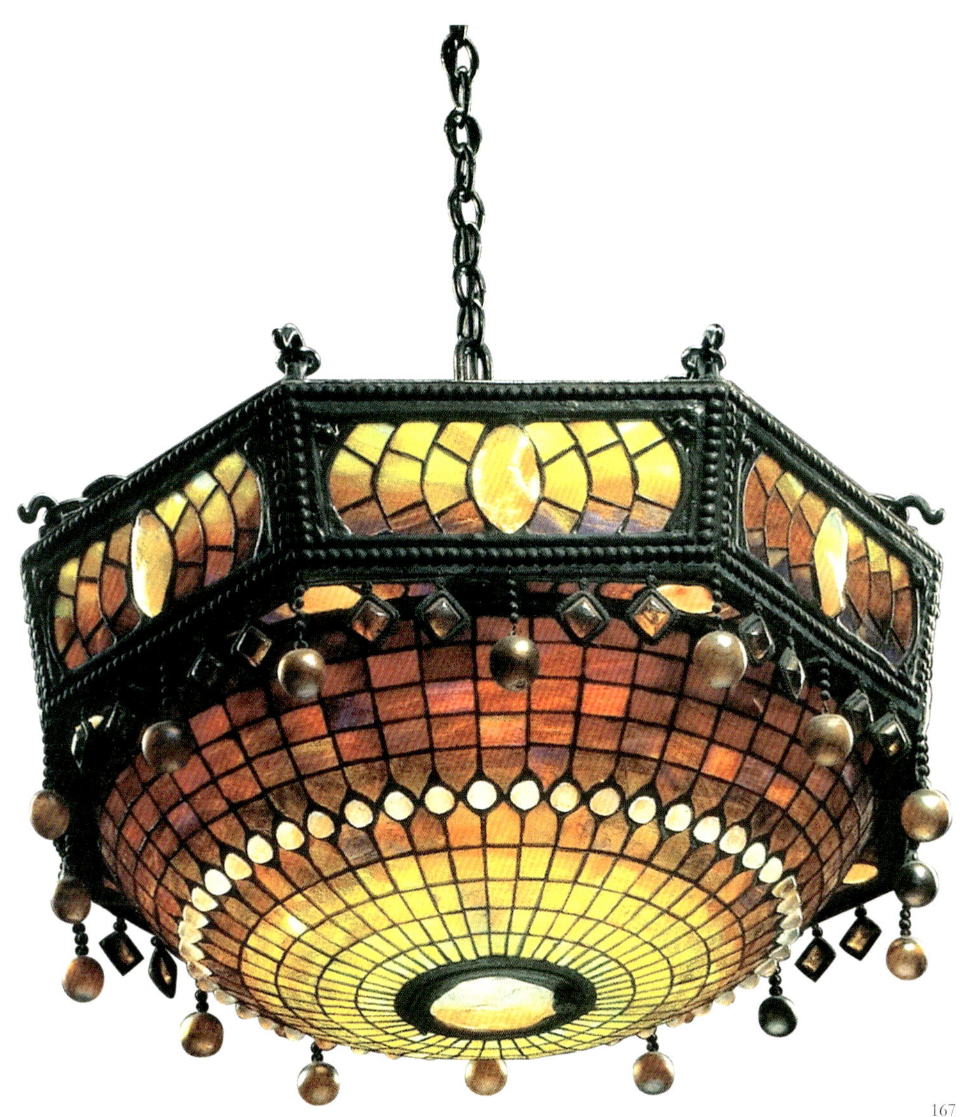

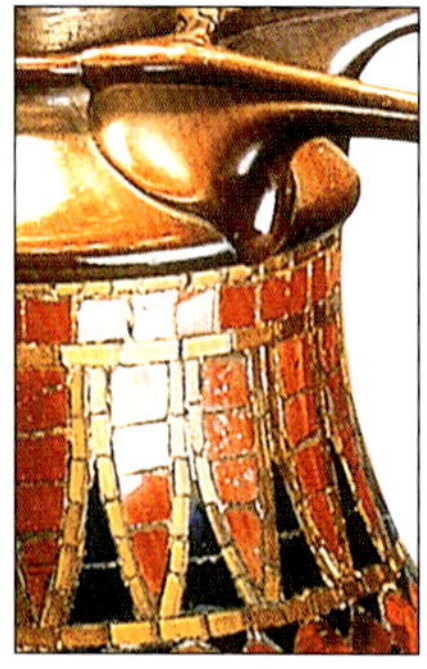

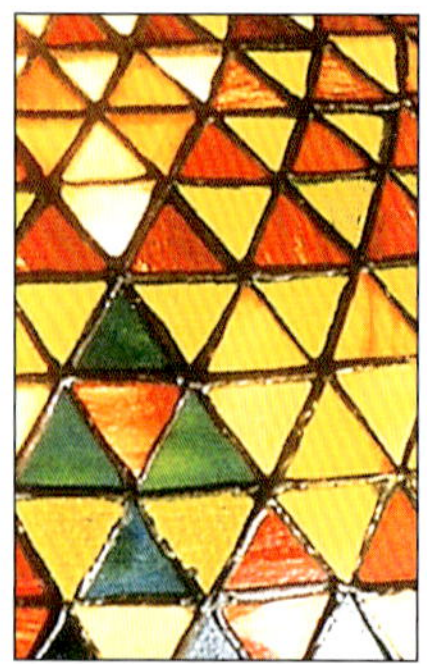

strange to say, is not common—must revel in the deep-set richness of hue offered by precious gems and love the tones so lavishly presented by nature in marbles, onyx, malachite, and carnelian; in various shells; in pearls, opals and coral; in old amber and tortoise shell. Enamels on copper, silver or gold afford an almost inexhaustible variety of background against which these semi-precious materials may stand

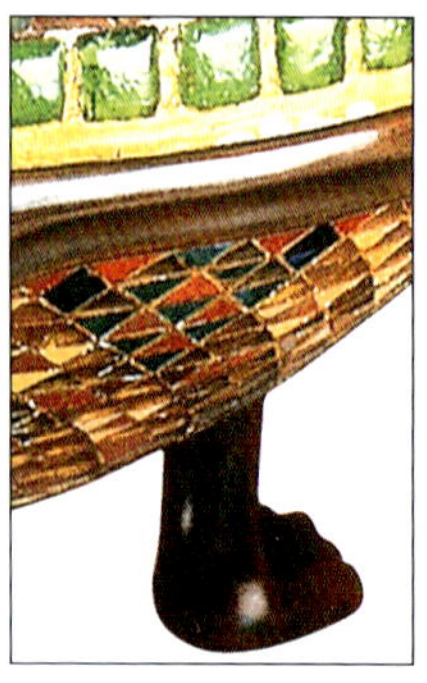

Hourglass-Shaped Oil Lamp with Mosaic Base
and Geometric Shade

Glass tile, leaded glass and bronze.

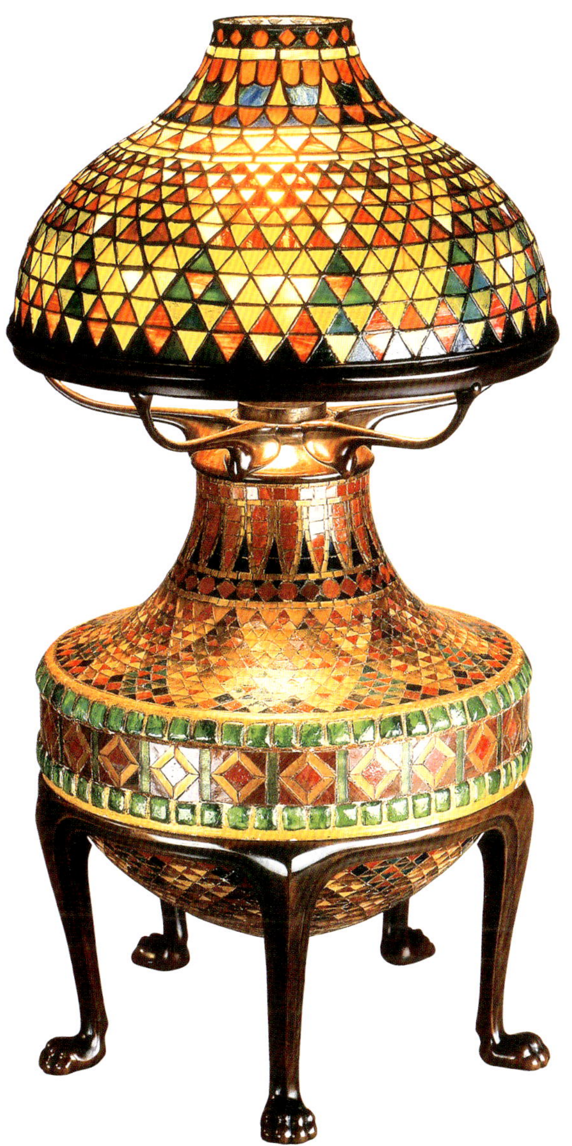

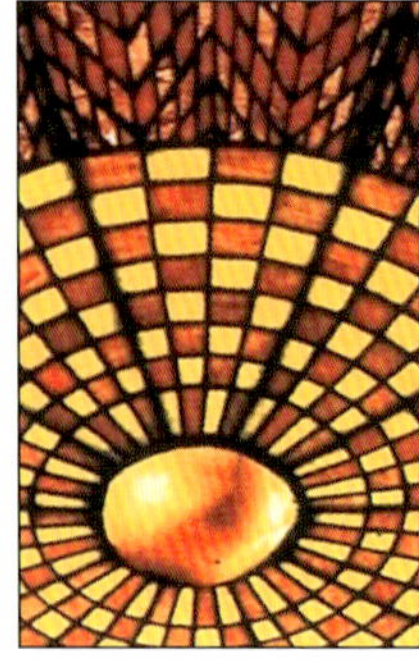

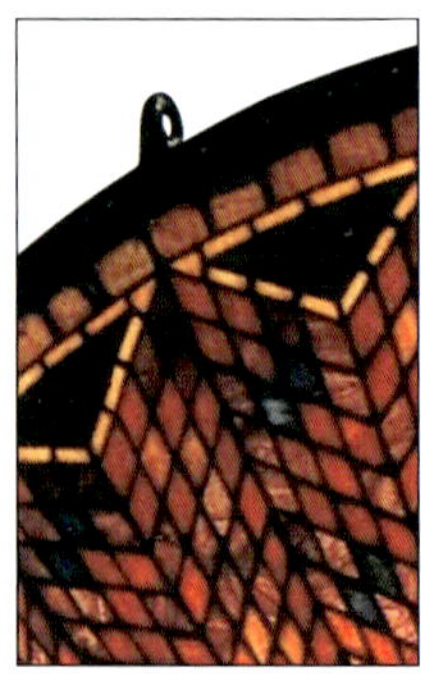

relieved—not to speak of harder stones like diamond, ruby, and sapphire.

It is not hard to imagine the enjoyment which an artist of Mr. Tiffany's nature, training, and antecedents obtained from the exercise of his faculties and taste in the designing of such rare and beautiful things. In addition to their flower-like colors, to their hues only rivaled by sunsets, rainbows and the northern aurora,

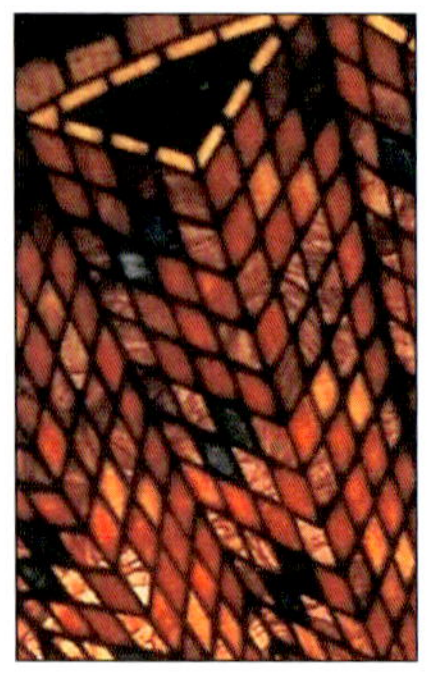

Geometric Sconce

Leaded glass and bronze.

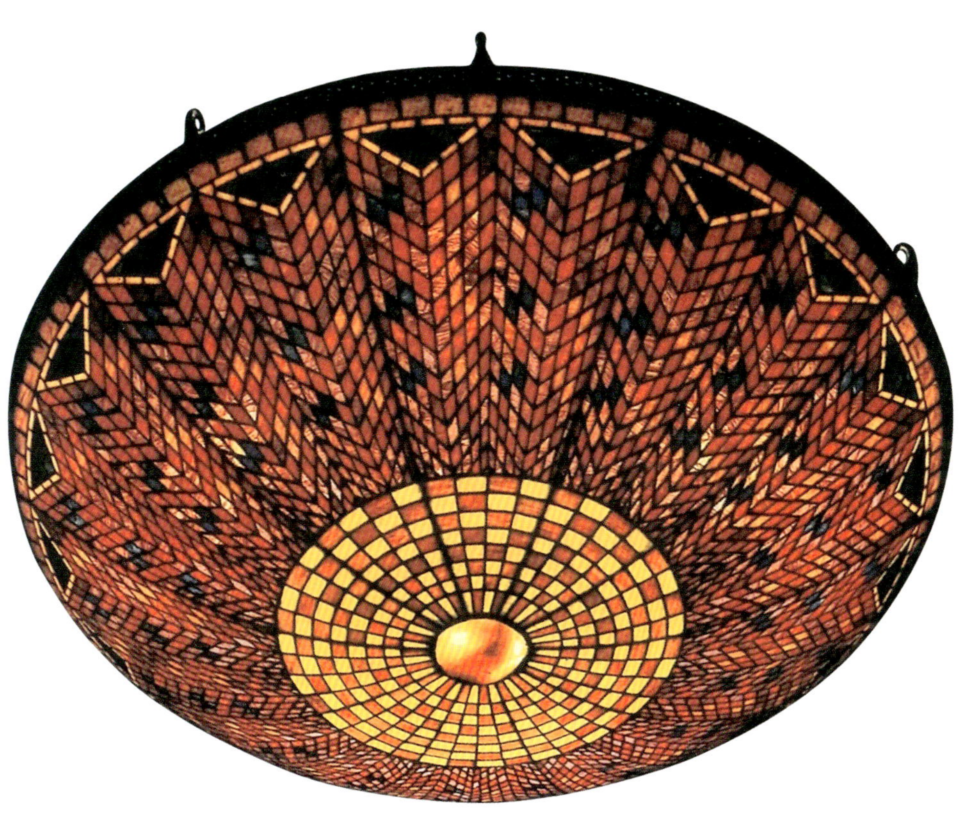

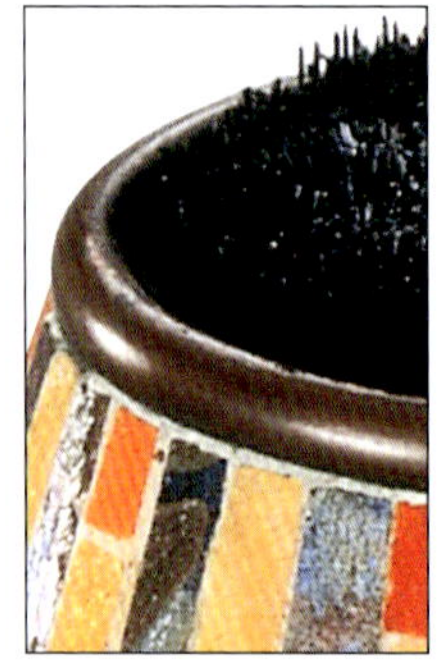

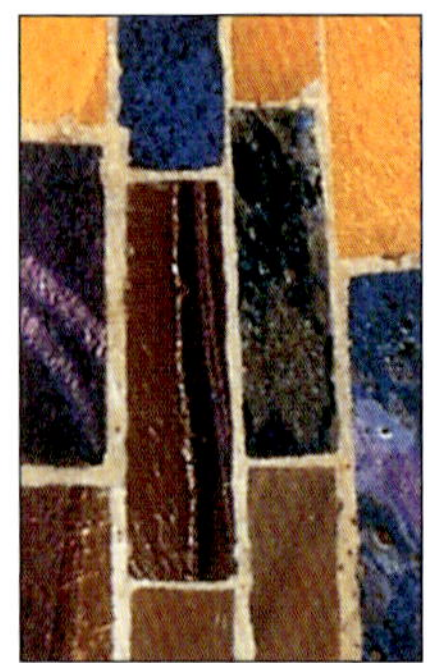

these objects have an indestructibility which is very appealing to most men and women. Along with a seeming fragility like that of petals and tendrils of the vine they have a solidity of material and a thoroughness in workmanship which place them in a high rank, considered merely from the craftsman's viewpoint. Tiffany, one may say without exaggeration, has been the foremost exponent of the Arts and Crafts in America.

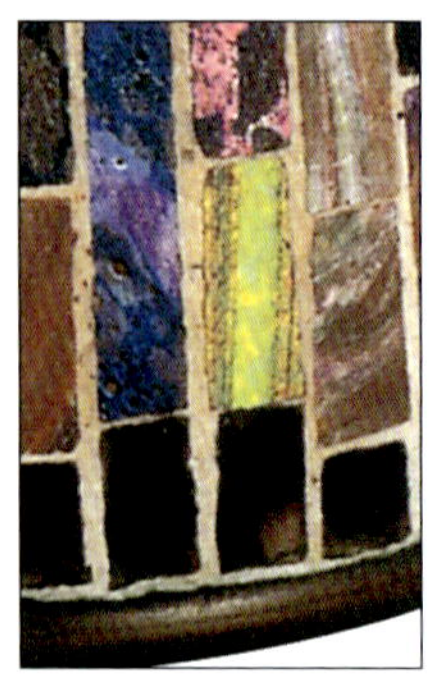

Mosaic Ink Blotter

Favrile glass and bronze.

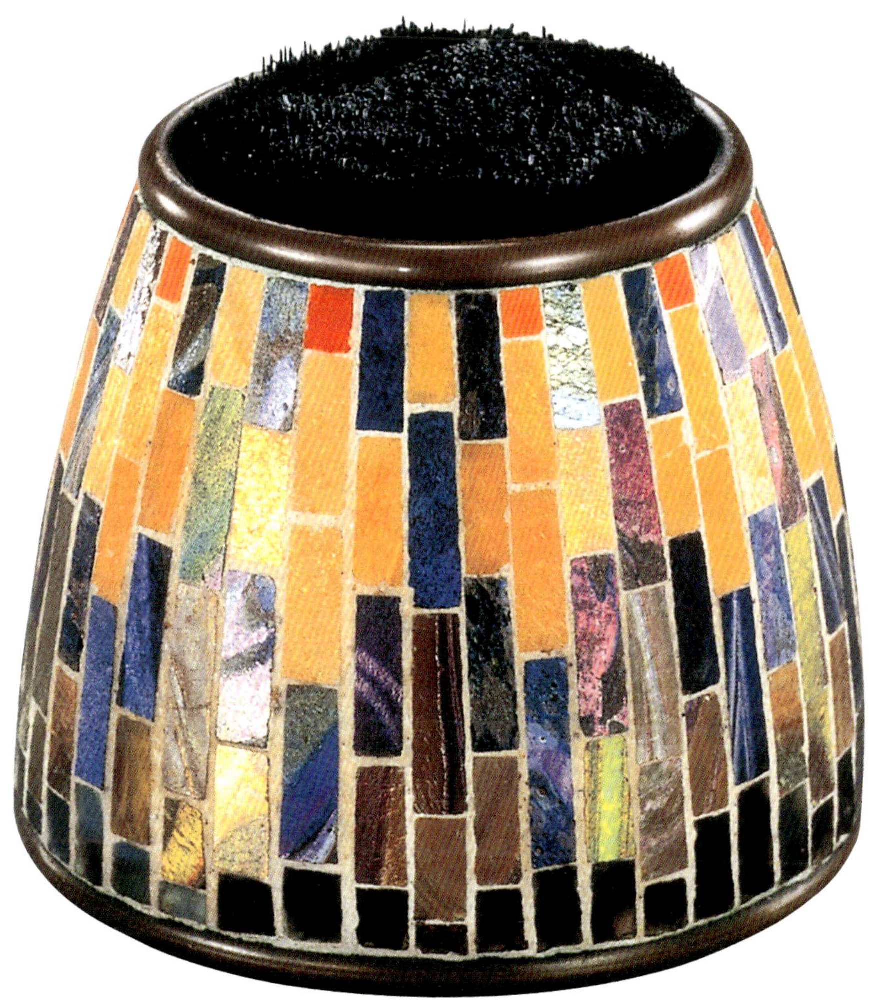

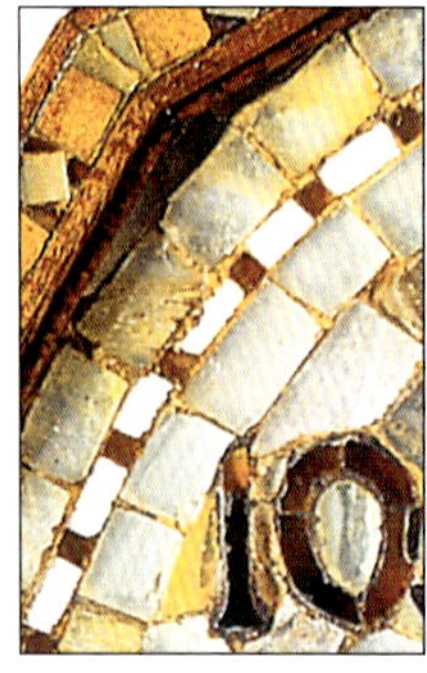

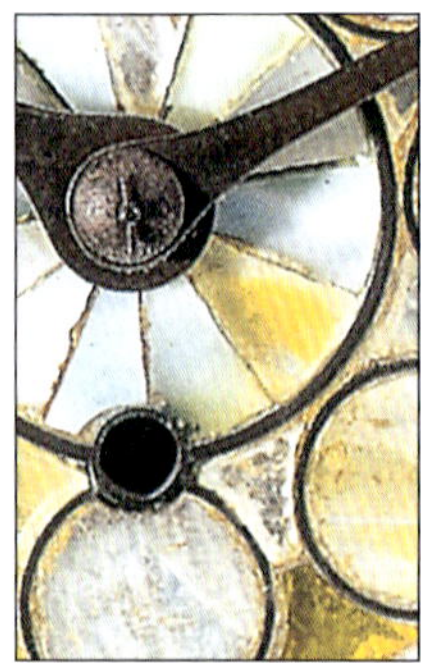

And in no point does he better deserve the title of *fabrum princeps* than in the technical soundness of these pretty pieces. It is not for nothing that he was the son of Charles L. Tiffany.

The sixth floor of the great building on Fifth Avenue known as Tiffany & Company contained the department of original—that is to say individual and unduplicated—enamels and jewels designed by Louis C. Tiffany.

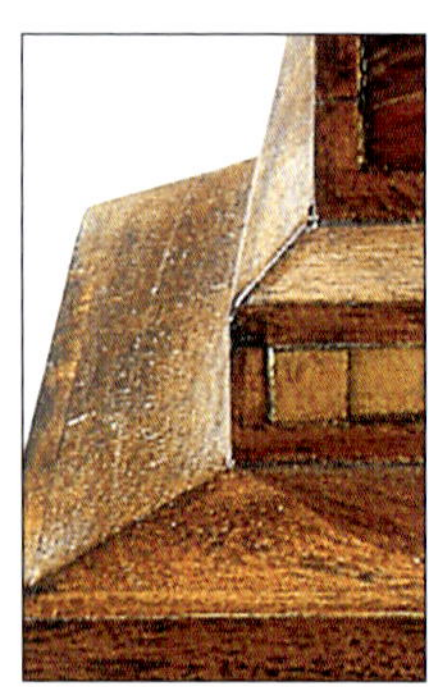

Mosaic Clock

Favrile glass and bronze.

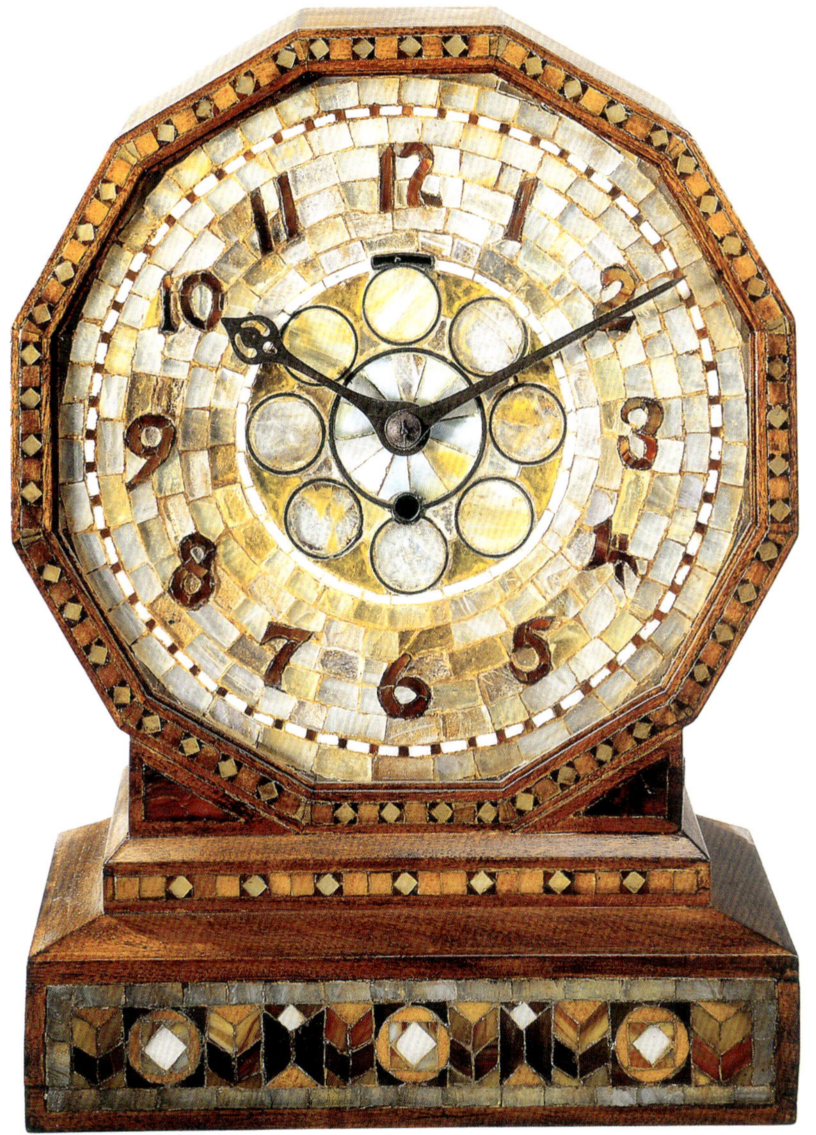

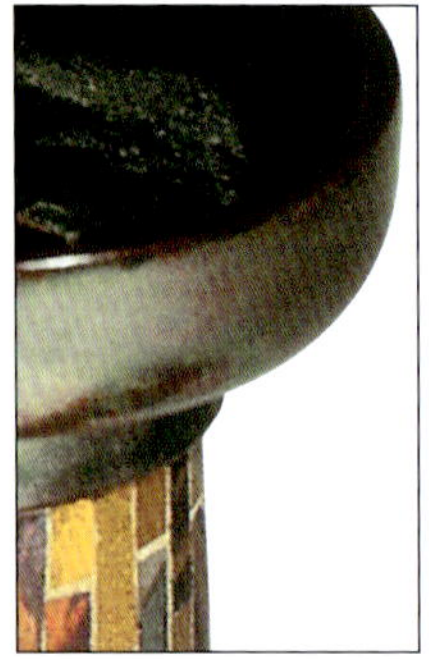

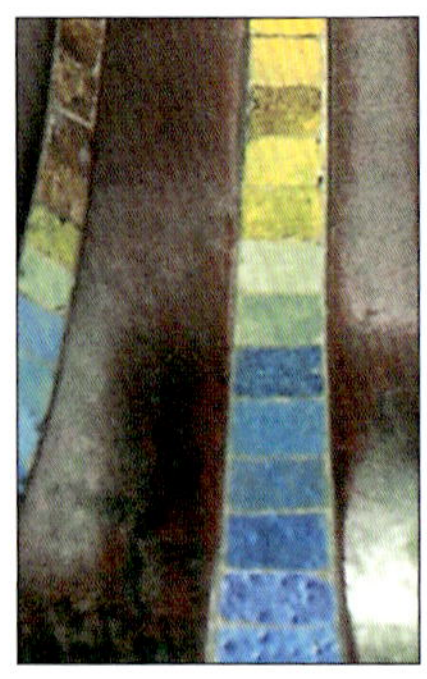

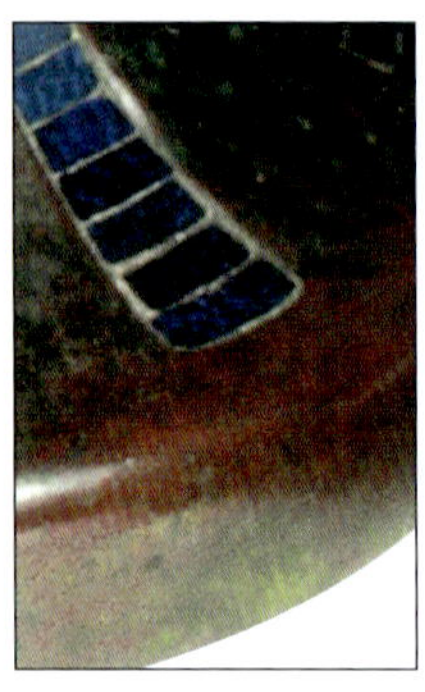

A sketch by the master is taken in hand; often a second watercolor cartoon is made and from this is built up with wax and various precious materials the model of the coming piece. At various stages in its development the master is consulted. The gold or platinum, the silver or copper framework is made from the wax model by trained craftsmen and craftswomen and the enamels are painted in and fired. Then the materials which will

Lighthouse Design Mosaic Candlestick

Favrile glass and bronze.

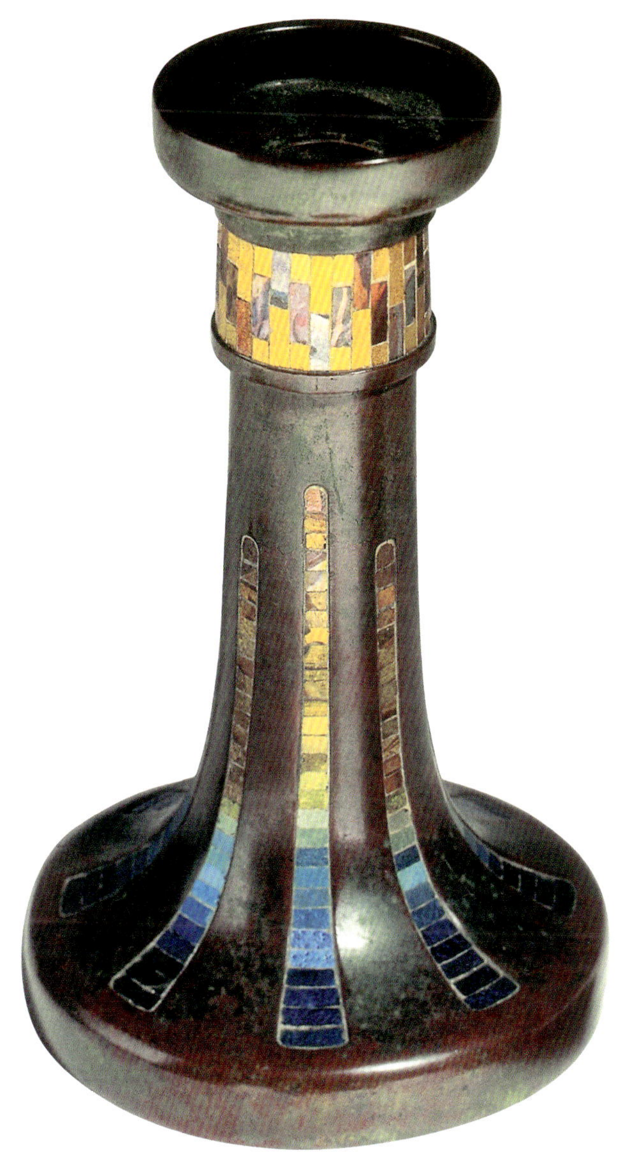

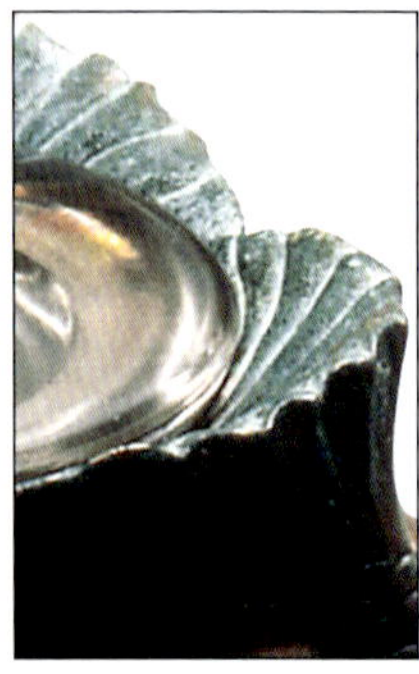

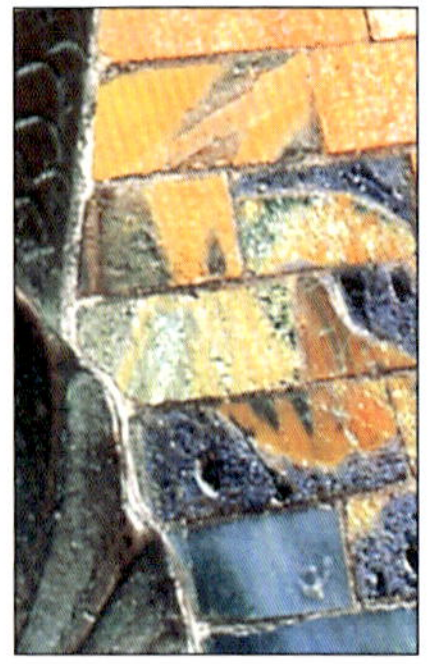

not bear the heat of firing are temporarily put in place for a last revision. When the master is satisfied, the final touches are applied, the jewels or semi-precious materials are solidly joined to their beds and the object, a result of many consultations and many expert hands, is ready for the show-case.

Not only the favrile glass pieces mentioned in a former chapter but objects like those alluded to above

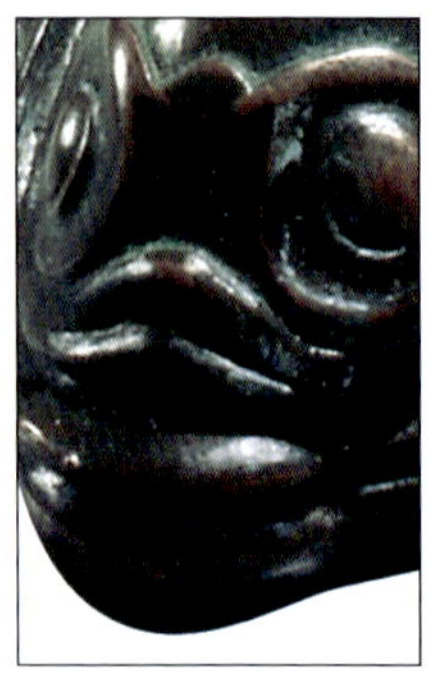

Mosaic Inkwell

Favrile glass and bronze.

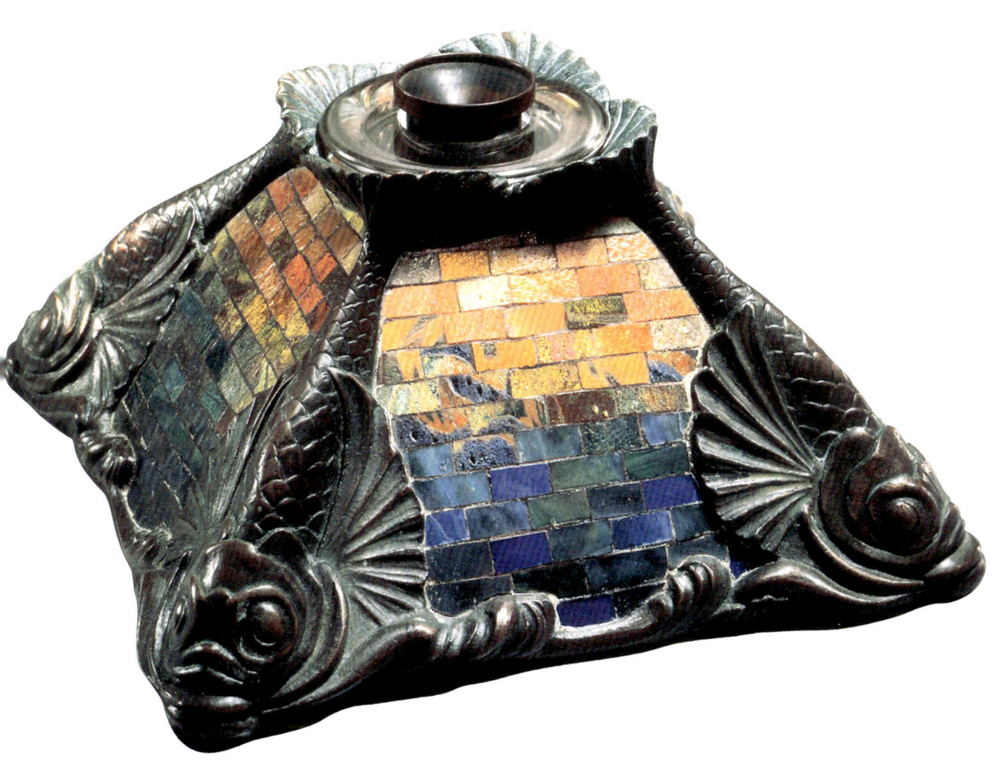

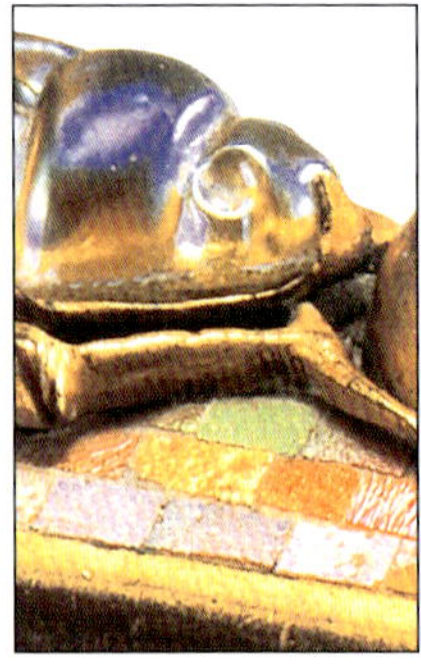

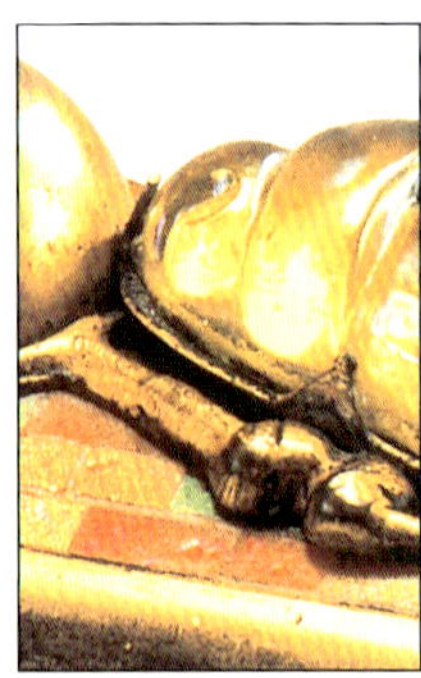

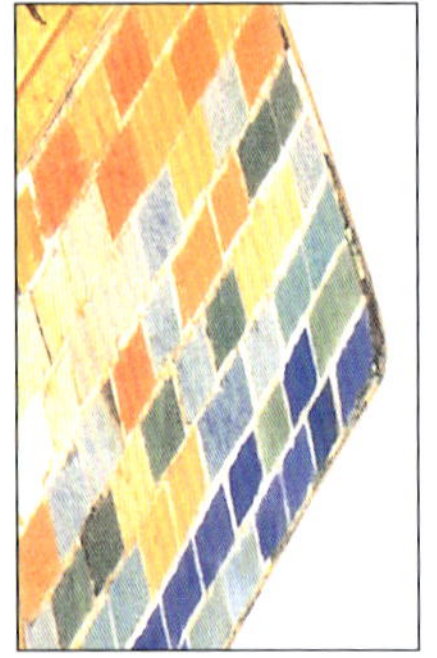

are permanent exhibits in many museums, such as the Musée des Arts Decoratifs in Paris, the Victoria and Albert Museum, South Kensington, London, the Metropolitan Museum, New York, and the Walters Gallery, Baltimore. Many luxurious private houses have Louis C. Tiffany's enameled objects. His constructions in color for personal jewelry are favorites in a host of households. Owing to the extraordinary collections of all sorts of gems and

Ornate Mosaic Box with Two Scarabs

Favrile glass and bronze.

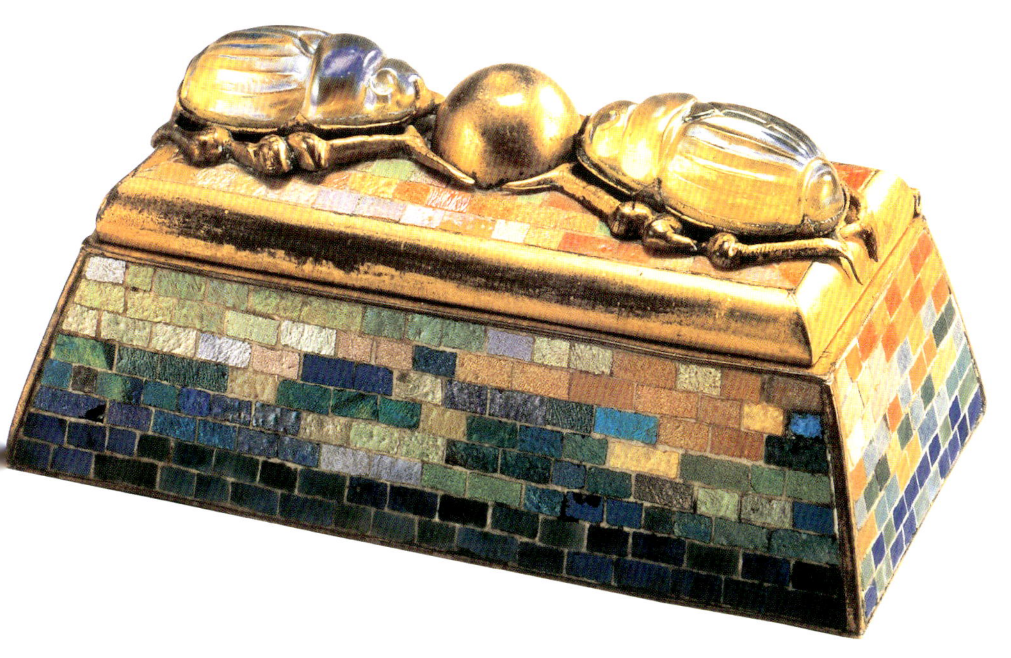

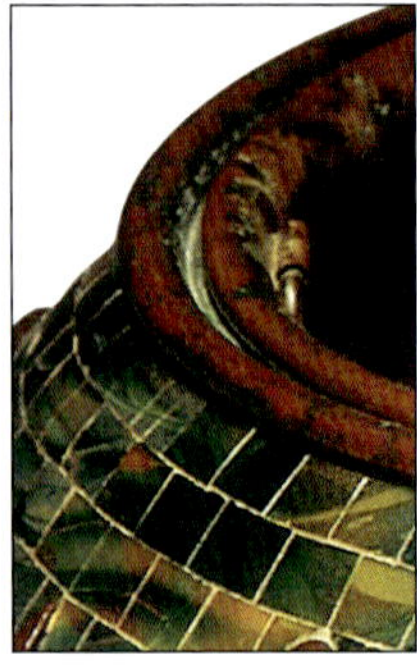

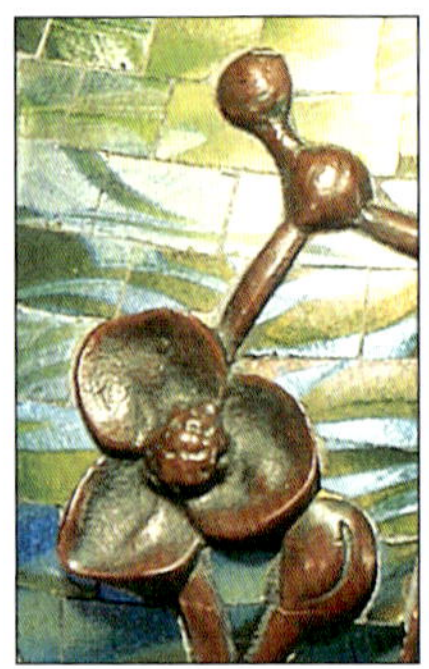

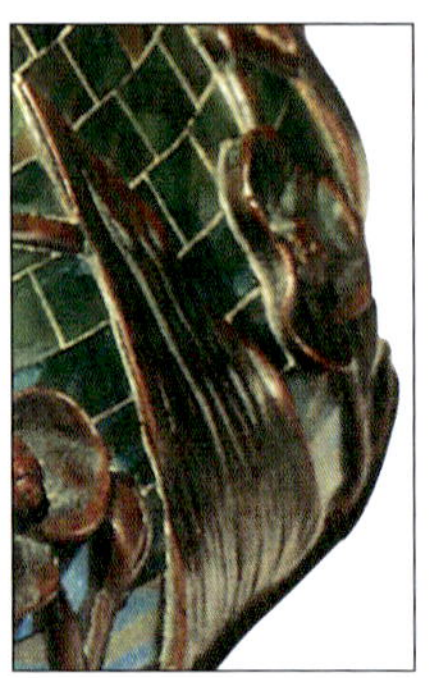

colored stones amassed by Tiffany & Company, this department has a variety and wealth of materials to choose from, the likes of which does not exist in America or in any known land.

One of the earliest designs for personal jewelry which occurred to Mr. Tiffany is the flower of the wild carrot, called Queen Anne's lace. This charming weed is found everywhere. Its unpretending wheel formed of

Arrowheads and Fern Mosaic Dish

Favrile glass and bronze.

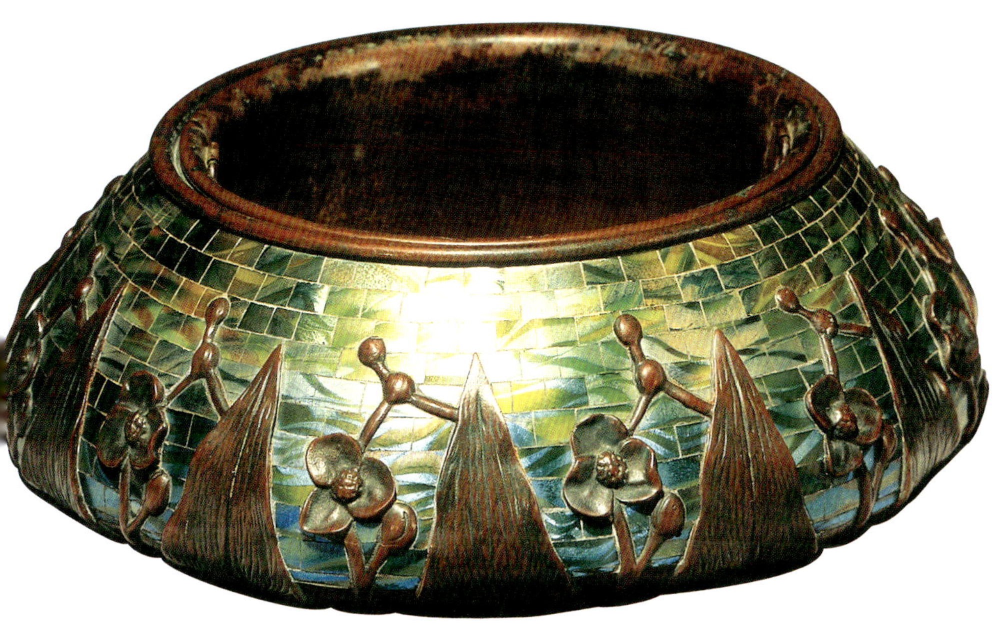

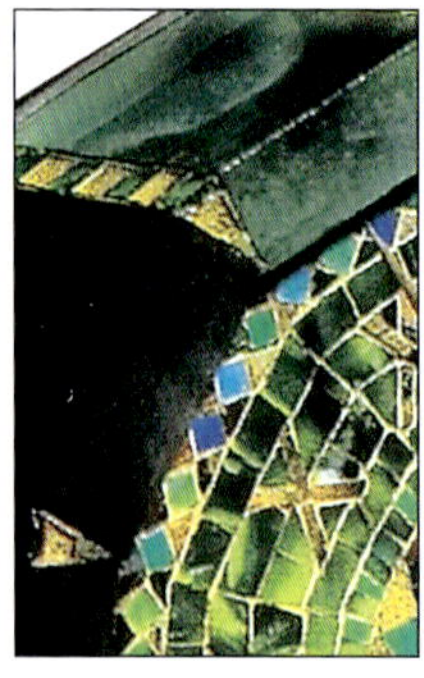

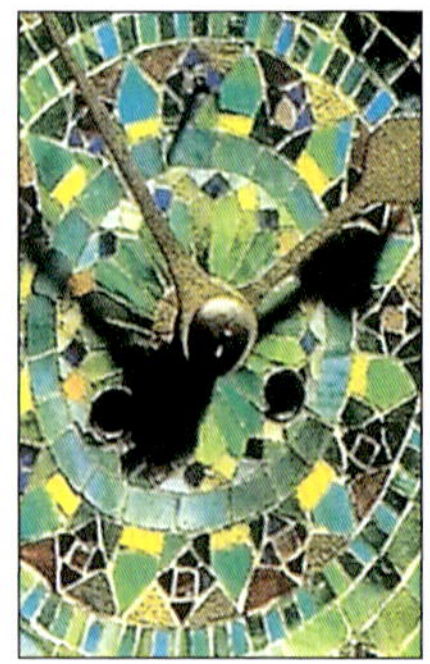

a great number of small white flowers, sometimes of a delicate mauve, will often carry a small dark floweret in the centre of the disk. This wheel is reproduced in white enamel on silver, with a garnet at the centre. A dragon fly for a hat-pin is enameled and set with opals on a platinum base. A marine motif, half crab, half octopus, with the writhing feet split into two or more special ends, is arranged for a brooch and set with opals,

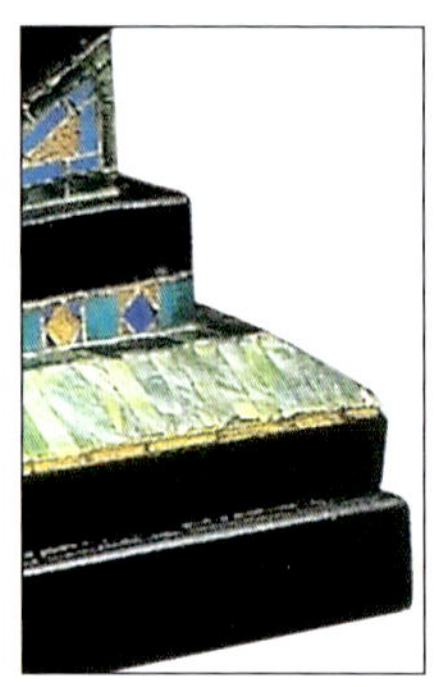

Mosaic Mantle Clock

Favrile glass and bronze.

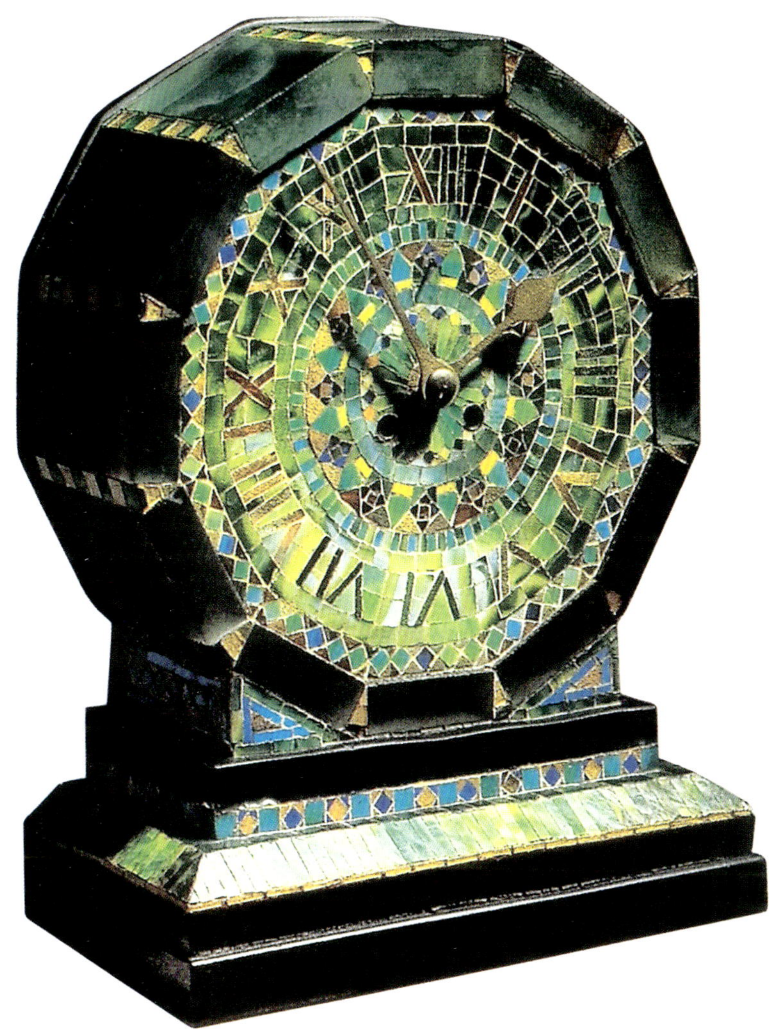

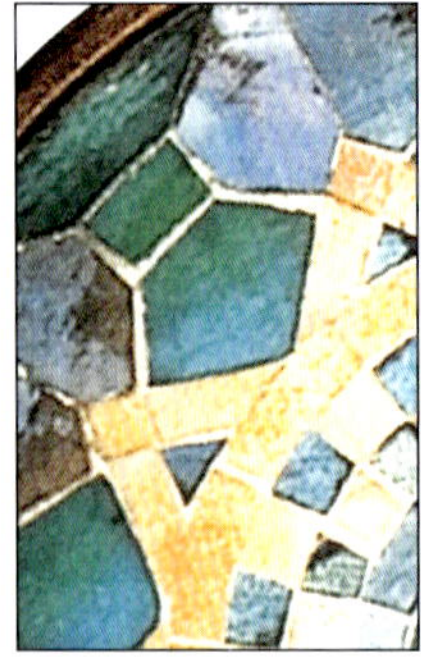

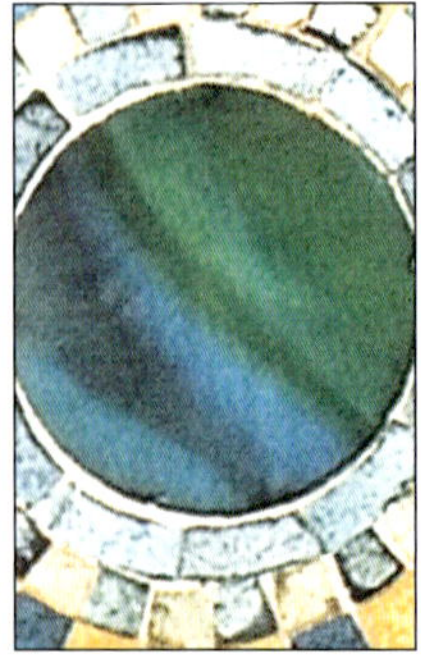

sapphires and rubies. This piece is now in the Walters Gallery. A girdle of silver ornamented with enamels, has berries formed of opals. A decoration for the head is a branch of blackberries, the leaves made of filigree of gold and silver, enameled, the berries composed of clusters of dark garnets. Another design is the dandelion full blown with seed. A third is a spray of the little *spirea* flower.

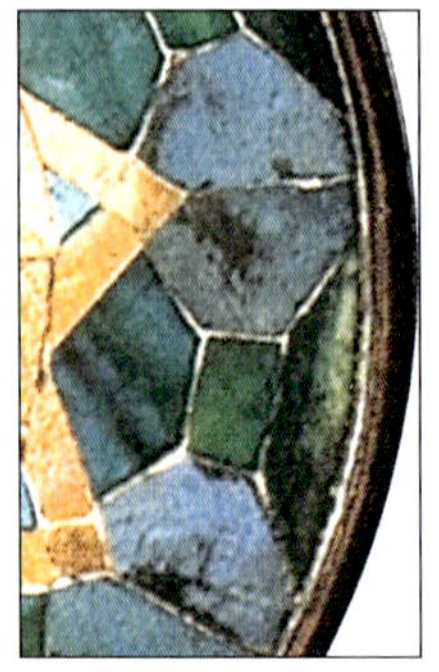

Ten Point Star Sconce

Leaded glass and bronze.

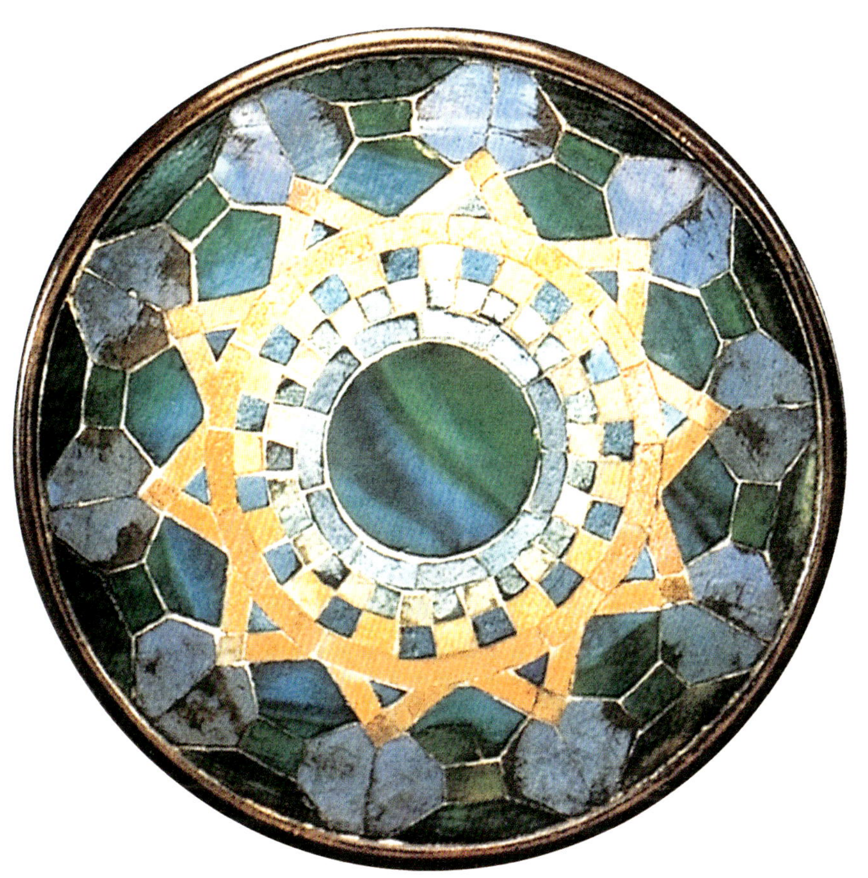

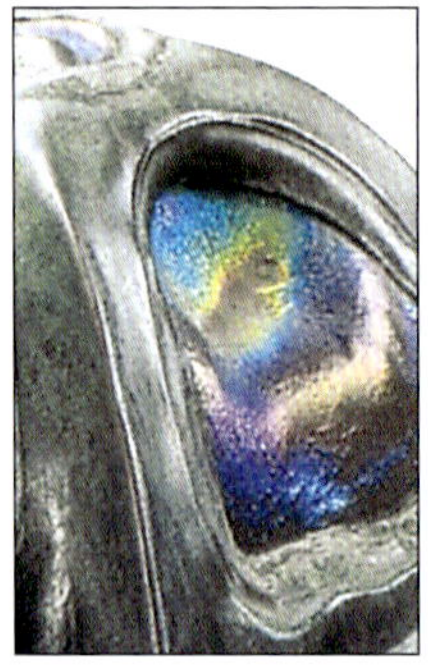

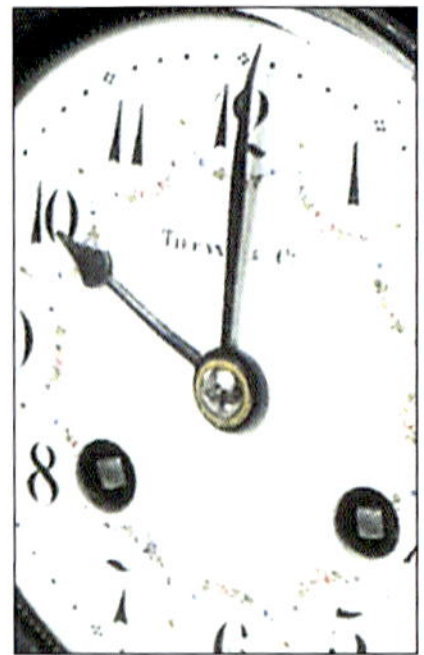

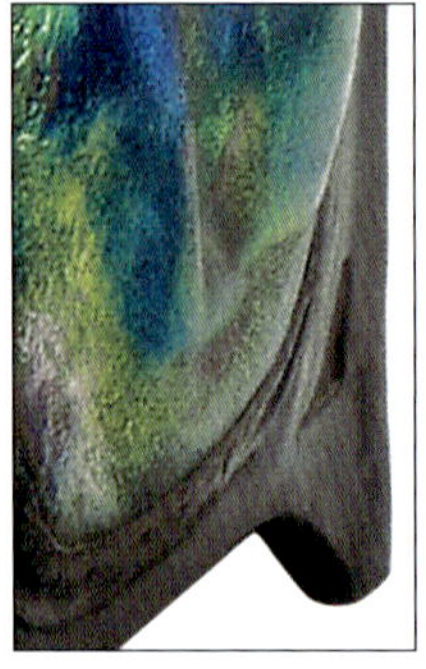

Another is the peacock necklace, the main piece of which is a mosaic of opals, amethysts and sapphires. The less large pieces that adjoin the centre are of enamel on gold repoussé work, lighted up with opals and rubies, emeralds being used to relieve the colors. The back of the big centrepiece has a decoration of flamingoes and the lowest point of the pendant below is a single large ruby, selected not for its costliness but for

Opalescent Glass Clock

Bronze and leaded opalescent glass.

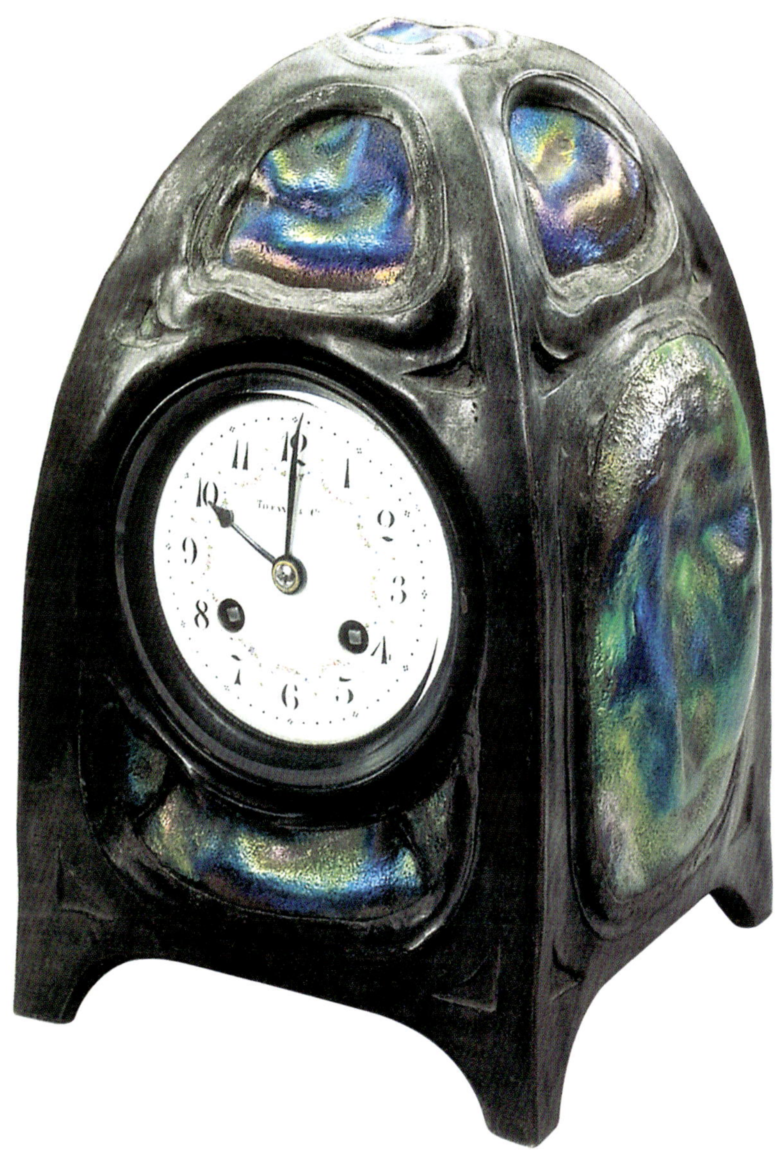

189

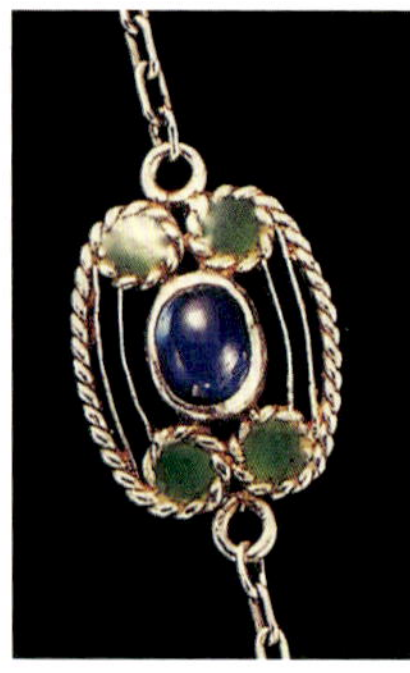

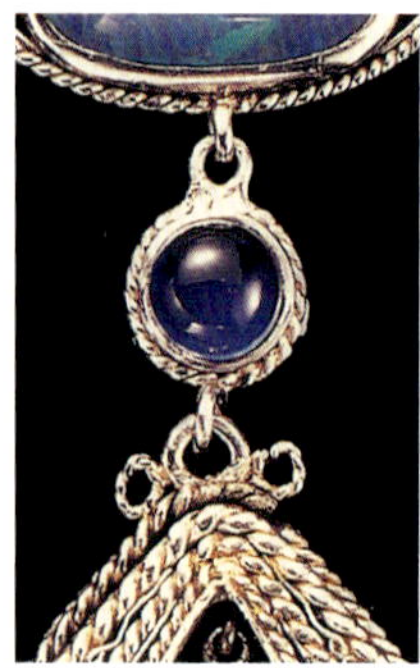

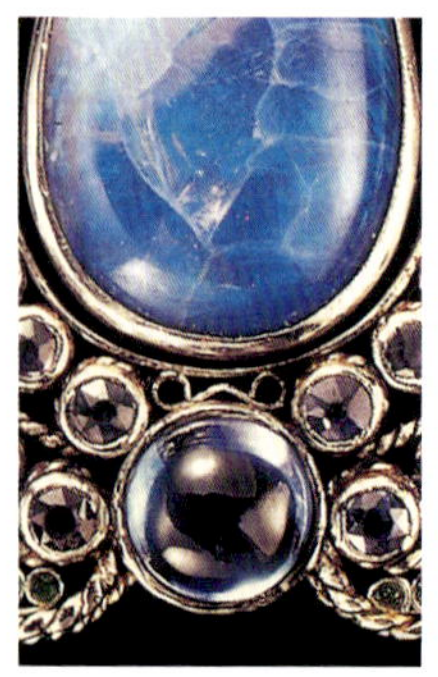

the exact shade of its red. Objects of this sort make one feel that the artist has studied well the enamels of China and Japan without losing sight of those of Byzantium and the Italian Renaissance. Neither color nor design is Oriental, but it is certain that the Orient has had a stimulating effect, as we perceive to have been the case with Whistler and La Farge and many French painters and decorators. Tiffany has taken the best, namely,

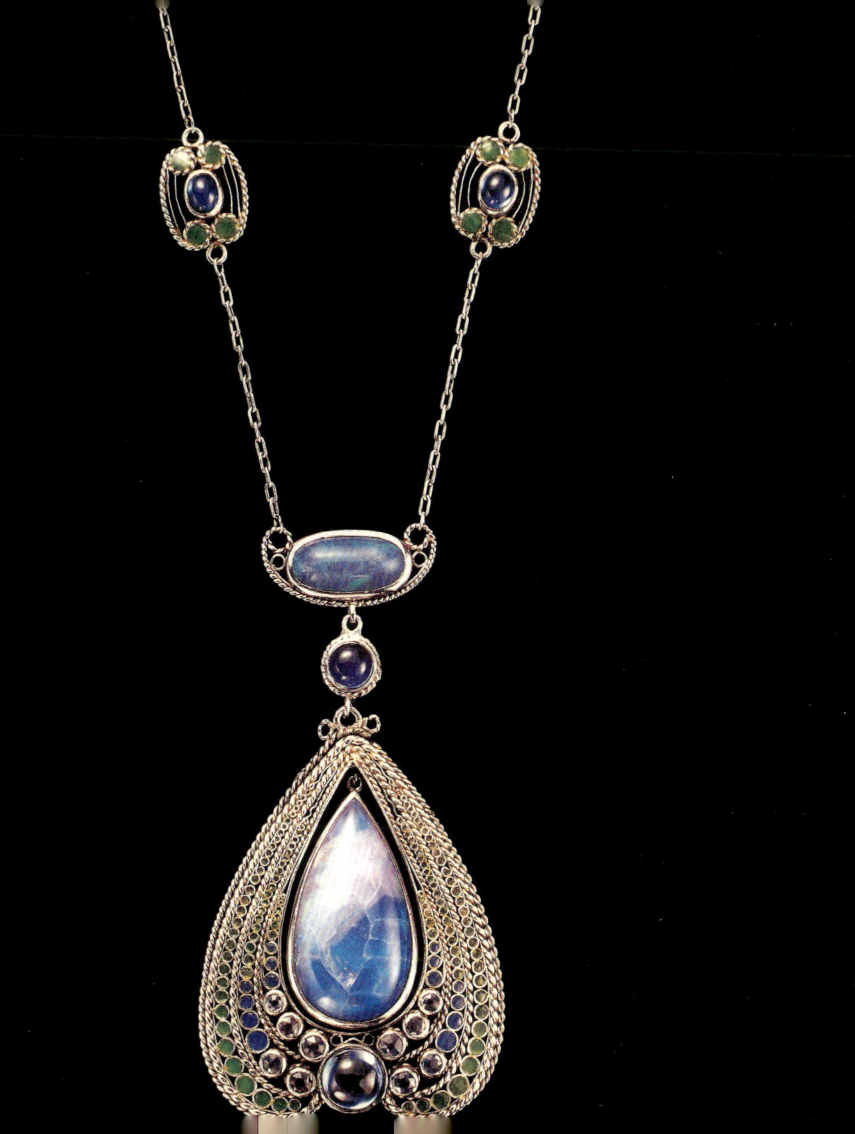

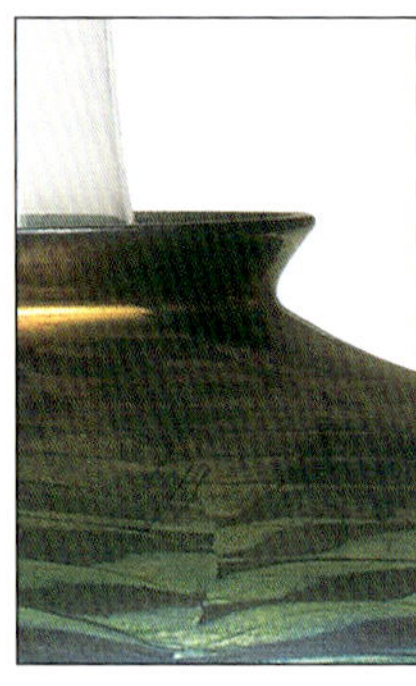

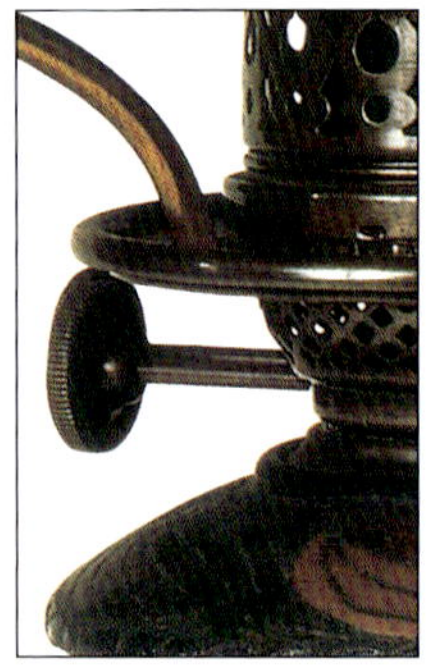

the spirit of the Oriental craftsmen, without falling so far under their spell as to become a copyist, and this independence and originality will be found in the form of his works as well as in the designs wrought upon them.

Among the most exquisite products of the Tiffany enamels are pieces meant to hold flower pots or cut flowers, decorative vases for the drawing room or dining table,

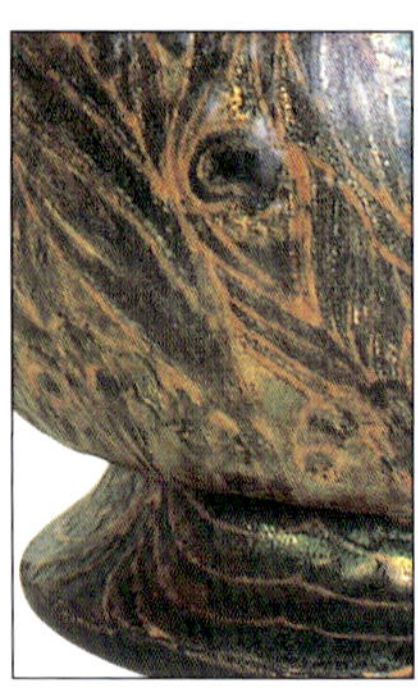

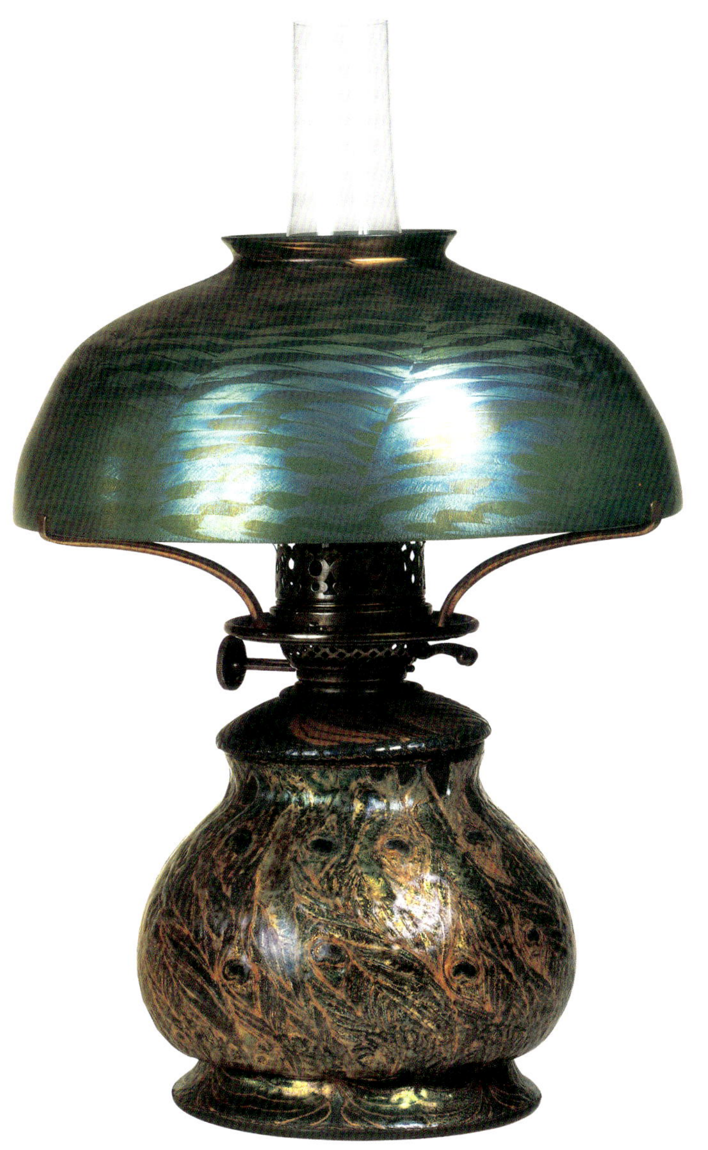

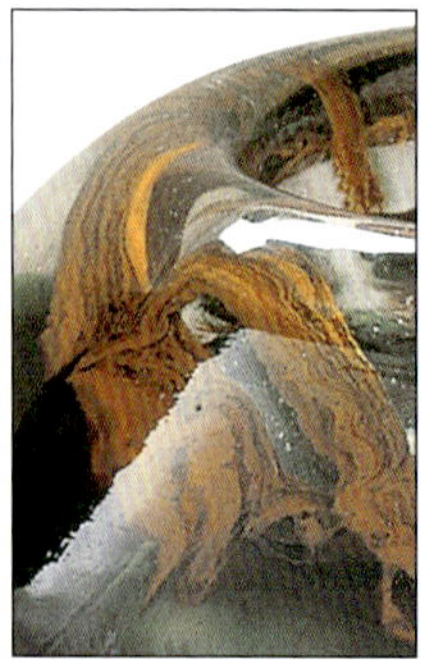

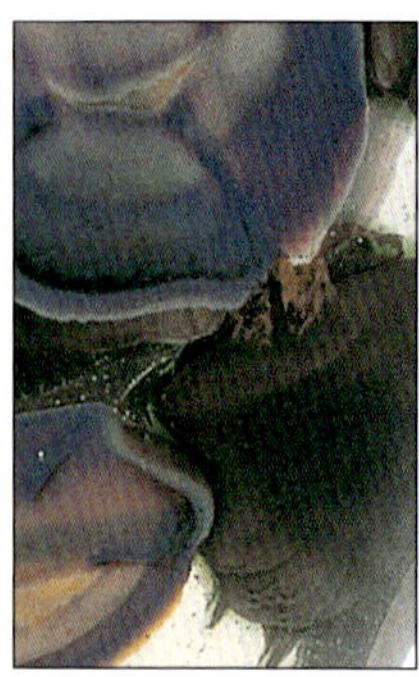

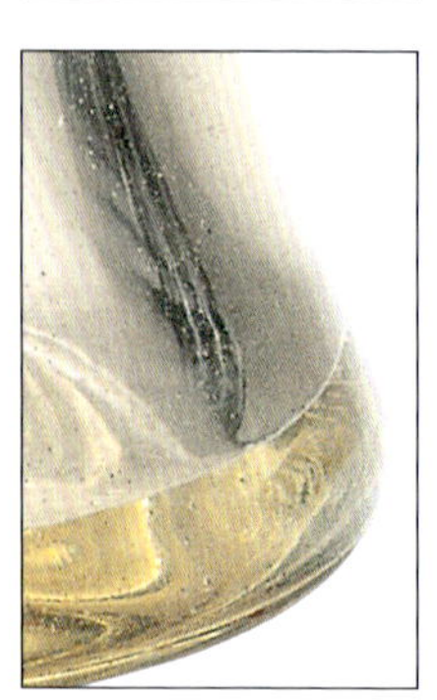

trinket-holders for the toilet table, bonbonnieres, etc. Beside these warm and resplendent enamels the tones of old Limoges ware look formal and cold. The designs are commonly flower motifs which recall Mr. Tiffany's paintings of roses, rhododendrons and peonies. They reflect the pleasure which the artist takes in color, analogous in music to the notes of the cello.

1917.
Glass, 15.9 x 11.1 x 11.1 cm.
Currier Museum of Art, Manchester.

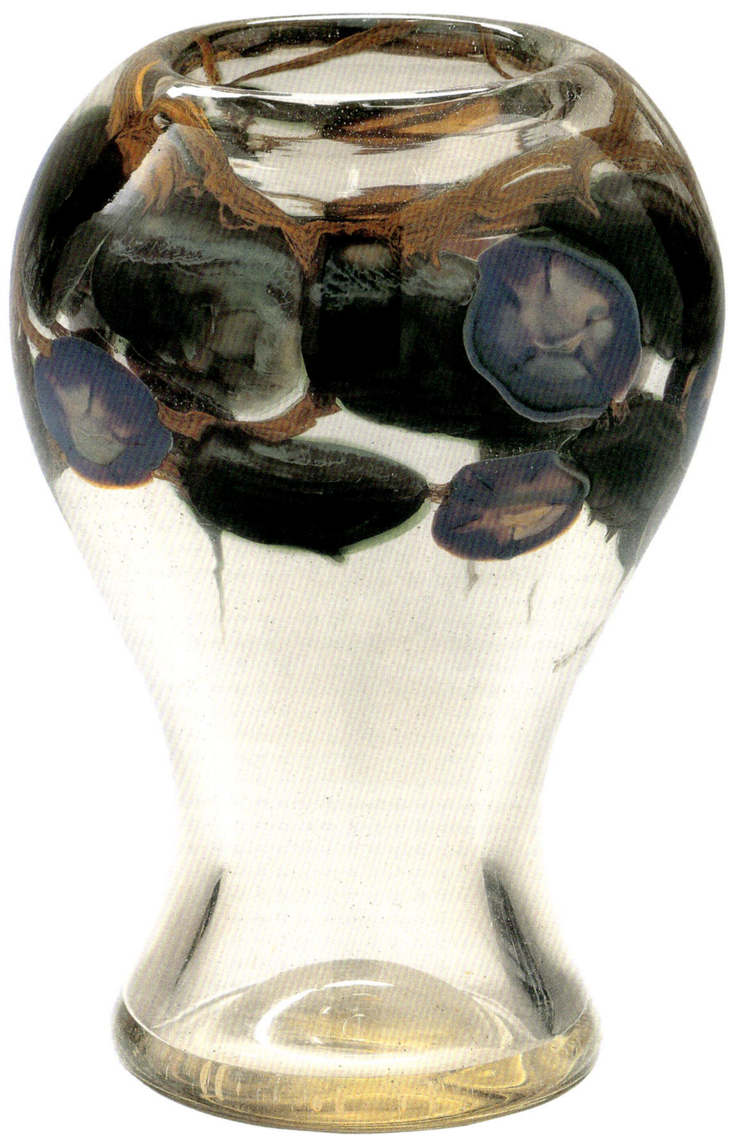

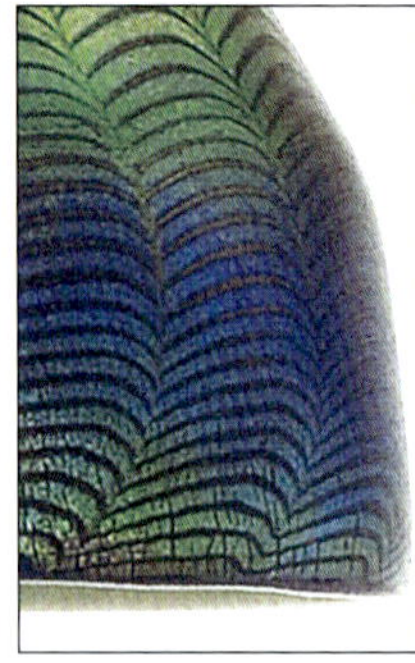

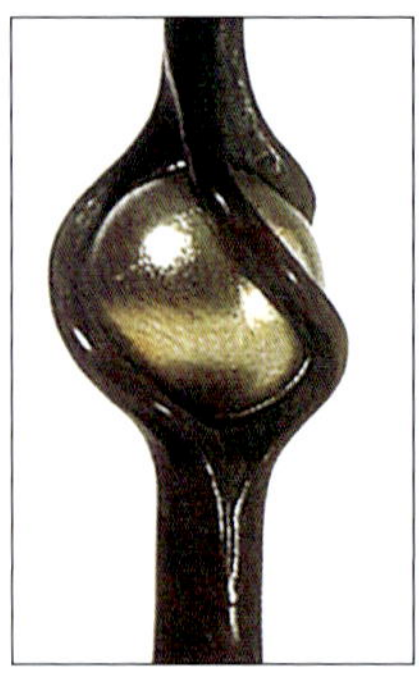

Take for example one small vase which has a number of toadstools in different stages of growth in repoussé relief. The artist has succeeded in suggesting the very texture of the fungus. The red and rose tints of the plants and the varied greens of the vase form a sumptuous color scheme and lend to the small object that precious quality which is so difficult to attain. A smaller round pot with decoration

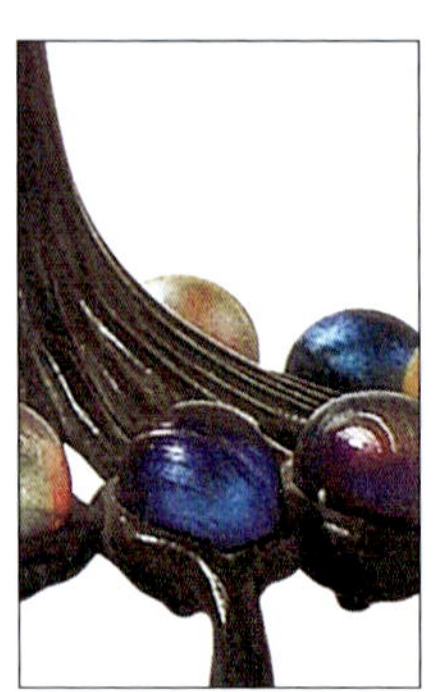

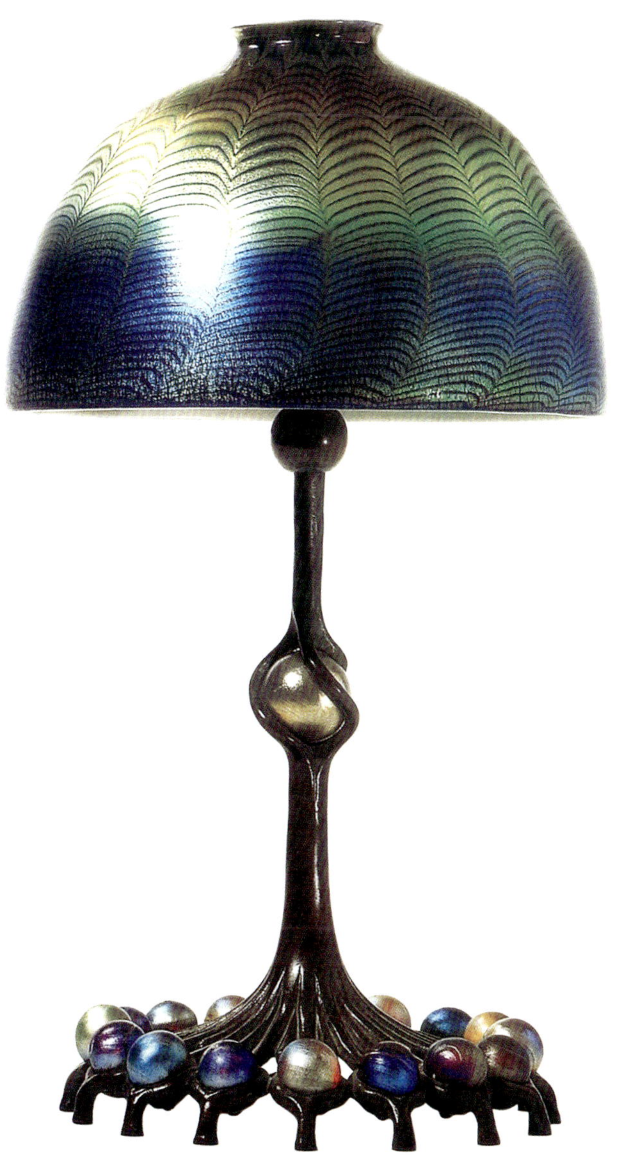

197

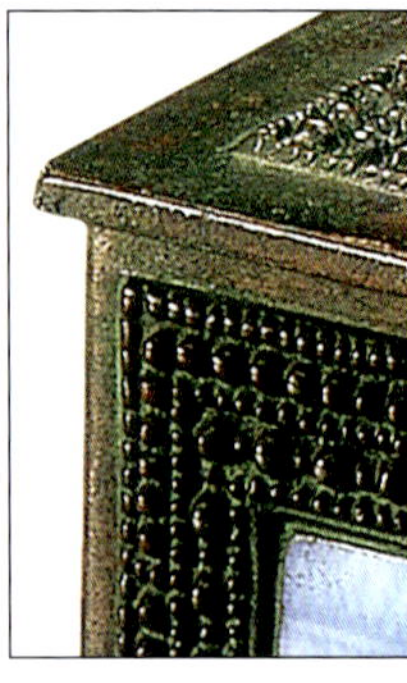

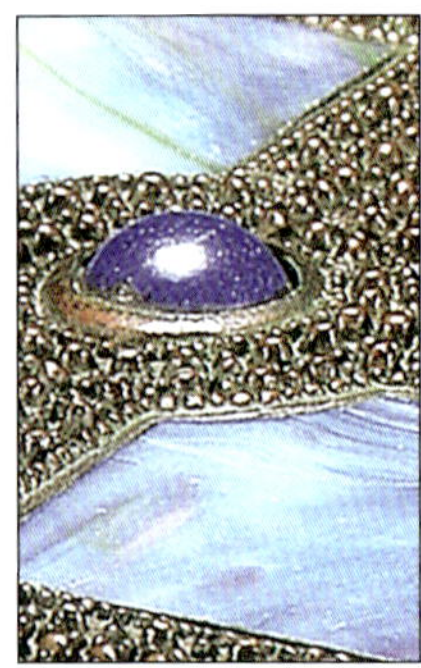

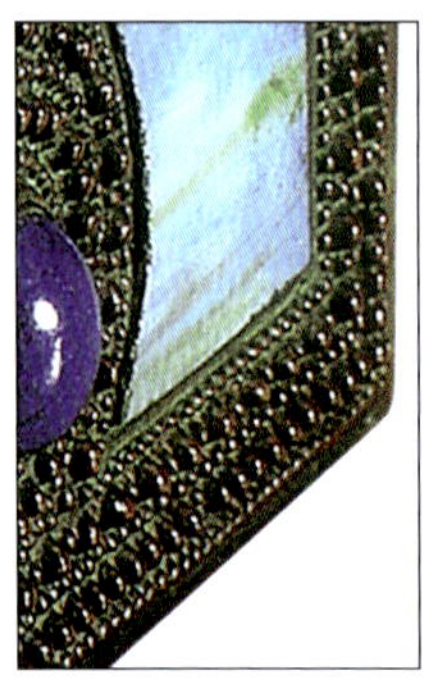

of red flowers in relief makes the same impression. A wide-mouthed bowl or cup with red flowers deep in the smooth surface (not repoussé) is notable for the simple elegance of its shape and the glow of the flower motif.

Next to the structure of the design is the color scheme in these and a minted other pieces. Long practice in selecting glass for windows trains an artist to a certainty of eye which makes him instantaneous in his judgment.

Byzantine Cigar Box

Favrile glass, bronze and lapis.

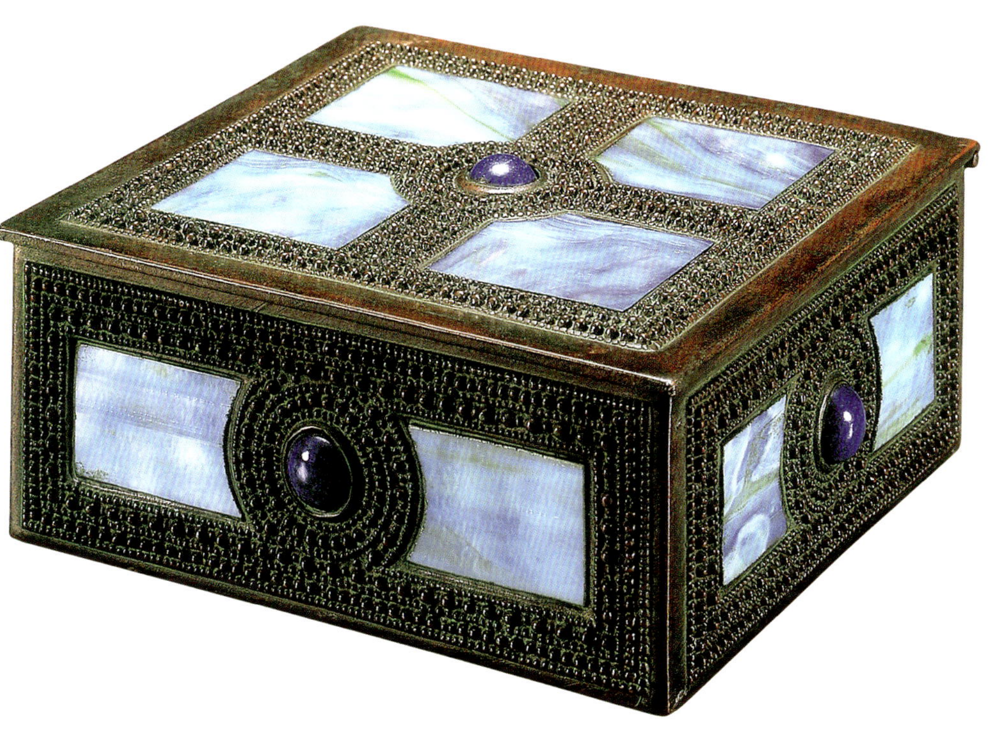

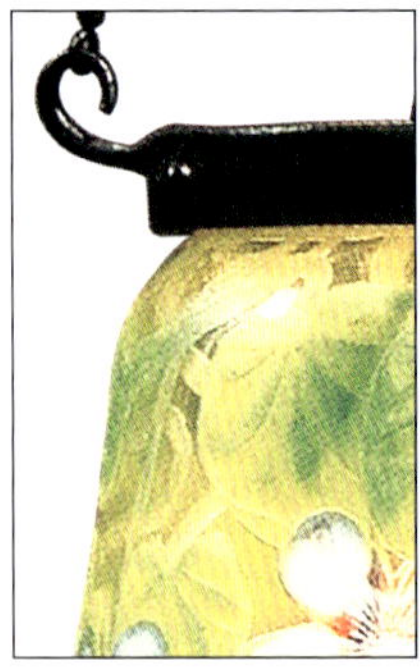

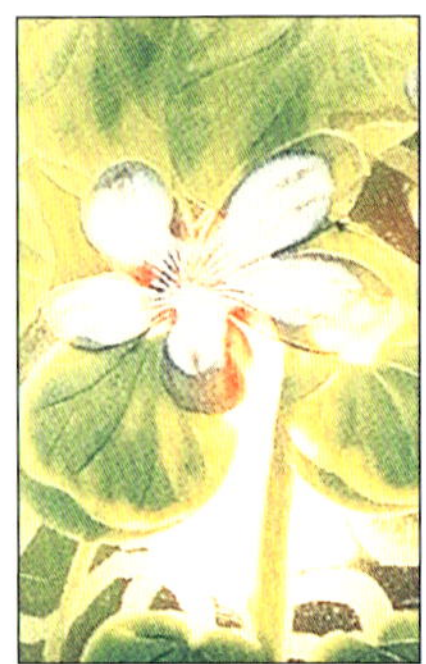

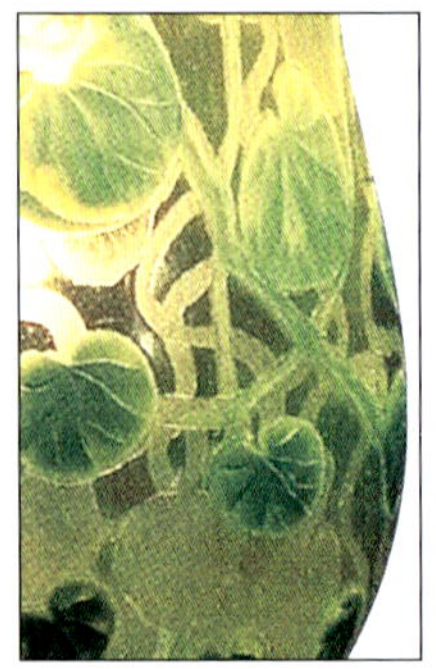

He does not require a rule of color adjustment; it is more like an instinct. This allows the master to get through a vast quantity of work in a given time. Mr. Tiffany has his helpers so well trained that he needs to devote but a few hours a day to enamels and jewelry. It is through his study of flowers as a painter interested in nature and his delight in the growing of flowers that he has come to many happy adaptations of flower forms

Floral Hanging Lamp

Glass and bronze.

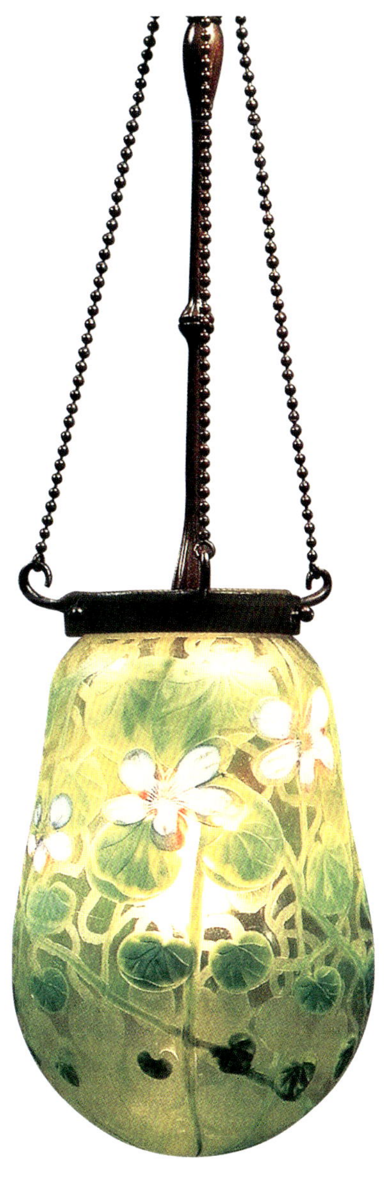

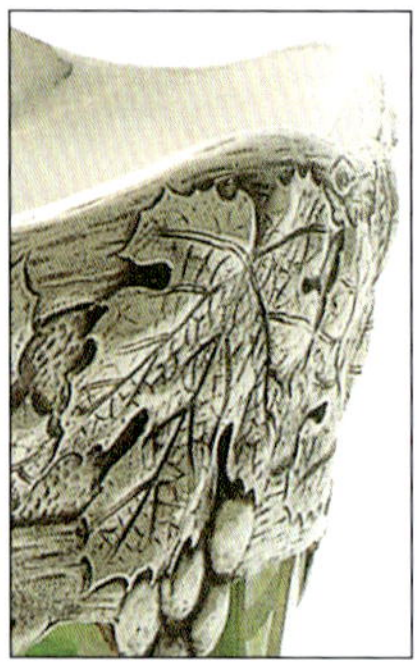

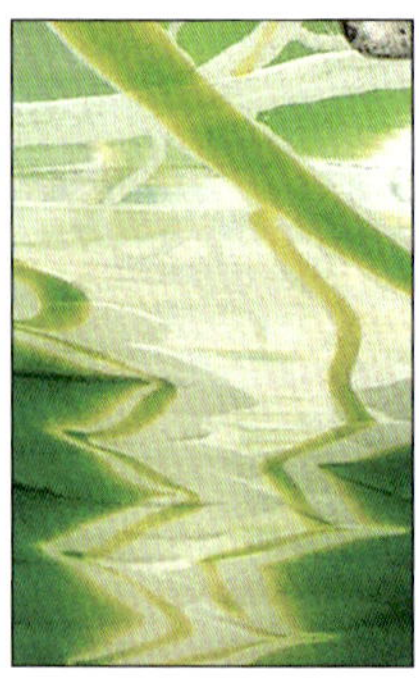

in enamel work and stained glass. Insect life and marine forms have suggested other combinations of lines and masses, hues and shades. He has followed the bidding "reach boldly out and grasp the life about you" as we may paraphrase one of Goethe's best known verses, and taken advantage of the endless wealth of precept and suggestion that lies around us in air

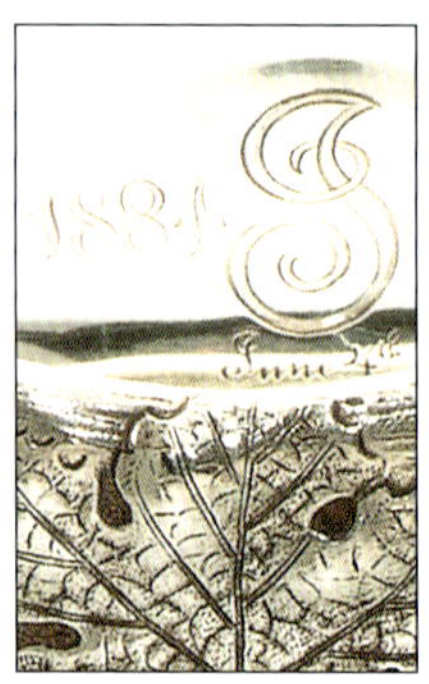

Bowl with Silver Rim in Grapevine Pattern

1909.
Glass, sterling silver, 12 x 27.3 x 27.3 cm.
The Chrysler Museum of Art, Norfolk.

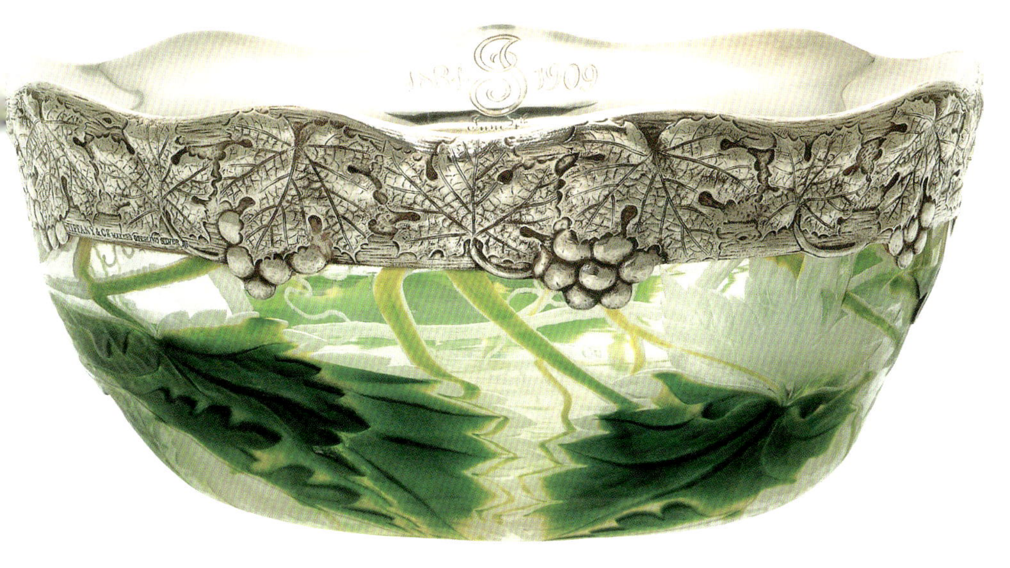

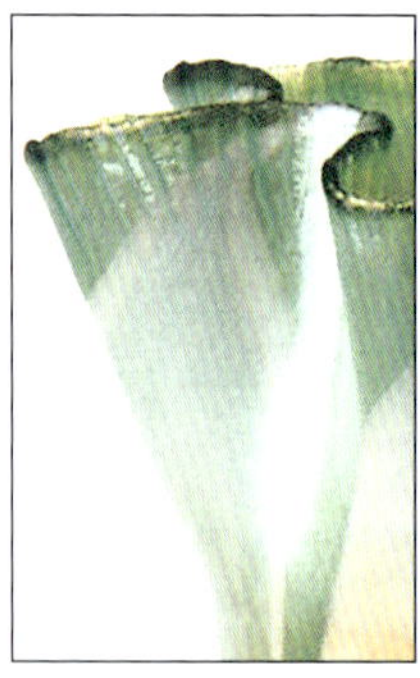

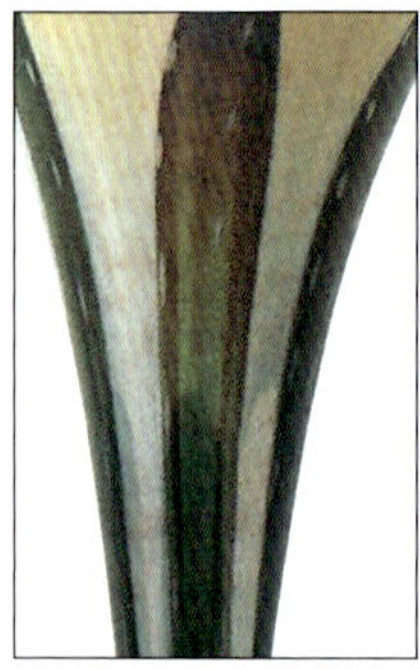

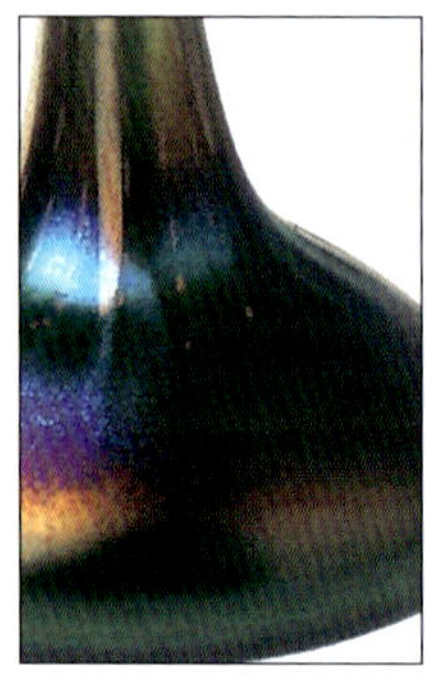

and water and earth, in all the vast, teeming bosom of nature.

Articles of personal adornment are wont to be rated low throughout the wide field of art in contradistinction to objects of the fine arts. One must not forget, however, that they appeal to the very widest imaginable circle of buyers. Practically all

Vase

———

1900.
Favrile glass, height: 51.1 cm.
The Museum of Modern Art, New York.

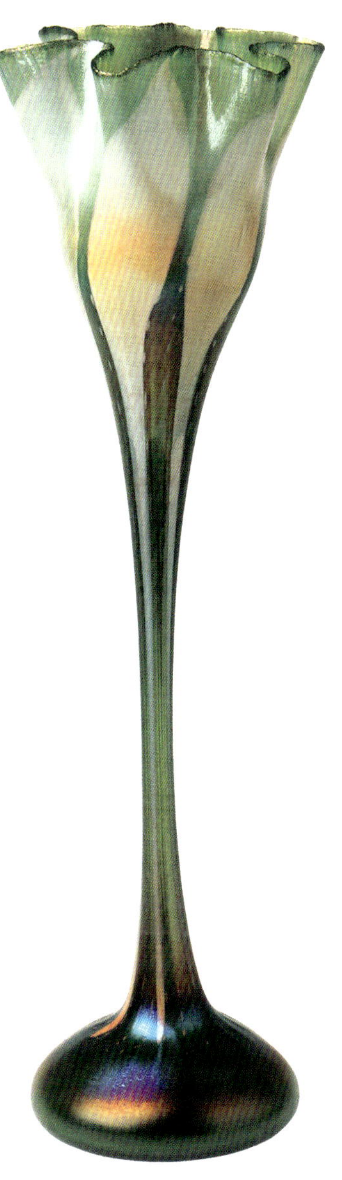

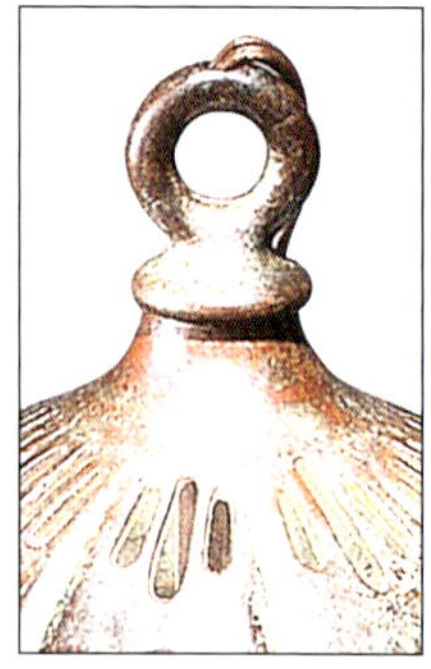

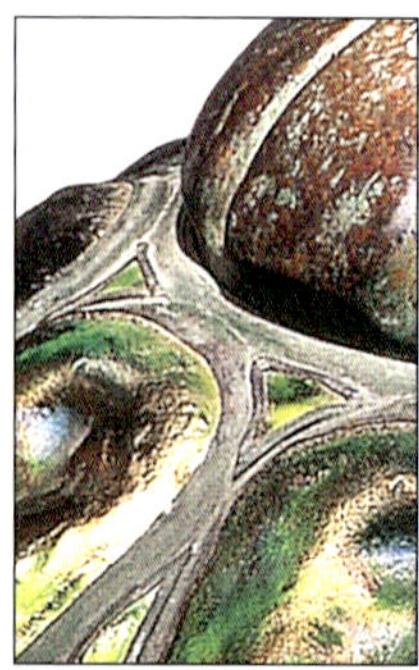

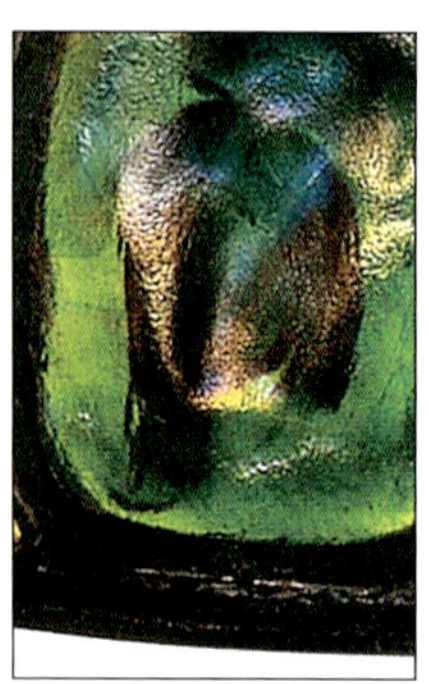

women and most men take an interest of a more or less lively sort in things which they carry about their persons. It is well, therefore, that objects of the sort should be beautiful or at any rate exhibit some taste. One may say that the quality, the artistic quality, of the jewelry which is found among a people goes far to measure that people's level in art.

Favrile glass and bronze.

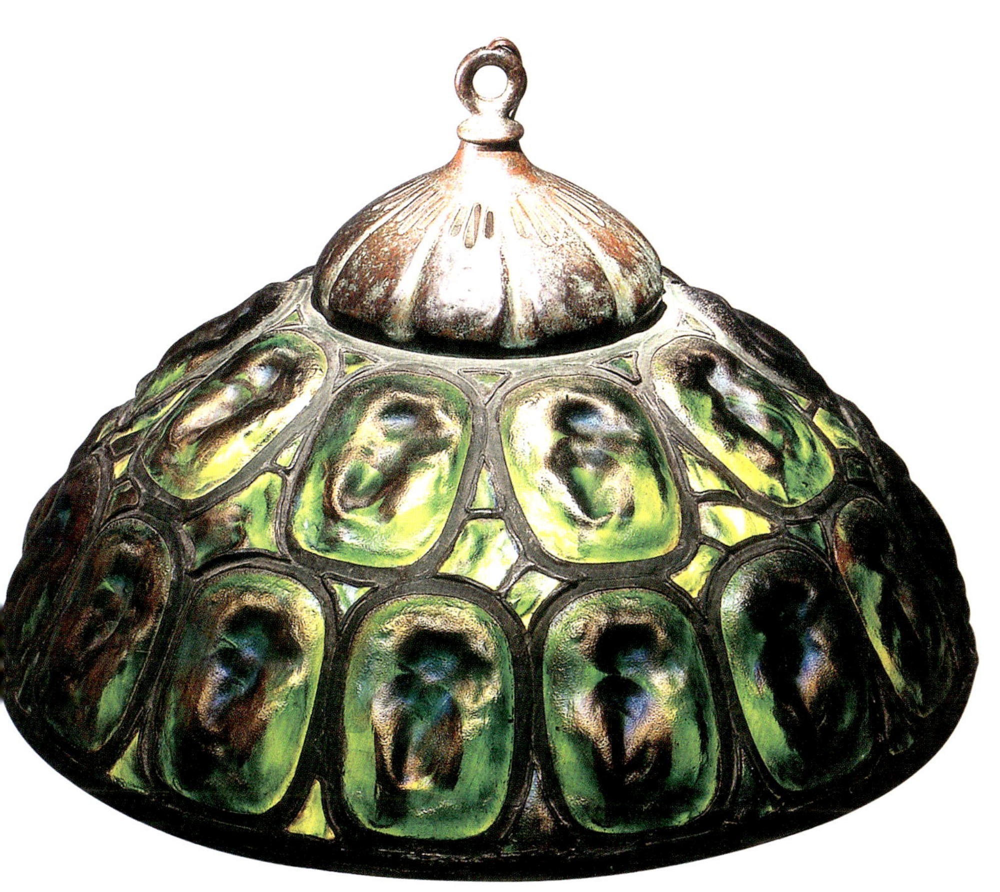

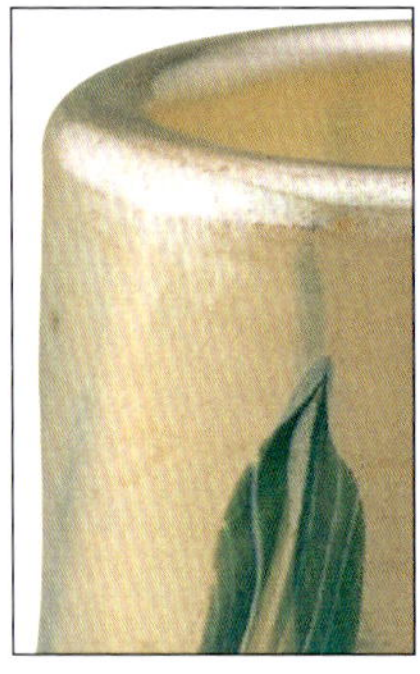

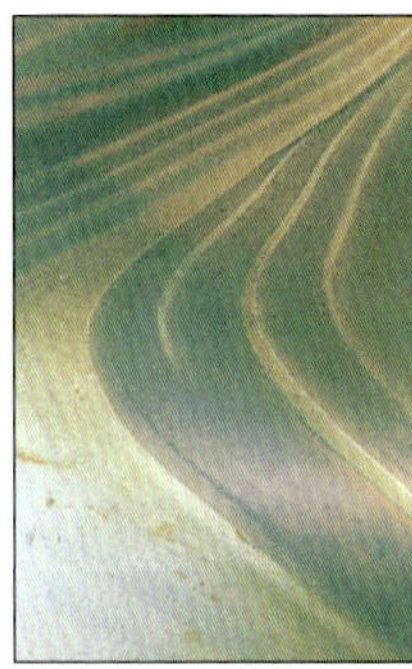

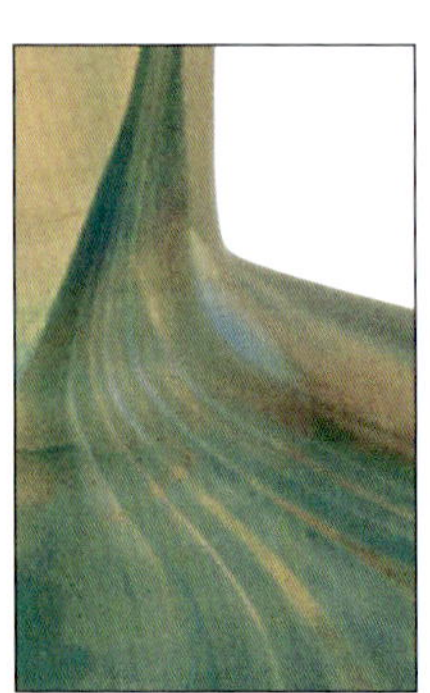

Hence the importance of having artists instead of untrained artisans to supply jewelers with designs; hence the value to the people of Mr. Tiffany's efforts to supply a class of jewelry not only original and individual, but often very beautiful. Each piece acts as a little missionary of art and tries in its own little way to convert the Philistine.

Vase

———

1892-1896.
Glass, height: 14.9 cm.
Museum of Art, University of Michigan, Ann Arbor.

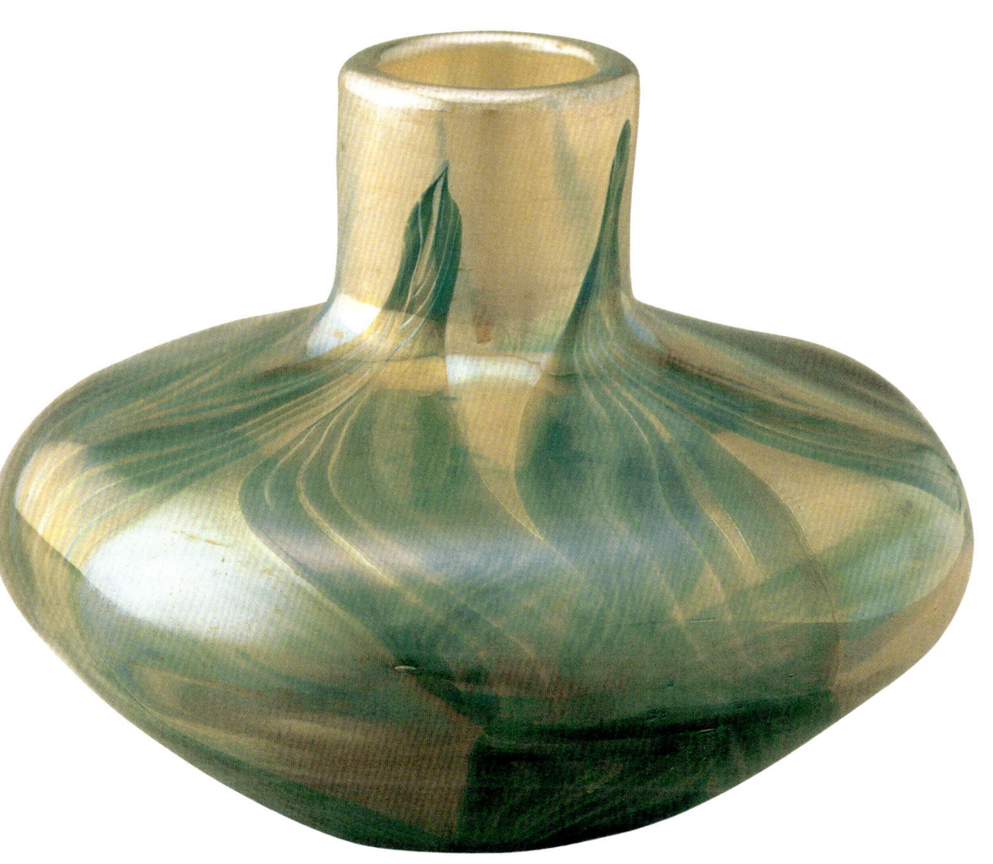

209

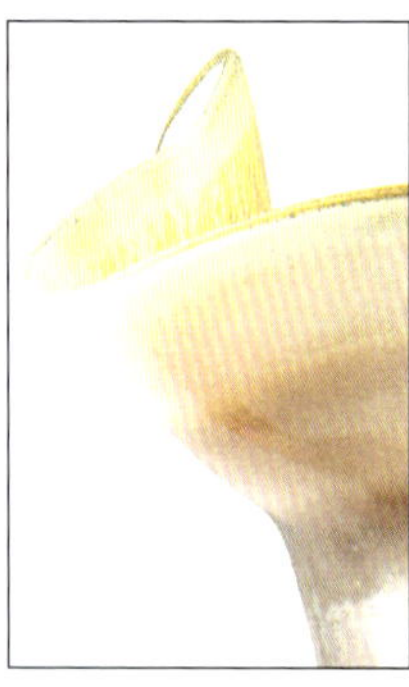

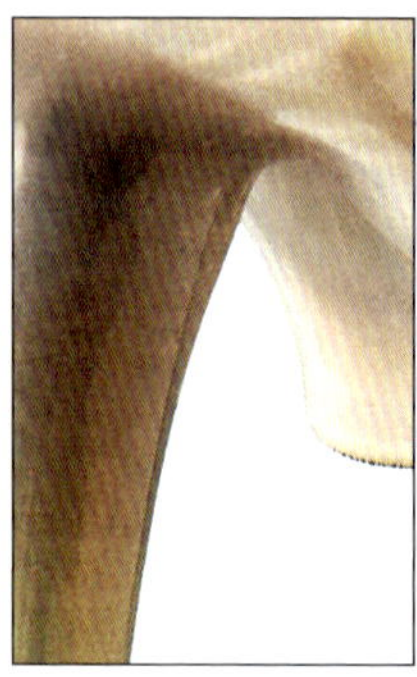

AFTERWORD

In the preceding pages, should they be thought worthy of a careful reading, it may be remarked that the words color, color-sense, color-feeling often recur. The value attributed to color has been denied by theorists who have started from an untenable assumption that there is a purity, there is a moral worth attached to

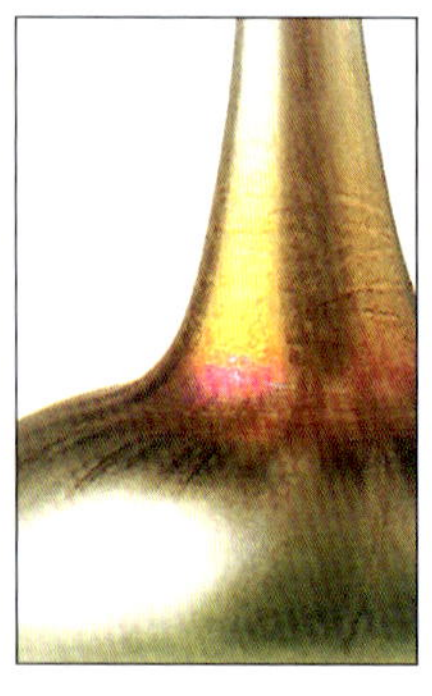

Vase

———

1900.
Favrile glass, height: 41.2 x 15.2 cm.
The Museum of Modern Art, New York.

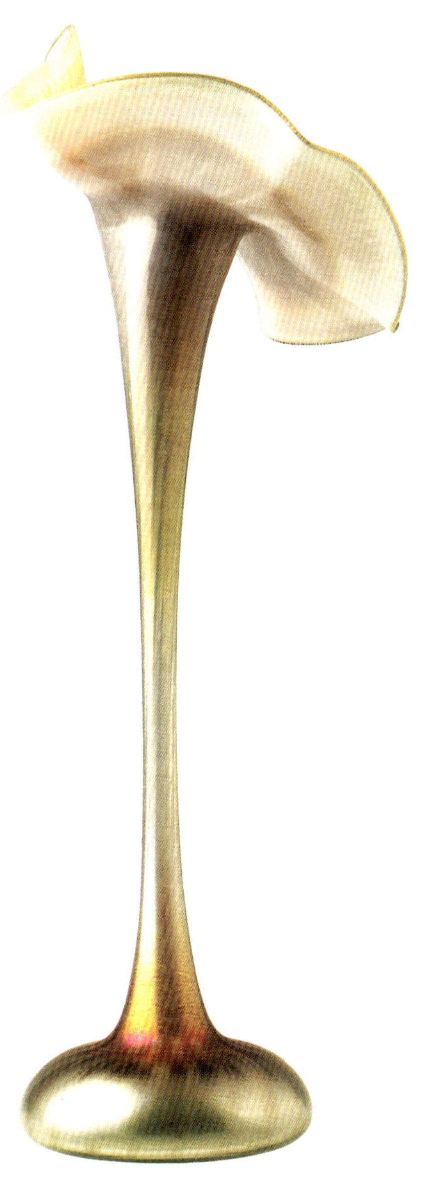

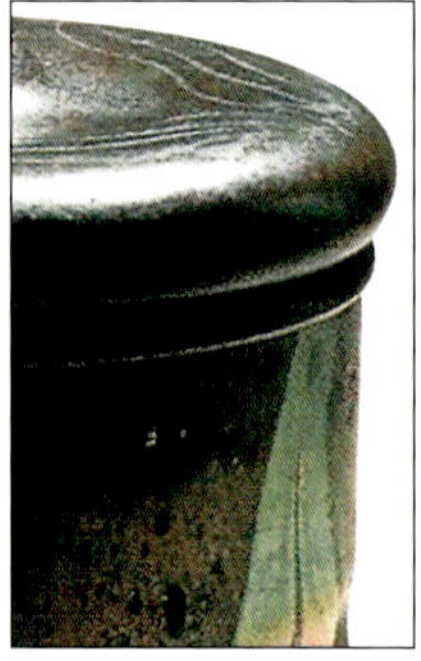

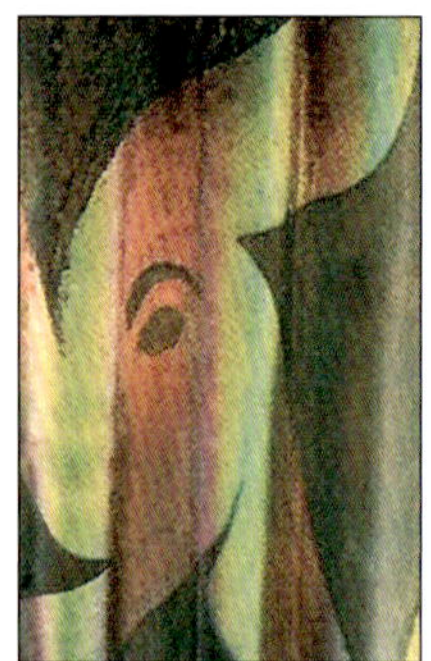

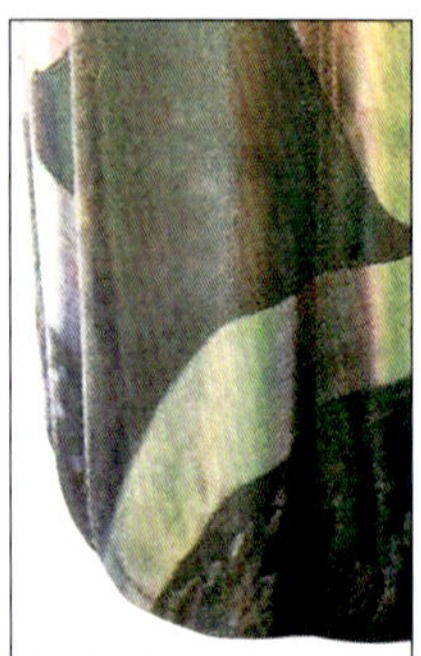

absence of color, in opposition to sensuousness and luxury in a bad sense attached to its presence. This is a convenient theory for a vast majority of artists who are born without the peculiar eyes and senses that distinguish values and respond with sympathy to the vibrations of light.

Tobacco Jar

Favrile glass with metal mounts.

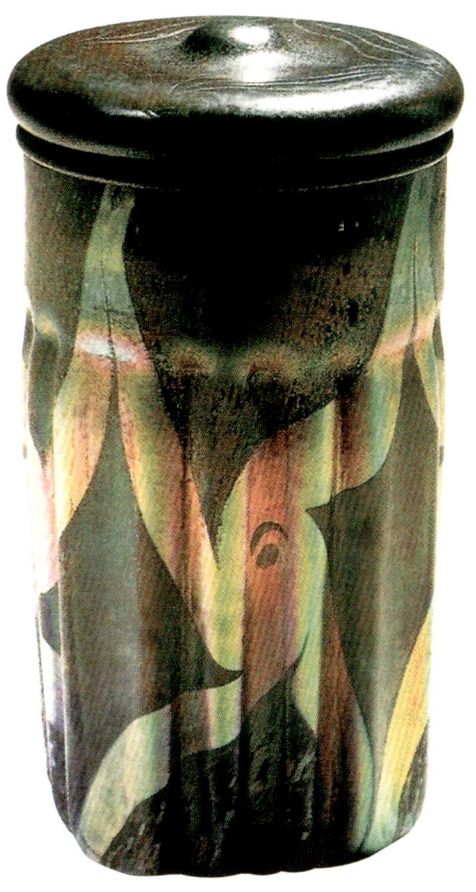

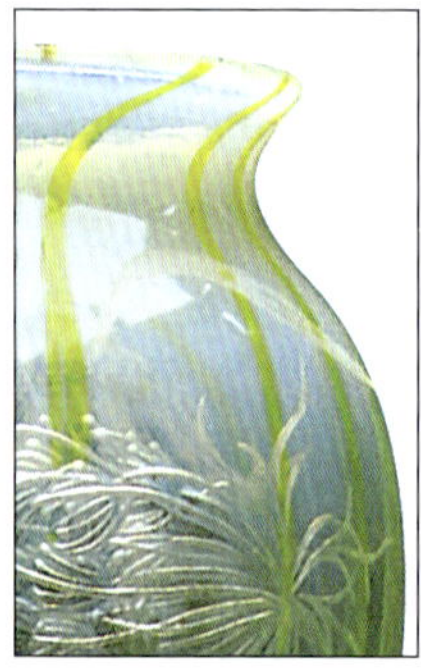

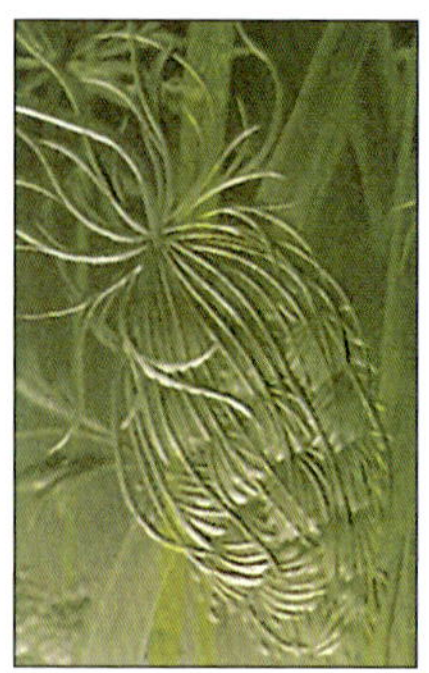

Persian textiles, Japanese watercolors, Chinese porcelain, Venetian paintings, the works of Rembrandt and Velásquez can be forced into appeals to sensuousness and luxuriousness only by a twist in the meaning of words which may satisfy the narrow-minded and the bigot. Some painters do make their mark without

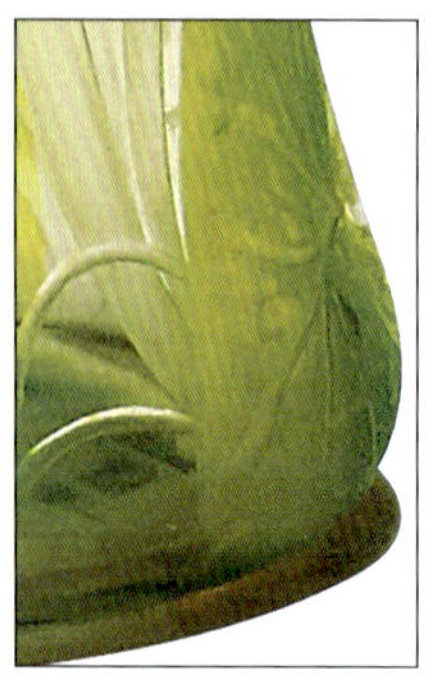

Vase

—

1895-1898.
Favrile glass, carved and etched, height: 31.1 cm.
Metropolitan Museum of Art, New York.

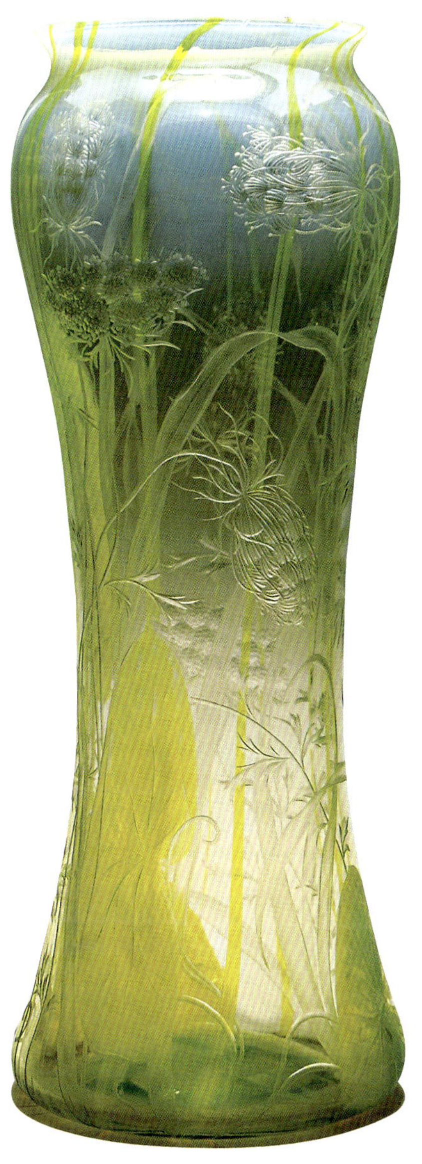

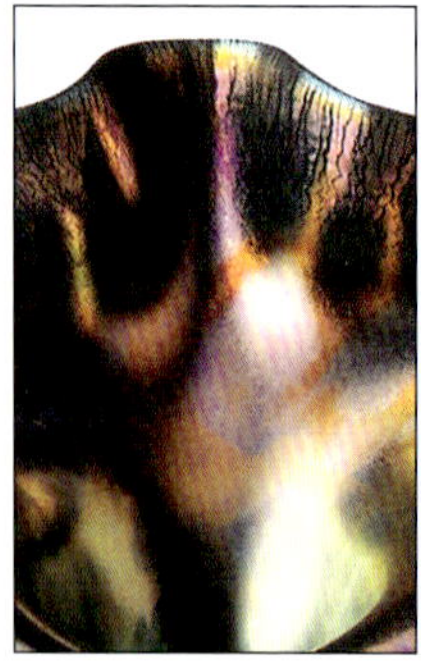

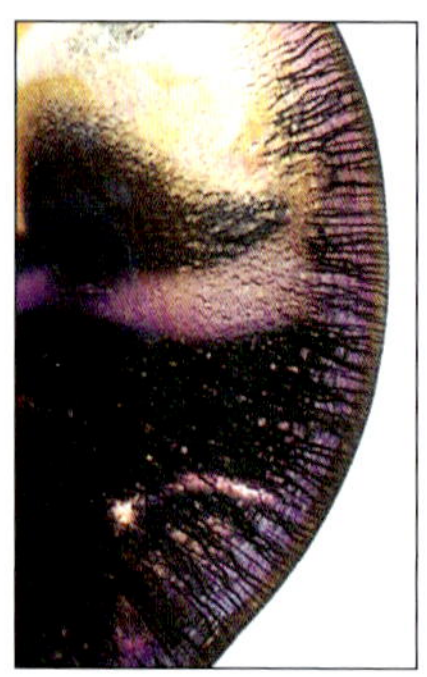

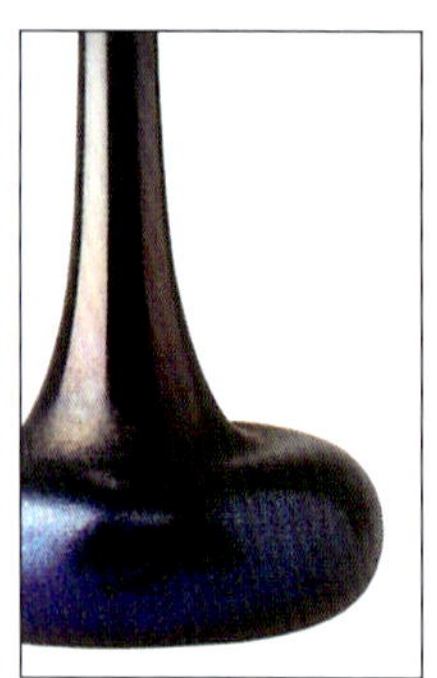

having this characteristic to any great extent, although it would appear from the nature of things that it ought to be the painter's strongest trait. Now Louis C. Tiffany belongs to the painters who can be embraced under the broad term of colorists; hence the frequent appearance of these words.

Vase

———

1900.
Favrile glass, height: 52.5 x 13 cm.
The Museum of Modern Art, New York.

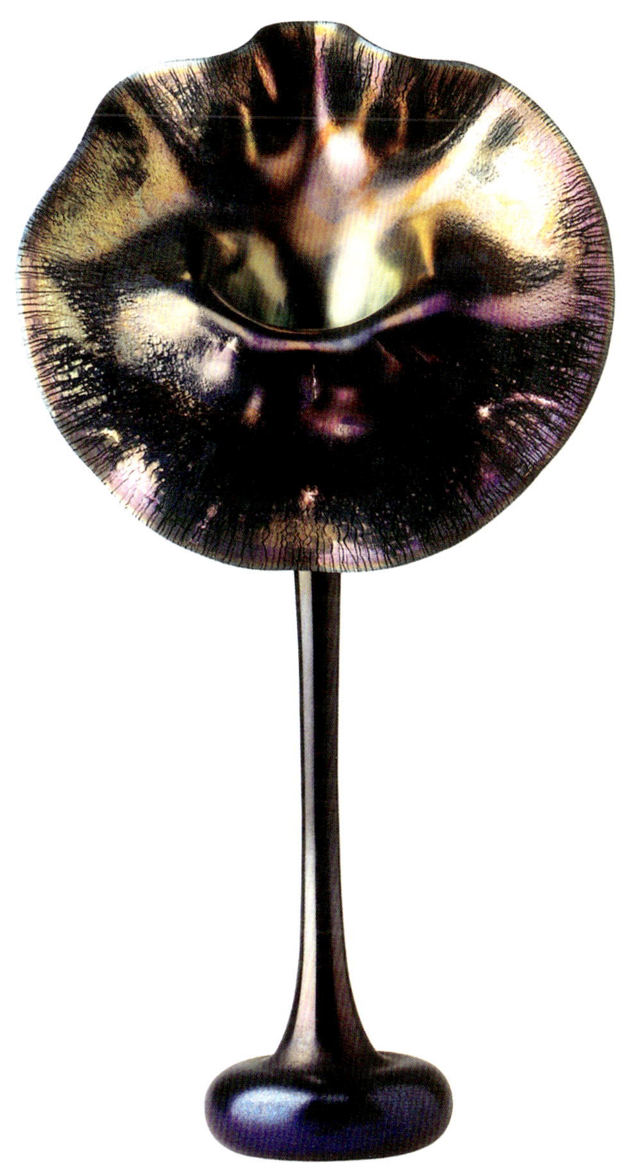

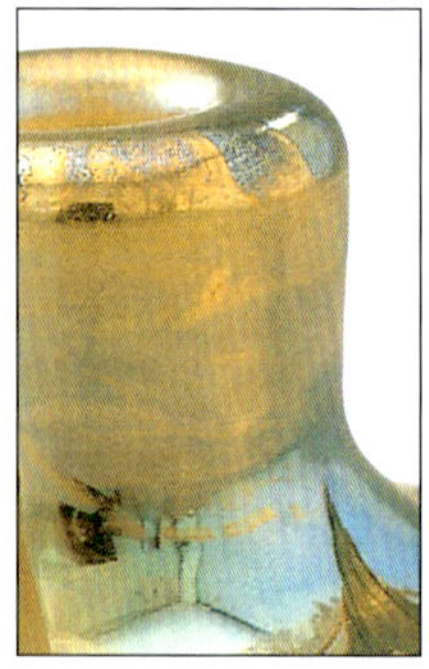

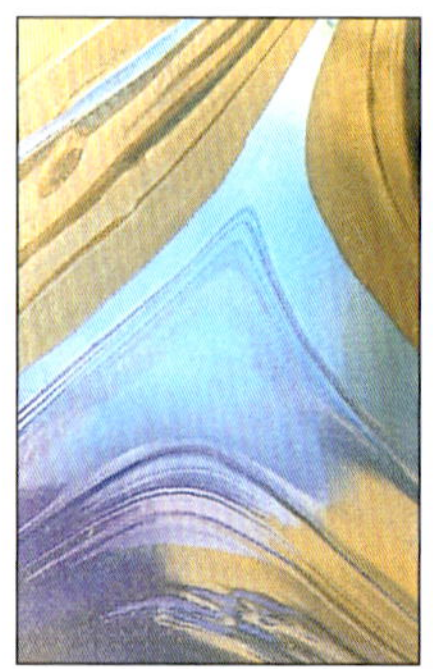

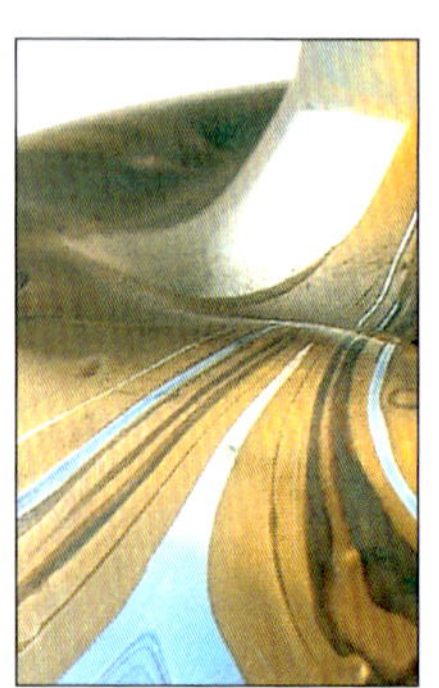

The United States have had more than their share of painters who come under the head of colorists, as, for instance in colony times, Gilbert Stuart and Malbone, and later on, Henry Peters Gray, George Inness, George Fuller and Whistler, John La Farge and Homer D. Martin, Albert P. Ryder and John Singer Sargent, It is to this group that Louis C. Tiffany belongs, and if the relationship is not always recognized the reason lies in

1892-1896.
Glass, height: 8.1 cm.
Museum of Art, University of Michigan, Ann Arbor.

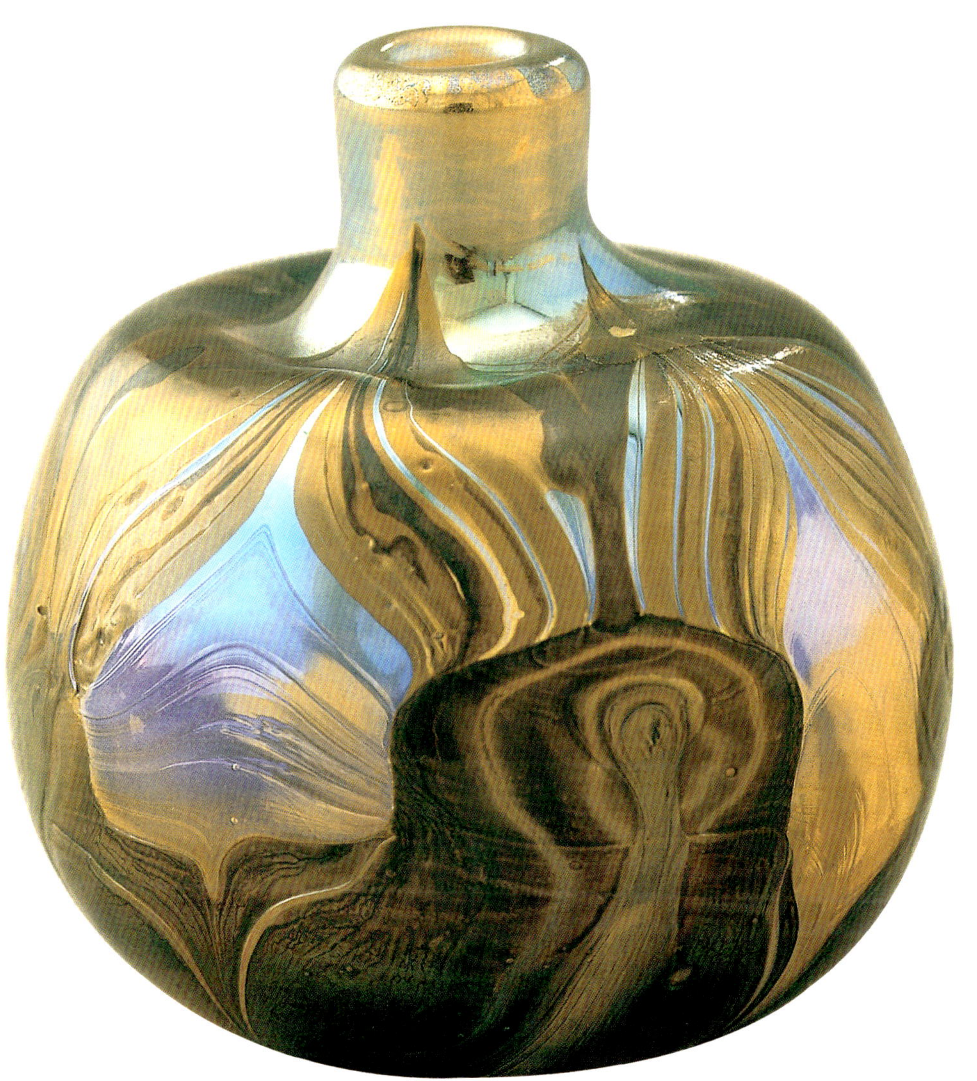

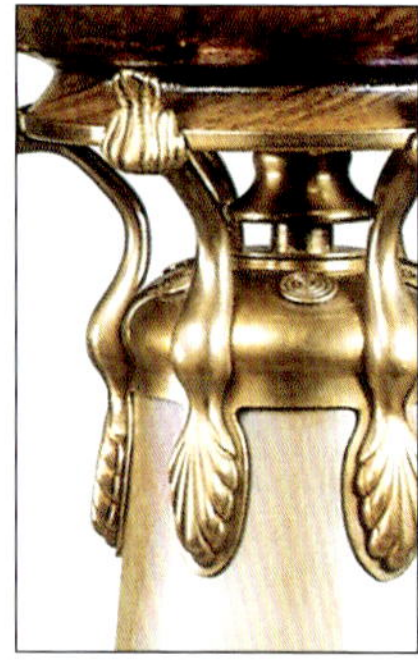

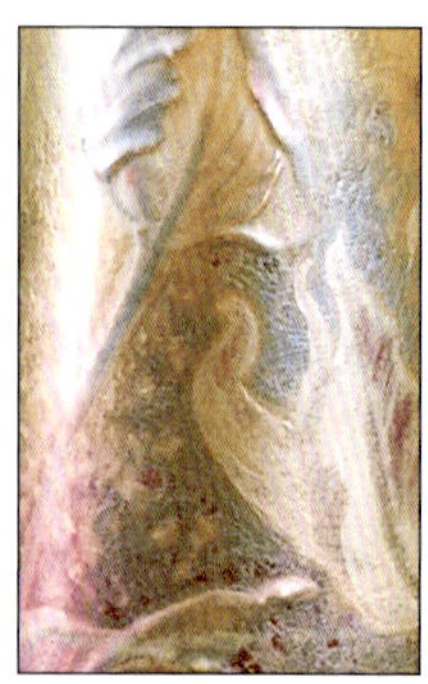

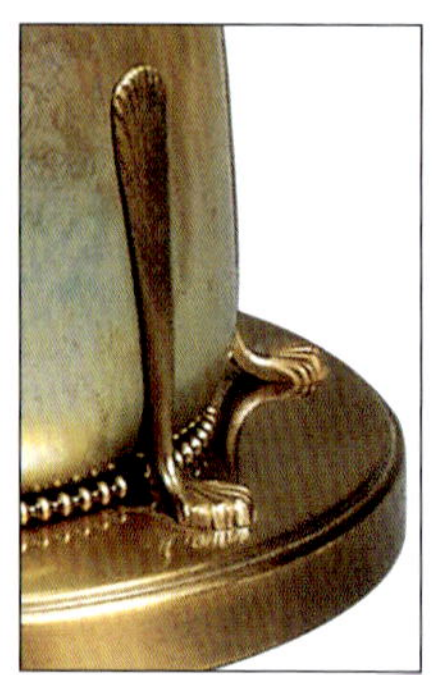

the fact that he made so great a name in the arts and crafts that his achievements in this field have thrown his work as a painter in the shade. There was a time, however, when his paintings and watercolors at the exhibitions of the National Academy, the Society of American Artists and the New York Water Color Society were recognized as the work of a colorist by those who

1900.
Ceramic, glass, bronze, height: 83.8 cm.
The Corning Museum of Glass, Corning.

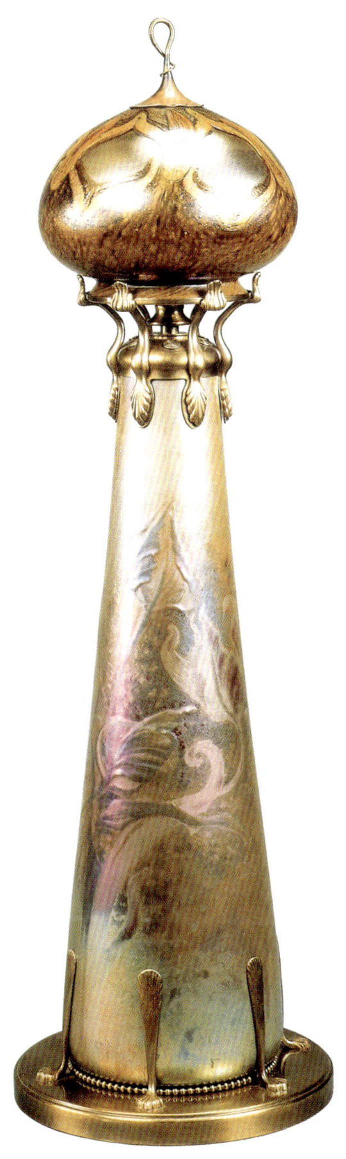

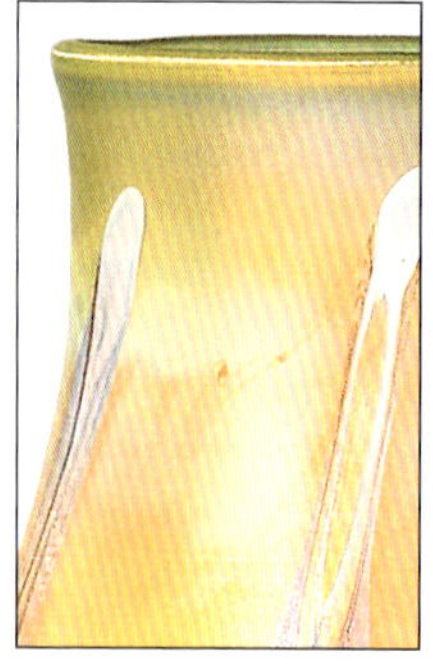

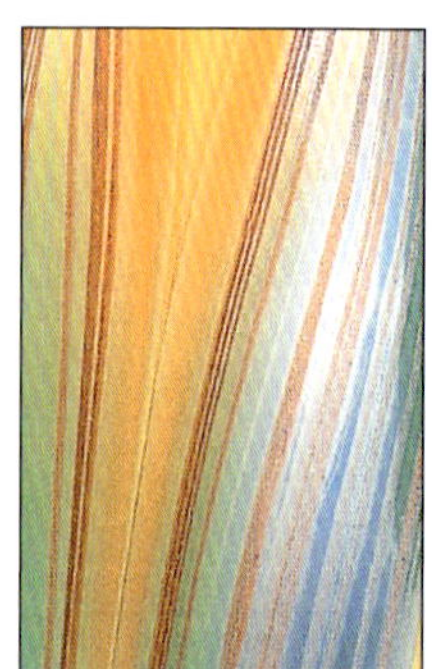

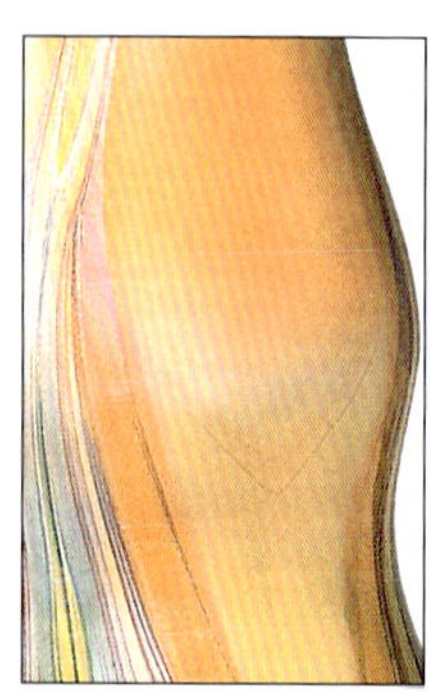

know enough to value the rare gifts of an eye for color and a hand capable of making color sing from the canvas.

It was with this uncommon endowment, so generally misunderstood, that he turned to forms of art which demand color-feeling in an artist even more than does oil painting; for they offer no methods of getting round

1897.
Glass, 47 x 22.9 cm.
Cincinnati Art Museum, Cincinnati.

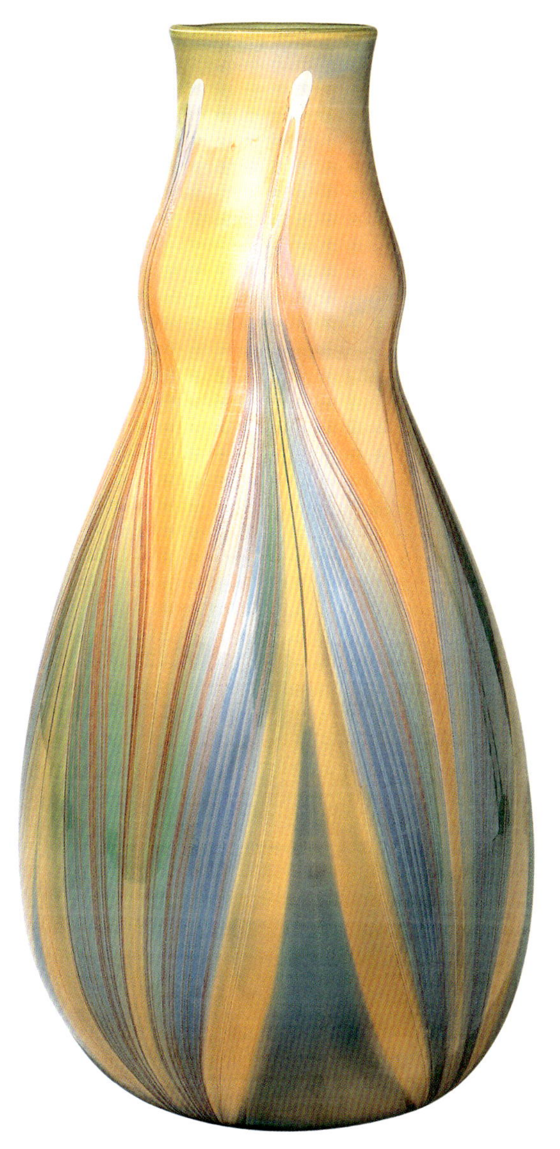

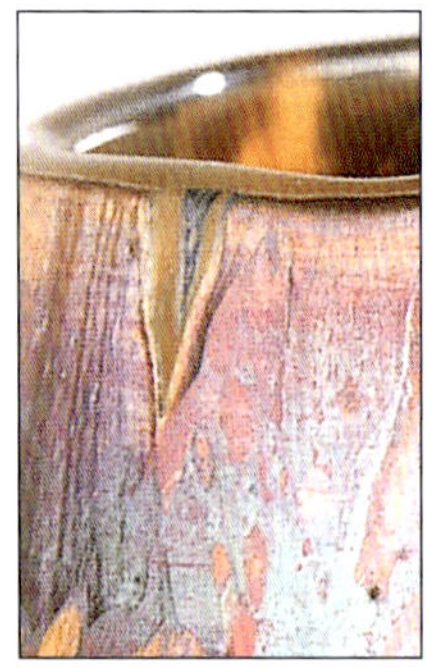

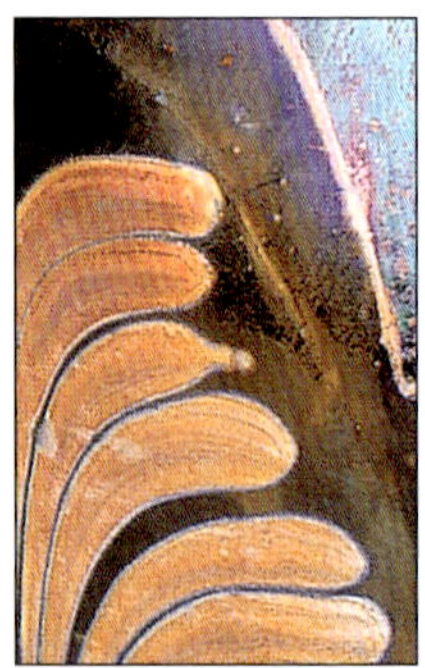

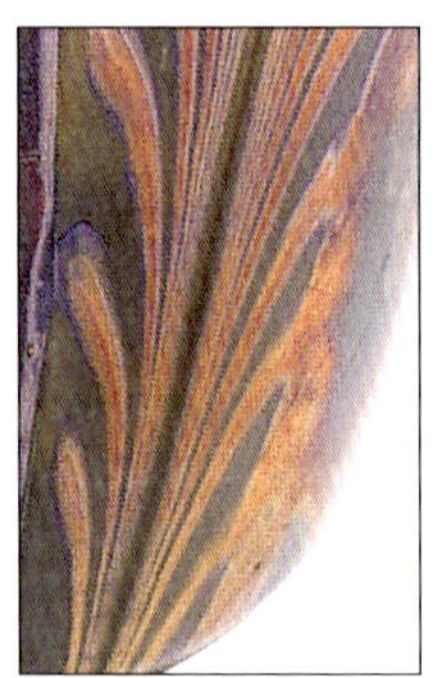

the issue as oil painting can be made to do for the near-colorist. Mosaics that admit of no shadows and confused lines, glass through which the light shines revealingly, textiles that are moved about in this or that light, these are things that test an artist on the color-side and permit of no evasion. In the queer, half-conscious faith of the artist, such works rank far below the painted canvas;

"Cypriote" Vase

1916.
Glass, 15.7 x 7.9 cm.
Design Museum, Smithsonian Institution, Washington, D.C.

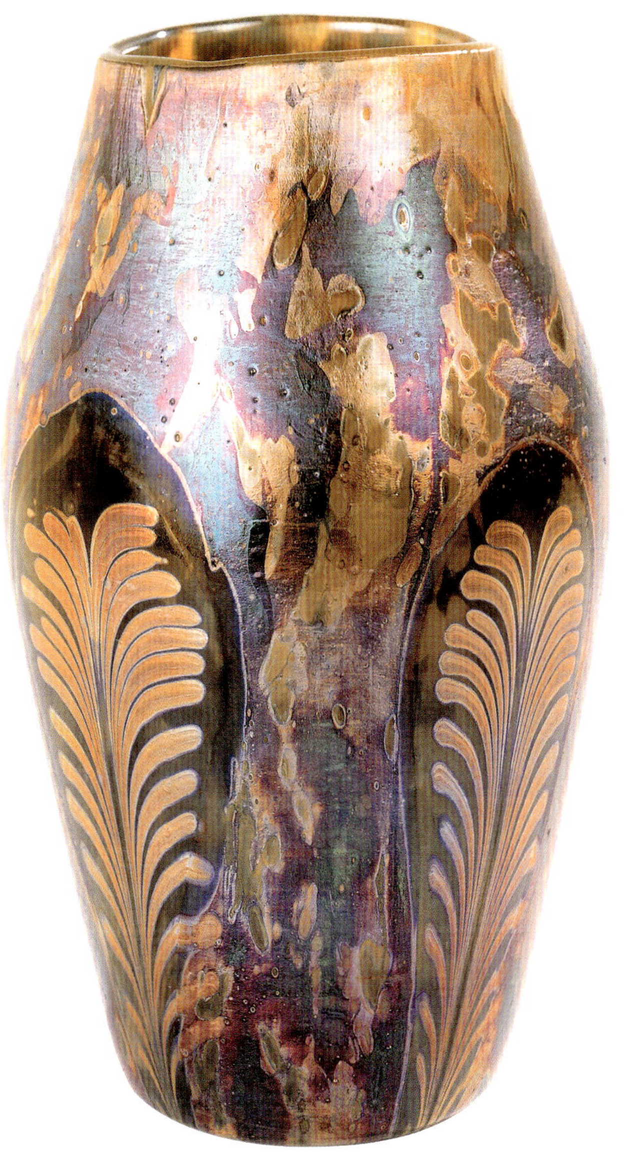

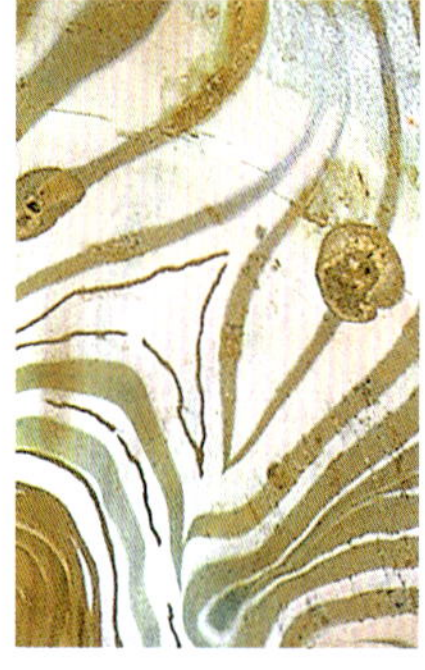

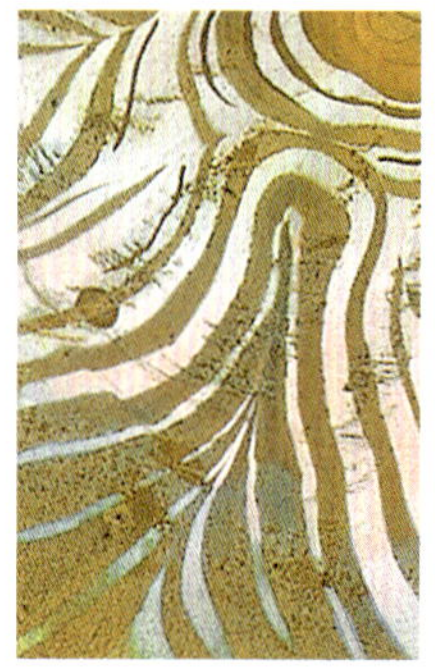

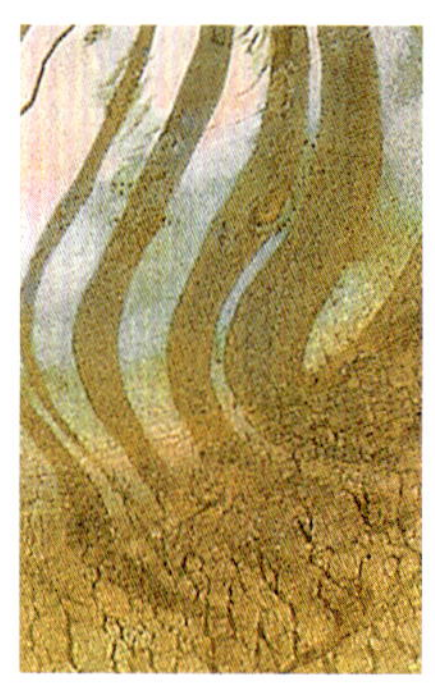

in their unwritten book of nobility the workmen in the arts and crafts are mere bons bourgeois, while they are the upper crust. Without reasoning on the matter, they take opinions ready-made like the generality of people and learn from their school days that the painters of easel pictures form the aristocracy of the profession. Without going farther into the matter and showing historically and sociologically how this odd situation

Plaque

———

1893.
Glass, 33.2 x 33.2 cm.
The Metropolitan Museum of Art, New York.

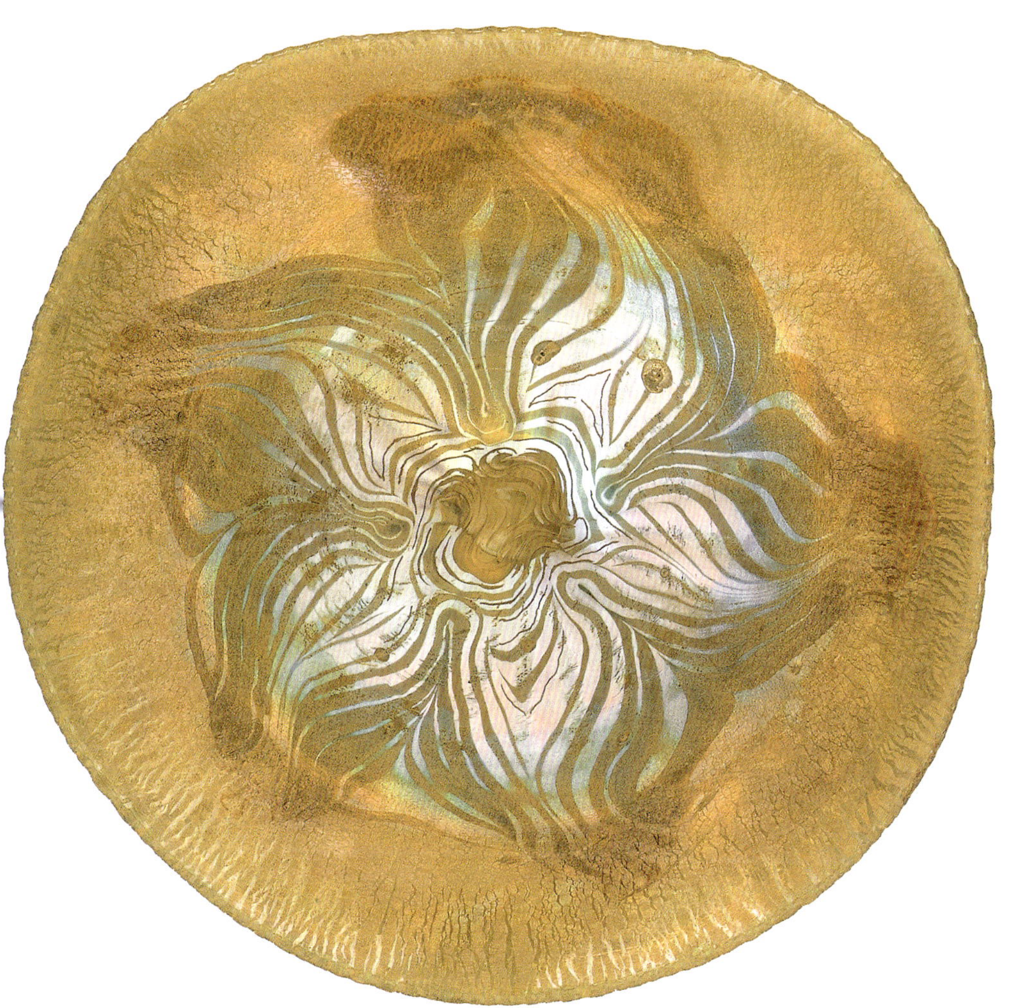

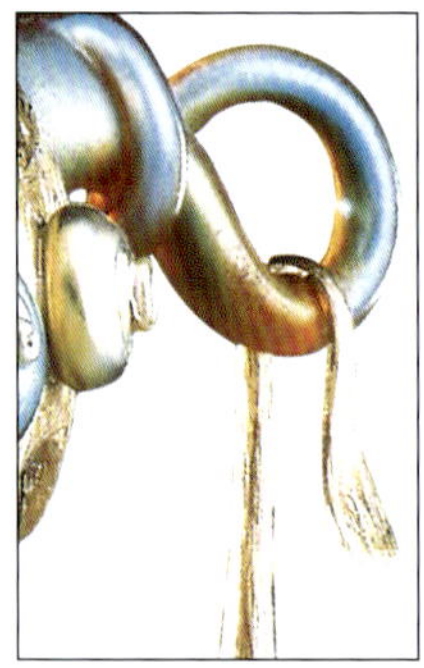

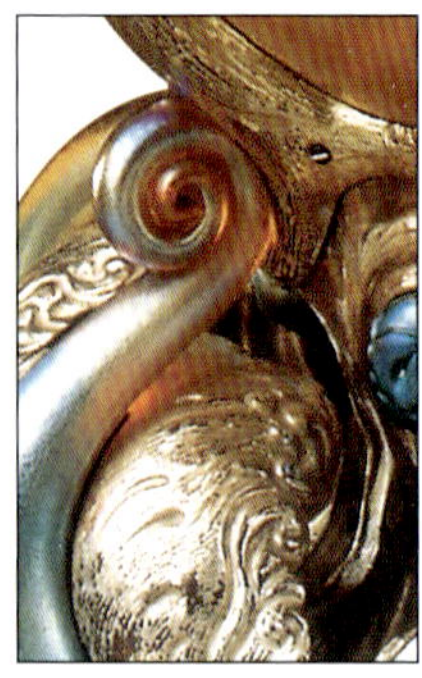

among painters has come about, let us merely note that Tiffany was too intelligent an artist to be thus deceived and being naturally of an inventive turn of mind, proceeded to devote himself to other lines of work which called upon his talent with even greater force.

It has been told how stained glass fascinated him and how he helped to place that exquisite form of art

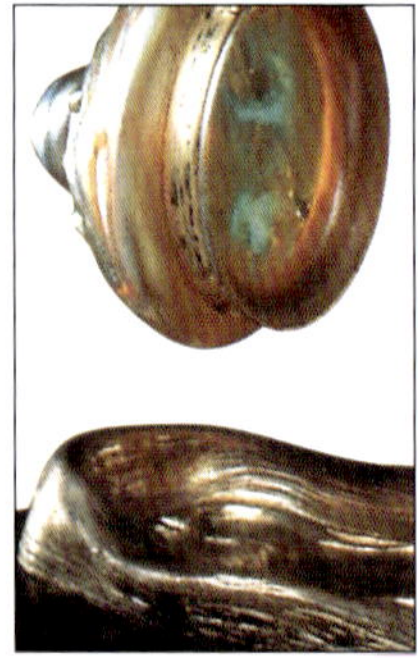

Punch Bowl with Three Ladles

1900.
Favrile glass, silver, gilding, copper, 36.8 x 61 cm.
Virginia Museum of Fine Arts, Richmond.

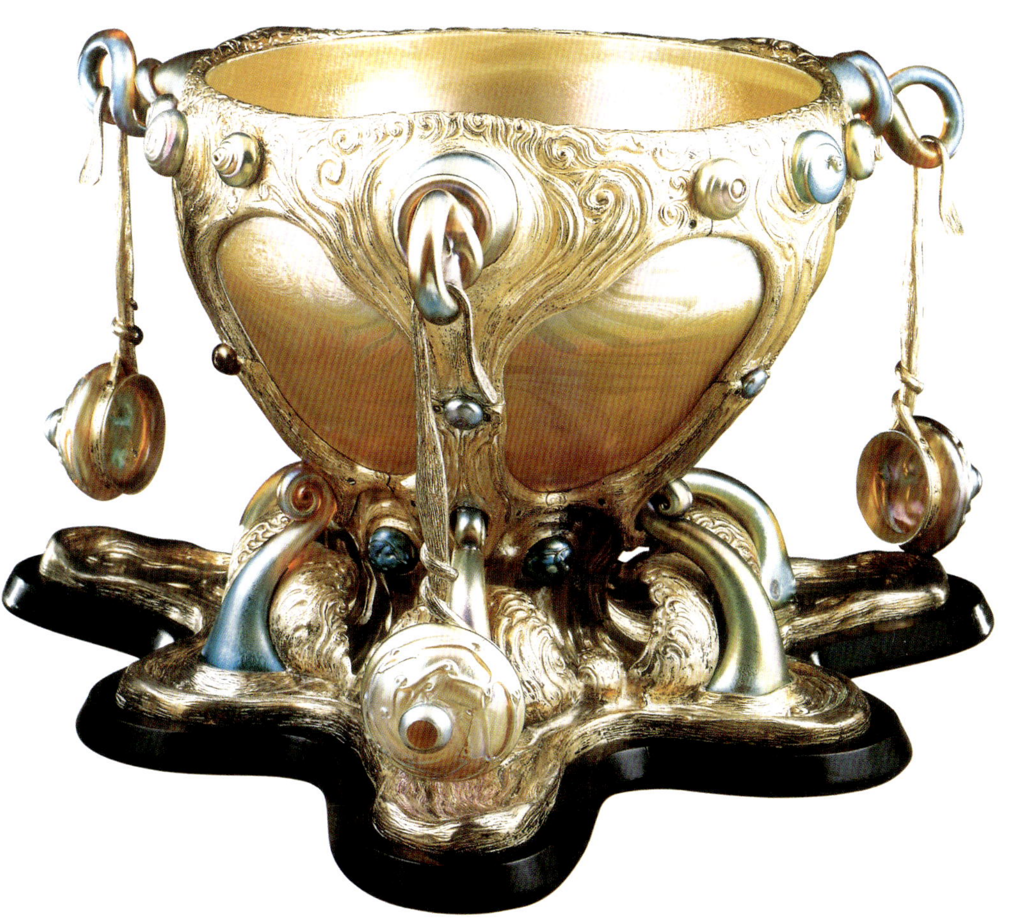

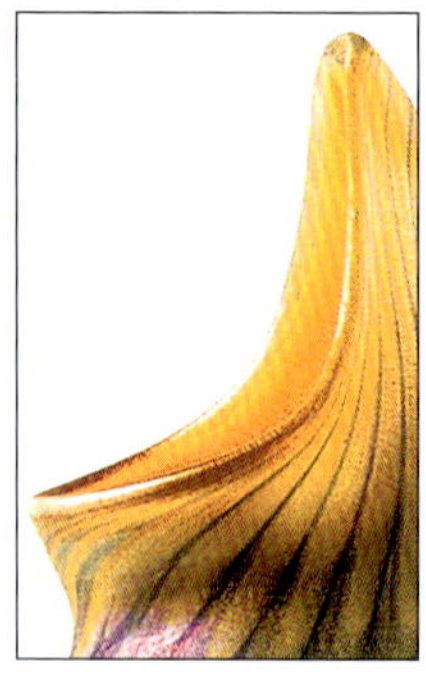

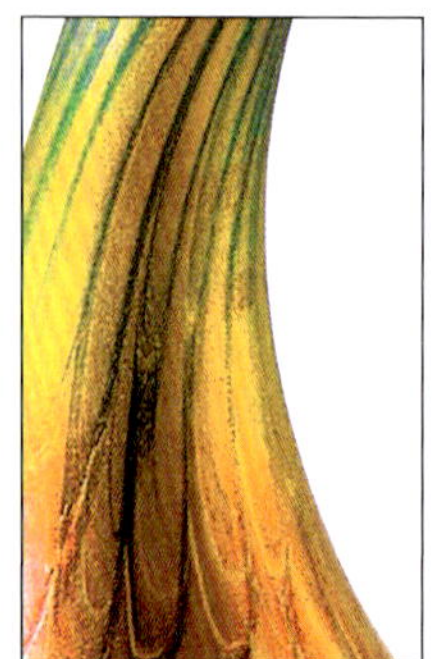

expression again before the world with a richness and magnificence of color only to be equalled by the men of the thirteenth century, who filled the great bays of Gothic aisles and chancels with splendor, so that America, not Europe, now makes stained glass for true connoisseurs. Out of this school of American painters in glass came, thanks to Tiffany's inventive mind, the small

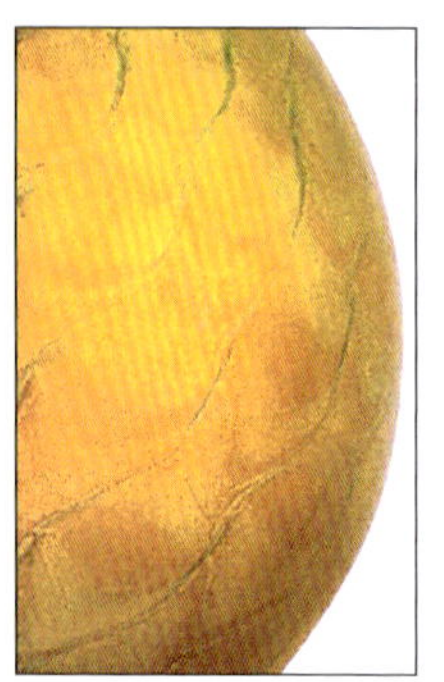

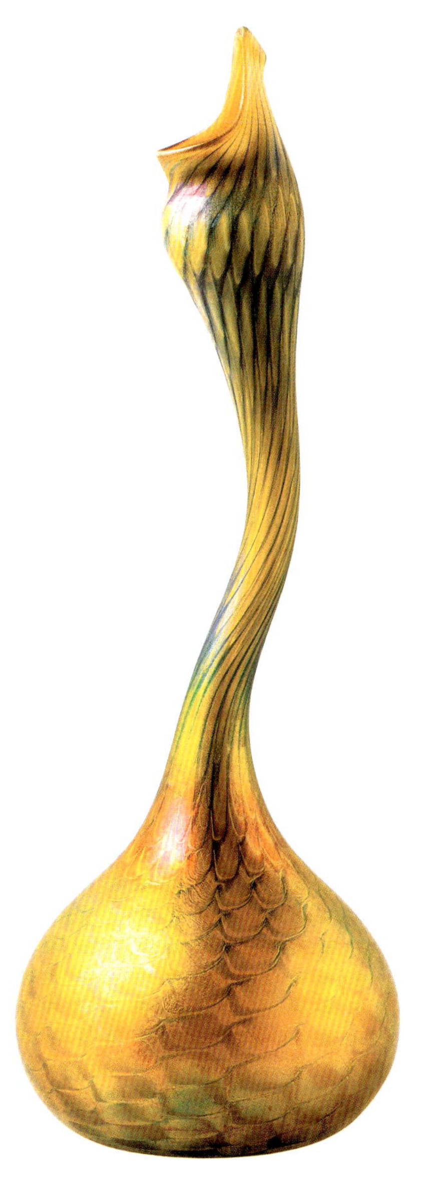

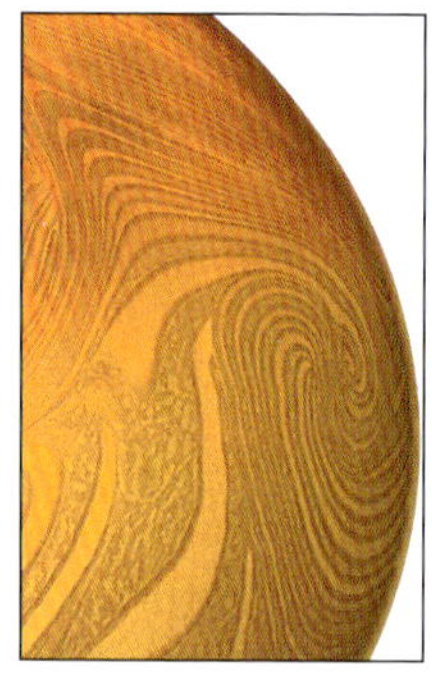

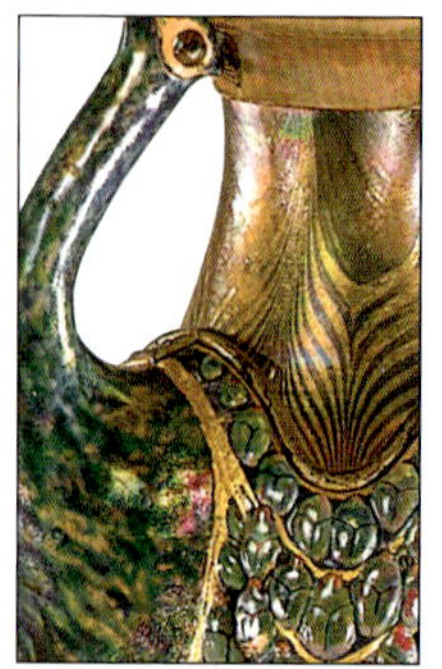

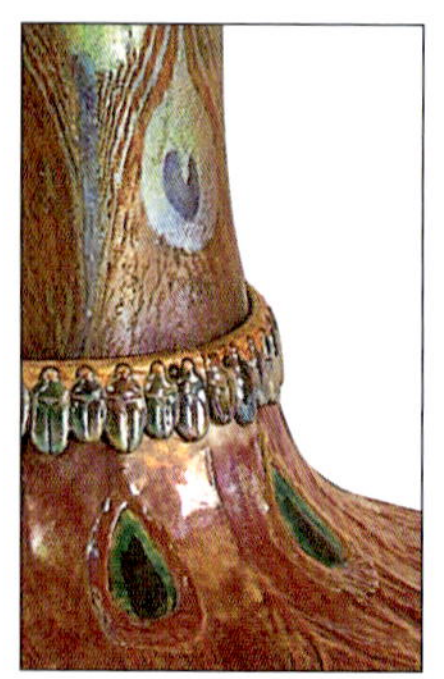

glass objects like the favrile and other styles, together with a variety of objects in glass too many for anything but a catalogue. Glazes on pottery claimed much of his time during certain years; enamels on copper were brought to public notice; jewelry of an original and individual kind found and still finds a big circle of admirers. Indeed, as time went on, the number of different artworks to which he gave attention became

Peacock Lamp

1898-1900.
Virginia Museum of Fine Arts, Richmond.

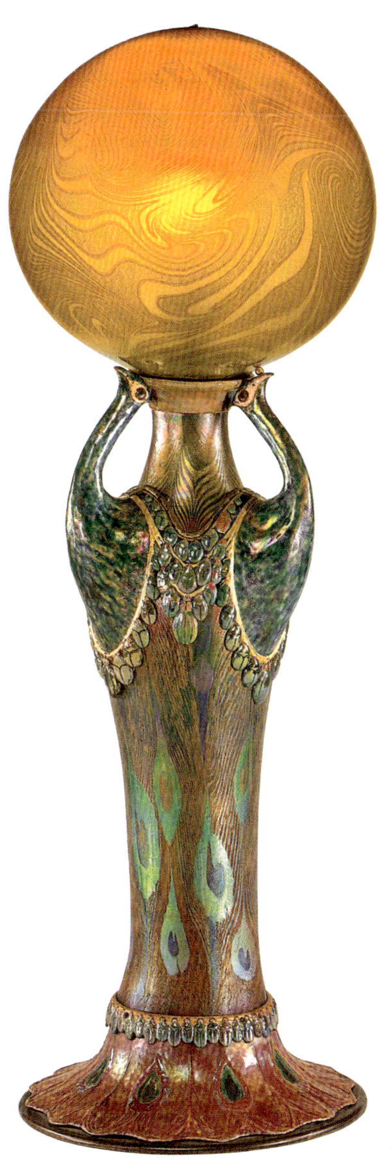

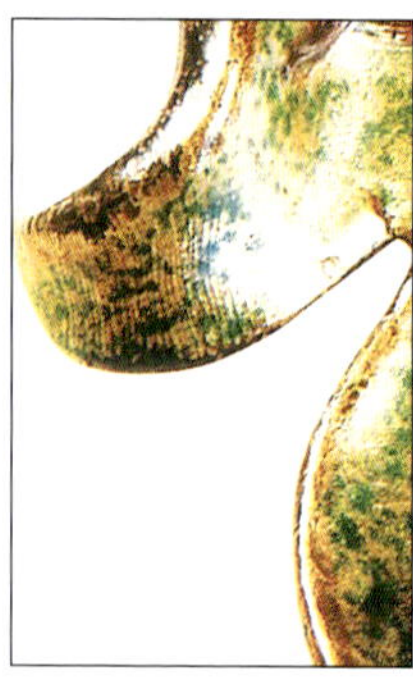

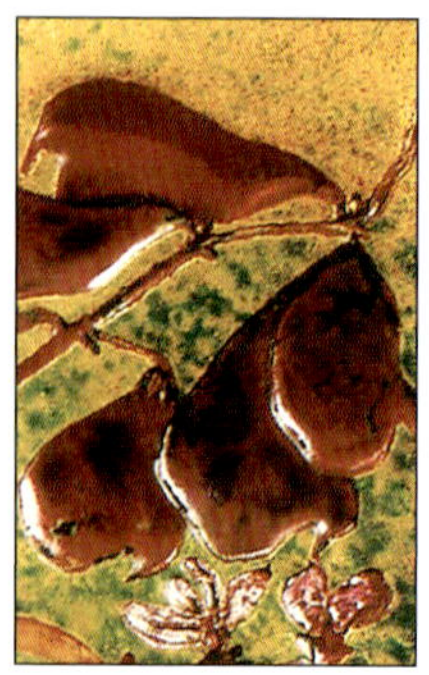

so great that it seemed marvelous that one man, however well supported by capable assistants, could find the waking hours in which to keep track of them all. No one could have done it all except a person who could double his existence as a creative artist with the life of a business man.

A vast amount of work was turned out in the quarters of the Tiffany Glass Company at Fourth Avenue

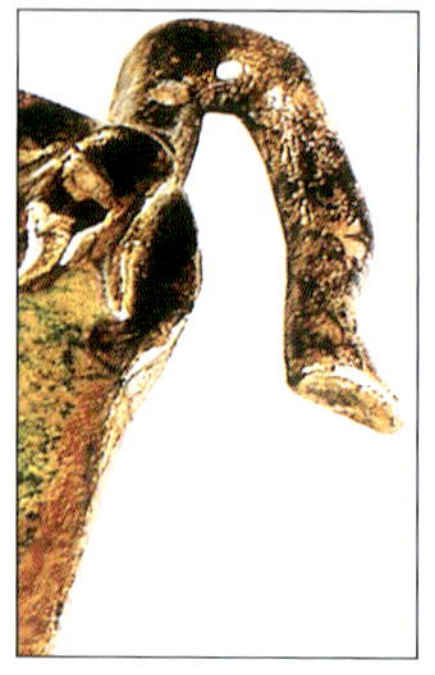

1900.
Enamel on brass.
Collection of Erwing and Joyce Wolf.

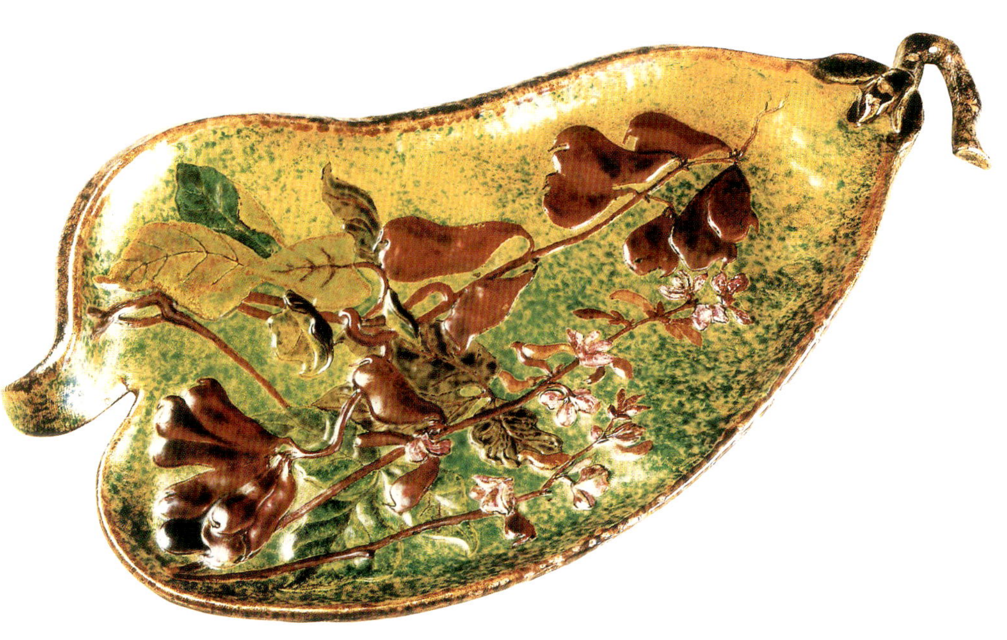

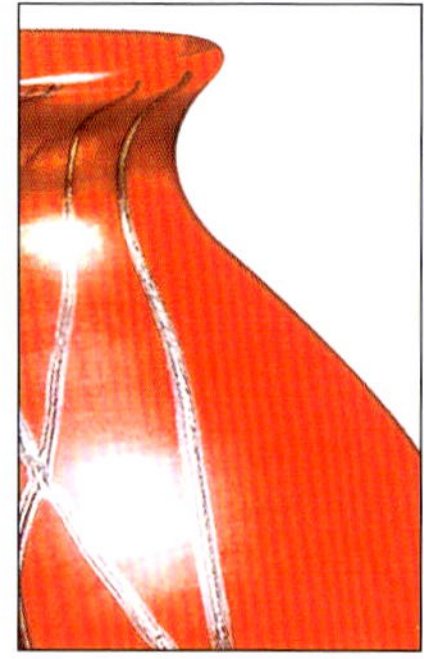

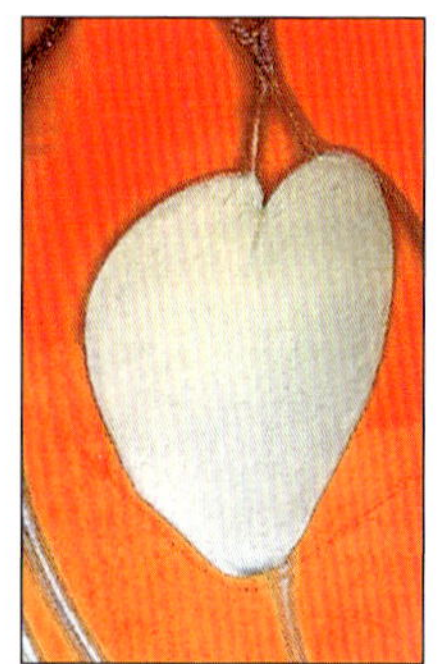

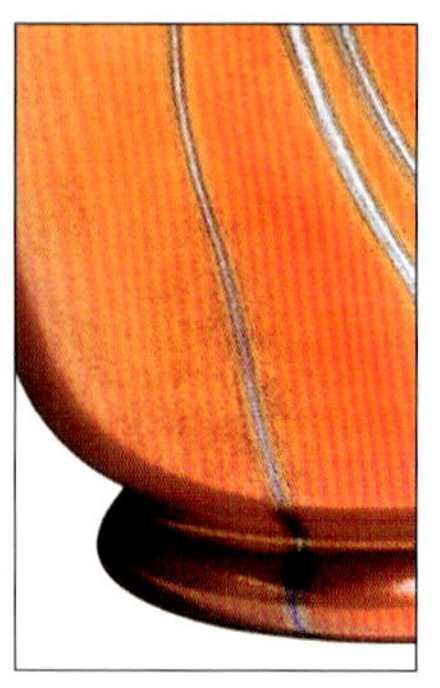

and Twenty-Fifth Street, but when he moved his art shops to Madison Avenue and Forty-Fifth Street, taking possession of the building erected for the Knickerbocker Athletic Club, the supervision of so great a business by itself made demands on the nerves which might seem enough for any man without the addition thereto of individual exertion.

1898-1899.
Favrile glass, height: 14 cm.
Victoria & Albert Museum, London.

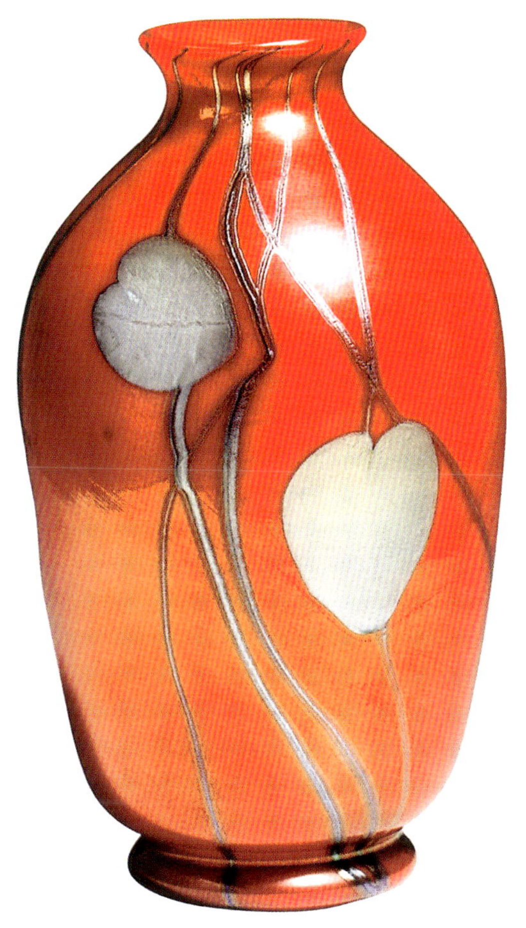

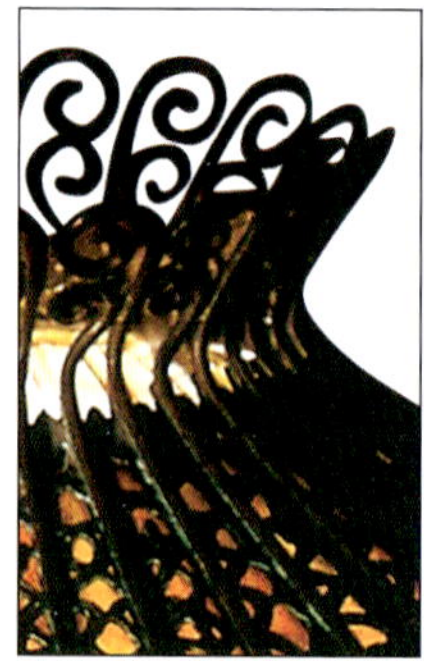

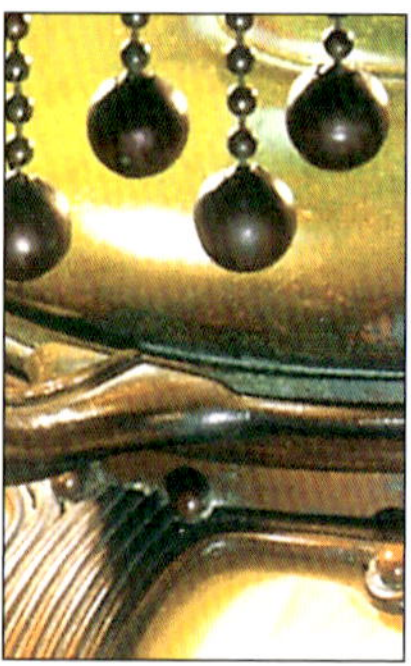

Yet all this while Mr. Tiffany was so far from neglecting home life under the stress of business plus creative art in the various fields of his endeavor that he found time to plan and carefully carry out no less than four homes in succession. Nor were these ordinary dwellings. Each apartment was the result of intense application as to its general scheme, and every part of

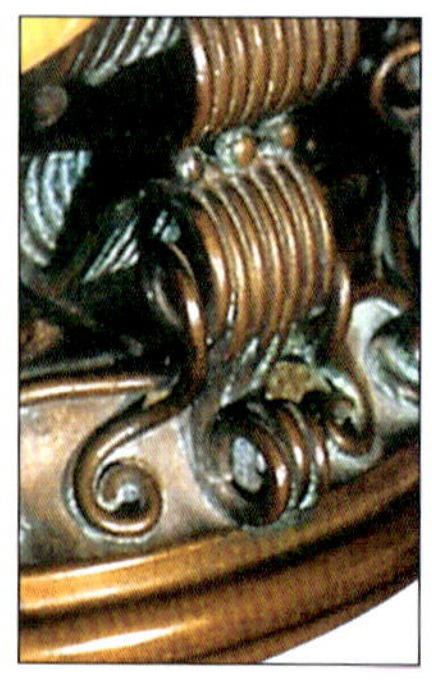

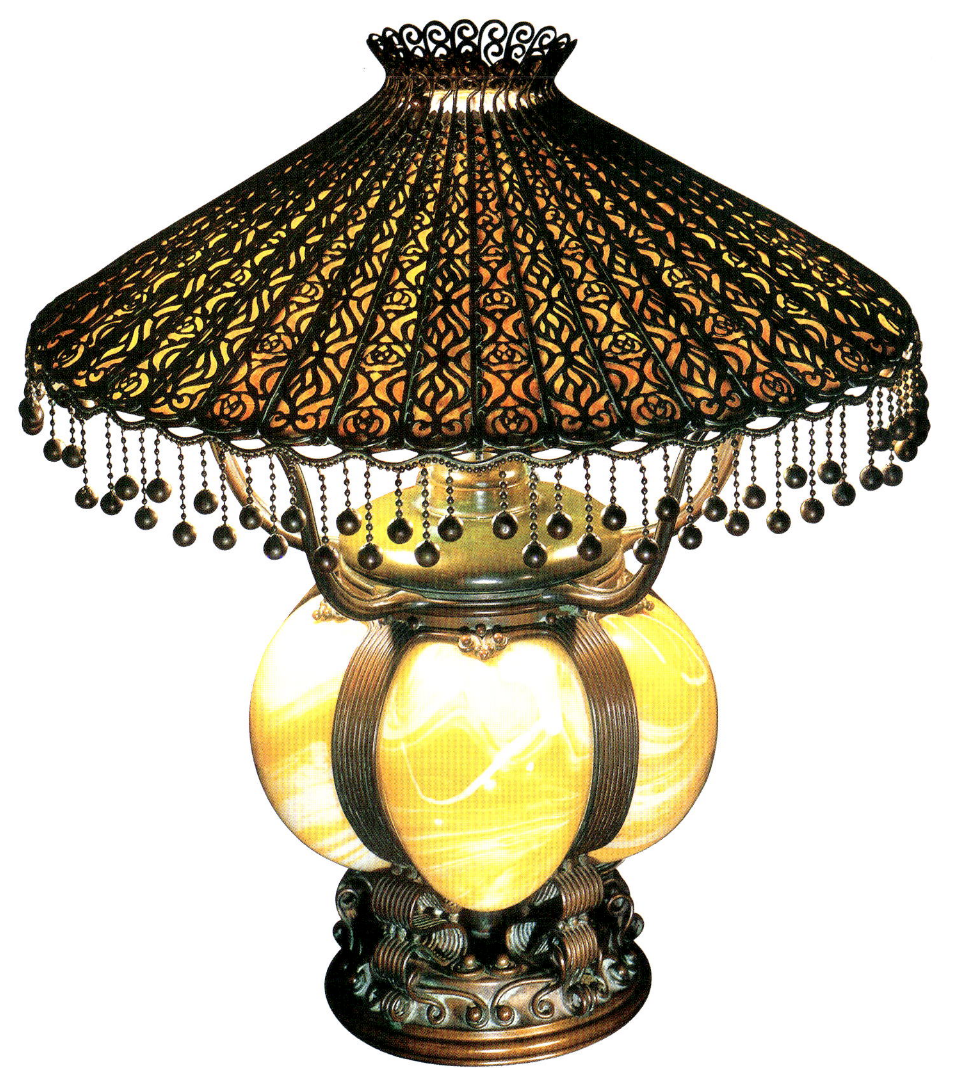

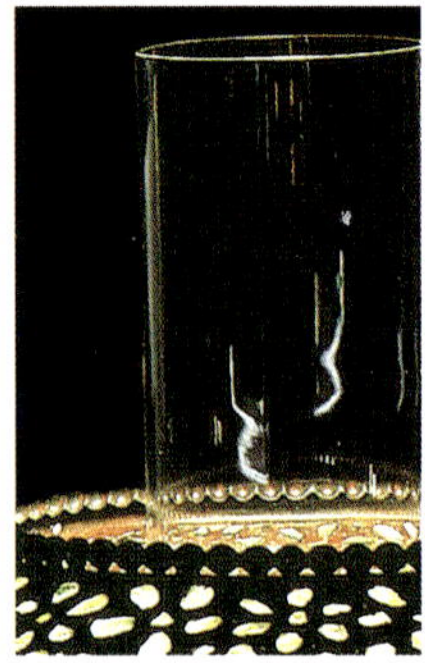

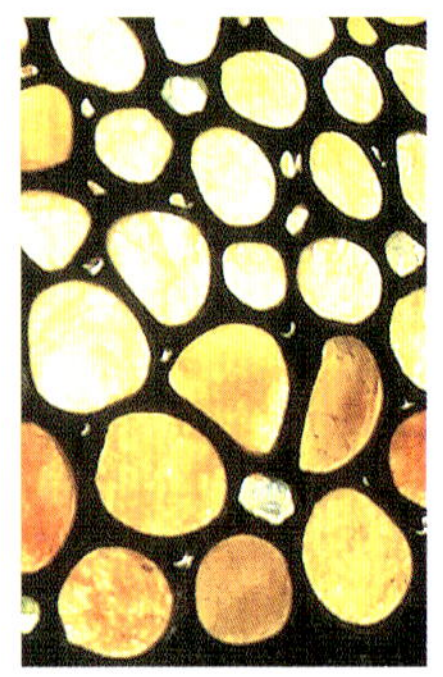

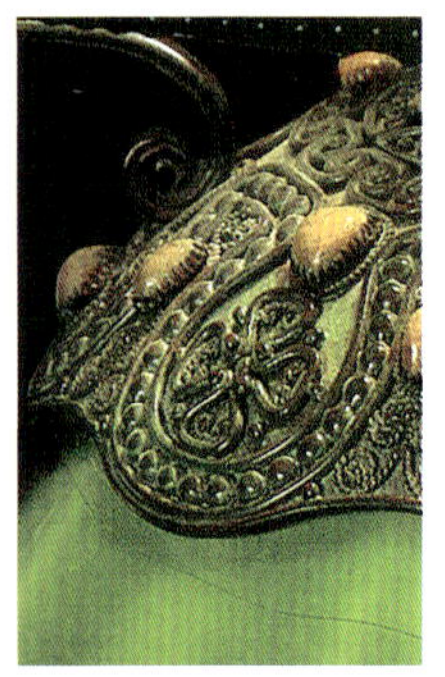

each room was studied for its color-scheme, the lighting by day and night, and the disposal of art objects of the greatest beauty and value. As to the two country houses as parts of the landscape, the matter has been treated in the last chapter. His delight in flowers has resulted in great attention to the growing of native and exotic plants, some for their blossoms, and others for their foliage.

Pumpkin, Pebble Decoration with Pebble Shade

Favrile glass, leaded glass, bronze, shade: 40.64 cm.

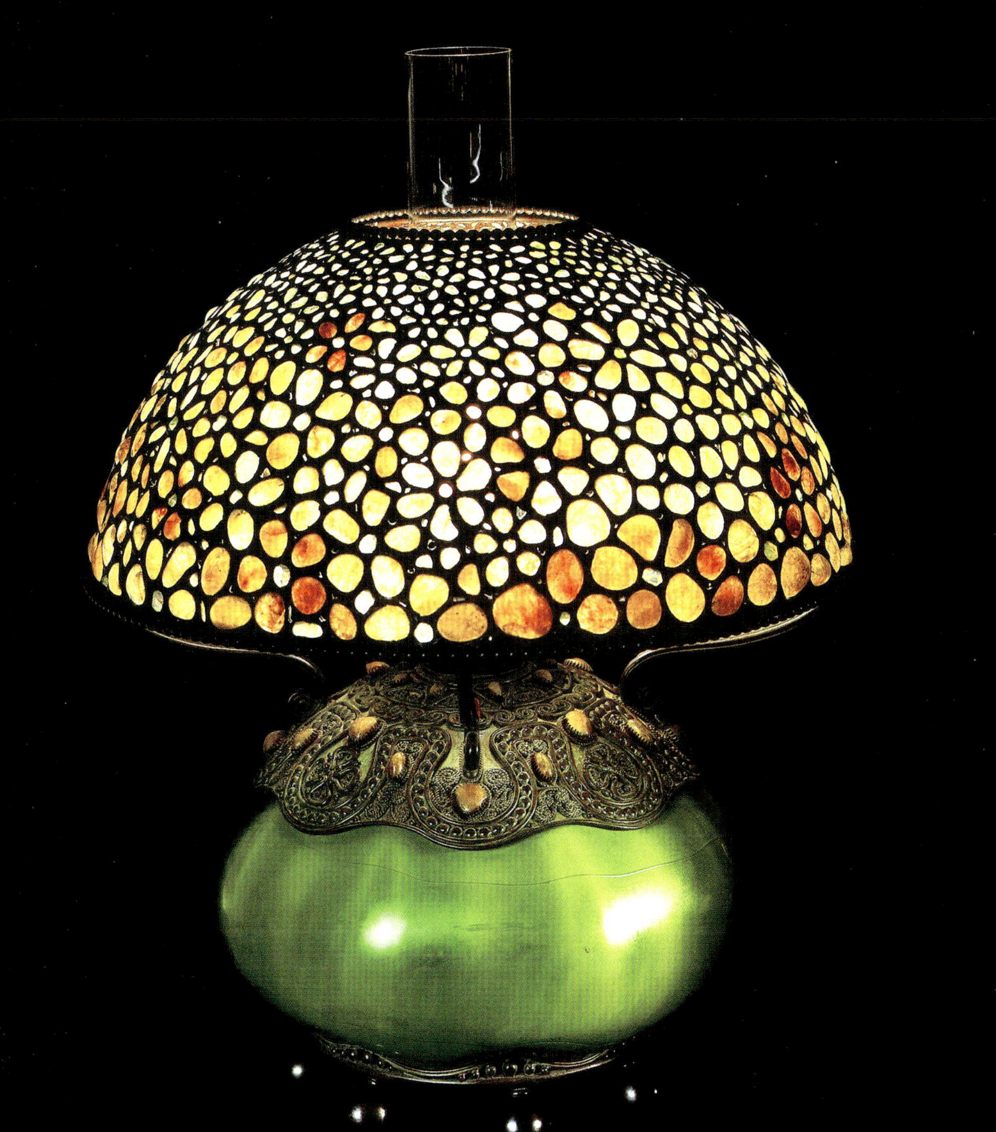

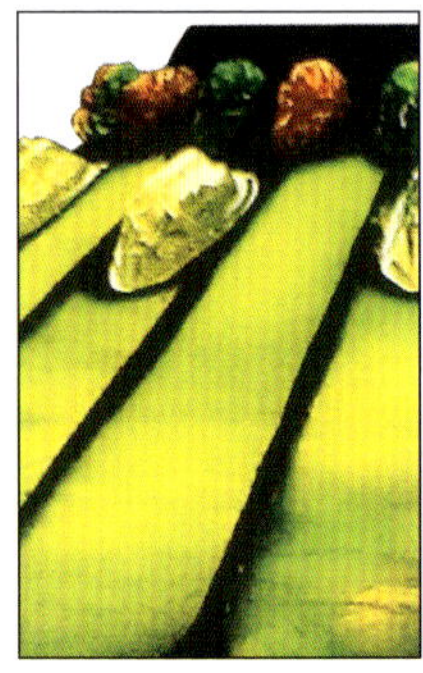

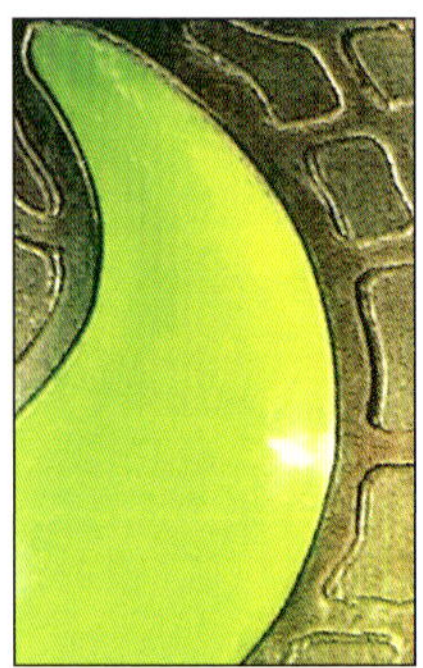

We may fairly ask how he could have made the time to attend to all these things in and out of town. It is true that he has denied himself distant travels. He had not visited Japan and India, though the pull in that direction must always have been very strong.

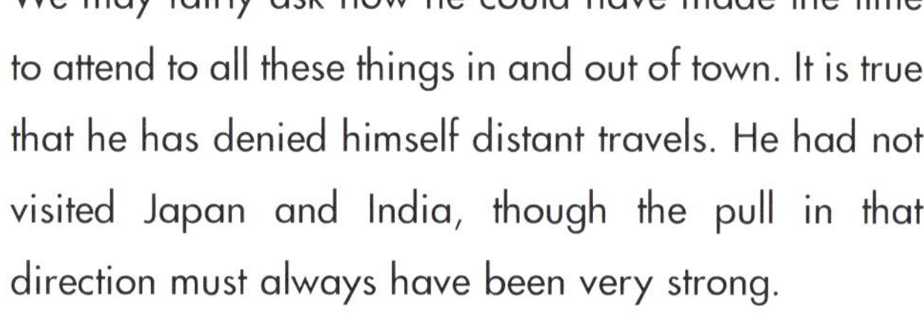

Favrile Glass Oil Lamp with Geometric Shade

Favrile glass, leaded glass and bronze.

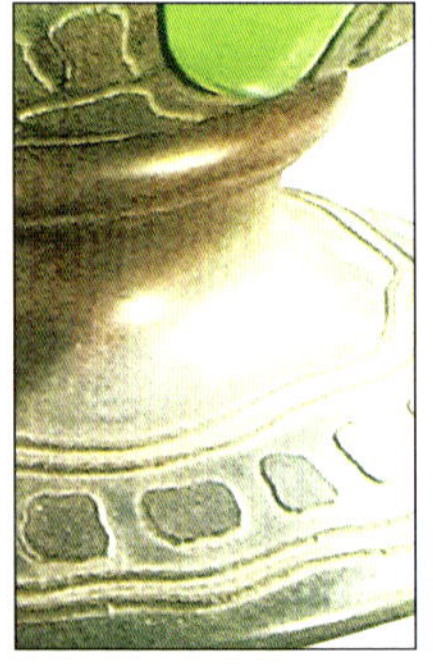

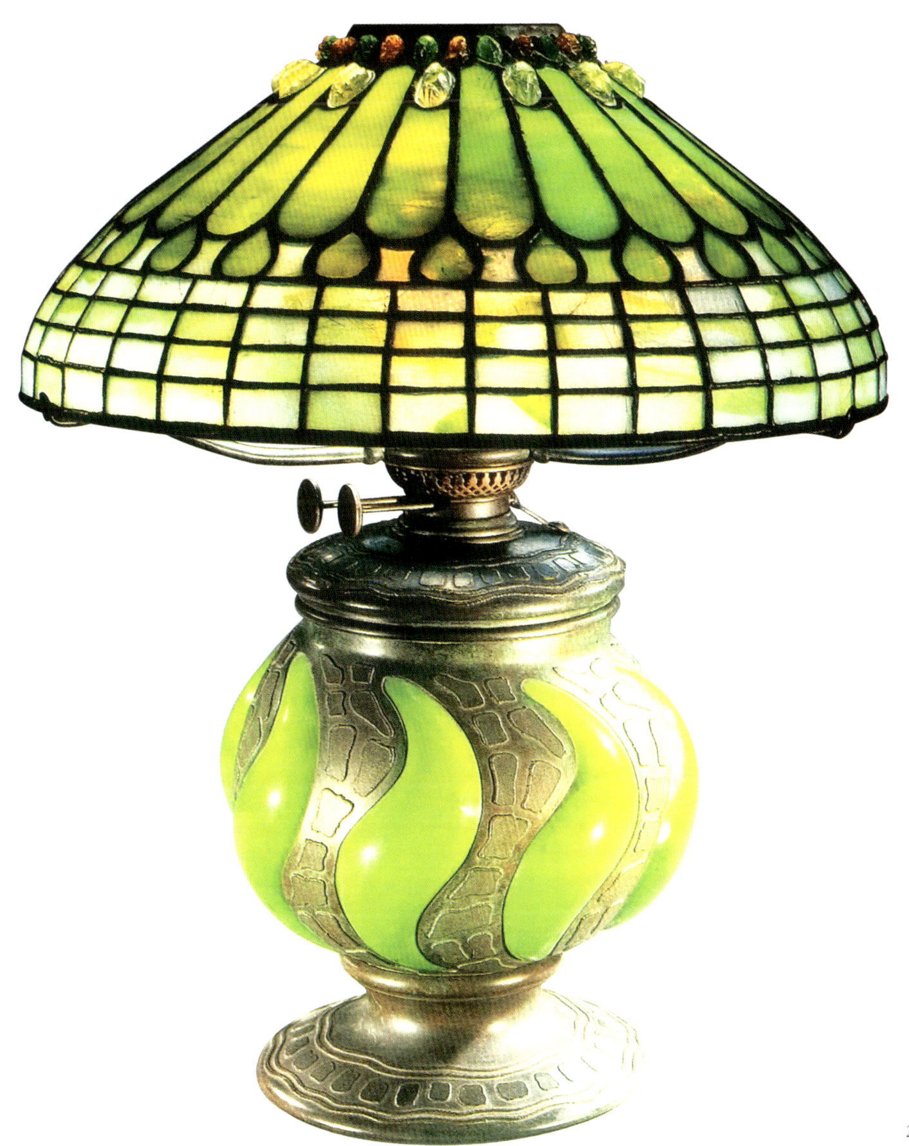

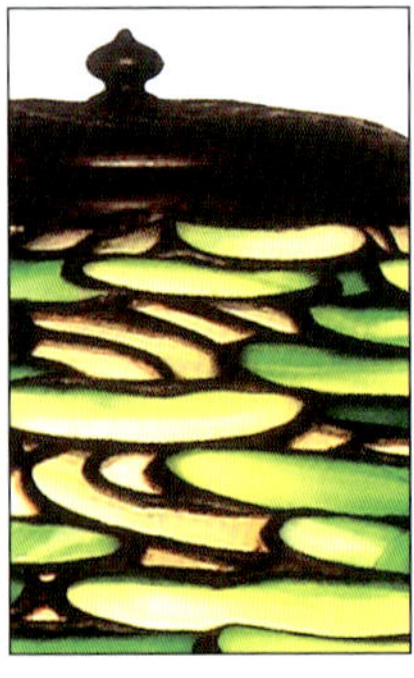

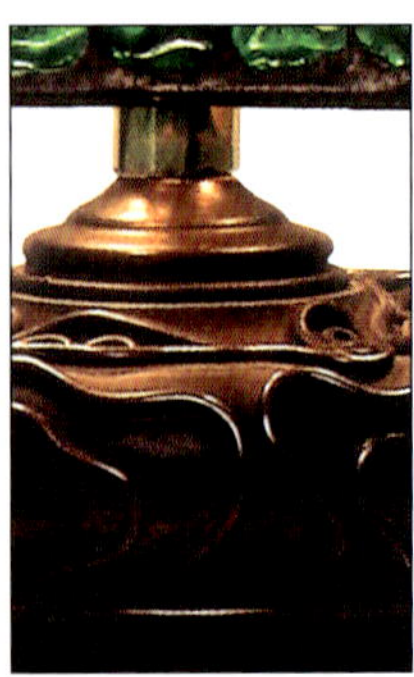

It was about one hundred fifty years ago that he showed in his art the influence of the Orient, yet Turkey and Algiers are the only parts of the East that he studied on the spot. In one sense his life may be said to have been uneventful, if we speak from the traveler's point of view,

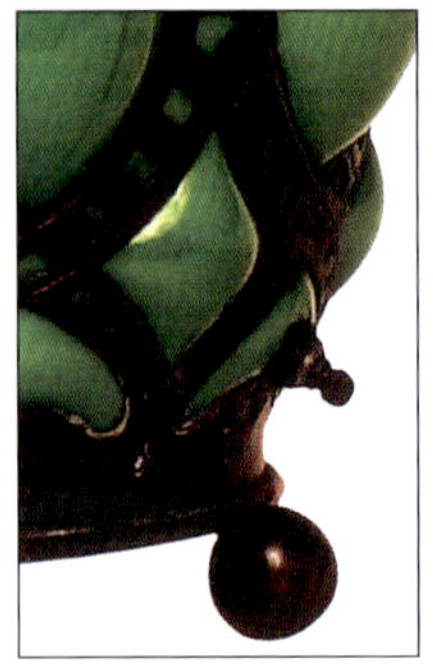

Lamp with Lily-Pad Motif

1899-1910.
Leaded glass, blown glass, bronze, 60.3 x 50.8 x 50.8 cm.
New York Historical Society, New York.

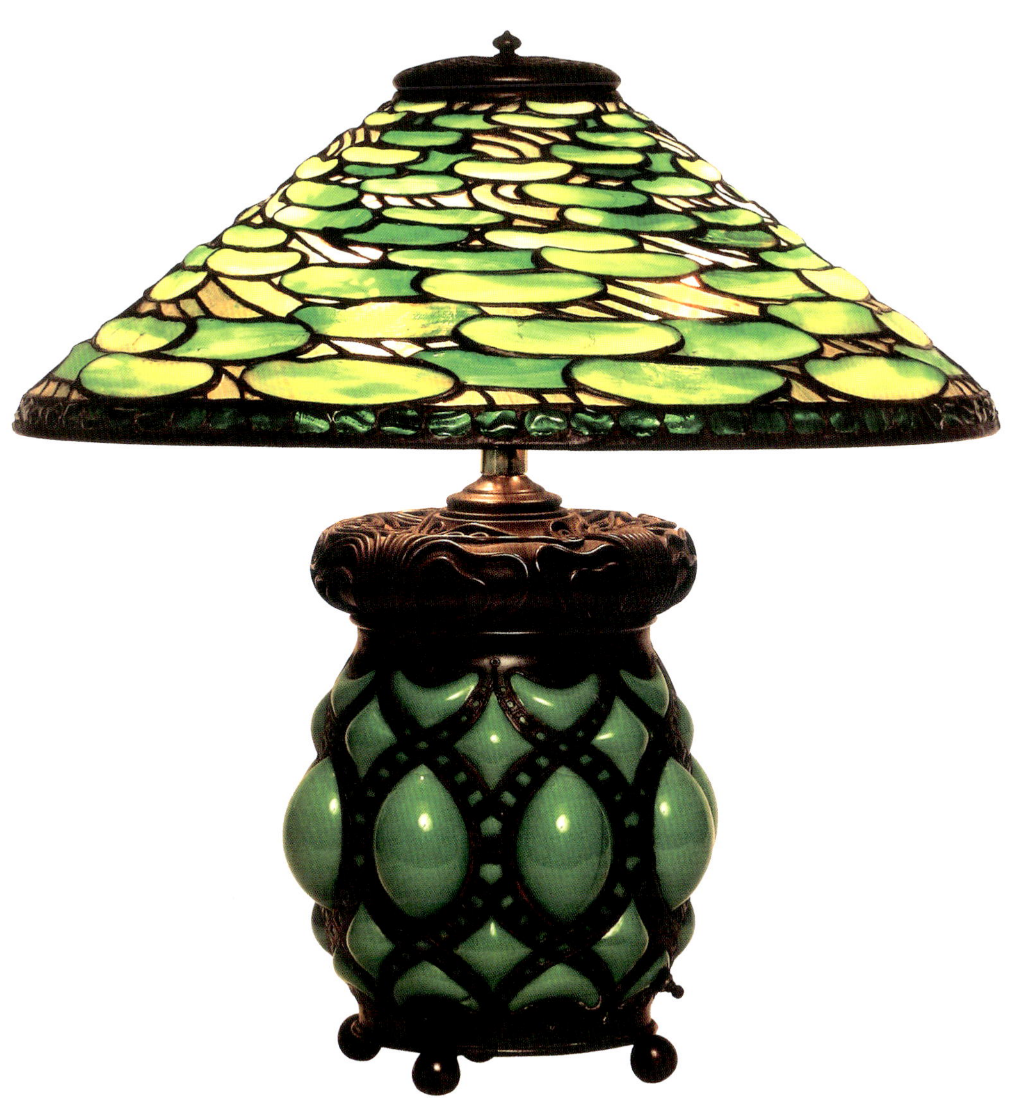

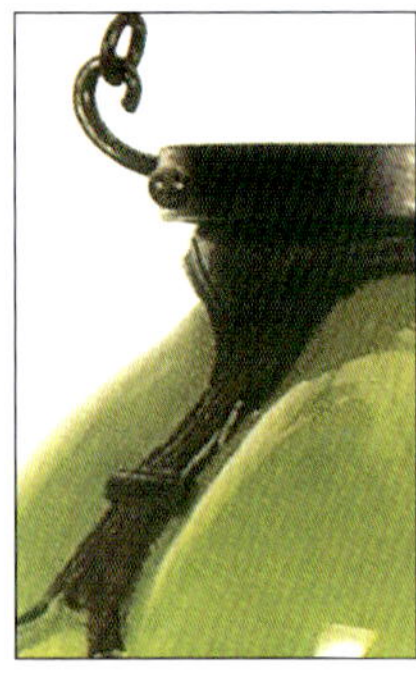

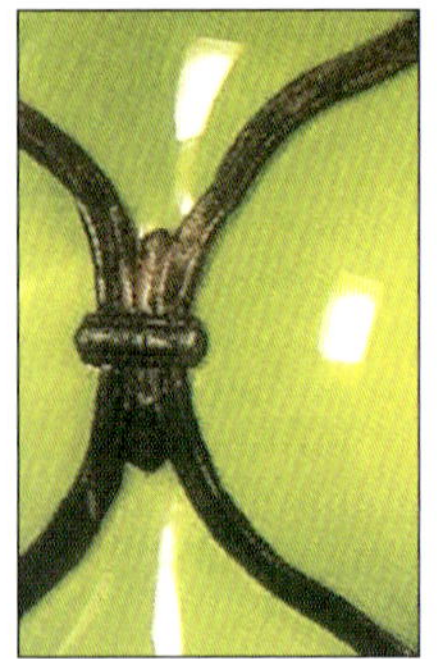

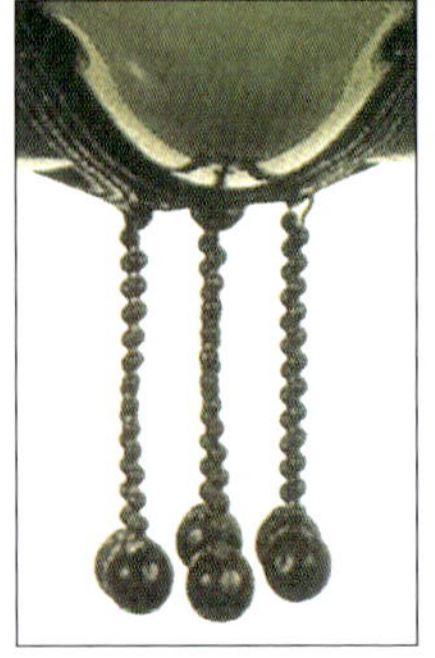

but not so if we put ourselves in the place of the artist and inventor. It can never be said of him that a rolling stone gathers no moss. When we think of the silent effect produced in a thousand families, and in more museums than could easily be named, by the inspiring artworks he has produced, we can say sincerely that he deserves the admiration of the republic.

Hanging Lamp

Glass and bronze.

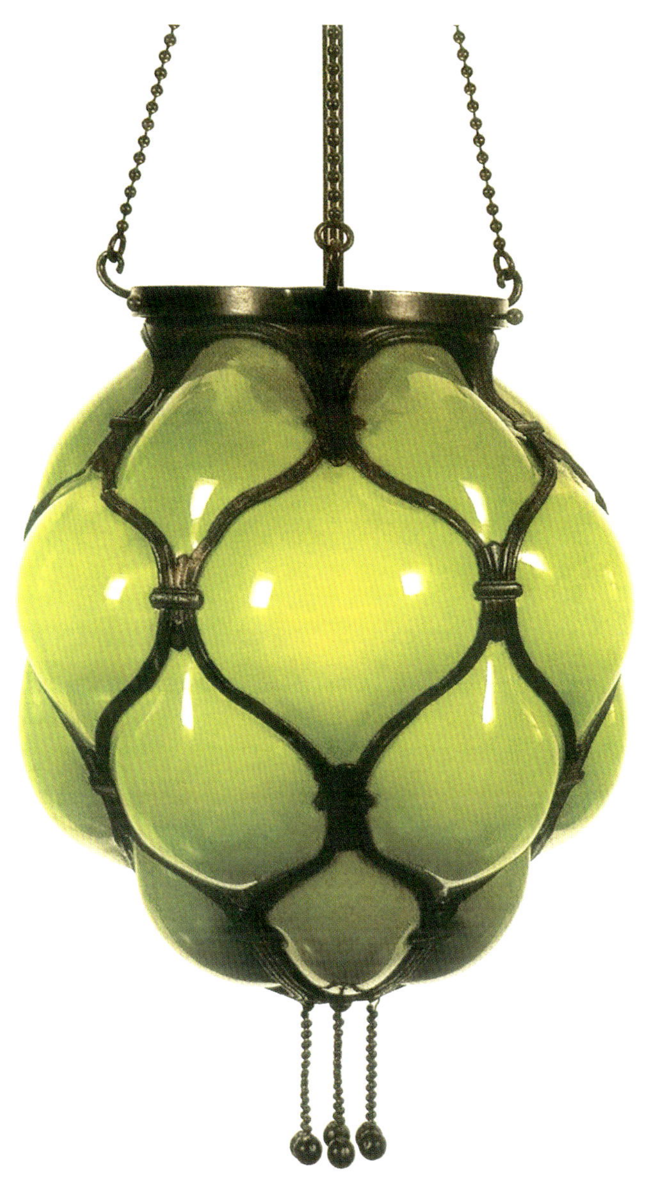

List of illustrations